KU-539-509

DR E. W. THORNTON

Neuropsychology
of Cardiovascular Disease

Neuropsychology of Cardiovascular Disease

Edited by

Shari R. Waldstein
University of Maryland, Baltimore County
University of Maryland School of Medicine
Baltimore Veterans Affairs Medical Center

Merrill F. Elias
Boston University and
Boston University Schools of Medicine
and Public Health

2001

LAWRENCE ERLBAUM ASSOCIATES, PUBLISHERS
Mahwah, New Jersey   London

Copyright © 2001 by Lawrence Erlbaum Associates, Inc.
All rights reserved. No part of this book may be reproduced in any form, by photostat, microfilm, retrieval system, or any other means, without prior written permission of the publisher.

Lawrence Erlbaum Associates, Inc., Publishers
10 Industrial Avenue
Mahwah, NJ 07430

Cover design by Kathryn Houghtaling Lacey

Library of Congress Cataloging-in-Publication Data

Neuropsychology of cardiovascular disease / edited by Shari R. Waldstein, Merrill F. Elias.
    p. cm.
    Includes bibliographical references and index.
ISBN 0-8058-3103-7 (alk. paper)
1. Neurobehavioral disorders. 2. Neurologic manifestations of general diseases. 3. Cardiovascular system—Diseases—Complications.
4. Cardiovascular system—Diseases—Psychological aspects.
I. Waldstein, Shari R. II. Elias, Merrill F., 1938– .
[DNLM: 1. Cardiovascular Diseases—complications. 2. Cognition Disorders—etiology. 3. Cardiovascular Agents—adverse effects.
4. Cardiovascular Surgical Procedures—adverse effects.
5. Dementia, Vascular—physiopathology. 6. Neuropsychology—methods. WG 120 N494 2000]
RC455.4.B5 N475   2000
616.1'001'9—dc21   00-042246
                                       CIP

Books published by Lawrence Erlbaum Associates are printed on acid-free paper, and their bindings are chosen for strength and durability.

Printed in the United States of America
10 9 8 7 6 5 4 3 2 1

To Matt and Penny …
and to the linking of hearts and minds.

Contents

Preface

Cardiovascular disease is the leading cause of morbidity and mortality in the United States and in many other countries worldwide (American Heart Association, 1998).[1] Recent statistics provided by the American Heart Association indicate that 41.4% of all deaths in the United States are attributable to cardiovascular disease. Furthermore, 58,800,000 Americans are estimated to have one or more types of cardiovascular disease.

Cerebrovascular events such as stroke and vascular dementia are commonly associated with other forms of cardiovascular disease. New or recurrent stroke affects approximately 600,000 Americans each year (American Heart Association, 1998) and is the leading cause of disability in adults. The neuropsychological sequelae of stroke and vascular dementia are well documented and can have a potentially devastating impact on the quality of life of affected individuals. However prior to the development of overt cerebrovascular complications, persons with cardiovascular disease or cardiovascular risk factors display neuropsychological difficulties that can range from mild to severe. Medical and surgical treatments for cardiovascular disease have also been found to affect cognitive functioning.

To date, the neuropsychological consequences of various dimensions of cardiovascular disease and its treatment have generally been examined in isolation. However, cardiovascular diseases, their associated risk factors, and the consequences of treatment often co-exist within the individual. Furthermore, persons who experience overt cerebrovascular events are often found to have a long-standing history of other cardiovascular diseases. Consideration of the nat-

---

[1]American Heart Association (1998). *1999 Heart and stroke statistical update*. Dallas, TX.

ural history of cardiovascular disease, and its gradual progression over the course of a lifespan, is critical in research and clinical evaluation of neuropsychological performance in affected individuals. By reviewing and summarizing the neuropsychological consequences of various dimensions of cardiovascular disease, cerebrovascular events, and associated treatments, this volume encourages researchers and clinicians to consider all relevant facets of vascular disease process in their evaluation, study, and treatment of patients with cardiovascular disease. The research described herein also highlights the brain as a target organ for damage associated with cardiovascular disease and further emphasizes the need for primary and secondary prevention efforts.

Accordingly, this volume provides an overview of the neuropsychology of cardiovascular disease. The chapters roughly follow in sequence with the natural progression of cardiovascular disease. The authors represent a broad range of professional disciplines including neuropsychology, behavioral medicine, epidemiology, public health, neurology, internal medicine, gerontology, and biostatistics.

In Part I "Cardiovascular Risk Factors, Cardiovascular Disease, and Neuropsychological Performance" eight chapters examine the neuropsychological consequences of cardiovascular risk factors and early manifestations of cardiovascular disease. Chapter 1, by Katzel and Waldstein, first provides an overview of cardiovascular disease classification. Next, Waldstein and Katzel (chap. 2), Muldoon, Flory, and Ryan (chap. 3), and Ryan (chap. 4) describe the relations of hypertension, serum lipid concentrations, and diabetes mellitus, respectively, to cognitive functioning. In chapter 5 by Elias, Elias, Robbins, Wolf, and D'Agostino, cardiovascular risk factors are considered in terms of their epidemiological significance and in terms of their cumulative impact.

The next three chapters describe the neuropsychological consequences of later manifestations of cardiovascular disease. Everson, Helkala, Kaplan, and Salonen (chap. 6) discuss the impact of atherosclerosis on cognitive function. Peripheral vascular disease is reviewed by Phillips (chap. 7), and Vingerhoets (chap. 8) examines cardiac arrhythmias, myocardial infarction, and cardiac arrest in relation to cognition.

In Part II "Treatment of Cardiovascular Disease and Neuropsychological Performance," four chapters examine the impact of several common treatments for cardiovascular disease on neuropsychological function. Jonas, Blumenthal, Madden, and Serra review literature on antihypertensive medications and cognitive function in chapter 9. Coronary artery bypass surgery is reviewed by Newman, Stygall, and Kong in chapter 10. Bornstein covers the cognitive sequelae of heart transplantation in chapter 11. Carotid endarterectomy is reviewed by Baird and Pieroth in chapter 12.

Part III, "Cerebrovascular Disease and Neuropsychological Performance" includes three chapters that describe the relation of cerebrovascular disease to neuropsychological performance. The section begins with an overview of cerebrovascular disease classification by Merino and Hachinski (chap. 13). Next, Kramer, Kemenoff, and Chui describe the cognitive correlates of subcortical ischemic vascular dementia (chap. 14). In chapter 15, Brown and Zorilla review the neuropsychological consequences of stroke.

We hope that this volume will stimulate further research on the neuropsychology of cardiovascular disease by focusing attention on critical areas of future investigation and by providing testable models for underlying causation. It is also our wish that this volume will promote multidisciplinary research efforts. We believe that collaboration among various disciplines such as neuropsychology, behavioral medicine, epidemiology, life-span psychology, gerontology, nursing, and medicine provides the key to advancing our understanding of the neuropsychology of cardiovascular disease and integrating research findings into clinical practice. Our ultimate goal should be to enhance the preservation of cognitive functioning across the lifespan.

—*Shari R. Waldstein*
—*Merrill F. Elias*

List of Contributors

Anne D. Baird, Ph.D., Neuropsychology Division, Henry Ford Health System, Detroit, MI.

James A. Blumenthal, Ph.D., Department of Psychiatry and Behavioral Sciences, Duke University Medical Center, and Department of Psychology: Social and Health Sciences, Duke University.

Robert A. Bornstein, Ph.D., Departments of Psychiatry and Neurology, The Ohio State University.

Gregory G. Brown, Ph.D., Psychology Service, Veterans Administration San Diego Healthcare System, and Department of Psychiatry, University of California, San Diego.

Helena C. Chui, M.D., Department of Neurology, University of Southern California.

Ralph B. D'Agostino, Ph.D., Statistics and Consulting Unit, Department of Mathematics and Statistics, Boston University.

Merrill F. Elias, Ph.D., M.P.H., Statistics and Consulting Unit, Department of Mathematics, Boston University, Boston University Schools of Medicine and Public Health, and the Department of Psychology, University of Maine.

Penelope K. Elias, Ph.D., Statistics and Consulting Unit, Department of Mathematics and Statistics, Boston University.

Susan A. Everson, Ph.D., M.P.H., Department of Epidemiology, University of Michigan School of Public Health.

Janine D. Flory, Ph.D., Behavioral Physiology Laboratory, Department of Psychology, University of Pittsburgh.

Vladimir Hachinski, M.D., FRCP(C), M.Sc. (DME), D.Sc. (Med), Department of Clinical Neurological Sciences, The University of Western Ontario.

Eeva-Liisa Helkala, Ph.D., Department of Public Health and General Practice and Research Institute of Public Health, University of Kuopio.

Deborah L. Jonas, Ph.D., Department of Psychology: Experimental, Duke University.

George A. Kaplan, Ph.D., Department of Epidemiology, University of Michigan School of Public Health.

Leslie I. Katzel, M.D., Ph.D., Division of Gerontology, Department of Medicine, University of Maryland School of Medicine, and Geriatrics Research Education and Clinical Center, Baltimore Veterans Affairs Medical Center.

Lada A. Kemenoff, Psy.D., Department of Neurology, University of California, San Francisco Medical Center.

Robert Kong, MBBS, FRCA, Unit of Health Psychology, Department of Psychiatry and Behavioural Sciences, University College London.

Joel H. Kramer, Psy.D., Department of Psychiatry, University of California, San Francisco Medical Center.

David J. Madden, Ph.D., Center for the Study of Aging and Human Development, and Department of Psychiatry and Behavioral Sciences, Duke University Medical Center.

José Merino, M.D., M. Phil., Department of Clinical Neurological Sciences, The University of Western Ontario.

Matthew F. Muldoon, M.D., M.P.H., Center for Clinical Pharmacology, University of Pittsburgh School of Medicine.

Stanton P. Newman, D. Phil., Dip Psych. AFBPS, Unit of Health Psychology, Department of Psychiatry and Behavioural Sciences, University College London.

Natalie A. Phillips, Ph.D., Department of Psychology, Concordia University.

Elizabeth M. Pieroth, Psy.D., Schwab Rehabilitation Hospital, Chicago, IL.

Michael A. Robbins, Ph.D., Department of Psychology, University of Maine.

Christopher M. Ryan, Ph.D., Department of Psychiatry, University of Pittsburgh School of Medicine, and Western Psychiatric Institute and Clinic, Pittsburgh, PA.

Jukka T. Salonen, M.D., Ph.D., M.Sc.P.H., Department of Public Health and General Practice and Research Institute of Public Health, University of Kuopio.

Matt Serra, Ph.D., Department of Psychology: Social and Health Sciences, Duke University

Jan Stygall, M.Sc., Unit of Health Psychology, Department of Psychiatry and Behavioural Sciences, University College London.

Guy Vingerhoets, Ph.D., Department of Psychiatry and Neuropsychology, University of Ghent.

Shari R. Waldstein, Ph.D., Department of Psychology, University of Maryland, Baltimore County, and Division of Gerontology, Department of Medicine, University of Maryland School of Medicine, and Geriatrics Research Education and Clinical Center, Baltimore Veterans Affairs Medical Center.

Philip A. Wolf, M.D., Department of Neurology, Boston University School of Medicine.

Lisa T. Eyler Zorilla, Ph.D., Psychology Service, Veterans Administration San Diego Healthcare System, and Department of Psychiatry, University of California, San Diego.

PART I

Cardiovascular Risk Factors,
Cardiovascular Disease, and
Neuropsychological Performance

CHAPTER ONE

Classification
of Cardiovascular Disease

LESLIE I. KATZEL
University of Maryland School of Medicine
and Baltimore Veterans Affairs Medical Center

SHARI R. WALDSTEIN
University of Maryland, Baltimore County;
University of Maryland School of Medicine;
and Baltimore Veterans Affairs Medical Center

Cardiovascular disease (CVD), in broad terms, comprises diseases of the heart, blood vessels, and circulation. The most common CVDs are hypertension, coronary artery disease (CAD), cerebrovascular disease, and peripheral vascular disease (aneurysms and peripheral arterial disease [PAD]; see Table 1.1). Other CVDs include congenital heart disease, rheumatic heart disease, valvular heart disease, congestive heart failure, and cardiac arrhythmias. Some researchers use the term *coronary heart disease* (*CHD*) interchangeably with CAD. However, CAD more specifically refers to atherosclerotic disease of the coronary arteries, whereas CHD can be caused by atherosclerotic and nonatherosclerotic (e.g., autoimmune, infectious) processes. This chapter provides an overview of the prevalence and clinical manifestations of hypertension and the atherosclerotic diseases examined in subsequent chapters of this book.

PREVALENCE OF CARDIOVASCULAR DISEASE

It is estimated that approximately 50 million adults in the United States have hypertension (Sixth Report of the Joint National Committee on Prevention, Detection, Evaluation, and Treatment of High Blood Pressure, 1997), 12 million

TABLE 1.1
Classification of Cardiovascular Disease

Disease	Prevalence	Comments
Hypertension	50 million	35% of all atherosclerotic cardiovascular events can be attributed to hypertension.
Coronary heart disease (CHD)	12 million	CHD accounts for half of all deaths in the United States.
Congestive heart failure (CHF)	4.6 million	75% of patients with CHF have a history of hypertension.
Peripheral arterial disease (PAD)	3.5 million	PAD is a major cause of ambulatory dysfunction.
Carotid artery disease	2 million	A major cause of stroke; one third of patients who have had a TIA have a stroke within 5 years.
Stroke	3.9 million	Stroke is the third leading cause of death and the leading cause of functional disability.

Note. TIA = transient ischemic attack.

people have CHD (American Heart Association, 1999), 3.5 million have PAD (Kannel, 1996b), and 3.9 million have had a stroke (National Heart, Lung, and Blood Institute, 1996; see Table 1.1). These estimates, based on national surveys, may be conservative, because hypertension, CAD, and peripheral vascular diseases are often clinically silent, particularly in elderly people, and these diseases may thus be present without accompanying symptoms.

In 1993 it was estimated that CVD accounted for $126 billion in health care expenditures in the United States (National Heart, Lung, and Blood Institute, 1996). CHD costs were estimated at $32.7 billion per year; stroke costs at $21.9 billion; hypertension at $19.1 billion; congestive heart failure at $17.8 billion; and other CVDS, including PAD, at $34.2 billion. One fourth of patients with CHD and more than 40% of patients who have had a stroke have functional disabilities related to their diseases. Collectively, the morbidity, mortality, and health care costs associated with CVD are substantial.

OVERVIEW OF ATHEROSCLEROSIS RISK FACTORS

Environmental as well as genetic factors play a role in the pathophysiology of atherosclerosis. The majority of the studies that have examined risk factors for atherosclerosis have focused specifically on risk for the development of CAD. Risk factors for atherosclerosis in the other vascular beds, resulting in carotid artery atherosclerosis, stroke, and PAD, are similar to those observed for CAD. Major well-established risk factors for CAD have been traditionally divided into nonmodifiable and modifiable risk factors (see Table 1.2). The nonmodifiable risk factors comprise age, male gender, and family history of premature CAD and genetic factors. The modifiable factors include dyslipidemia (elevated total and low density lipoprotein cholesterol, reduced levels of high-density lipoprotein cholesterol); cigarette smoking; hypertension; diabetes; obesity; a sedentary lifestyle; and psychosocial factors, including hostility and depression. In addition, a number of other metabolic abnormalities, including prothrombogenic (blood clotting) and coagulation factors may increase CVD risk (see Table 1.3). The evidence linking these factors to CVD risk is not as comprehensive as that for the factors listed in Table 1.2. In addition, recent studies also suggest that inflammation and infection may play a role in atherogenesis (see chaps. 5 and 6).

There is a propensity for many of these CVD risk factors to cluster in given individuals, resulting in atherogenic phenotypes. An example of this is the metabolic syndrome *X*, or the *insulin resistance syndrome*, in which individuals often have the "deadly quartet" of central obesity, dyslipidemia, hypertension, and glucose intolerance or diabetes mellitus (Kaplan, 1989). The CVD risk factors

TABLE 1.2
Established Nonmodifiable and Modifiable Cardiovascular Disease Risk Factors

Nonmodifiable Factors	*Modifiable Factors*
Age	Dyslipidemia
Male gender	Elevated levels of low-density lipoprotein cholesterol
Family history / genetics	Reduced levels of high-density lipoprotein cholesterol
	Hypertension
	Cigarette smoking
	Diabetes
	Obesity
	Physical inactivity
	Psychosocial factors
	Hostility
	Depression

TABLE 1.3
Proposed Cardiovascular Disease Risk Factors*

Proatherogenic	*Prothrombogenic*
Elevated homocysteine levels	Lipoprotein (a)
Oxidized lipoprotein particles	Plasminogen
Hyperinsulinemia	Fibrinogen
Small, dense, low-density lipoprotein particles	Factor VII
Elevated triglycerides	Plasminogen activator inhibitor 1
Abnormal cholesteryl ester transfer proteins	

Note. Adapted from Hoeg (1997).

increase risk for atherosclerosis in an additive fashion. Multivariate analyses of CVD risk factor and cardiovascular outcome data in the Framingham Heart Study have produced gender specific risk factor scores for the development of CAD (Wilson et al., 1998). These risk assessment scores provide information on both the absolute and relative risk of a patient developing CAD and can be used as a guide in patient education and treatment. It should be noted that the risk scores underestimate an individual's true risk when there are severe abnormalities in the given risk factors; for example, heavy smoking, severe hypertension, and hyperlipidemia confer much greater absolute and relative risk than the scores would indicate. Data from the Framingham Heart Study demonstrate that, over 8 years of follow-up, individuals in the top 10% of risk scores account for one fifth of new cases of CAD and one third of cases of new stroke and PAD. The risk factors for CVD (see chaps. 2–5) and the pathogenesis of atherosclerosis (see chap. 6) are explored in greater detail in subsequent chapters.

OVERVIEW OF HYPERTENSION

Hypertension is defined as a systolic blood pressure >140 millimeters of mercury (mm Hg) and or diastolic blood pressure >90 mm Hg (Sixth Report of the Joint National Committee on Prevention, Detection, Evaluation, and Treatment of High Blood Pressure, 1997). The prevalence of hypertension increases with age and is greater in Black people than in White people. At younger ages, women have lower blood pressures than men; however, the increase of blood pressure with aging is greater in women such that the prevalence of hypertension is higher in older women than in older men. In the third National Health and Nutrition Examination Survey, more than 60% of the respondents who were above the age of 60 years had hypertension (Burt et al., 1995). It is estimated that 90% of hypertension in adults is *essential hypertension,* also known as *primary hypertension of unknown cause* (see chap. 2)—2%–5% due to chronic renal disease; 1%–4% due to renovascular hypertension; and the rest due to a variety of causes, including aortic coarctation, Cushing's disease, primary aldosteronism, pheochromocytoma, and other miscellaneous causes.

There is a strong positive graded relationship among systolic blood pressure; diastolic blood pressure; and all of the major atherosclerotic diseases and clinical outcomes, including CAD, PAD, stroke, and carotid atherosclerosis. Hypertension is the fourth largest cause of functional disability. Hypertension causes left ventricular hypertrophy and increased myocardial fibrosis, and some patients progress to hypertensive cardiomyopathy and congestive heart failure. Indeed, 75% of patients with congestive heart failure have a history of hypertension. It is estimated that 4.8 million Americans have congestive heart failure.

Hypertension also causes damage in other organs, leading to aortic aneurysm or dissection, retinopathy, renal nephrosclerosis and nephropathy, and lacunar infarcts. Even well-controlled hypertensive patients may develop brain white matter disease and neurocognitive impairment (Salerno et al., 1995; see chap. 2). Hypertension is also a risk factor for vascular dementia (see chap. 14). Data from the Framingham Heart Study suggest that perhaps 35% of all athero-sclerotic cardiovascular events can be attributed to hypertension (Kannel, 1996a).

As noted previously, hypertension tends to occur in association with other atherogenic risk factors. Patients with hypertension have a higher prevalence of hyperinsulinemia, glucose intolerance, abdominal obesity and hyperuricemia. Some believe that hyperinsulinemia plays an integral part in the pathogenesis of hypertension. Treatments to reduce risk for atherosclerosis in patients with hypertension should be directed both at reducing blood pressure and correcting these other metabolic abnormalities.

OVERVIEW OF CHD

Epidemiology

CHD has been the leading cause of death in the United States since the 1920s and accounts for approximately half of all deaths in the United States (Henne-kens, 1998; Levy & Thom, 1998; Thom, Kannel, Silbershatz, & D'Agostino, 1998). Approximately 12 million people in the United States have CHD, a category that includes angina pectoris, myocardial infarction, and sudden cardiac death. This includes 800,000 new heart attacks and about 450,000 recurrent heart attacks. The prevalence and mortality rates from CHD increase exponentially with age, doubling roughly every 5 years. The prevalence of CHD is estimated to be 61.8 per 1,000 for middle-aged adults and 138.5 per 1,000 for people older than 65 years (Thom et al., 1998).

The age-adjusted death rate from CHD has declined by more than 50% in the United States since the late 1960s (Levy & Thom, 1998). Much of this decline has been due to a reduction in the incidence rates for myocardial infarction. There has also been a decline in the case fatality rates; that is, the death rate of people who have suffered a heart attack has declined because of improved medical care. However, because of the aging of the population, the overall prevalence of patients with CHD is increasing (Hennekens, 1998).

Manifestations

The cardinal symptoms of CHD include dyspnea (shortness of breath at rest or with exertion), chest pain (angina), syncope (loss of consciousness), palpitations (unpleasant awareness of forceful or rapid heartbeat), cough, edema (swelling in lower extremities), hemoptysis (blood-streaked expectoration), and fatigue. Many of these symptoms can also be caused by noncardiac diseases, such as gastritis, pulmonary disease, and musculoskeletal disorders. Therefore, in the clinical evaluation and management of the patient it is imperative that the noncardiac causes of these symptoms be distinguished from the cardiac causes.

Angina Pectoris. When atherosclerosis affects the coronary arteries (i.e., CAD) the clinical manifestations of the disease reflect both the chronic and the acute effects of luminal narrowing on coronary blood flow. Coronary blood flow that inadequately meets metabolic demands results in myocardial ischemia, with angina pectoris being the pathognomonic symptom. More abrupt or severe disruption of the blood supply that is due to a rupture of an atheromatous plaque or to a superimposed thrombus can result in an acute myocardial infarction (see chap. 8). The clinical manifestations of CAD include asymptomatic silent myocardial ischemia, angina, unstable angina, myocardial infarction, arrhythmias, heart failure, and death. Sequelae of CAD and myocardial infarction include cardiomyopathy, congestive heart failure, left ventricular aneurysms, mitral valve regurgitation, arrhythmias, and other abnormalities in the conduction system. The presenting cardiac event is more likely to be a myocardial infarction or sudden death in men and angina in women. More than half of all coronary events are sudden events. Approximately 300,000 people die suddenly in the United States each year, and many of these people are in apparently good health without a prior history of symptomatic heart disease. Data from the Framingham Heart Study demonstrate that in one third of patients the first, only, and last symptom of CAD is sudden death (Schatzkin et al., 1984).

Angina pectoris classically refers to chest pain or pressure produced by myocardial ischemia. It typically occurs in the setting of exertion resulting in increased demand that cannot be met adequately by diseased coronary arteries, thus leading to ischemia. Angina pain typically leads to a pressurelike sensation in the chest, but the pain may radiate to the left arm, jaw, teeth, or throat. Some patients describe a burning sensation. Accompanying symptoms often include dyspnea, tachycardia (rapid heart rate), and diaphoresis (sweating). The symptoms usually begin at a low intensity, increase over 2 to 3 minutes and last less than 15 minutes. Angina can also occur at rest, or it can be due to vasospasm of the coronary arteries. The pathophysiology of the pain is uncertain, because studies that have used Holter monitors to examine ischemia during activities of daily living demonstrate that the majority of ischemic episodes are clinically silent.

Medical therapy for angina is directed at decreasing myocardial oxygen demand, increasing myocardial blood flow, or both. A large number of drugs are used to treat angina. These include beta blockers, nitrates, calcium channel blockers, vasodilators, and antiplatelet drugs. The beta blockers, calcium channel blockers, and vasodilators are also used to treat hypertension (see chap. 9) and some cardiac arrhythmias. Surgical and interventional cardiology procedures to treat CAD include angioplasty, arthrectomy, and coronary artery bypass graft surgery (see chap. 10). Promising techniques currently under evaluation for treatment of angina and CAD include angiogenesis (induction of the growth of new blood vessels) and laser therapy to increase collateral blood flow.

Myocardial Infarction. The term *myocardial infarction* refers to the death of cardiac tissue because of a relative or absolute insufficiency of blood supply. In the United States there are approximately 1.5 million patients who have a myocardial infarction each year, and it is the leading cause of death. The pathophysiology of myocardial infarction is discussed further in chapter 8. In the classic, acute myocardial infarction, the initial presenting symptoms are similar to angina but are more severe, more persistent, and are unrelieved by nitroglycerin. Sweating, nausea, and vomiting are also common. The presenting signs and symptoms may be different in elderly people. The predominant symptoms may be the sudden onset of dyspnea, confusion, worsening of heart failure, and syncope, as opposed to crushing chest pain. Data from the Framingham Heart Study suggest that one third of all myocardial infarctions may be clinically silent or may present with atypical features that are not recognized as being cardiac in nature. The severity of the acute myocardial infarction can be classified on the basis of the presence or absence of congestive heart failure using the Killip classification scale. In Class I there are no signs of heart failure, Class II patients have mild to moderate rales, Class III patients have pulmonary edema, and Class IV patients are in cardiogenic shock. Patients in Class III and IV have an acute mortality are of more than 30%, whereas Class I patients have a mortality rate of less than 5%. It is important to note, however, that one third of patients with acute myocardial infarction die before reaching a hospital.

Cardiac Arrhythmias

The cardiac arrhythmias consist of a number of acute and chronic disorders of heart rate and rhythm. In 1993 it was estimated that there were 3.6 million visits to physicians for cardiac arrhythmias (Myerburg, Kessler, & Castellano, 1998). Broad categories include disorders that cause slow ventricular heart rates (bradycardias, with rates of fewer than 60 beats/min) and fast ventricular heart rates (tachycardias, with rates of more than 100 beats/min). Some of the more prevalent brady-arrhythmias are sinus bradycardia and atrioventricular electrical impulse conduction delays, including first-degree atrial-ventricular block; second-degree atrial-ventricular block (Mobitz I and II); and third-degree, or complete heart block. The symptoms of bradycardia include fatigue and other symptoms of inadequate cardiac output, such as dizziness (presyncope), syncope, confusion, and symptoms of heart failure. Persistent symptoms may necessitate pacemaker placement.

The tachycardias are generally distinguished as being supraventricular (narrow-complex) tachycardias, with the conduction abnormality before the atrial ventricular node, or ventricular (wide-complex) tachycardias. Common narrow-complex tachycardias include sinus tachycardia, atrial fibrillation, and atrial flutter. Atrial fibrillation is the most common sustained arrhythmia for which patients seek treatment. Its prevalence increases markedly with aging, and it is a major cause of thromboembolic events. Common wide-complex tachycardias include ventricular tachycardia and ventricular fibrillation. Ventricular tachycardia is the most commonly encountered life-threatening arrhythmia. Symptoms of the tachycardias include palpitations, shortness of breath, lightheadedness, angina, and syncope. Untreated ventricular tachycardia may degenerate into ventricular fibrillation, causing hemodynamic compromise and ultimately death. Treatment involves a number of classes of antiarrhythmic drugs, electrical cardioversion, ablative therapy (destruction of the source of the arrhythmias using electric current), pacemakers, implantable defibrillators, and anticoagulation therapy with warfarin to prevent embolic events. Interested readers are referred to Myerburg et al.'s (1998) chapter in *Hurst's The Heart, Arteries and Veins,* or other standard internal medicine textbooks, for a more comprehensive discussion of the pathophysiology and medical management of the cardiac arrhythmias.

OVERVIEW OF PERIPHERAL VASCULAR DISEASES

The two most common diseases that affect the peripheral arteries are aneurysms and arterial occlusions, both of which in most cases are due to atherosclerosis.

Aneurysm

An aneurysm is a permanent dilatation of an artery, which is usually due to a weakness in the arterial wall. Aneurysms most commonly involve the larger arteries, such as the aorta, but they can also occur in smaller arteries. Hypertension and atherosclerosis can cause aneurysms, particularly abdominal aortic aneurysms. Abdominal aortic aneurysms can be detected by physical examination and confirmed by a variety of imaging studies, including ultrasound, magnetic resonance imaging, computerized tomography, and arteriography. Studies of the natural history of abdominal aortic aneurysms suggest that 80% of these aneurysms expand over time. The risk of acute rupture is related to the diameter of the aneurysm (Bickerstaff, Hollier, & Van Peenen, 1984). Patients with abdominal aortic aneurysms typically have no chronic symptoms attributable to the aneurysm prior to rupture. Given the very high mortality associated with the rupture, patients with abdominal aneurysms larger than 4 to 5 cm should be evaluated for elective surgical resection.

PAD

Symptomatic PAD afflicts approximately 6% of the U.S. population above the age of 55 years. It is estimated that there are more than 40,000 deaths related to PAD annually in the United States (primarily from coexistent CAD), 267,000 hospitalizations, and 2.7 million office visits at an estimated cost of more than $3.3 billion (Kannel, 1996b). Thus, PAD is associated with significant morbidity, mortality, and health care costs.

PAD is characterized by stenoses and occlusions of the arteries of the lower extremities. The reduction in blood flow distal to the occlusion(s) results in diminished blood pressure in the dorsalis pedis and posterior tibial arteries at the level of the ankle. A reduction in the ratio of the blood pressure in the brachial artery in the arm to the pressure in the ankle arteries (ankle-to-brachial pressure index [ABI]) is the hallmark of PAD. The presence of PAD is defined by ABI values of less than .97, with values greater than .97 considered in the normal range. Routine evaluation includes measurement of segmental blood pressures and blood flow using Doppler ultrasound. Arteriography is generally reserved for patients considered for surgical reconstruction or balloon angioplasty.

In the early stages of PAD, the reduction in blood flow does not cause any noticeable symptoms and is defined as Stage I (asymptomatic PAD) according to the Fontaine classification system. However, population studies demonstrate that a higher percentage of older women with low ABI reported difficulty in performing heavy housework and walking two to three blocks than women with higher ABI (Vogt, Cauley, Kuller, & Nevitt, 1994). This suggests that even mild subclinical PAD may result in decreased mobility and functional status.

As PAD progresses (Stage II), ischemic pain in the lower musculature occurs with walking, and the patients have symptoms of intermittent claudication. Patients with disease of the iliac arteries may have cramping or tightness in the hips, buttocks, and thighs. In more advanced stages of the disease, blood flow is reduced to such an extent that there is ischemic pain at rest (Stage III), and limb-threatening ischemia with ischemic ulcerations and gangrene or necrosis (Stage IV). Patients with severe PAD have a very poor long-term prognosis. In one study, the 5-year mortality rate in patients with critical limb-threatening ischemia was over 60% (Criqui et al., 1992). The poor prognosis is attributed to the high prevalence of CAD, hypertension, hyperlipidemia, diabetes, stroke, and other comorbid conditions in patients with PAD. Medical and surgical management of PAD is discussed in greater detail in chapter 7.

OVERVIEW OF CAROTID ARTERY DISEASE

Atherosclerotic disease of the carotid arteries and vertebrobasilar arteries affects approximately 5% of older adults in the United States. The signs and symptoms of carotid artery disease differ somewhat from those of vertebrobasilar disease, but both may mimic other diseases. The major clinical manifestations of disease of the carotid and vertebrobasilar arteries range from asymptomatic bruits discovered on physical examinations to transient ischemic attacks (TIA), amaurosis fugax (temporary blindness in one eye), reversible ischemic neurologic disability, syncope, headache, paresthesias, and ultimately stroke.

Studies indicate that approximately one third of patients who have had a TIA will subsequently have a stroke within 5 years. The relative risk of stroke in patients who have had a TIA is approximately five times higher than that in age-matched patients who have not had a TIA (Brown, 1997). As a result of this heightened risk for stroke, it has been proposed that carotid endarterectomy may decrease the risk for subsequent stroke in patients who have suffered a TIA or in asymptomatic patients with significant stenoses of the carotid arteries. Therefore, a series of clinical trials examined the effect of carotid endarterectomy on the subsequent incidence of stroke in symptomatic patients—that is, those who have had recent TIAs or nondisabling strokes—and in asymptomatic patients (see chap. 12). Collectively, these data suggest that patients with symptomatic disease with severe stenosis derive the greatest overall benefit from carotid endarterectomy (Chassin, 1998).

OVERVIEW OF STROKE

It is estimated that 3.9 million people in the United States have had strokes, with more than 700,000 new strokes occurring each year. Stroke is the third leading cause of death in the United States, accounting for 200,000 deaths per year, and is the number-one cause of disability in adults (National Heart, Lung, and Blood Institute, 1996). The overall mortality rate from stroke is about 25% in the first month and approximately 50% at 5 years, primarily because of coexistent CAD. Among long-term stroke survivors, 48% have hemiparesis, 22% cannot walk, 25% to more than 50% report difficulty or dependence in the activities of daily living, and 32% are clinically depressed (Helgason & Wolf, 1997).

In the United States, approximately 80%–85% of strokes are ischemic, with the remainder being hemorrhagic (see chap. 13). Ischemic cerebrovascular disease is divided into two broad categories: TIAs (cerebral ischemia) and stroke (cerebral infarction). Strokes in turn may be divided into those that are acutely presenting with worsening of focal ischemia (stroke in evolution) and those with stable neurologic symptoms (completed strokes). The most common causes of cerebral ischemia and infarction are atherosclerosis with thromboembolism and cardiogenic emboli. Other causes of stroke include valvular heart disease, cardiac arrhythmia, vasculitis, arterial dissection, hemorrhagic disorders (polycythemia, sickle cell disease, etc.), hypercoagulable states, vasoconstriction, infection, and other assorted causes. The clinical manifestations of stroke are related to the area of the brain affected and the magnitude of tissue necrosis and cerebral edema. The pathophysiology of stroke is further discussed in chapters 13 and 15.

The risk factors for stroke are similar to those for CAD; however, hypertension plays a more prominent role as a risk factor for stroke than for CHD (Kannel, 1996a). Hypertension adversely affects the prognosis of survival after a stroke. Hypertension also causes a number of vascular syndromes, including lacunar infarctions and hypertensive intracerebral hemorrhage, as well as direct damage to the cerebral vasculature that causes subtle cognitive impairment (Salerno et al., 1995; see chap. 2). The presence of carotid artery disease, cardiac disease, atrial fibrillation, and congestive heart failure significantly increase the risk for stroke. Like CHD, the age-adjusted death rate for stroke has declined 55% since the late 1960s, but there are indications that the incidence rate of stroke has actually increased slightly since the early 1990s.

SUMMARY

CVD remains a major cause of morbidity and mortality, killing more people each year than the next seven leading causes of death combined. The age-adjusted death rate from CVD is declining; however, because of the aging of the U.S. population, the prevalence of hypertension and atherosclerotic diseases is actually increasing. Therefore, as people live longer, CVDs will remain critically important in terms of added years of cumulative risk for disability. Continued efforts aimed at lifestyle and pharmaceutical interventions to treat hypertension and other risk factors for atherosclerosis are necessary to reduce the disability and health care costs attributable to CVD.

ACKNOWLEDGEMENT

Preparation of this chapter was supported in part by National Institute of Aging Grants 1K24A600930–01 and 1R29AG15112 and by a Veterans Affairs Merit Grant.

REFERENCES

American Heart Association. (1999). *2000 Heart and stroke statistical update*. Dallas, TX: American Heart Association.

Bickerstaff, L. K., Hollier, L. H., & Van Peenen, H. J. (1984). Abdominal aortic aneurysms: The changing natural history. *Journal of Vascular Surgery, 1*, 6–16.

Brown, R. D. (1997). Cerebrovascular disease. In R. B. Conn, W. Z. Borer, & J. W. Snyder (Eds.), *Current diagnosis* (9th ed., pp. 313–321). Philadelphia: Saunders.

Burt, V. L., Whelton, P., Roccella, E. J., Brown, C., Cutler, J. A., Higgins, M., Horan, M. J., & Labarthe, D. (1995). Prevalence of hypertension in the US adult population: Results from the third National Health and Nutrition Examination Survey, 1988–1991. *Hypertension, 25,* 305–313.

Chassin, M. R. (1998). Appropriate use of carotid endarterectomy. *New England Journal of Medicine, 339,* 1468–1470.

Criqui, M. H., Langer, R. D., Fronek, A., Fergelson, H. S., Klauber, M. S., McCann, T. J., & Browner, D. (1992). Mortality over a period of 10 years in patients with peripheral arterial disease. *New England Journal of Medicine, 325,* 381–386.

Helgason, C. M., & Wolf, P. A. (1997). American Heart Association Prevention Conference IV: Prevention and rehabilitation of stroke. Executive summary. *Circulation, 96,* 701–707.

Hennekens, C. H. (1998). Increasing burden of cardiovascular disease: Current knowledge and future directions for research on risk factors. *Circulation, 97,* 1095–1102.

Hoeg, J. M. (1997). Evaluating coronary heart disease risk. *Journal of the American Medical Association, 277,,* 1387–1390.

Kannel, W. B. (1996). Blood pressure as cardiovascular risk factor: Prevention and treatment. *Journal of the American Medical Association, 275,* 1571–1576.

Kannel, W. B. (1996). The demographics of claudication and the aging of the American population. *Journal of Vascular Medicine, 1,* 60–64.

Kaplan, N. M. (1989). The deadly quartet: Upper-body obesity, glucose intolerance, hypertriglyceridemia, and hypertension. *Archives of Internal Medicine, 149,* 1514–1520.

Levy, D., & Thom, T. J. (1998). Death rates from coronary disease—Progress and a puzzling paradox. *New England Journal of Medicine, 339,* 915–916.

Myerburg, R. S., Kessler, K. M., & Castellano, A. (1998). Recognition, clinical assessment and management of arrhythmias and conduction disturbances. In R. W. Alexander, R. Schlant, & V. Fuster (Eds.), *Hurst's the heart, arteries and veins* (9th ed., pp. 873–941). New York: McGraw-Hill.

National Heart, Lung, and Blood Institute. (1996). *Morbidity and mortality chartbook on cardiovascular, lung, and blood diseases/1996.* Washington, DC: U.S. Department of Health and Human Services.

Salerno, J. A., Grady, C., Mentis, M., Gonzalez-Aviles, A., Wagner, E., Schapiro, M. B., & Rapoport, S. I. (1995). Brain metabolic function in older men with chronic essential hypertension. *Journal of Gerontology, 150A,* M147–M154

Schatzkin, A., Cupples, A., Heeren, T., Morelock, S., Mucatel, M., & Kannel, W. B. (1984). The epidemiology of sudden unexpected death: Risk factors for men and women in the Framingham Heart Study. *American Heart Journal, 24,* 1300–1306.

Sixth Report of the Joint National Committee on Prevention, Detection, Evaluation, and Treatment of High Blood Pressure. (1997). *Archives of Internal Medicine, 157,* 2413–2446.

Thom, T. J., Kannel, W. B., Silbershatz, H., D'Agostino, R. B. (1998). Incidence, prevalence and mortality of cardiovascular diseases in the United States. In R. W. Alexander, R. C. Schlant, & V. Fuster (Eds), *Hurst's the heart, arteries and veins* (9th ed., pp. 3–17). New York: McGraw-Hill.

Vogt, M. T., Cauley, J. A., Kuller, L. H., & Nevitt, M. C. (1994). Functional status and mobility among elderly women with lower extremity arterial disease: The study of osteoporotic fractures. *Journal of the American Geriatrics Society, 42,* 923–929.

Wilson, P. W. F., D'Agostino, R. B., Levy, D., Belanger, A. M., Silbershatz, W., & Kannel, W. B. (1998). Prediction of coronary heart disease using risk factor categories. *Circulation, 97,* 1837–1847.

CHAPTER TWO

Hypertension and Cognitive Function

SHARI R. WALDSTEIN
University of Maryland, Baltimore County;
University of Maryland School of Medicine;
and Baltimore Veterans Affairs Medical Center

LESLIE I. KATZEL
University of Maryland School of Medicine
and Baltimore Veterans Affairs Medical Center

Hypertension is one of the earliest manifestations of cardiovascular disease (CVD). In the United States, *hypertension* is currently defined as a systolic and diastolic blood pressure (BP) greater than or equal to 140 millimeters of mercury (mm Hg) and or 90 mm Hg, respectively, as measured on at least two separate occasions (Joint National Committee on Prevention, Detection, Evaluation, and Treatment of High Blood Pressure [JNC], 1997). These criteria reflect a lowering, over time, of the BP cutoffs used to define hypertension. Cross-cultural differences in hypertension criteria are also common.

Hypertension is a major risk factor for atherogenesis, coronary heart disease (CHD), and stroke (Stamler, 1992). The brain is thus one of several target organs (e.g., heart, kidneys, eyes) that are damaged by hypertension. However, prior to clinically evident cerebrovascular complications, hypertension-related changes in the brain and cognition are detectable with methods such as neuropsychological assessment and neuroimaging.

In this chapter we provide a select review of the literature on hypertension and cognitive (or neuropsychological) performance. A detailed review of the association between hypertension (or BP levels) and the dementias (e.g., vascular dementia, Alzheimer's disease) is beyond the scope of this chapter. We first provide a brief overview of hypertension epidemiology and pathophysiology. Next, we review case control and cross-sectional, population-based studies of hypertension and neuropsychological function and consider several variables that may moderate hypertension–performance relations. We then review the longitudinal association of hypertension (or BP levels) with cognition. We next discuss potential mechanisms underlying the relation between hypertension and cognitive function and conclude with a general summary, consideration of clinical significance, and suggestions for future research.

HYPERTENSION EPIDEMIOLOGY AND PATHOPHYSIOLOGY

It is estimated that one in five Americans, or 50 million individuals, has hypertension (American Heart Association, 1998). Approximately 90%–95% of all cases of adult-onset hypertension are *essential* (or *primary*) *hypertension,* a term that refers to a sustained BP elevation of unknown (idiopathic) cause. Elevated BP that is attributable to a known medical disorder is called *secondary hypertension.* Prevalence estimates of secondary hypertension include 2%–5% due to chronic renal disease; 1%–4% due to renal artery stenosis; and 1%–2% due to a variety of other causes, including aortic coarctation, Cushing's disease, primary aldosteronism, and pheochromocytoma (JNC, 1997).

Essential hypertension is thought to be determined by a complex interplay of genetic and environmental factors (Kaplan, 1998). Thus, a positive familial history of hypertension is a known risk factor. Indeed, BP levels have been observed to aggregate in families, with a polygenic mode of inheritance suggested. Recent findings indicate the involvement of numerous candidate genes in the determination of interindividual variability in BP (Krushkal et al., 1999).

Hypertension incidence and prevalence increase with age. Male gender is a risk factor until the age of 55, after which prevalence rates are greater among women. Hypertension is also more common among African Americans than among Whites. Numerous lifestyle and behavioral risk factors for hypertension are suggested; they include excess body weight; physical inactivity; dietary factors, such as high sodium and low potassium or calcium intake; excessive alcohol consumption; oral contraceptive use; various psychosocial factors; and stress-related cardiovascular reactivity (American Heart Association, 1998; JNC, 1997; Kaplan, 1998).

The complexity of BP regulation is highlighted in Fig. 2.1. As just discussed, the pathogenesis of hypertension is multifactorial, and numerous abnormalities have been ascribed to the renal, endocrine, and cardiovascular regulatory systems. BP is ultimately determined by the cardiac output multiplied by the peripheral vascular resistance, each of which is influenced by numerous neural, hormonal, local (e.g., autoregulatory), reflexive (e.g, baroreceptor), cardiac, and renal factors. Hypertension can thus result from an increased cardiac output, an increased peripheral resistance, or both. Several of the potential mechanisms

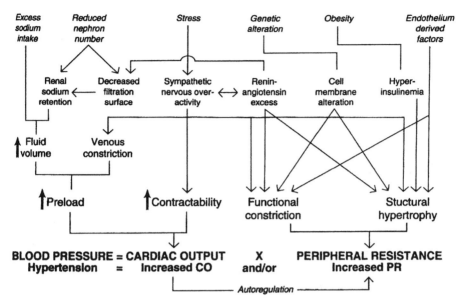

FIG. 2.1. Some of the factors involved in the control of blood pressure that affect the basic equation: Blood pressure = cardiac output × peripheral resistance. From Kaplan, N. M. (1998). *Clinical Hypertension* (7th ed., p. 45), Baltimore: Williams & Wilkins. Copyright 1998 by Williams & Wilkins. Reprinted with permission.

underlying essential hypertension are briefly reviewed below. In most instances it remains unclear whether these factors are a primary cause or a consequence of essential hypertension. A more detailed discussion is beyond the scope of this chapter, and interested readers are referred to Kaplan's (1998) book *Clinical Hypertension* for a comprehensive description of the pathogenesis of essential hypertension.

Increased Cardiac Output

An increased cardiac output, perhaps due to increased contractility, is observed in a subset of younger individuals who are early in the course of hypertension. However, long-standing hypertensives typically display a normal or even decreased cardiac output and an increased peripheral vascular resistance (Cowley, 1992). It has therefore been posited that elevated cardiac output may play a role in the initiation of hypertension, whereas elevated peripheral vascular resistance plays a more central role in the maintenance of hypertension, particularly among older hypertensives who experience vascular remodeling and arterial stiffness.

Increased Sympathetic Nervous System Activity

Enhanced sympathetic and decreased parasympathetic nervous system activity can, by several direct and indirect mechanisms, result in tonic BP elevations and acute pressor responses to a variety of stressors, including mental stress. Putative markers of sympathetic overactivity may include increased cardiac output, increased peripheral vascular resistance, elevated plasma renin and norepinephrine levels, or some combination of these.

Renin-Angiotensin System

A subset of hypertensives display high plasma renin levels. Renin, a proteolytic enzyme released from the juxtaglomerular cells of the kidney, cleaves angiotensinogen to angiotensin I, which is in turn cleaved by angiotensin converting enzyme to form angiotensin II. Angiotensin II is a potent vasoconstrictor and stimulator of aldosterone synthesis. Increased synthesis of aldosterone enhances sodium retention by the kidney. Angiotensin II also activates receptors in the heart and central and autonomic nervous systems that amplify its vasoconstrictive effects.

Renal Mechanisms

Renal function is thought to be altered in virtually all hypertensives. In normotensive individuals, when BP rises the excretion of sodium and water by the kidney increases, thus reducing fluid volume and lowering BP—a relationship called pressure–natriuresis. Hypertensives display a resetting of the arterial pressure–natriuresis relation toward higher BPs so that the kidney excretes less sodium for a given arterial BP (Cowley & Roman, 1996). This alteration in set point could result from changes both intrinsic and extrinsic to the kidney. Indeed, multiple alterations in feedback loops involving the renin–angiotensin system and sympathetic nervous system in hypertensive patients promote sodium retention and volume expansion. Defective sodium transport mechanisms may also play a role in renal retention of sodium.

Salt Sensitivity

Excessive salt intake increases BP among a subset of salt sensitive individuals (Graudal, Galloe, & Garred, 1998). Genetic factors are suggested in salt sensitivity with demonstrable heritability and associations of salt sensitivity with candidate genes. Potential mechanisms linking high sodium intake and hypertension among salt sensitive individuals include reduced renal sodium excretion, increased intracellular calcium, increased sympathetic nervous system activity, and various abnormalities in the renin–angiotensin system.

Increased Peripheral Vascular Resistance

As noted earlier, hypertensives typically have a normal cardiac output and elevated peripheral vascular resistance. The increased peripheral vascular resistance is attributed to changes in the structure and function of the larger arteries, smaller arterioles and microcirculation, increased vascular tone, and endothelial dysfunction. Hypertensives experience hypertrophy and stiffening of the arteries associated with extensive remodeling of the arterial structure. Large- and small-vessel arteriosclerosis causes much of the end organ damage characteristic of long-standing hypertension. Endothelial-derived growth factors, alterations in cell membrane structure and function, hyperinsulinemia, and abnormalities in the renin–angiotensin system, combined with increased hypertension-related shear forces, tend to increase peripheral resistance.

Insulin Resistance

Insulin resistance (impaired ability of insulin to stimulate the uptake and disposal of glucose by muscle), glucose intolerance, and diabetes mellitus are common in hypertensives and have been associated with both genetic and environmental determinants. It has been proposed that insulin resistance and associated sympathetic nervous system abnormalities may lead to hypertension (Reaven, Lithell, & Landsberg, 1996). In this model hyperinsulinemia directly causes damage to the peripheral arteries, accompanied by impaired endothelial function and vasoconstriction (Baron, 1996). Hyperinsulinemia also increases sympathetic nervous system activity. In addition to direct effects on the vasculature, increased sympathetic nervous system activity, in combination with hyperinsulinemia, adversely affects fluid and water balance, leading to increased sodium reabsorption by the kidneys, increased cardiac output, and other metabolic and endocrinologic changes that can result in hypertension.

HYPERTENSION AND COGNITIVE FUNCTION

Case Control Studies

The impact of hypertension on the brain has long been recognized in the form of severe disturbances termed *hypertensive encephalopathy* (Oppenheimer & Fischberg, 1928). The relation of hypertension to cognitive function has also been the subject of investigation for more than 50 years, and several recent reviews of the literature are available (M. F. Elias & Robbins, 1991; Waldstein, 1995; Waldstein, Manuck, Ryan, & Muldoon, 1991).

Case control studies of hypertension and cognition generally compare the performance of persons with normal BP (normotensives) with that of unmedicated essential hypertensives. The hypertensives are either newly diagnosed or are removed from antihypertensive therapy prior to neuropsychological assessment. The impact of antihypertensive medications on cognitive performance has been discussed elsewhere (Muldoon, Manuck, Shapiro, & Waldstein, 1991; Muldoon, Waldstein, & Jennings, 1995) and is discussed in chapter 9.

Because hypertension is often one of the earliest manifestations of CVD and frequently occurrs without substantial occult comorbidities, there is an opportunity to conduct tightly controlled investigations of hypertension and cognition. Hypertension has thus been one of the most extensively investigated of the CVDs with respect to cognitive functioning (Waldstein, Snow, Muldoon, & Katzel, in press). Neuropsychological investigations of hypertensives and normotensives typically control for numerous confounding variables by statistical adjustment or matching procedures. These variables most commonly include age, education, alcohol consumption, anxiety, and depression. Individuals with medical, neurological, or psychiatric comorbidities are generally excluded. As a result of the frequent exclusion of persons with major hypertension-related end organ damage, the impact of hypertension on cognition may be underestimated, particularly among older adults.

Nonetheless, results of the numerous available case control studies of hypertension and cognition generally reveal that hypertensives perform more poorly than normotensives across multiple domains of neuropsychological function (see Waldstein, Manuck, et al., 1991). Some of the most prominent and consistent findings are noted within the domains of learning and memory, attention, abstract reasoning, and other executive functions (e.g., Boller, Vrtunski, Mack, & Kim, 1977; M. F. Elias, Robbins, Schultz, & Pierce, 1990; M. F. Elias, Robbins, Schultz, Streeten, & Elias, 1987; Robbins, Elias, Croog, & Colton, 1994; Waldstein, Ryan, Manuck, Parkinson, & Bromet, 1991; Waldstein et al., 1996). Compromised performance is also evident on tests of visuospatial, visuoconstructive, perceptual, and psychomotor abilities (e.g., Blumenthal, Madden, Pierce, Siegel, & Appelbaum, 1993; Boller et al., 1977; M. F. Elias et al., 1987; Robbins et al., 1994; Shapiro, Miller, King, Ginchereau, & Fitzgibbon, 1982; Waldstein et al., 1996). However, relatively less support has been found for a relation between hypertension and performance on tests of general verbal intelligence or language abilities (e.g., Blumenthal et al., 1993; Boller et al., 1977; Waldstein, Ryan, et al., 1991; Waldstein et al., 1996).

In several investigations, dose–response relations have been noted between progressive increments in BP level and reduced cognitive performance (e.g., M. F. Elias, Schultz, et al., 1990; Robbins et al., 1994). However, there is recent evidence to suggest that low levels of BP also predict poorer cognitive function. In this regard, Costa, Stegagno, Schandry, and Ricci Bitti (1998) found that young female hypotensives (systolic BP <100 mm Hg and diastolic BP <60 mm Hg) performed more poorly than normotensives on tests of attention and memory. These and other similar findings (discussed later) may explain some of the inconsistencies in prior research and suggest the need to apply curvilinear statistics to evaluate the potential presence of an inverted-U or J-shaped cross-sectional relation between BP and cognitive function in persons of all ages.

Moderator Variables

Although most case-control studies reveal lowered average levels of neuropsychological function among hypertensives, substantial interindividual variability in performance also has been noted within groups of hypertensives (Waldstein, 1995). An examination of relevant effect sizes reveals that the impact of hypertension can range from small (or absent), with $ds < 0.10$, to large, with $ds > 1.0$ (see Waldstein, Manuck, et al., 1991). This variability may be explained in part by relevant moderators. Below we consider several demographic influences (e.g., age, education) and variables related to hypertension heterogeneity.

Demographic Variables. *Age:* Although hypertension-related cognitive deficits have been noted in individuals of all ages, several studies have revealed more pronounced performance differences between young (less than 40 or 50 years of age) than middle-aged (upper limits ranging from 56 to 72 years) hypertensive and normotensive groups on tests of attention, memory, executive functions, and psychomotor abilities (M. F. Elias, Schultz, et al., 1990; Schultz, Dineen, Elias, Pentz, & Wood, 1979; Waldstein et al., 1996). However, Madden and Blumenthal (1998) found that both young (ages 18–40) and middle-aged (ages 41–59) hypertensives showed a slightly greater error rate on a test of visual selective attention than did age-matched normotensives, whereas older (ages 60–78) hypertensives and normotensives performed comparably.

In contrast to the significant interactive effects of age and hypertension (or BP) described above, such interactions were not noted among three age cohorts (55–64, 65–74, and 75–88 years) in a sample of 1,695 participants in the Framingham Heart Study (M. F. Elias, D'Agostino, Elias, & Wolf, 1995). Outcome measures included tests of memory, visual organization, attention, verbal comprehension, and concept formation.

In sum, when interactive effects of age and hypertension (or BP) are noted, poorer performance tends to aggregate among the younger individuals in any particular study. Investigations of young (less than 40 to 50 years of age) hypertensives and normotensives have yielded the most pronounced differences in terms of effect size. Waldstein (1995) suggested that such trends may reflect survival effects and selective attrition from studies, because individuals with early-onset hypertension typically go on to develop cardiovascular and cerebrovascular complications. Furthermore, early-onset hypertension may confer greater risk for cognitive impairment than late-onset hypertension (see section on Longitudinal Investigations).

Approaching the study of age and hypertension from a somewhat different perspective, several investigators have examined whether hypertension (or BP levels) partially mediates age-related variance in cognitive performance. In this regard, Madden and Blumenthal (1998) found that systolic and diastolic BP attenuated by almost 58% the age-related variance in performance of an attention-shift reaction time task involving visual selective attention. Similarly, M. F. Elias et al. (1998) found a reduction of 50% in the relation between age and performance of Wechsler Adult Intelligence Scale (WAIS) subtests reflecting Visualization–Performance ability, but not Verbal–Crystallized ability or Digit Symbol Substitution Test performance, associated with a longitudinally assessed composite of systolic BP measures. These findings suggest that BP is an important mediator of cognitive aging.

Education: Interactive effects of education and hypertension have been noted such that, among hypertensives, relatively lower levels of education (12–15 years) are associated with poorer neuropsychological function, whereas more highly educated hypertensives and normotensives (more than 16 years) show comparable performance (M. F. Elias et al., 1987). Relative preservation of cognitive function among more highly educated persons has also been noted in other contexts and may reflect an enhanced "cognitive reserve" (Katzman, 1993). This finding may also more generally suggest protective effects of higher socioeconomic status (SES). In this regard, potential interactions of hypertension with SES, and with race–ethnicity and gender, are warranted.

Hypertension-Related Variables. *Hypertension heterogeneity and comorbidities:* As discussed earlier, hypertension is a heterogeneous disorder with multiple determinants and thus identifiable subgroups (e.g., persons with renal disturbances that lead to blood volume expansion vs. those with neural influences, such as an increased sympathetic tone). It is possible that particular subgroups of hypertensives are vulnerable to diminished neuropsychological performance. For example, there is some suggestion that hypertensives who are characterized by markers of high levels of sympathetic nervous system activity (plasma renin activity) may perform particularly poorly on certain psychomotor tests (Light, 1975, 1978).

Another subgroup of hypertensives is characterized by a clustering of metabolic risk factors for CVD, including hyperinsulinemia. In this regard, hyperinsulinemic hypertensives have been found to perform more poorly on tests of memory and executive functions than either normoinsulinemic hypertensives or normotensives (Kuusisto et al., 1993).

Hypertension may also interact with other CVD and metabolic diseases to affect cognitive function. In this regard, data from the Framingham Heart Study reveal an interaction of BP with non-insulin-dependent diabetes mellitus (NIDDM) such that hypertensives with NIDDM showed the poorest performance on tests of visual organization and memory (P. K. Elias et al., 1997). The impact of multiple cardiovascular risk factors (or diseases) on cognition is discussed further in chapter 5.

Duration of hypertension: It remains unclear whether a certain duration of hypertension is necessary to produce cognitive deficits. However, duration is a problematic variable to quantify, because hypertension is typically a "silent" disease and may therefore exist undetected for long periods of time. It is estimated that approximately 32% of individuals with high BP are unaware of their condition (American Heart Association, 1998). In addition, once hypertension is detected most individuals are prescribed antihypertensive agents. Although the hypertensives who participate in case control studies are typically removed from their medications prior to testing, any chronic medication effects are unknown. The degree of BP normalization achieved by antihypertensive therapy is thought to be a critical, long-term determinant of cognitive performance. In this regard, it is estimated that approximately 26% of hypertensives taking medication do not have their BP under control.

Cross-Sectional, Population-Based Studies

Results of cross-sectional, population-based studies have been mixed regarding the relation of BP to cognition. These studies have generally focused on older adults. Some studies have found minimal to no relation between BP and cognitive function (Farmer et al., 1987; Scherr, Hebert, Smith, & Evans, 1991). However, Wallace et al. (1985) found an association between higher BP and poorer memory performance among an elderly sample ($n = 2,433$). In contrast, Guo, Fratiglioni, Winblad, and Viitanen (1997) noted an association between lower BP levels and lower mental status scores in an elderly cohort ($n = 1,736$). Low BP levels have also been related to diagnosed dementia (e.g., Alzheimer's disease, vascular dementia; Guo, Viitanen, Fratiglioni, & Winblad, 1996); however, it has been noted that dementia may lead to decreased BP levels as a result of weight loss and dietary factors. Interpretation of the cross-sectional studies described in this section is limited by their measurement of BP on a single occasion, which greatly limits reliability (Llabre et al., 1988) and precludes hypertension classification (JNC, 1997).

Longitudinal Investigations

Results of longitudinal (or follow-up) studies, including the Framingham Heart Study and the Cardiovascular Health Study, indicate that deficits in neuropsychological performance persist, or worsen, over time among hypertensives (e.g., Haan, Shemanski, Jagust, Manolio, & Kuller, 1999; Miller, Shapiro, King, Ginchereau, & Hosutt, 1984; M. F. Elias, Robbins, & Elias, 1996: M. F. Elias, Robbins, Schultz, & Streeten, 1986; M. F. Elias, Schultz, Robbins, & Elias, 1990; Wilkie & Eisdorfer, 1971). Chronicity of hypertension has been identified as a critical variable in such investigations—that is, lifetime exposure to BP elevation may be a more important predictor of poor cognitive outcome in older adults than cross-sectionally measured BP. In this regard, late-life-onset hypertension is very common (and frequently attributable to arterial stiffness) and may have different implications for cognitive function than BP elevation of earlier onset (Swan, Carmelli, & La Rue, 1998; Waldstein, 1995).

The importance of chronicity was emphasized in a reanalysis of data from the Framingham Heart Study ($n = 1,695$). Findings indicated that persistent BP elevation, measured at five biennial examinations, predicted poorer performance on a cognitive composite measure, composed primarily of tests of attention and memory, at a 12- to 14-year follow-up (M. F. Elias, Wolf, D'Agostino, Cobb, & White, 1993). In another longitudinal study, BP measures averaged across 19 years of follow-up predicted decline on WAIS subtests measuring Visualization–Performance and Speed but not Verbal–Crystallized abilities (M. F. Elias et al., 1998).

Swan et al. (1998) described the importance of persistent BP elevation with respect to cognitive outcomes. They studied a sample of 717 participants from the Western Collaborative Group Study (WCGS) who underwent BP assessment in midlife (mean age = 45) and old age (mean age = 75). Participants were defined as having persistently high systolic BP in both middle age and old age ("trackers"); "normals" had normal systolic BP on both occasions or increased from normal to high; "decreasers" showed a decrease in systolic BP from middle to old age. The trackers showed poorer verbal learning and memory performance than the normals or the decreasers in old age. However, systolic BP decreasers showed slower speeded performance than normals. Swan et al. posited that the trackers may have experienced long-term neuropathological consequences of hypertension, whereas the decreasers had comorbidities (e.g., depression, coronary heart disease) that might explain their poorer performance.

Also pertinent to the issue of chronicity of BP elevation (and lifetime exposure) is a series of recent epidemiological studies that reveal that higher BP levels during middle age predict poorer cognitive outcomes in older age. In an analysis of data from the WCGS, Swan, Carmelli, and La Rue (1996) found that both systolic and diastolic BP assessments obtained during middle age predicted poorer performance on cognitive screening measures at a 25- to 30-year follow-up. Also predicted was self-reported dementia or documented morbidity or mortality due to dementia. Midlife BP also predicted poorer performance on a cognitive screening measure in older age ($n = 3,735$) in the Honolulu–Asia Aging Study (Launer, Masaki, Petrovitch, Foley, & Havlik, 1995) and on tests of mental status and mental flexibility in the Uppsala study (Kilander, Nyman, Boberg, Hansson, & Lithell, 1998).

Findings from another recent epidemiologic study of 2,068 individuals suggest a curvilinear (U-shaped) relation of BP to performance on a mental status measure, but not with respect to memory function, at both a baseline assessment and at 9-year follow-up (Glynn et al., 1999). However, in this study BP was measured on only one occasion at each assessment period.

In general, longitudinal studies control for many critical confounding variables, such as age, education, alcohol consumption, smoking, and use of antihypertensive medications, but they do not always control for comorbid diseases such as diabetes mellitus or CHD. This is important, because hypertension may bear a relatively stronger or weaker relation to cognition in the presence of more severe cardiovascular or metabolic diseases. As noted previously, P. K. Elias et al. (1997) found significant synergistic effects of hypertension and NIDDM. In contrast, Desmond, Tatemichi, Paik, and Stern (1993) did not find a relation between hypertension and cognitive performance in a community-based sample of older adults (*n* = 249), whereas other cardiovascular risk factors, such as hypercholesterolemia and diabetes mellitus, did predict poorer cognitive function. However, assessment of risk factors in this study was accomplished by means of self-report. Similarly, Phillips and Mate-Kole (1997) did not find hypertension to be a predictor of cognitive function in peripheral vascular disease patients.

UNDERLYING MECHANISMS

Numerous biological mechanisms have been proposed to underlie the relation between hypertension and diminished cognitive function (see M. F. Elias & Robbins, 1991; Waldstein, 1995; Waldstein, Manuck, et al., 1991). We propose a working model that posits a multiplicity of influences on cognitive performance in hypertensives (see Fig. 2.2). These include, first, a series of genetic and environmental factors that may indirectly influence cognition through the development of hypertension and associated factors such as the metabolic syndrome and stress-induced cardiovascular and neuroendocrine responses (i.e., reactivity). These latter factors may, alone or in combination, promote neuroanatomical and neurophysiological alterations in the brain that lead to diminished cognitive performance. Other direct and indirect influences of these variables on cognition also are possible. Each portion of the model is considered briefly here. It is important that the relative influences of these proposed mechanisms may vary over the course of the life span and among different subgroups of hypertensives (Waldstein, 1995).

Genetics and Environment

As mentioned earlier, both genetic and environmental influences are thought to play a role in the development of hypertension and factors associated with hypertension, such as the metabolic syndrome (e.g., hyperinsulinemia, dyslipidemia, central adiposity) and cardiovascular and neuroendocrine responses to stress (Turner, Sherwood, & Light, 1992). Genetic and environmental factors may thus bear an indirect association to poor cognitive performance in hypertensives by promoting a cascade of neurobiological changes that are associated with BP

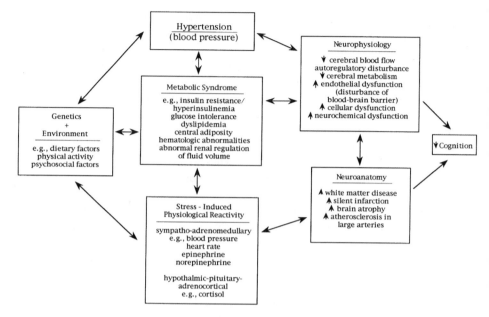

FIG. 2.2.   Working model of potential mechanisms underlying the relation of hypertension to cognitive function. For the purpose of simplicity, single bidirectional arrows are placed between proximal components of the model. However, each of these factors can also affect more distal components of the model in a bidirectional fashion. For example, hypertension is associated with enhanced stress-induced physiological reactivity, and genetic and environmental factors may directly influence neurophysiology and neuroanatomy. The relative importance of the various components of this working model may vary among different sociodemographic groups (e.g., by age, race, socioeconomic status) or among different biological subgroups of hypertensives.

elevation, metabolic syndrome, and stress reactivity. This model therefore suggests that there are characteristics of hypertensives, other than elevated BP per se, that are important to the development of diminished cognitive functioning.

Genetic and environmental factors may also exert more direct influences on brain structure and function and cognitive performance. First, with regard to genetic factors, it has been noted that subtly lowered neuropsychological test performance precedes BP elevation in a subgroup of individuals who are at genetic risk for the development of hypertension. Specifically, normotensive young adults who have a parental history of hypertension show lower levels of performance on tests of visuoperceptual, spatial, and constructional skill and speed of short-term memory search compared to the young adult offspring of normotensive parents (Pierce & Elias, 1993; Waldstein, Ryan, Polefrone, & Manuck, 1994). It is thus possible that genetic and or environmental factors act as third variables that influence both the development of hypertension and altered cognitive function, perhaps by means of similar neurobiological mechanisms (e.g., cellular mechanisms, cerebral metabolism).

In this instance, a portion of performance variability among hypertensives should thus be attributable to genetic variation. Indirect evidence was provided by Thyrum, Blumenthal, Madden, and Siegel (1994), who found that hypertensives with a positive family history of hypertension performed more poorly on neuropsychological tests than hypertensives without a family history. It is important that these findings could also reflect environmental factors that aggregate among families and predispose individuals to hypertension. In this regard, a number of lifestyle factors, such as fitness and various nutritional factors, bear an association to cognitive performance.

Hypertension, Metabolic Syndrome, and Stress Reactivity

Hypertension-related BP elevation may directly alter neuroanatomical structure and neurophysiological function (see subsequent discussion), thus leading to poorer cognitive outcomes. However, as indicated previously, characteristics of certain subgroups of hypertensives may further promote neurobiological changes that produce cognitive dysfunction. Two such factors that have demonstrable association with hypertension are metabolic syndrome and enhanced stress-induced cardiovascular and neuroendocrine reactivity (Fredrikson & Matthews, 1990; Kaplan, 1998).

Dimensions of metabolic syndrome (e.g., hyperinsulinemia) have been associated with neuropathological outcomes such as carotid atherosclerosis (Folsom et al., 1994). Indexes of metabolic syndrome have also been associated with the potentiation of stress-induced cardiovascular reactivity (Waldstein, Burns, Toth, & Poehlman, 1999). Repeated episodes of cardiovascular and neuroendocrine reactivity may, by means of the sympathoadrenomedullary and hypothalamic–pituitary–adrenocortical axes, promote neuropathology and accompanying cognitive changes. For example, stress-induced cortisol responses have been related to neuronal loss in hippocampal regions (Sapolsky, 1996); higher cortisol levels have also been associated with decreased memory performance (Seeman, McEwan, Albert, & Rowe, 1997). Mental-stress-induced BP reactivity has also been related to enhanced carotid atherosclerosis (Kamarck et al., 1997). Indeed, cardiovascular and neuroendocrine reactivity may promote atherosclerosis and vascular damage by numerous mechanisms (Manuck, 1994). Associations between indexes of autonomic dysfunction and neuropathology are further discussed.

Neurobiological Mechanisms

Neurophysiology

A variety of alterations in neurophysiological functioning have been associated with hypertension and may promote cognitive dysfunction. Many of these factors are likely interrelated. For example, cerebral metabolic dysfunction or cellular dysfunction may be reflected in a decreased cerebral blood flow.

Cerebral Blood Flow and Cerebral Metabolism. Decreased cerebral blood flow, metabolism, or both, has been noted in hypertensives, with some suggestion that frontal, temporal, "watershed," and subcortical (e.g., basal ganglia) regions are most affected (Fujishima, Ibayashi, Fujii, & Mori, 1995; Mentis et al., 1994; Rodriguez et al., 1987; Salerno et al., 1995). Fujishima et al. (1995) found that spontaneously hypertensive rats, as compared to normotensive rats, had decreased cerebral blood flow and glucose utilization in a variety of cortical and subcortical regions that correlated with poorer spatial learning and memory in maze tests. However, these changes were reversible with antihypertensive treatment. Cerebral perfusion has also been found to be better among treated than untreated hypertensives (Nobili et al., 1993). Reductions in cerebral perfusion are thought to predispose individuals to the neuroanatomical changes described later.

Recent findings have also noted that hypertensives show smaller cerebral blood flow responses during memory tasks (Jennings et al., 1998). More specifically, hypertensives displayed less activation in right hemisphere regions but enhanced (possibly compensatory) left hemisphere activation during two memory tasks.

Autoregulation of Cerebral Blood Flow. Hypertension is known to affect the autoregulation of cerebral blood flow (Baumbach & Heistad, 1988). Specifically, hypertension shifts both the lower and upper limits of the autoregulatory range to the right (i.e., toward a higher BP), at least in part as a result of vascular hypertrophy and remodeling. This can lead to impairment in autoregulatory vasodilation during episodes of hypotension, thus rendering hypertensives vulnerable to hypoxic effects associated with decreases in perfusion pressure. Such effects may be particularly pertinent to issues of BP lowering with antihypertensive medications.

Endothelial Dysfunction. An intact endothelium in the cerebral blood vessels is critical to adequate functioning of the blood–brain barrier. Baumbach and Heistad (1992) posited that hypertension-related endothelial dysfunction disrupts the blood–brain barrier, thus leading to "leakiness." Hypertension also impairs vasodilatory responses to endothelium-dependent agonists.

Cellular or Neurochemical Disturbances. Disturbances in several basic cellular functions, such as ion-transport mechanisms, have been associated with hypertension (Kaplan, 1998). Such abnormalities may lead to increased intracellular sodium and calcium and may promote hypertrophy and vasoconstriction. Additionally, disturbances of central neurochemical systems (e.g, catecholaminergic, serotonergic) are suggested (Chalmers & Pilowsky, 1991).

Neuroanatomy

It is well established that hypertension is associated with subtle alterations in brain structure that mark the gradual emergence of cerebrovascular disease. In this regard, hypertensives display increased hyperintensities in periventricular and deep white matter on magnetic resonance imaging that indicate the presence of cerebral white matter disease (Liao et al., 1996; Manolio et al., 1994; Schmidt et al., 1995; van Swieten et al., 1991). Treated hypertensives display less white matter disease than untreated hypertensives (Fukuda & Kitani, 1995). Among treated hypertensives, those who exhibit poorer BP control show the most extensive pathology (Liao et al., 1996). Also noted among hypertensives is a greater prevalence of silent lacunar infarction (Hougaku et al, 1992), a greater degree of cerebral atrophy and ventricular enlargement (Manolio et al., 1994; Salerno et al., 1992; Schmidt et al., 1995), and increased carotid atherosclerosis (Ferrara et al., 1995) as compared to normotensives. Each of these neuroanatomical findings has been related independently to poorer cognitive function in some, though not all, studies (see chap. 6; see also Boone et al., 1992; Breteler, Claus, Grobbee, & Hofman, 1994; DeCarli et al., 1995; Raz, Gunning-Dixon, Head, Dupuis, Acker, 1998; Schmidt et al., 1993). However, it is unusual for these factors to be examined specifically as mediators of cognitive dysfunction in hypertensives. In this regard, two of the studies just cited indicated that hypertensives with significant white matter disease showed poorer neuropsychological performance than either normotensives or hypertensives without notable white matter disease (Schmidt et al., 1995; van Swieten et al., 1991).

There is some suggestion that not only resting BP but also variability in BP may indirectly affect cognition by means of neuroanatomical mechanisms. In this regard, Shimada, Kawamoto, Matsubayashi, and Ozawa (1990) found that variability in ambulatory measures of BP was a better predictor of magnetic resonance abnormalities than were resting BP measurements obtained in an office setting. Goldstein, Bartzokis, Hance, and Shapiro (1998) found both casual and ambulatory BP measures to predict such abnormalities. It is important to note that increased variability in ambulatory BP may, in part, reflect increased sympathetic or decreased parasympathetic nervous system function. Others indexes of autonomic dysfunction that have been examined are either extreme nocturnal falls in BP or "nondipping" of BP, both of which have been associated with an increased prevalence of silent lacunar infarction and white and gray matter hyperintensities (Goldstein et al., 1998; Kario et al., 1997; Kohara et al., 1997).

SUMMARY AND CLINICAL SIGNIFICANCE

To summarize, there is now extensive evidence, emanating from studies of varying methodologies, indicating that hypertension is associated with poorer cognitive performance on tests of attention; learning and memory; executive functions; and visuospatial, visuoconstructional, psychomotor, and perceptual abilities and that chronic hypertension also predicts cognitive decline over time. Low BP has also been related to poorer cognitive function.

The findings, in general, suggest that uncomplicated essential hypertensive individuals should not be characterized as clinically impaired on neuropsychological measures (M. F. Elias et al., 1987). Nevertheless, the findings can be considered clinically significant, both at the population level and at the individual level. In this regard, results of numerous case control studies have indicated that, in some instances, the performance of hypertensives falls below that of normotensives by up to one standard deviation (Waldstein, Manuck, et al., 1991; Waldstein, Ryan, et al., 1991). At the individual level, this magnitude of difference could, for example, translate into a below-average versus average (or average vs. above-average) test score. Among individuals, even subtle alterations in cognitive functioning can have negative consequences. Such changes can be distressing and may affect quality of life.

Lowering of cognitive performance associated with hypertension is also considered significant at the population level, with significantly increased risk for poor cognitive performance, both cross-sectionally and longitudinally, associated with hypertension or progressive increments in BP (see chap. 5). For example, data from the Framingham Heart Study reveal that chronic hypertensives had an increased risk for their scores on several learning and memory tests to fall in the lower quartile of the distribution. Significant odds ratios ranged from 1.19 to 1.62 (P. K. Elias et al., 1995). Adequate treatment of hypertension may thus be critical to the preservation of cognitive function.

Despite an overall increase in hypertension-related risk for poor cognitive function, the pronounced interindividual variability in performance noted within hypertensive groups indicates that it is important to continue to identify pertinent predictors of poor cognitive function among hypertensives and to seek to determine potential areas for prevention or intervention efforts. Thus far, age and education have been identified as important moderator variables. However, many other sociodemographic, lifestyle, and biomedical factors may also be pertinent.

The cognitive changes associated with hypertension are likely determined by a complex interplay of factors. Predictors of cognitive functioning, and the mechanisms underlying these difficulties, may differ among subgroups of hypertensives and at distinct points in the life span. Future studies should seek to sample numerous mechanistic variables in conjunction with measures of cognitive function and use sophisticated statistical methods, such as structural equation modeling, to determine interrelations among these variables. Several exciting mechanistic studies are at present in progress in various laboratories. As one example, our ongoing study of hypertension and cognition seeks to determine interrelations among genetic and environmental factors, BP, metabolic syndrome, cardiovascular reactivity, neuroanatomy, neurophysiology, and cognition. Preliminary findings from a subset of variables indicate a relation of hypertension in older adults to increased white matter disease, decreased cerebral perfusion, and diminished cognitive performance, with significant correlations between the cerebral pathology and reduced cognitive function (Waldstein et al., 1997)

FUTURE DIRECTIONS

Despite the fact that the association between hypertension and cognition has been investigated extensively for more than 50 years, many questions remain. First, identifying patterns, predictors, and mechanisms of cognitive function (or dysfunction) among subgroups of hypertensives of differing ages remains critical. Further elucidation of the complicated underlying mechanisms also is necessary. Consideration of long-term antihypertensive therapy and relative degree of BP control is important, particularly in longitudinal investigations. Further study of the relation of low BP to cognitive performance (and associated mechanisms) is also necessary. Future studies should also determine the impact of hypertension on cognition in the presence of other cardiovascular risk factors and diseases, because such comorbidities are common among hypertensives. Finally, it would be useful to determine whether hypertensives who display the lowest levels of cognitive performance are at greatest risk for future cerebrovascular events.

ACKNOWLEDGMENT

Preparation of this chapter was supported in part by National Institute of Aging Grants 1R29AG15112 and 1K24A600930–01 and by a Veterans Affairs Merit Grant. We thank Merrill Elias for his helpful comments on this chapter.

REFERENCES

American Heart Association. (1998). *1999 Heart and stroke statistical update*. Dallas, TX: Author.

Baron, A. D. (1996). Insulin and the vasculature—Old actors, new roles. *Journal of Investigative Medicine, 44*, 406–412.

Baumbach, G. L., & Heistad, D. D. (1988). Cerebral circulation in chronic arterial hypertension. *Hypertension, 12*, 89–95.

Blumenthal, J. A., Madden, D. J., Pierce, T. W., Siegel, W. C., & Appelbaum, M. (1993). Hypertension affects neurobehavioral function. *Psychosomatic Medicine, 55*, 44–50.

Boller, F., Vrtunski, P. B., Mack, J. L., & Kim, Y. (1977). Neuropsychological correlates of hypertension. *Archives of Neurology, 34*, 701–705.

Boone, K. B., Miller, B. L., Lesser, I. M., Mehringer, C. M., Hill-Gutierrez, E., Goldberg, M. A., & Berman, N. G. (1992). Neuropsychological correlates of white-matter lesions in healthy elderly subjects: A threshold effect. *Archives of Neurology, 49,* 549–554.

Breteler, M. M. B., Claus, J. J., Grobbee, D. E., & Hofman, A. (1994). Cardiovascular disease and distribution of cognitive function in elderly people: The Rotterdam study. *British Medical Journal, 308,* 1604–1608.

Chalmers, J., & Pilowsky, P. (1991). Brainstem and bulbospinal neurotransmitter systems in the control of blood pressure. *Journal of Hypertension, 9,* 675–694.

Costa, M., Stegagno, L., Schandry, R., & Ricci Bitti, P. E. (1998). Contingent negative variation and cognitive performance in hypotension. *Psychophysiology, 35,* 737–744.

Cowley, A. W. (1992). Long-term control of arterial blood pressure. *Physiology Reviews, 72,* 231–300.

Cowley, A. W., & Roman, R. J. (1996). The role of the kidney in hypertension. *Journal of the American Medical Association, 275,* 1581–1589.

DeCarli, C., Murphy, D. G. M., Tranh, M., Grady, C. L., Haxby, J. V., Gillette, J. A., Salerno, J. A., Gonzales-Aviles, A., Horwitz, B., Rapoport, S. I., & Schapiro, M. B. (1995). The effect of white matter hyperintensity volume on brain structure, cognitive performance, and cerebral metabolism of glucose in 51 healthy adults. *Neurology, 45,* 2077–2084.

Desmond, D. W., Tatemichi, T. K., Paik, M., & Stern, Y. (1993). Risk factors for cerebrovascular disease as correlates of cognitive function in a stroke-free cohort. *Archives of Neurology, 50,* 162–166.

Elias, M. F., D'Agostino, R. B., Elias, P. K., & Wolf, P. A. (1995). Neuropsychological test performance, cognitive functioning, blood pressure, and age: The Framingham Study. *Experimental Aging Research, 21,* 369–391.

Elias, M. F., & Robbins, M. A. (1991). Cardiovascular disease, hypertension, and cognitive function. In A. P. Shapiro & A. Baum (Eds.), *Behavioral aspects of cardiovascular disease* (pp. 249–285). Hillsdale, NJ: Lawrence Erlbaum Associates.

Elias, M. F., Robbins, M. A., & Elias, P. K. (1996). A 15-year longitudinal study of Halstead–Reitan neuropsychological test performance. *Journal of Gerontology: Psychological Sciences, 51B,* P331–P334.

Elias, M. F., Robbins, M. A., Elias, P. K., & Streeten, D. H. P. (1998). A longitudinal study of blood pressure in relation to performance on the Wechsler Adult Intelligence Scale. *Health Psychology, 17,* 486–493.

Elias, M. F., Robbins, M. A., Schultz, N. R., & Pierce, T. W. (1990). Is blood pressure an important variable in research on aging and neuropsychological test performance? *Journal of Gerontology: Psychological Sciences, 45,* 128–135.

Elias, M. F., Robbins, M. A., Schultz, N. R., & Streeten, D. H. P. (1986). A longitudinal study of neuropsychological test performance for hypertensive and normotensive adults: Initial findings. *Journal of Gerontology, 41,* 503–505.

Elias, M. F., Robbins, M. A., Schultz, N. R., Streeten, D. H. P., & Elias, P. K. (1987). Clinical significance of cognitive performance by hypertensive patients. *Hypertension, 9,* 192–197.

Elias, M. F., Schultz, N. R., Robbins, M. A., & Elias, P. K. (1990). A longitudinal study of neuropsychological performance by hypertensives and normotensives: A third measurement point. *Journal of Gerontology: Psychological Sciences, 44,* 25–28.

Elias, M. F., Wolf, P. A., D'Agostino, R. B., Cobb, J., & White, L. R. (1993). Untreated blood pressure level is inversely related to cognitive functioning: The Framingham Study. *American Journal of Epidemiology, 138,* 353–364.

Elias, P. K., D'Agostino, R. B., Elias, M. F., & Wolf, P. A. (1995). Blood pressure, hypertension, and age as risk factors for poor cognitive performance. *Experimental Aging Research, 21,* 393–417.

Elias, P. K., Elias, M. F., D'Agostino, R. B., Cupples, L. A., Wilson, P. W., Silbershatz, H., & Wolf, P. A. (1997). NIDDM and blood pressure as risk factors for poor cognitive performance. *Diabetes Care, 20,* 1388–1395.

Farmer, M. E., White, L. R., Abbott, R. D., Kittner, S. J., Kaplan, E., Wolz, M. M., Brody, J. A., &

Wolf, P. A. (1987). Blood pressure and cognitive performance: The Framingham Study. *American Journal of Epidemiology, 126,* 1103–1114.

Ferrara, L. A., Mancini, M., Iannuzzi, R., Marotta, T., Gaeta, I., Pasanisi, F., Postiglione, A., & Guida, L. (1995). Carotid diameter and blood flow velocities in cerebral circulation in hypertensive patients. *Stroke, 26,* 418–421.

Folsom, A. R., Eckfeldt, J. H., Weitzman, S., Ma, J., Chambless, L. E., Barnes, R. W., Cram, K. B., & Hutchinson, R. G., for the ARIC study investigators. (1994). Relation of carotid artery wall thickness to diabetes mellitus, fasting glucose and insulin, body size, and physical activity. *Stroke, 25,* 66–73.

Fredrikson, M., & Matthews, K. A. (1990). Cardiovascular responses to behavioral stress and hypertension: A meta-analytic review. *Annals of Behavioral Medicine, 12,* 30–39.

Fujishima, M., Ibayashi, S., Fujii, K., & Mori, S. (1995). Cerebral blood flow and brain function in hypertension. *Hypertension Research, 18,* 111–117.

Fukuda, H., & Kitani, M. (1995). Differences between treated and untreated hypertensive subjects in the extent of periventricular hyperintensities observed on brain MRI. *Stroke, 26,* 1593–1597.

Glynn, R. J., Beckett, L. A., Hebert, L. E., Morris, M. C., Scherr, P. A., & Evans, D. A. (1999). Current and remote blood pressure and cognitive decline. *Journal of the American Medical Association, 281,* 438–445.

Goldstein, I. B., Bartzokis, G., Hance, D. B., & Shapiro, D. (1998). Relationship between blood pressure and subcortical lesions in healthy elderly people. *Stroke, 29,* 765–772.

Graudal, N. A., Galloe, A. M., & Garred, P. (1998). Effects of sodium restriction on blood pressure, renin, aldosterone, catecholamines, cholesterols, and triglyceride: A meta-analysis. *Journal of the American Medical Association, 279,* 1383–1391.

Guo, Z., Fratiglioni, L., Winblad, B., & Viitanen, M. (1997). Blood pressure and performance on the Mini-Mental State Examination in the very old: Cross-sectional and longitudinal data from the Kungsholmen Project. *American Journal of Epidemiology, 145,* 1106–1113.

Guo, Z., Viitanen, M., Fratiglioni, L., & Winblad, B. (1996). Low blood pressure and dementia in elderly people: The Kungsholmen Project. *British Medical Journal, 312,* 805–808.

Haan, M. N., Shemanski, L., Jagust, W. J., Manolio, T. A., & Kuller, L. (1999). The role of APOE e4 in modulating effects of other risk factors for cognitive decline in elderly persons. *Journal of the American Medical Association, 282,* 40–46.

Hougaku, H., Matsumoto, M., Kitagawa, K., Harada, K., Oku, N., Itoh, T., Maeda, N., & Kamada, T. (1992). Silent cerebral infarction as a form of hypertensive target organ damage in the brain. *Hypertension, 20,* 816–820.

Jennings, J. R., Muldoon, M. F., Ryan, C. M., Mintun, M. A., Meltzer, C. C., Townsend, D. W., Sutton-Tyrrell, K., Shapiro, A. P., & Manuck, S. B. (1998). Cerebral blood flow in hypertensive patients: An initial report of reduced and compensatory blood flow responses during performance of two cognitive tasks. *Hypertension, 31,* 1216–1222.

Joint National Committee on Prevention, Detection, Evaluation, and Treatment of High Blood Pressure. (1997). The sixth report of the Joint National Committee on Prevention, Detection, Evaluation, and Treatment of High Blood Pressure. *Archives of Internal Medicine, 157,* 2413–2446.

Kamarck, T. W., Everson, S. A., Kaplan, G. A., Manuck, S. B., Jennings, J. R., Salonen, R., & Salonen, J. T. (1997). Exaggerated blood pressure responses during mental stress are associated with enhanced carotid atherosclerosis in middle-aged Finnish men: Findings from the Kuopio Ischemic Heart Disease Study. *Circulation, 96,* 3842–3848.

Kaplan, N. M. (1998). *Clinical hypertension* (7th ed.). Baltimore: Williams & Wilkens.

Kario, K., Motai, K., Mitsuhashi, T., Suzuki, T., Nakagawa, Y., Ikeda, U., Matsuo, T., Nakayama, T., Shimada, K. (1997). Autonomic nervous system dysfunction in elderly hypertensive patients with abnormal diurnal blood pressure variation: Relation to silent cerebrovascular disease. *Hypertension, 30,* 1504–1510.

Katzman, R. (1993). Education and the prevalence of dementia and Alzheimer's disease. *Neurology,* *43,* 13–20.

Kilander, L., Nyman, H., Boberg, M., Hansson, L., & Lithell, H. (1998). Hypertension is related to cognitive impairment: A 20-year follow-up of 999 men. *Hypertension, 31,* 780–786.

Kohara, K., Igase, M., Yinong, J., Fukuoka, T., Maguchi, M., Okura, T., Kitami, Y., & Hiwada, K. (1997). Asymptomatic cerebrovascular damages in essential hypertension in the elderly. *American Journal of Hypertension, 10,* 829–835.

Krushkal, J., Ferrell, R., Mockrin, S. C., Turner, S. T., Sing, C. F., & Boerwinkle, E. (1999). Genome-wide linkage analyses of systolic blood pressure using highly discordant siblings. *Circulation, 99,* 1407–1410.

Kuusisto, J., Koivisto, K., Mykkanen, L., Helkala, E. L., Vanhanen, M., Hanninen, T., Pyorala, K., Riekkinen, P., & Laakso, M. (1993). Essential hypertension and cognitive function: The role of hyperinsulinemia. *Hypertension, 22,* 771–779.

Launer, L. J., Masaki, K., Petrovitch, H., Foley, D., & Havlik, R. J. (1995). The association between midlife blood pressure levels and late-life cognitive function. *Journal of the American Medical Association, 274,* 1846–1851.

Liao, D., Cooper, L., Cai, J., Toole, J. F., Bryan, N. R., Hutchinson, R. G., & Tyroler, H. A. (1996). Presence and severity of cerebral white matter lesions and hypertension, its treatment, and its control: The ARIC study. *Stroke, 27,* 2262–2270.

Light, K. C. (1975). Slowing of response time in young and middle-aged hypertensive patients. *Experimental Aging Research, 1,* 209–227.

Light, K. C. (1978). Effects of mild cardiovascular and cerebrovascular disorders on serial reaction time performance. *Experimental Aging Research, 4,* 3–22.

Llabre, M. M., Ironson, G. H., Spitzer, S. B., Gellman, M. D., Weidler, D. J., & Schneiderman, N. (1988). How many blood pressure measurements are enough? An application of generalizability theory to the study of blood pressure reliability. *Psychophysiology, 25,* 97–106.

Madden, D. J., & Blumenthal, J. A. (1998). Interaction of hypertension and age in visual selective attention performance. *Health Psychology, 17,* 76–83.

Manolio, T. A., Kronmal, R. A., Burke, G. L., Poirier, V., O'Leary, D. H., Gardin, J. M., Fried, L. P., Steinberg, E. P., & Bryan, P. N. (1994). Magnetic resonance abnormalities and cardiovascular disease in older adults: The Cardiovascular Health Study. *Stroke, 25,* 318–327.

Manuck, S. B. (1994). Cardiovascular reactivity in cardiovascular disease: "Once more unto the breach." *International Journal of Behavioral Medicine, 1,* 4–31.

Mentis, M. J., Salerno, J., Horwitz, B., Grady, C., Schapiro, M. B., Murphy, D. G. M., & Rapoport, S. I. (1994). Reduction of functional neuronal connectivity in long-term treated hypertension. *Stroke, 25,* 601–607.

Miller, R. E., Shapiro, A. P., King, H. E., Ginchereau, E. H., & Hosutt, J. A. (1984). Effect of antihypertensive treatment on the behavioral consequences of elevated blood pressure. *Hypertension, 6,* 202–208.

Muldoon, M. F., Manuck, S. B., Shapiro, A. P., & Waldstein, S. R. (1991). Neurobehavioral effects of antihypertensive medications. *Journal of Hypertension, 9,* 549–559.

Muldoon, M. F., Waldstein, S. R., & Jennings, J. R. (1995). Neuropsychological consequences of antihypertensive medication use. *Experimental Aging Research, 21,* 353–368.

Nobili, F., Rodriguez, G., Marenco, S., De Carli, F., Gambaro, M., Castello, C., Pontremoli, R., & Rosadini, G. (1993). Regional cerebral blood flow in chronic hypertension. A correlative study. *Stroke, 24,* 1148–1153.

Oppenheimer, B. S., & Fischberg, A. M. (1928). Hypertensive encephalopathy. *Archives of Internal Medicine, 41,* 264.

Phillips, N. A., & Mate-Kole, C. C. (1997). Cognitive deficits in peripheral vascular disease: A comparison of mild stroke patients and normal control subjects. *Stroke, 28,* 777–784.

Pierce, T. W., & Elias, M. F. (1993). Cognitive function and cardiovascular responsivity in subjects with a parental history of hypertension. *Journal of Behavioral Medicine, 16,* 277–294.

Raz, N., Gunning-Dixon, F. M., Head, D., Dupuis, J. H., & Acker, J. D. (1998). Neuroanatomical correlates of cognitive aging: Evidence from structural magnetic resonance imaging. *Neuropsychology, 12,* 95–114.

Reaven, G. M., Lithell, H., & Lansberg, L. L. (1996). Hypertension and associated metabolic abnormalities: The role of insulin resistance and the sympathoadrenal system. *New England Journal of Medicine, 334,* 374–381.

Robbins, M. A., Elias, M. F., Croog, S. H., & Colton, T. (1994). Unmedicated blood pressure levels and quality of life in elderly hypertensive women. *Psychosomatic Medicine, 56,* 251–259.

Rodriguez, G., Arvigo, F., Marenco, S., Nobili, F., Romano, P., Sandini, G., & Rosadini, G. (1987). Regional cerebral blood flow in essential hypertension: Data evaluation by a mapping system. *Stroke, 18,* 13–20.

Salerno, J. A., Grady, C., Mentis, M., Gonzalez-Aviles, A., Wagner, E., Schapiro, M. B., & Rapoport, S. I. (1995). Brain metabolic function in older men with chronic essential hypertension. *Journal of Gerontology: Medical Sciences, 50A,* M147–M154.

Salerno, J. A., Murphy, D. G. M., Horwitz, B., DeCarli, C., Haxby, J. V., Rappoport, S. I., & Schapiro, M. B. (1992). Brain atrophy in hypertension: A volumetric magnetic resonance imaging study. *Hypertension, 20,* 340–348.

Sapolsky, R. M. (1996). Stress, glucocorticoids, and damage to the nervous system: The current state of confusion. *Stress, 1,* 1–19.

Scherr, P. A., Hebert, L. E., Smith, L. A., & Evans, D. A. (1991). Relation of blood pressure to cognitive function in the elderly. *American Journal of Epidemiology, 134,* 1303–1315.

Schmidt, R., Fazekas, F., Koch, M., Kapeller, P., Augustin, M., Offenbacher, H., Fazekas, G., & Lechner, H. (1995). Magnetic resonance imaging cerebral abnormalities and neuropsychologic test performance in elderly hypertensive subjects: A case-control study. *Archives of Neurology, 52,* 905–910.

Schmidt, R., Fazekas, F., Offenbacher, H., Dusek, T., Zach, E., Reinhart, B., Grieshofer, P., Freidl, W., Eber, B., Schumacher, M., Koch, M., & Lechner, H. (1993). Neuropsychologic correlates of MRI white matter hyperintensities: A study of 150 normal volunteers. *Neurology, 43,* 2490–2494.

Schultz, N. R., Dineen, J. T., Elias, M. F., Pentz, C. A., & Wood, W. G. (1979). WAIS performance for different age groups of hypertensive and control subjects during the administration of a diuretic. *Journal of Gerontology, 34,* 246–253.

Seeman, T. E., McEwen, B. S., Albert, M. S., & Rowe, J. W. (1997). Urinary cortisol and decline in memory performance in older adults: MacArthur Studies of Successful Aging. *Journal of Clinical Endocrinology and Metabolism, 82,* 2458–2465.

Shapiro, A. P., Miller, R. E., King, H. E., Ginchereau, E. H., & Fitzgibbon, K. (1982). Behavioral consequences of mild hypertension. *Hypertension, 4,* 355–360.

Shimada, K., Kawamoto, A., Matsubayashi, K., & Ozawa, T. (1990). Silent cerebrovascular disease in the elderly. *Hypertension, 16,* 692–699.

Stamler, J. (1992). Established major coronary risk factors. In M. Marmot & P. Elliott (Eds.), *Coronary heart disease epidemiology* (pp. 35–65). New York: Oxford University Press.

Swan, G. E., Carmelli, D., & La Rue, A. (1996). Relationship between blood pressure during middle age and cognitive impairment in old age: The Western Collaborative Group Study. *Aging, Neuropsychology, and Cognition, 3,* 241–250.

Swan, G. E., Carmelli, D., & La Rue, A. (1998). Systolic blood pressure tracking over 25 to 30 years and cognitive performance in older adults. *Stroke, 29,* 2334–2340.

Thyrum, E. T., Blumenthal, J. A., Madden, D. J., & Siegel, W. (1994). Family history of hypertension influences neurobehavioral function in hypertensive patients. *Psychosomatic Medicine, 57,* 496–500.

Turner, J. R., Sherwood, A., & Light, K. C. (1992). *Individual differences in cardiovascular response to stress*. New York: Plenum.

van Swieten, J. C., Geyskes, G. G., Derix, M. M. A, Beeck, B. M., Ramos, L. M. P., van Latum, J. C., & van Gijn, J. (1991). Hypertension in the elderly is associated with white matter lesions and cognitive deficits. *Annals of Neurology, 30,* 825–830.

Waldstein, S. R. (1995). Hypertension and neuropsychological function: A lifespan perspective. *Experimental Aging Research, 21,* 321–352.

Waldstein, S. R., Burns, H. O., Toth, M. J., & Poehlman, E. T. (1999). Cardiovascular reactivity and central adiposity in older African-Americans. *Health Psychology, 18,* 221–228.

Waldstein, S. R., Jennings, J. R., Ryan, C. M., Muldoon, M. F., Shapiro, A. P., Polefrone, J. M., Fazzari, T. V., & Manuck, S. B. (1996). Hypertension and neuropsychological performance in men: Interactive effects of age. *Health Psychology, 15,* 102–109.

Waldstein, S. R., Manuck, S. B., Ryan, C. M., & Muldoon, M. F. (1991). Neuropsychological correlates of hypertension: Review and methodologic considerations. *Psychological Bulletin, 110,* 451–468.

Waldstein, S. R., Ryan, C. M., Manuck, S. B., Parkinson, D. K., & Bromet, E. J. (1991). Learning and memory function in men with untreated blood pressure elevation. *Journal of Consulting and Clinical Psychology, 59,* 513–517.

Waldstein, S. R., Ryan, C. M., Polefrone, J. M., & Manuck, S. B. (1994). Neuropsychological performance of young men who vary in familial risk for hypertension. *Psychosomatic Medicine, 56,* 449–456.

Waldstein, S. R., Siegel, E. L., Holder, L. E., Snow, J., Rothman, M. I., Zoarski, G. H., & Katzel, L. I. (1997). Neuropsychological, neuroanatomical, and neurophysiological correlates of hypertension in older adults: Preliminary findings. *Psychosomatic Medicine, 59,* 90.

Waldstein, S. R., Snow, J., Muldoon, M. F., & Katzel, L. I. (in press). Neuropsychological consequences of cardiovascular disease. In R. E. Tarter, M. A. Butters, & S. R. Beers (Eds.), *Medical neuropsychology* (2nd ed.). New York: Plenum.

Wilkie, F., & Eisdorfer, C. (1971, May). Intelligence and blood pressure in the aged. *Science, 172,* 959–962.

CHAPTER THREE

Serum Cholesterol, the Brain, and Cognitive Functioning

MATTHEW F. MULDOON
University of Pittsburgh School of Medicine

JANINE D. FLORY
University of Pittsburgh

CHRISTOPHER M. RYAN
University of Pittsburgh School of Medicine

Cholesterol plays a well-known role in atherosclerosis, yet it is an important nutrient and is found in every cell in the human body. In this chapter we consider cholesterol's potential relationships to aspects of cognitive functioning. We review studies of (a) healthy young adults; (b) older individuals with and without cognitive impairment or Alzheimer's disease (AD); and (c) cholesterol's relationship to stroke, a major medical cause of overt neurological deficits. Following a brief overview of cholesterol, related fats, and lipid metabolism, each literature is presented and followed by a discussion of potential biologic mechanisms. We consider only normative variability in serum cholesterol concentration. The rare, inherited disorders of lipid metabolism can be associated with central nervous system (CNS) pathology but are not included in this review.

Cholesterol is a waxy, water-insoluble substance with a chemical composition of a sterol: interconnected rings of five or six carbon atoms each. It is found in all cell membranes and is both consumed in the diet and synthesized by the body. Cholesterol metabolism is closely integrated with that of triglycerides, the more traditional and common fat molecule. Triglycerides are esters of glycerol (a 3-carbon chain) to which are attached three fatty acids. The fatty acids are an important source of energy and serve additional, specific roles. For example, arachadonic acid, present in cell membrane lipids, is used to synthesize prostaglandins as well as related compounds important for intercellular communication. The most prevalent lipids in cell membranes are phospholipids, which are variants of triglycerides in which one fatty acid has been replaced by a phosphate-containing molecule. A common example is lecithin, which contains choline, the precursor of acetylcholine.

Because cholesterol, triglycerides, and phospholipids are all insoluble in water they are transported together in the bloodstream in spherical, macromolecular complexes surrounded by specialized proteins. The resulting lipoprotein particles vary in size, protein coating, and relative concentrations of proteins and lipids. High-density lipoprotein (HDL) particles have a higher protein concentration than very-low- or low-density lipoprotein (VLDL or LDL) particles. The surface proteins on lipoprotein particles are called *apoproteins;* notable examples include apoA (found in HDL particles), apoB (found in VLDL and LDL particles), and apoE (found in all lipoprotein particles but also synthesized in the brain and implicated in AD). Fat-soluble micronutrients, such as ubiquinone (co-Q) and vitamins A and E also travel in lipoprotein particles. Cholesterol, free fatty acids, and micronutrients are continuously being exchanged between the bloodstream and cells throughout the body. The liver plays the central role in the release and uptake of lipoprotein particles to and from the bloodstream. The simplest and most common measure of serum lipids is total cholesterol concentration, with <200 mg/dl being low, 200 to 240 being borderline, and over 240 considered to be high.

SERUM CHOLESTEROL AND COGNITIVE PERFORMANCE IN NONELDERLY ADULTS

Epidemiologic and Clinical Studies

Investigations assessing the relationship between cholesterol level and cognitive functioning in healthy samples indicate that certain abilities may be inversely associated with serum cholesterol, whereas other aptitudes appear to be positively correlated with cholesterol concentration. In an early study of male high school students, Kasl, Brooks, & Rogers (1970) found small but statistically significant negative correlations between serum cholesterol and IQ, school grades, and performance on a word generation task, suggesting that lower cholesterol is associated with better performance. Also, in a study that used neuropsychological assessment, low cholesterol concentration was associated with better performance than high cholesterol on memory tests but was not significantly related to four other performance domains (Desmond, Tatemichi, Paik, & Stern, 1993). Although conflicting evidence exists (Perrig, Perrig, & Stahelin, 1997), data from our own laboratory corroborate this pattern. Wechsler Adult Intelligence Scale–Revised (WAIS–R) Information and Vocabulary subtests were both inversely correlated with total cholesterol in 177 healthy White adults (see Fig. 3.1; Muldoon, Ryan, Matthews, & Manuck, 1997). These findings were not attributable to age or gender. Also, on the basis of the 90-minute neuropsychological assessment in the same investigation, individuals in the low-cholesterol group performed better on tests of working memory than did the average- and high-cholesterol groups (Muldoon, Ryan, Flory, Matthews, & Manuck, 1999). Compared to other participants, the low-cholesterol group had more education, weighed less, smoked less, and had lower blood pressure. Adjustment for education lessened the association between cholesterol group and working memory. In any case, taken together these data suggest that performance on indexes of memory and "crystallized intelligence" (Horn & Cattell, 1967) is best in individuals with relative hypo-cholesterolemia.

On the other hand, Benton (1995) found a direct relationship between serum total cholesterol and speed of mental processing. Specifically, elevated cholesterol was associated with faster decision and movement times on a choice reaction time task in 279 undergraduates. Similarly, compared to low cholesterol, high serum cholesterol was associated with less decline in digit–symbol substitution test performance over 5 years in a middle-aged twin sample (Swan, La-Rue, Carmelli, Reed, & Fabsitz, 1992). In our own analyses of data derived from healthy adults 25 to 60 years old with widely varying cholesterol levels, better performance on WAIS–R Block Design—a test that requires rapid, adaptive problem solving—was associated with higher total cholesterol, provided that scores were corrected for intelligence (estimated from WAIS–R Information scores; see Fig. 3.1.) Relatedly, a neurophysiologic test sensitive to cognitive function (the event-related auditory P-300 potential latency) was reported to be inversely proportional to total serum cholesterol concentration, suggesting that low cholesterol is associated with abnormal responses (Wada, Matsubayashi, Okumiya, Osaki, & Doi, 1997). These studies, therefore, indicate that high serum cholesterol may be associated with optimal mental speed and/or flexibility, sometimes labeled *fluid intelligence.*

Clinical studies of cholesterol-lowering interventions and cognitive performance have only recently begun to appear in the literature. Preliminary evidence from studies of relatively young and healthy individuals indicates that adoption of calorie-restricted diets—which lower both serum cholesterol and triglyceride levels—may slightly impair mental efficiency (Green & Rogers, 1995; Kretsch, Green, Fong, Elliman, & Johnson, 1997; Wing, Vazquez, & Ryan, 1995). On the other hand, poor dietary habits, and high dietary fat intake in particular, have been associated with lower cognitive functioning in elderly samples in observational studies (Kalmijn et al., 1997; Ortega et al., 1997), although in these studies it is not known whether premorbid factors, such as intelligence or socioeconomic factors, may account for the findings. Reitan and Shipley (1963) reported that cholesterol lowering improves cognitive function in men over, but not under, 40 years of age. Here too, interpretation is limited by lack of randomization,

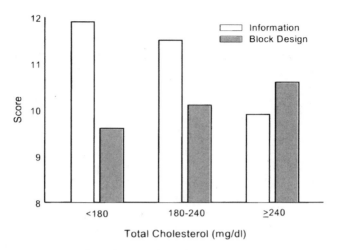

FIG. 3.1. Age-adjusted mean Information and Block Design Wechsler
Adult Intelligence Scale–Revised scores according to serum total cholesterol: data from 177 healthy White adults, aged 25 to 60 years. From
"Serum Cholesterol and Intellectual Performance," by M. F. Muldoon,
C. M. Ryan, K. A. Matthews, and S. B. Manuck, 1997, *Psychosomatic Medicine, 59*, p. 385. Copyright 1997 by Lipincott, Williams & Wilkins. Reprinted with permission.

lack of blinding, and baseline differences between treatment and control groups
in cholesterol level.

Companies manufacturing and marketing "statin" cholesterol-lowering medications have sponsored several studies evaluating cognitive functioning during
pharmacologic cholesterol reduction. Three of four such investigations found
no treatment effects (Gengo, Cwudzinski, Kinkel, Block, & Stauffer, 1995; Harrison & Ashton, 1994; Kostis, Rosen, & Wilson, 1994). The fourth reported that
lovastatin, but not pravastatin, significantly lowered scores on tests of attentional processes in normocholesterolemic volunteers (Roth et al., 1992). Each of
these studies involved relatively brief treatment periods and fewer than 25 individuals per condition. Muldoon, Ryan, Flory, Matthews, & Manuck (1997) recently completed a study involving a more thorough neuropsychological assessment. On the basis of a randomized, double-blind design, 196 adults 25 to 60
years of age received either lovastatin or a placebo for 6 months. Compared to
their placebo-treated counterparts, hypercholesterolemic individuals who received lovastatin had small but significant treatment-related performance decrements on neuropsychological tests measuring attentional processes and psychomotor speed. It is notable that large doses of statin-class drugs produce overt
behavioral pathology in dogs (Berry et al., 1988).

Potential Mechanisms

As a first general question, is it biologically plausible that serum cholesterol concentration could affect cognitive functioning in the absence of any pathological condition? Although fat is not an important energy substrate for the brain, brain lipids are intricately involved with most cellular processes and are susceptible to external manipulation. In fact, variation in serum cholesterol could alter the brain's composition and cellular activity through a number of well-accepted biological pathways. First, the brain has a very high lipid content, and although it has traditionally been taught that the cholesterol and phospholipid composition of neuronal and glial membranes and myelin sheaths is constant in adult mammals, contemporary laboratory research has suggested that the brain lipids are, in fact, vulnerable to variations in serum lipids (Connor, Neruinger, & Lin, 1990; Geiser, 1990; Hershkowitz, Heron, Samuel, & Shinitzky, 1982; Lin, Connor, Anderson, & Neuringer, 1990; McGee & Greenwood, 1989). Normal brain growth and development are dependent on good general nutrition, specifically on adequate dietary fat and cholesterol (Hardy & Kleinman, 1994; Miller, 1994). The CNS and peripheral nervous system synthesize a variety of compounds called *neurosteroids* from cholesterol and sterol precursors that may be affected by manipulations in lipid metabolism (Baulieu, 1997). Modification of dietary lipids alters (a) cortical lipoprotein uptake (Sparks, Liu, Gross, & Scheff, 1995), (b) synaptic membrane phosphorylation and neurotransmitter receptor binding (Hershkowitz et al., 1982), and (c) monoamine oxidase and acetylcholinesterase activity (Crane & Greenwood, 1987; Foot, Cruz, & Clandinin, 1983).

Therefore, it is plausible that manipulations in serum lipids, even if only to a small degree, might influence cognitive functioning in either a positive or a negative fashion (Mann, 1990). The precise biological mechanism(s) cannot be established by available research, but several candidate processes can be identified. Circulating triglycerides and phospholipids supply the CNS with important substrates for cell membranes, prostaglandins, and neurotransmitter synthesis (i.e., specific fatty acids and choline). Therefore, intra- and interindividual differences in the composition or concentration of lipoprotein particles could affect fat-soluble micronutrient supply, structural lipids, or intercellular communication.

What might explain why low cholesterol is associated with superior memory or crystallized intelligence, whereas high serum cholesterol is related to optimal mental flexibility or fluid intelligence? Muldoon, Ryan, Matthews, and Manuck (1997) found that, compared to people with high cholesterol, those with relative hypo-cholesterolemia have more education, lower body mass index, lower blood pressure, and are less likely to smoke. Statistical adjustment for education weakened the relationship between cholesterol and working memory. One possibility is that people with a wide fund of knowledge (*crystallized intelligence*) are most aware of the health risks of certain behaviors and thus are more likely to adopt lifestyles that maintain lower cholesterol levels. Causality, according to this hypothesis, is in the direction of crystallized intelligence affecting health-related behaviors, resulting in reduced serum cholesterol concentration. The cognitive processes of learning–memory and mental speed–executive functions use different brain structures; therefore, another possibility is that certain brain structures or circuits might be differentially affected by serum lipids. This latter hypothesis is somewhat unlikely given the uniformity of serum lipid levels throughout individual vascular beds. Serum cholesterol may differentially affect neurotransmitter systems. As noted earlier, choline, the precursor of acetylcholine, is delivered to the CNS in lipoprotein particles, and several groups of researchers have proposed a link between low cholesterol and reduced brain serotonin (e.g., Kaplan et al., 1998). Fluid intelligence and crystallized intelligence are not correlated perfectly within individuals, and it is conceivable that some fat-soluble nutrients, such as certain fatty acids, may have differing effects on the various dimensions of cognitive performance. Exciting new research indicates a role for omega-3 fatty acids, measured in the diet or blood, in psychiatric disorders, ranging from depression to antisocial behavior (Hibbeln et al., 1998; Peet, Murphy, Edwards, Shay, & Horrobin, 1998). Nutrient supply of certain fatty acids may similarly influence aspects of cognitive functioning; in that sense, serum cholesterol concentration may be viewed as only a general marker of individual differences in lipid metabolism.

SERUM CHOLESTEROL, COGNITIVE DECREMENTS, AND ALZHEIMER'S DISEASE IN STROKE-FREE ELDERLY ADULTS

Epidemiological and Clinical Studies

Despite some evidence to the contrary (Orengo et al., 1996; Paganini-Hill & Henderson, 1996; Wieringa, Burlinson, Rafferty, Gowland, & Burns, 1997), most cross-sectional studies indicate that AD (late-onset sporadic) or otherwise-classified cognitive dysfunction is associated with relative hypo-cholesterolemia (Cattin et al., 1997; Kuusisto et al., 1997; Postiglione et al., 1989; Scacchi et al., 1998; Wada et al., 1997). Compared to 153 controls, 80 individuals with probable AD had significantly lower age- and sex-adjusted total serum cholesterol levels (Scacchi et al., 1998). In a similar investigation of consecutive medical admissions of elderly patients, and additional adjustment for level of education, cognitive impairment was found to be inversely proportional to serum cholesterol concentration (see Fig. 3.2; Cattin et al., 1997). Finally, a report based on a population-based sample of 980 individuals aged 69 to 78 years noted that low cholesterol was associated with AD, independent of age and socioeconomic status (Kuusisto et al., 1997).

It is important to note that AD, particularly when severe, can result in a catabolic state from reduced caloric intake, in turn causing nutritional deficiency

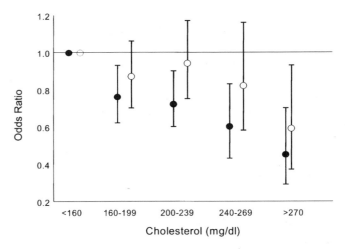

FIG. 3.2. Odds ratio of impaired cognition according to total serum cholesterol. Data points identified by filled circles are adjusted for age, gender, and education; data in open circles are additionally adjusted for duration of hospitalization, smoking status, weight, albumin, and lymphocyte level. Cognitive impairment is defined as a score of ≤6 out of 10 on the Hodkinson Abbreviated Mental Test (Cattin et al., 1997).

and a fall in serum cholesterol level. Therefore, low serum cholesterol in cross-sectional studies of demented patients may represent a spurious observation. In one study, however, adjustment for multiple indicators of illness severity and nutritional status (duration of hospitalization, weight, albumin level, and lymphocyte count) did not eliminate the association between low cholesterol and AD (Fig. 3.2; Cattin et al., 1997). Furthermore, marked hypercholesterolemia seemed to be protective, which would not be expected if the finding were due solely to a spurious association between AD and low cholesterol attributable to poor nutrition.

Another strategy for overcoming potential confounding by disease-related cholesterol reduction involves measurement of serum cholesterol years before dementia screening or cognitive testing. Wada, Matsubayashi, Okumiya, Kimura, et al. (1997) categorized 93 individuals with a mean age of 79 years as having cholesterol levels either greater than, or less than, 200 mg/dl and found that 3 years later, compared to their hypercholesterolemic counterparts, individuals with low cholesterol declined more on the Mini-Mental Status Examination (MMSE; Folstein, Folstein, & McHugh, 1974). Also, in an elderly population sample, referred to earlier (Kuusisto et al., 1997), dementia was associated (on multivariate analysis controlling for age and socioeconomic status) with relative hypo-cholesterolemia on the basis of blood samples obtained 3.5 years before dementia screening. More intriguing still, elderly men with AD were found to have had relative *hyper*cholesterolemia between 15 and 30 years prior to diagnosis, followed by a sharp decline in cholesterol concentration to levels below that of comparison groups (see Fig. 3.3; Notkola et al., 1998). This decline in cholesterol appears to have preceded the clinical manifestations of dementia and any associated compromise in nutritional status.

In the only germane treatment study, 431 hypercholesterolemic but generally healthy adults over the age of 65 received lovastatin or placebo for 6 months. Cholesterol reduction was not associated with any change in WAIS–R Digit–Symbol Substitution scores (the only cognitive test administered) or with any decline in self-reported cognitive function (Santanello et al., 1997). We are not aware of any studies of cholesterol-lowering interventions and cognitive functioning in demented, or dementia-prone, individuals.

In the previous section, in which we discussed young and middle-aged individuals, low serum cholesterol was noted to be associated with superior crystallized intelligence (or memory) and poorer fluid intelligence, whereas there is evidence that in the elderly low cholesterol is predictive of general cognitive decline and AD. How these findings may be reconciled remains unclear. If, as suggested, greater education and a larger fund of knowledge lead to lower

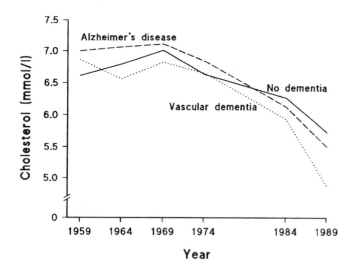

FIG. 3.3. Age-adjusted mean serum total cholesterol concentration during 1959 to 1989 according to dementia status determined in 1989. Dementia onset was generally between 1984 and 1989. Alzheimer's disease: $n = 27$, vascular dementia: $n = 13$, no dementia: $n = 397$. To convert cholesterol in mmol/L to mg/dl, multiply by 38.67. From "Serum Total Cholesterol, Apolipoprotein E & 4allele, and Alzheimer's Disease," by I. Notkola et al., 1998, *Neuroepidemiology, 17*, p. 17. Copyright 1998 by Karger. Reprinted with permission.

cholesterol in youth, other factors must underlie the association between low cholesterol and cognitive decline with aging. Several possibilities are outlined later, in the Potential Mechanisms section.

Great interest has recently developed in apolipoprotein (apo) E, as more than 100 studies have demonstrated an association between the apolipoprotein E polymorphism (*APOE*) and AD (see Roses, 1996). This association is most consistently present in Asian and North American Caucasian samples and less consistently in African American, African, and Hispanic samples (e.g., Tang et al., 1998). The gene for apo E is encoded on chromosome 19, and three common isoforms—designated ε2, ε3, and ε4—have been identified, distinguished by a single amino acid substitution in the receptor-binding region of apo E (Weisgraber, Innerarity, & Mahley, 1982). Homozygosity for the *APOE* ε4 allele, which occurs in 2% to 3% of the Caucasian population (Mahley, 1988), is associated with a five- to eight-fold greater risk for AD, and *APOE* ε4 heterozygosity is associated with a two- to three-fold greater risk, relative to individuals with no ε4 allele (Corder et al., 1993).

Evidence is accumulating that the *APOE* ε4 allele might be more important for the timing of the progressive cognitive decline characteristic of AD than for the risk of developing the disease. For example, the *APOE* ε4 genotype lowers the age at onset of AD in a dose-dependent fashion (Blacker et al., 1997; Meyer et al., 1998). The age at onset for *APOE* ε4 homozygotes is typically less than 70 years, whereas people with no ε4 allele show signs of the disorder after age 80. Moreover, in community samples of older adults (average age ≥ 65 years), most of whom are nondemented, the *APOE* ε4 allele is associated with lower scores on cognitive status examinations (e.g., MMSE; e.g., Alstiel, Greenberg, Marin, Lantz, & Mohs, 1997; Feskens et al., 1994; Henderson et al., 1995) and worse performance on tasks that measure learning and memory (e.g., Bondi et al., 1995; Carmelli et al., 1998; Henderson et al., 1995; Reed et al., 1994) and psychomotor speed (e.g., Henderson et al., 1995; Yaffe, Cauley, Sands, & Browner, 1997). Negative associations between the *APOE* ε4 allele and cognitive performance measures have been reported (e.g., Hyman et al., 1996), but the evidence for decrements in memory and learning abilities is fairly consistent and similar to data from a sample of 220 Caucasian younger adults, aged 24 to 60 (Flory, Manuck, Ferrell, Ryan, & Muldoon, 1999). In that study, Flory et al. (1999) observed lower scores on a cluster of learning and memory tasks in individuals with an ε4 allele, relative to individuals with no ε4 allele. In contrast, they did not observe an effect of *APOE* genotype on measures of psychomotor speed or attention. These data are intriguing, because the average age of the sample was 45 years. Together, these reports suggest that the *APOE* polymorphism is associated with an age-related decline in cognitive performance, which may include the development of AD at upper age levels. An alternative explanation is that the *APOE* genotype is a marker for poorer ability across the life span. These hypotheses await testing in a large, age-stratified sample.

Because the *APOE* ε4 isoform is also associated with at least mildly elevated serum cholesterol concentration, it has been hypothesized that hypercholesterolemia may also play a role in the development of AD (Chandra & Pandav, 1998). Although evidence is limited, the relatively rare *APOE* ε2 allele (which is associated with lower serum cholesterol) may be protective against AD (e.g., Corder et al., 1994; Talbot et al., 1994). Two groups of investigators have found evidence of a statistical interaction between the *APOE* genotype and cholesterol with respect to cognitive function. Specifically, in a case control study of more than 400 individuals, men under 80 years old with AD and hypercholesterolemia had the highest ε4 allele frequency (Jarvik et al., 1995), and in a community sample of 353 elderly men who underwent the MMSE twice 3 years apart, high serum cholesterol was a risk factor for a two-point decline among individuals with an ε4 allele (Kalmijn, Feskens, Launer, & Kromhout, 1996). However, such interactions between cholesterol concentration and the *APOE* polymorphism have not been noted in several other large studies (Kuusisto et al., 1997; Notkola et al., 1998; Wieringa et al., 1997).

Potential Mechanisms

Apo E is the major apolipoprotein found in the CNS and is synthesized in the brain (Mahley et al., 1988). Much of the work on mechanisms linking apo E to cognitive performance has been conducted in the context of AD and does not concern serum lipid levels per se. Overall, this research has demonstrated that apo E is associated with the characteristic neuropathology of AD (see Higgins, Large, Rupniak, & Barnes, 1997, for a review). Amyloid plaques and neurofibrillary tangles contain apo E, and the *APOE* ε4 allele product binds more strongly than the ε3 product to the beta amyloid protein. In addition, the *APOE* ε4 product does not bind as readily to tau, a protein necessary for cytoskeletal stability. The development of plaques and tangles is thought to begin many years before the clinical symptoms of AD appear and may occur earlier, develop more rapidly among individuals with the *APOE* ε4 genotype, or both (Ohm et al., 1995). Consistent with these observations, several reports have shown lesser hippocampal volume (Plassman et al., 1997; Soininen et al., 1995) and decreased blood flow in the temporal and parietal lobes of the brain (Reiman et al., 1996; Small et al., 1995) in cognitively normal middle-aged adults who have at least one *APOE* ε4 allele. Finally, in the presence of VLDL, the *APOE* ε4 isoform is associated with reduced neurite outgrowth in vitro, relative to the common ε3 isoform (Nathan et al., 1994), suggesting a role for apo E in neuronal plasticity and the response to neuronal injury. These data might also explain why individuals who inherit an *APOE* ε4 allele and suffer head trauma are particularly vulnerable to AD (Jordan et al., 1997; Mayeux et al., 1995).

Even aside from apo E, brain lipids may play a role in age-related cognitive decline and AD. The various biologic pathways discussed in the previous section also apply here. In addition, structural changes in the cortex of AD patients are mediated, in part, by reductions in the membrane cholesterol:phospholipid ratio (Mason, Shoemaker, Shajenko, Chambers, & Herbette, 1992). Supplementing phospholipids (e.g., phosphatidylserine) in the diet of AD patients can alter cerebrospinal fluid dopamine and serotonin metabolite levels and increase activated regional brain metabolism assessed by positron emission tomography scanning and may improve cognitive performance (Argentiero & Tavolato, 1980; Crook, Petrie, Wells, & Massari, 1992; Heiss et al., 1993).

Vitamin E is transported to the CNS in lipoprotein particles, and low levels have been associated with more rapid progression of AD (Schmidt et al., 1998). Analogously, choline supply may be reduced in individuals with significant hypocholesterolemia. Cholinergic receptor blockade induces a transient memory deficit in humans that mimics aspects of AD (Gitelman & Prohovnik, 1992), and hippocampal long-term potential of synaptic transmission—the primary model of learning and memory—is inhibited in vitro by a "statin" cholesterol-lowering medication (Matthies, Schulz, Hollt, & Krug, 1997). Other in vitro research, on the other hand, suggests that cholesterol depletion inhibits the generation of beta-amyloid, a pathologic marker of AD (Simons, Keller, de Strooper, Beyreuther, Dotti, & Simons, 1998).

CHOLESTEROL LEVELS, THE CEREBRAL VASCULATURE, STROKES, AND VASCULAR DEMENTIA

Epidemiological and Clinical Studies

Although serum cholesterol, and particularly LDL cholesterol, is widely accepted as playing a causal role in coronary artery disease, a consensus has not yet been reached on whether hypercholesterolemia is a risk factor for cerebral infarction or stroke. In a recent effort to bring together as much evidence as possible, the Prospective Studies Collaborators enlisted investigators of 33 prospective observational studies involving a total of 45 cohorts from around the world (Prospective Studies Collaboration, 1995). The collective data pool included nearly 45,000 adults of varying ages, 39% of whom were female. The average length of follow-up was 16 years, during which time more than 13,000 strokes were recorded. No association between blood cholesterol and stroke was found to exist. (See top of Fig. 3.4.) This lack of association was not influenced by adjustment for age, sex, ethnicity, or blood pressure.

However, because information on stroke subtypes was not generally available in these studies, the lack of an overall association might conceal a positive association between cholesterol and ischemic stroke that is offset by a negative association with respect to hemorrhagic stroke. Indeed, as illustrated in the bottom panel of Fig. 3.4, this was found to be the case in the single largest cohort

A.

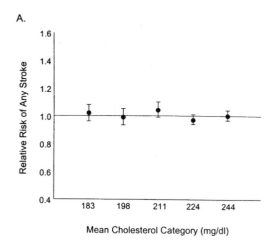

Mean Cholesterol Category (mg/dl)

B.

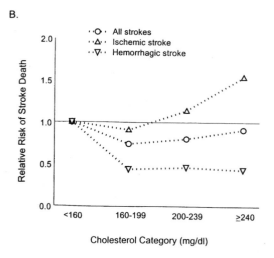

FIG. 3.4. Panel A: Floating absolute risk of stroke and 99% confidence intervals by total cholesterol, adjusted for age, sex, diastolic blood pressure, history of coronary heart disease, and race. These are data from 45 prospective observational cohorts comprising 450,000 individuals with 5 to 30 years of follow-up (Prospective Studies Collaboration, 1995). Panel B: Relative risk of stroke death by total cholesterol, adjusted for age, diastolic blood pressure, tobacco use, and race. Low cholesterol level is used as referent. These are data from 350,000 men who were followed for 12 years (Neaton et al., 1992).

study distinguishing among stroke subtypes (Neaton et al., 1992). Additional evidence linking high serum cholesterol with at least ischemic stroke derives from studies imaging the extracranial carotid arteries using duplex ultrasound. Some, though not all, cross-sectional studies using this methodology have found that concentrations of total and LDL cholesterol are significantly related to either carotid artery thickness (Sharret et al., 1994; Zanchetti et al., 1998) or stenotic lesions (P. W. F. Wilson et al., 1997). Interestingly, however, the limited data on diet suggest that saturated fat protects against ischemic strokes (Gillman, Cupples, Millen, Ellison, & Wolf, 1997).

The foregoing observational or correlational studies can only infer causal relationships between serum cholesterol and cognitive dysfunction due to vascular disease, whereas investigations of cholesterol-lowering interventions more directly test such hypotheses. Early randomized clinical trials of cholesterol-lowering therapies failed to demonstrate any reduction in stroke risk, even with meta-analysis (Herbert, Gaziano, & Hennekens, 1995). Indeed, some evidence suggested that a particular class of medication—fibric acid derivatives—might actually increase stroke risk. However, since 1990 older cholesterol-lowering drugs have been largely supplanted by "statin" drugs (e.g., lovastatin [Mevacor], pravastatin [Pravachol], and simvastatin [Zocor]). These potent medications block intracellular cholesterol synthesis, substantially lower serum cholesterol levels, prevent heart attacks, and produce few obvious side effects. Randomized clinical studies using duplex ultrasound to assess carotid artery morphology have now shown that statin therapy retards the progression of carotid artery atherosclerosis (Furberg et al., 1994; MacMahon et al., 1998; Salonen et al., 1995). Moreover, a meta-analysis of stroke incidence in large clinical trials indicates that treating hypercholesterolemia with a statin-class medication lowers stroke risk by 27% in high-risk populations (Crouse, Byington, Hoen, & Furberg, 1997). (Hemorrhagic strokes did not increase, as might have been expected from epidemiologic studies.) To date, no clinical trials of cholesterol reduction in stroke-prone individuals have included cognitive or neuropsychological testing.

Distinct from large-vessel atherosclerosis and large strokes, lacunar (small) infarcts and white matter lesions (areas of hyperintensity on magnetic resonance imaging) are also quite common in elderly people. Moreover, lacunar infarcts are currently understood to cause multi-infarct (or vascular) dementia, the most common form of intellectual deterioration attributable to vascular disease. White matter lesions may also contribute to age-related cognitive decline. Little if any evidence links hypercholesterolemia with lacunar or small-vessel cerebral infarcts. Several cross-sectional studies of brain imaging in clinical sample populations of 140 to 200 individuals each found no association between hyperlipidemia and either areas of white matter low attenuation or lacunar infarcts (Amar, Lewis, Wilcock, Scott, & Bucks, 1995; Fukui, Sugita, Kawamura, Takeuchi, & Hasegawa, 1997; Kario, Matsuo, Kobayashi, Asada, & Matsuo, 1996; Olicheny et al., 1995). Similarly, the mean cholesterol level of 53 patients with vascular dementia was not different from that of 153 age-equivalent controls (Scacchi et al., 1998), and even cholesterol levels measured two decades before dementia screening failed to implicate hyperlipidemia in vascular dementia (Notkola et al., 1998). Indeed, among Japanese-Americans, preference for an American diet (high in saturated fat) over an Asian diet has been associated with fewer small vessel lesions and a lower risk of vascular dementia (Ross et al., 1999).

Potential Mechanisms

Stroke or cerebral infarction—the permanent loss of focal areas of brain tissue—most often results from loss of blood flow to that area. Often, this loss of perfusion is the result of atherosclerosis in large arteries supplying the brain, or it is due to embolization of atherosclerotic plaque or thrombus from more distant arteries or the heart. A second cause of stroke is bleeding from ruptured blood vessels within the cranium (i.e., intracerebral hemorrhage). Although overall stroke rate is not influenced by serum cholesterol concentration, the weight of the evidence does implicate hypercholesterolemia in carotid artery atherosclerosis and resulting large ischemic strokes. Just as in coronary arteries, the carotid and cerebral arteries can develop atheromatous plaque. Macrophages and smooth-muscle cells within the walls of the arteries abnormally accumulate cholesterol intracellularly, forming foam cells, which eventually rupture, leaving large deposits of cholesterol that progressively occlude the vessel's lumen.

In addition to observational epidemiologic evidence linking high cholesterol to atherosclerotic strokes, there is strong evidence from clinical trials showing that cholesterol-lowering statin drugs retard carotid artery disease progression and reduce ischemic stroke risk, at least in high-risk populations. It should be noted that statin-class medications have other (nonlipid) actions that may be anti-atherogenic (Rosenson & Tangney, 1998). If statins are found to prevent stroke through mechanisms other than cholesterol reduction, it would diminish the strongest evidence that hypercholesterolemia contributes to ischemic stroke.

In the United States, roughly 20% to 25% of large strokes, and roughly half of all fatal strokes, are due to intracerebral hemorrhage. Prospective epidemiologic evidence links hemorrhagic strokes with hypo-cholesterolemia. It is suggested that low serum cholesterol compromises the strength or integrity of vessel walls (by means of angionecrosis), predisposing the aneurysmal dilation and rupture. Small or lacunar strokes are due to a microscopic process referred to as *hyaline arteriolosclerosis,* which usually affects small penetrating arteries of deep brain structures and subcortical white matter. This disorder is distinct from atherosclerosis, and no epidemiologic evidence links cholesterol levels with either lacunar strokes or their ultimate clinical manifestation: vascular (multi-infarct) dementia. Finally, the origins of white matter lesions are still poorly understood, although they are suspected to be due to cerebral hypoperfusion. Here, also, a relationship to serum cholesterol concentration has not been demonstrated to exist.

SUMMARY AND COMMENT

From this summary of existing literatures, it appears that multiple relationships exist between serum lipids and cognitive function. Two general neurobiological models are proposed in Table 3.1. With respect to cerebral infarction or stroke, serum cholesterol concentration does not modify an individual's overall stroke risk. Nonetheless, a body of both observational and clinical trial evidence suggests that hypercholesterolemia plays a causal and reversible role in carotid artery atherosclerosis and large-vessel stroke. Viewed from the vantage point of

TABLE 3.1
Putative Models of Relationships Between Serum Cholesterol
and Cognitive Functioning

Model	Description
Nutrient supply	Lipoprotein particles deliver a large number of fat-soluble compounds to the brain, some of which are essential to optimal cognitive functioning and some of which may be deleterious. Therefore, variability in serum lipid concentrations can affect cognitive functioning by means of biologically plausible yet unspecified mechanisms involving nutrient delivery.
Atherosclerosis	Hypercholesterolemia causes carotid atherosclerosis and strokes, and through this mechanism high cholesterol levels are associated with diminished cognitive functioning in older adults. Furthermore, lowering serum cholesterol will retard cerebrovascular atherosclerosis, prevent strokes, and help preserve optimal cognitive functioning.

atherosclerosis as a major degenerative disease of aging, it is logical to posit that hypercholesterolemia adversely affects cognitive functioning. By promoting the development of atherosclerosis in the arteries of the head and neck, elevated serum cholesterol levels cause cerebral infarctions and, in that manner, contribute in an important way to the cognitive dysfunction in populations over 50 years of age. Moreover, current cholesterol-lowering drugs appear to prevent large ischemic strokes. There is not a parallel body of mechanistic research to suggest that hypercholesterolemia should predispose individuals to lacunar strokes or white matter lesions; neither do available epidemiologic studies implicate high cholesterol in these lesions or vascular (multiple, small-infarct) dementia.

If the above-summarized literature pertaining to cerebrovascular disease, stroke, and serum cholesterol is at least reasonably cohesive, broader issues of serum lipids in relation to cognitive abilities and age-related cognitive decline remain largely unresolved. Several studies of stroke-free elderly individuals have revealed an association between low serum cholesterol and either minor cognitive decrements or AD. Although it may be supposed that such findings merely reflect a catabolic state resulting from cognitive impairment, that does not sufficiently explain the findings. Relative hypo-cholesterolemia appears to predate cognitive impairment by several years. Moreover, some preliminary evidence from studies of dietary and pharmacologic interventions in nonelderly adults also suggests that serum cholesterol reduction may induce mild cognitive decrements.

How might low or lowered serum cholesterol predispose a person to varying degrees of cognitive dysfunction? The nutritional-supply model recognizes cholesterol as a single component of chemically complex lipoprotein particles and acknowledges that serum cholesterol concentration is but one measure of diverse processes involved in lipid metabolism. The brain is dependent on the bloodstream for all nutrients, and it may be that serum cholesterol concentration correlates with one or more essential compounds involved, for example, in neurotransmitter synthesis or neuronal membrane composition. Accordingly, serum cholesterol levels may be directly or indirectly related to aspects of cognitive function. Much more general than the atherosclerosis model, this suggests that interplay occurs between lipid-soluble substances transported in the bloodstream and the brain but does not specify the particular biological processes involved or the direction of effect(s) on cognitive performance. Although still general, this model is supported by several observational and randomized treatment studies in nonelderly adults indicating that low cholesterol and cholesterol-lowering interventions may be associated with some reduction in performance on tests of psychomotor speed, mental flexibility, and attentional processes. Such a view conflicts with evidence in nonelderly samples that memory and fund of knowledge is poorer in persons with high, compared to low, cholesterol levels. Possible biologic mechanisms were presented, but clarification of these issues awaits additional research.

It should be noted that several cited studies report neuropsychological performance differences that are small in magnitude Clinical interpretation of such findings is difficult. Standard neuropsychological tests have the advantages of sensitivity and the logical decomposition of cognitive functioning into its component skills and abilities (memory, attention, psychomotor speed, executive functioning, etc.). However, although these assessments have proven clinically useful in localization of CNS pathology, they tend to have unknown ecological validity (Heinrichs, 1990; B. A. Wilson, 1993). Moreover, the relevance of small changes on such tests for optimal responding to the cognitive challenges typical of daily life requires substantial extrapolation. This is not a problem as long as the neuropsychological measures are being used to diagnose brain dysfunction. However, these measures may be less appropriate when applied to clinical studies designed to determine how a particular intervention influences everyday cognitive processes (Harris & Morris, 1984). Some of the small performance differences as a function of serum cholesterol concentration may be truly inconsequential. On the other hand, a series of different cognitive decrements could conceivably aggregate to affect performance on tasks such as automobile driving, which require the integration of a broad array of cognitive abilities (e.g., sustained attention, speed and accuracy of psychomotor performance).

As we strive for a clearer understanding of the relationships between serum lipids and cognitive functioning, several key studies are required. Additional prospective studies of elderly people should use serial nutritional assessments in conjunction with longitudinal cognitive testing to determine the exact relationship among serum cholesterol, nutritional status, and cognitive decline. Studies of nutritional factors in animal models of dementia would be helpful in this regard. Sensitive neuropsychological testing is needed in diet- and drug-based clinical trials of cholesterol reduction, but such assessments must be complemented by measures that are interpretable with respect to everyday cognitive demands. Examples might include the pre-employment exams widely administered by the human resources industry and automobile driving simulation. The current national recommendations to lower the serum cholesterol concentration of millions of individuals (NCEP) compels us to complete these additional studies.

ACKNOWLEDGMENT

Preparation of this chapter and related research was supported by National Institutes of Health Public Health Service Grant HL46328.

REFERENCES

Alstiel, L. D., Greenberg, D. A., Marin, D., Lantz, M., & Mohs, R. (1997). Apolipoprotein E genotype and cognition in the very old. *The Lancet, 349*, 1451.

Amar, K., Lewis, T., Wilcock, G., Scott, M., & Bucks, R. (1995). The relationship between white matter low attenuation on brain CT and vascular risk factors: A memory clinic study. *Age and Aging, 24*, 411–415.

Argentiero, V., & Tavolato, B. (1980). Dopamine (DA) and serotonin metabolic levels in the cerebrospinal fluid (CSF) in Alzheimer's presenile dementia under basic conditions and after stimulation with cerebral cortex phospholipids. *Journal of Neurology, 224*, 53–58.

Baulieu, E. E. (1997). Neurosteroids: Of the nervous system, by the nervous system, for the nervous system. *Recent Progress in Hormone Research, 52*, 1–32.

Benton, D. (1995). Do low cholesterol levels slow mental processing? *Psychosomatic Medicine, 57*, 50–53.

Berry, P. H., MacDonald, J. S., Albert, A. W., Molon-Noblot, S., Chen, J. S., Lo, C.-Y. L., Greenspan, M. D., Allen, H., Durand-Cavagna, G., Jensen, R., Bailly, Y., Delort, P., & Duprat, P. (1988). Brain and optic system pathology in hypocholesterolemic dogs treated with a competitive inhibitor of 3-hydroxy-3-methylglutaryl coenzyme A reductase. *American Journal of Pathology, 132*, 427–443.

Blacker, D., Haines, J. L., Rodes, L., Terwedow, H., Go, R. C. P., Harrell, L. E., Perry, R. T., Bassett, S. S., Chase, G., Meyers, D., Albert, M. S., & Tanzi, R. (1997). ApoE ε4 and age at onset of Alzheimer's disease: The NIMH Genetics Initiative. *Neurology, 48*, 139–147.

Bondi, M. W., Salmon, D. P., Monsch, A. U., Galasko, K., Butters, N., Klauber, M. R., Thal, L. J., & Saitoh, T. (1995). Episodic memory changes are associated with the APOE–ε4 allele in nondemented older adults. *Neurology, 45*, 2203–2206.

Carmelli, D., Swan, G. E., Reed, T., Miller, B., Wolf, P. A., Jarvik, G. P., & Schellenberg, G. D. (1998). Midlife cardiovascular risk factors, ApoE, and cognitive decline in elderly male twins. *American Academy of Neurology, 50*, 1580–1585.

Cattin, L., Bordin, P., Fonda, M., Adamo, C., Barbone, F., Bovenzi, M., Manto, A., Pedone, C., & Pahor, M. (1997). Factors associated with cognitive impairment among older Italian inpatients. *Journal of the American Geriatrics Society, 45*, 1324–1330.

Chandra, V., & Pandav, R. (1998). Gene–environment interaction in Alzheimer's disease: A potential role for cholesterol. *Neuroepidemiology, 17*, 225–232.

Connor, W. E., Neruinger, M., & Lin, D. S. (1990). Dietary effects on brain fatty acid composition:

The reversibility of n-3 fatty acid deficiency and turnover of docosahexaenoic acid in the brain, erythrocytes, and plasma of rhesus monkeys. *Journal of Lipid Research, 31,* 237–247.

Corder, E., Saunders, A., Risch, N., Strittmatter, W. J., Schmechel, D. E., Gaskell, P. C., Rimmler, J. B., Locke, P. A., Conneally, P. M., Schmader, K. E., Small, G. W., Roses, A. D., Haines, J. L., & Pericak-Vance, M. A. (1994). Protective effect of apolipoprotein E type 2 allele for late onset Alzheimer disease. *Nature Genetics, 7,* 180–183.

Corder, E., Saunders, A., Strittmatter, W., Schmechel, D. E., Gaskell, P. C., Small, G. W., Roses, A. D., Haines, J. L., & Pericak-Vance, M. A. (1993, August). Gene dose of apolipoprotein E type 4 allele and the risk of Alzheimer's disease in late onset families. *Science, 261,* 921–923.

Crane, S. B., & Greenwood, C. E. (1987). Dietary fat source influences neuronal mitochondrial monoamine oxidase activity and macronutrient selection in rats. *Pharmacology, Biochemistry, and Behavior, 27,* 1–6.

Crook, T., Petrie, W., Wells, C., & Massari, D. C. (1992). Effects of phosphatidylserine in Alzheimer's disease. *Psychopharmacology Bulletin, 28,* 61–66.

Crouse, J. R. III, Byington, R. P., Hoen, H. M., & Furberg, C. D. (1997). Reductase inhibitor monotherapy and stroke prevention. *Archives of Internal Medicine, 157,* 1305–1310.

Desmond, D., Tatemichi, T., Paik, M., & Stern, Y. (1993). Risk factors for cerebrovascular disease as correlates of cognitive function in a stroke-free cohort. *Archives of Neurology, 50,* 162- 166.

Feskens, E. J. M., Havekes, L. M., Kalmijn, S., de Knijff, P., Launer, L. J., & Kromhout, D. (1994). Apolipoprotein e4 allele and cognitive decline in elderly men. *British Medical Journal, 309,* 1202–1206.

Flory, J. D., Manuck, S. B., Ferrell, R. E., Ryan, C. M., & Muldoon, M. F (1999). APOE e4 allele is associated with lower memory scores in middle-aged adults. *Psychosomatic Medicine, 61,* 257.

Folstein, M. F., Folstein, S. E., McHugh, P. R. (1974). A practical method for grading the cognitive state of patients for the physician. *Journal of Psychiatric Research, 16,* 965–969.

Foot, M., Cruz, T. F., & Clandinin, M. T. (1983). Effect of dietary lipid on synaptosomal acetylcholinesterase activity. *Biochemical Journal, 211,* 507–509.

Fukui, T., Sugita, K., Kawamura, M., Takeuchi, T., & Hasegawa, Y. (1997). Differences in factors associated with silent and symtomatic MRI T_2 hyperintensity lesions. *Journal of Neurology, 244,* 293–298.

Furberg, C. D., Adams, H. P. Jr., Applegate, W. B., Byington, R. P., Espeland, M. A., Hartwell, T., Hunninghake, D. B., Lefkowitz, D. S., Probstfield, J., Riley, W. A., & Young, B. (1994). Effect of lovastatin on early carotid atherosclerosis and cardiovascular events. *Circulation, 90,* 1679–1687.

Geiser, F. (1990). Influence of polyunsaturated and saturated dietary lipids on adipose tissue, brain and mitochondrial membrane fatty acid composition of a mammalian hibernator. *Biochimica et Biophysica Acta, 1046,* 159–166.

Gengo, F., Cwudzinski, D., Kinkel, P., Block, G., & Stauffer, L. (1995). Effects of treatment with ovastatin and pravastating on daytime cognitive performance. *Clinical Cardiology, 18,* 209- 214.

Gillman, M. W., Cupples, L. A., Millen, B. E., Ellison, R. C., & Wolf, P. A. (1997). Inverse association of dietary fat with development of ischemic stroke in men. *Journal of the American Medical Association, 278,* 1245–1250.

Gitelman, D. R., & Prohovnik, I. (1992). Muscarinic and nicotine contributions to cognitive function and cortical blood flow. *Neurobiology of Aging, 13* (Part 2), 313–318.

Green, M. W., & Rogers, P. J. (1995). Impaired cognitive functioning during spontaneous dieting. *Psychosomatic Medicine, 25,* 1003–1010.

Hardy, S. C., & Kleinman, R. E. (1994). Fat and cholesterol in the diet of infants and young children: Implications for growth, development, and long-term health. *Journal of Pediatrics, 25* (Part 2), S69–S77.

Harris, J. E., & Morris, P. E. (1984). *Everyday memory, actions, and absent-mindedness.* London: Academic Press.

Harrison, R. W. S., & Ashton, C. H. (1994). Do cholesterol-lowering agents affect brain activity? A comparison of simvastatin, pravastatin, and placebo in healthy volunteers. *British Journal of Clinical Pharmacology, 37,* 231–236.

Heinrichs, R. W. (1990). Current and emergent applications of neuropsychological assessment: Problems of validity and utility. *Professional Psychology: Research and Practice, 21,* 171–176.

Heiss, W. D, Kessler, J., Slansky, I., Mielke, S. R., Szelies, B., & Herholz, K. (1993). Activation PET as an instrument to determine therapeutic efficacy in Alzheimer's disease. *Annals of the New York Academy of Sciences, 695,* 327–331.

Henderson, A. S., Eastel, S., Jorm, A. F., Mackinnon, A. J., Korten, A. E., Christensen, H., Croft, L., & Jacomb, P. A. (1995). Apolipoprotein E allele ε4, dementia, and cognitive decline in a population sample. *The Lancet, 346,* 1387–1390.

Herbert, P. R., Gaziano, J. M., & Hennekens, C. H. (1995). An overview of trials of cholesterol lowering and risk of stroke. *Archives of Internal Medicine, 155,* 50–55.

Hershkowitz, M., Heron, D., Samuel, D., & Shinitzky, M. (1982). The modulation of protein phosphorylation and receptor binding in synaptic membranes by changes in lipid fluidity: Implications for aging. *Progress in Brain Research, 56,* 419–434.

Hibbeln, J. R., Uwhau, J. C., Linnoila, M., George, D. T., Regan, P., Shosf, S., Vaughan, M., Rawlings, R., & Salem, N. Jr. (1998). A replication study of violent and non-violent subjects: CSF metabolites of serotonin and dopamine are predicted by plasma essential fatty acids. *Biological Psychiatry, 44* (Part 4), 243–249.

Higgins, G. A., Large, C. H., Rupniak, H. T., & Barnes, J. C. (1997). Apolipoprotein E and Alzheimers disease: A review of recent studies. *Pharmacology, Biochemistry and Behavior, 56,* 675–685.

Horn, J. L., & Cattell, R. B. (1967). Age differences in fluid and crystallized intelligence. *Acta Psychologica, 26,* 107–129.

Hyman, B. T., Gomez-Isla, T., Briggs, M., Chung, H., Nichols, S., Kohout, F., & Wallace, R. (1996). Apolipoprotein E and cognitive change in an elderly population. *Annals of Neurology, 40,* 55–66.

Jarvik, G. P., Wijsman, E. M., Kukull, W. A., Schellenberg, G. D., Yu, C., & Larson, E. B. (1995). Interactions of apoliopoprotein E genotype, total cholesterol level, age, and sex in prediction of Alzheimer's disease: A case-control study. *Neurology, 45,* 1092–1096.

Jordan, B. D., Relkin, N. R., Raudin, L. D., Jacobs, A. R., Bennett, A., & Gandy, S. (1997). Apolipoprotein E ε4 associated with chronic traumatic brain injury in boxing. *Journal of the American Medical Association, 278* (Part 2), 136–140.

Kalmijn, S., Feskens, E. J. M., Launer, L. J., & Kromhout, D. (1996). Cerebrovascular disease, the apolipoprotein e4 allele, and cognitive decline in a community-based study of elderly men. *Stroke, 27,* 2230–2235.

Kalmijn, S., Launer, L. J., Ott, A., Witteman, J. C. M., Hofman, A., & Breteler, M. M. B. (1997). Dietary fat intake and the risk of incident dementia in the Rotterdam study. *Annals of Neurology, 42,* 776–782.

Kaplan, J. R., Manuck, S. B., Fontenot, M. B., Muldoon, M. F., Shively, S. A., & Mann, J. J. (1998). The cholesterol–serotonin hypothesis: Interrelationships among dietary lipids, central serontonergic activity, and antagonistic behavior in monkeys. In M. Hillbrand & R. T. Spitz (Eds.), *Lipids, health, and behavior* (pp. 139–166). Washington, DC: American Psychological Association.

Kario, K., Matsuo, T., Kobayashi, H., Asada, R., & Matsuo, M. (1996). "Silent" cerebral infarction is associated with hypercoagulability, endothelial cell damage, and high Lp(a) levels in elderly Japanese. *Arteriosclerosis, Thrombosis, and Vascular Biology, 16,* 734–741.

Kasl, S. V., Brooks, G. W., & Rogers, W. L. (1970). Serum uric acid and cholesterol in achievement behavior and motivation. *Journal of the American Medical Association, 213,* 1158–1164.

Kostis, J. B., Rosen, R. C., & Wilson, A. C. (1994). Entral nervous system effects of HMG CoA reductase inhibitors: Lovastatin and pravastatin on sleep and cognitive performance in patients with hypercholesterolemia. *Clinical Pharmacology, 34,* 989–996.

Kretsch, M. J., Green, M. W., Fong, A. K. H., Elliman, N. A., & Johnson, H. (1997). Cognitive effects of a long-term weight reducing diet. *International Journal of Obesity, 21,* 4–21.

Kuusisto, J., Koivisto, K., Mykkanen, L., Helkala, E., Matti, V., Hanninen, T., Kervinen, K., Kesaniemi, Y., Riekkinen, P., & Laaakso, M. (1997). Association between features of the insulin resistance syndrome and Alzheimer's disease independently of apolipoprotein E4 phenotype: Cross sectional population based study. *British Medical Journal, 315,* 1045–1049.

Lin, D. S., Connor, W. E., Anderson, G. J., & Neuringer, M. (1990). Effects of dietary n-3 fatty acids on the phospholipid molecular species of monkey brain. *Journal Neurochemistry, 5,* 1200–1207.

MacMahon, S., Sharpe, N., Gamble, G., Hart, H., Scott, J., Simes, J., & White, H. (1998). Effects of lowering average or below-average cholesterol levels on the progression of carotid atherosclerosis. *Circulation, 97,* 1784–1790.

Mahley, R. W. (1988, April). Apolipoprotein E: Cholesterol transport protein with expanding role in cell biology. *Science, 240,* 622–630.

Mann, F. (1990). The dynamics of free cholesterol exchange may be critical for endothelial cell membranes in the brain. *Perspectives in Biology and Medicine, 33* (Part 4), 531–534.

Mason, R. P., Shoemaker, W. J., Shajenko, L., Chambers, T. E., & Herbette, L. G. (1992). Evidence for changes in the Alzheimer's disease brain cortical membrane structure mediated by cholesterol. *Neurobiology of Aging, 13,* 413–419.

Matthies, H. Jr., Schulz, S., Hollt, V., & Krug, M. (1997). Inhibition by compactin demonstrates a requirement of isoprenod metabolism for long-term potentiation in rat hippocampal slices. *Neuroscience, 79,* 2.

Mayeux, R., Ottman, R., Maestre, G., Ngai, C., Tang, M. X., Ginsberg, H., Chun, M., Tycko, B., & Shelanski, M. (1995). Synergistic effects of traumatic head injury and apolipoprotein-ε4 in patients with Alzheimers disease. *Neurology, 45,* 555–557.

McGee, C. D., & Greenwood, C. E. (1989). Effects of dietary fatty acid composition on macronutrient selection and synaptosomal fatty acid composition in rats. *Journal of Nutrition, 119,* 1561–1568.

Meyer, M. R., Tschanz, J. T., Norton, M. C., Welsh-Bohmer, K. A., Steffens, D. C., Wyse, B. W., & Breitner, J. C. S. (1998). APOE genotype predicts when—Not whether—One is predisposed to develop Alzheimer disease. *Nature Genetics, 19,* 321–322.

Miller, E. M. (1994). Intelligence and brain myelination: A hypothesis. *Personality and Individual Differences, 17,* 803–832.

Muldoon, M. F., Barger, S. D., Ryan, C. M., Flory, J. D., Lehoczky, J. P., Matthews, K. A., Manuck, S. B. (2000). Effects of lovastatin on cognitive function and psychological well-being. *American Journal of Medicine, 108,* 538–547.

Muldoon, M. F., Ryan, C. R., Flory, J. D., Matthews, K. A., & Manuck, S. B. (1999). Hypo-cholesterolemia associated with superior working memory in healthy adult men. *Circulation, 99,* 1123.

Muldoon, M. F., Ryan, C. M., Matthews, K. A., & Manuck, S. B. (1997). Serum cholesterol and intellectual performance. *Psychosomatic Medicine, 59,* 382–387.

Nathan, B. P., Bellosta, S., Sanan, D. A., Weisgraber, K. H., Mahley, R. W., & Pitas, R. E. (1994, May). Differential effects of apolipoproteins E3 and E4 on neuronal growth in vitro. *Science, 264,* 850–852.

Neaton, J. D., Blackburn, H., Jacobs, D., Kuller, L., Lee, D.-J., Sherwin, R., Shih, J., Stamler, J., & Wentworth, D. (1992). Serum cholesterol level and mortality findings for men screened in the multiple risk factor intervention trial. *Archives Internal Medicine, 152,* 1490–1500.

Notkola, I., Sulkava, R., Pekkanen, J., Erkinjunti, T., Ehnholm, C., Kivinen, P., Tuomilehto, J., & Nissinen, A. (1998). Serum total cholesterol, apolipoprotein E e4 allele, and Alzheimer's disease. *Neuroepidemiology, 17,* 14–20.

Ohm, T. G., Kirca, M., Bohl, J., Scharnagle, H., Gro, W., & Marz, W. (1995). Apolipoprotein E polymorphism influences not only cerebral senile plaque load but also Alzheimer-type neurofibrillary tangle formation. *Neuroscience, 66,* 583–587.

Olicheny, J. M., Hansen, L. A., Hofstetter, C. R., Grundman, M., Katzman, R., & Thal, L. J. (1995). Cerebral infarction in Alzheimer's disease is associated with severe amyloid angiopathy and hypertension. *Archives of Neurology, 52,* 702–708.

Orengo, C., Kunik, M. E., Molinari, V. A., Teasdale, T. A., Workman, R. H., & Yudofsky, S. C. (1996). Association of serum cholesterol and triglyceride levels with agitation and cognitive function in a geropsychiatry unit. *Journal of Geriatric Psychiatry and Neurology, 9*, 53–56.

Ortega, R., Requejo, A. M., Andres, A., Lopez-Sobaler, A. M., Quintas, M. E., Redondo, M. R., Navia, B., & Rivas, T. (1997). Dietary intake and cognitive function in a group of elderly people. *American Journal of Clinical Nutrition, 66*, 803–809.

Paganini-Hill, A., & Henderson, V. W. (1996). The effects of hormone replacement therapy, lipoprotein cholesterol levels, and other factors on a clock drawing task in older women. *Journal of the American Geriatrics Society, 44*, 818–822.

Peet, M., Murphy, B., Edwards, R., Shay, J., & Horrobin, D. (1998). Depletion of docosahexaenoic acid in erythrocyte membranes of depressed patients. *Biological Psychiatry, 43*, 315–319.

Perrig, W. J., Perrig, P., & Stahelin, H. B. (1997). The relation between antioxidants and memory performance in the old and very old. *Journal of the American Geriatrics Society, 45*, 718–724.

Plassman, B. L., Welsh-Bohmer, K. A., Biger, E. D., Johnson, S. C., Anderson, C. V., Helms, M. J., Saunders, A. M., & Breitner, J. C. S. (1997). Apolipoprotein E ε4 allele and hippocampal volume in twins with normal cognition. *Neurology, 48*, 985–988.

Postiglione, A., Cortese, C., Fischetti, A., Cicerano, U., Gnasso, A., Gallota, G., Grossi, D., & Mancini, M. (1989). Plasma lipids and geriatric assessment in a very aged population of south Italy. *Atherosclerosis, 80*, 63–68.

Prospective Studies Collaboration. (1995). Cholesterol, diastolic blood pressure, and stroke: 13,000 strokes in 450,000 people in 45 prospective cohorts. *The Lancet, 346*, 1647–1653.

Reed, T., Carmelli, D., Swan, G. E., Breitner, J. C. S., Welsh, K. A., Jarvik, G. P., Deeb, S., & Auwerx, J. (1994). Lower cognitive performance in normal older adult male twins carrying the apolipoprotein E ε4 allele. *Archives of Neurology, 51*, 1189–1192.

Reiman, E. M., Caselli, R. J., Yun, L. S., Chen, K., Bandy, D., Minoshima, S., Thibodeau, S. N., & Osborne, B. (1996). Preclinical evidence of Alzheimer's disease in persons homozygous for the ε4 allele for apolipoprotein E. *New England Journal of Medicine, 334*, 752–758.

Reitan, R. M., & Shipley, R. E. (1963). The relationship of serum cholesterol changes to cognitive abilities. *Journal of Gerontology 18*, 350–355.

Rosenson, R. S., & Tangney, C. C. (1998). Antiatherothrombotic properties of statins: Implications for cardiovascular event reduction. *Journal of the American Medical Association, 279*, 1643–1650.

Roses, A. D. (1996). Apolipoprotein E alleles as risk factor in Alzheimer's disease. *Annual Review of Medicine, 47*, 387–400.

Ross, G. W., Petrovitch, H., White, L. R., Masaki, K. H. L., Curb, J. D., Yano, K., Rodriguez, B. L., Foley, D. J., Blanchette, P. L., & Havik, R. (1999). Characterization of risk factors for vascular dementia: The Honolulu-Asia study. *Neurology, 337*, 337–343.

Roth, T., Richardson, G. R., Sullivan, J. P., Lee, R. M., Merlotti, L., & Roehrs, T. (1992). Comparative effects of pravastatin and lovastatin on nighttime sleep and daytime performance. *Clinical Cardiology, 15*, 426–432.

Salonen, R., Nyyssonen, K., Porkkala, E., Rummukainen, J., Belder, R., Park, J., & Salonen, J. (1995). Kuopio Atherosclerosis Prevention Study (KAPS): A population-based primary preventive trial of the effect of LDL lowering on atherosclerotic progression in carotid and femoral arteries. *Circulation, 92*, 1758–1764.

Santanello, N. C., Barber, B. L., Applegate, W. B., Elam, J., Curtis, C., Hunningbake, D. B., & Gordon, D. J. (1997). Effect of pharmacologic lipid lowering on health-related quality of life in older persons: Results from the Cholesterol Reduction In Seniors Program (CRISP) pilot study. *Journal of the American Geriatics Society, 45*, 8–14.

Scacchi, R., De Bernardini, L., Vilardo, T., Donini, L. M., Ruggeri, M., Gemma, A. T., Pascone, R., & Corbo, R. M. (1998). DNA polymorphisms of Apolipoprotein B and Angiotensin I-converting enzyme genes and relationships with lipid levels in Italian patients with vascular dementia or Alzheimer's disease. *Dementia and Geriatric Cognitive Disorders, 9*, 186–190.

Schmidt, R., Hayn, M., Reinhart, B., Roob, G., Schmidt, H., Schumacher, M., Watzinger, N., &
Launer, L. J. (1998). Plasma antioxidants and cognitive performance in middle-aged and older
adults: Results of the Austrian Stroke Prevention Study. *Journal of the American Geriatrics Society*
46, 1407–1410.

Sharret, A. R., Patsch, W., Sorlie, P. D., Heiss, G., Bond, M. G., & Davis, C. E. (1994). Associations of
lipoprotein cholesterols, Apolipoproteins A-I and B, and triglycerides with carotid atherosclerosis and coronary heart disease: The ARIC study. *Arteriosclerosis and Thrombosis, 14*, 1098–1104.

Simons, M., Keller, P., de Strooper, B., Beyreuther, K., Dotti, C. G., & Simons, K. (1998). Cholesterol
depletion inhibits the generation of beta-amyloid in hippocampal neurons. *Proceedings of the
National Academy of Sciences, 95*, 6460–6464.

Small, G. W., Mazziotta, J. C., Collins, M. T., Baxter, L. R., Phelps, M. E., Mandelkern, M. A., Kaplan,
A., LaRue, A., Adamsonk C. F., Chang, L., Guze, B. H., Corder, E. H., Saunders, A. M., Haines,
J. L., Pericak-Vance, M. A., & Roses, A. D. (1995). Apolipoprotein E type 4 allele and cerebral glu-
cose metabolism in relatives at risk for familial Alzheimer disease. *Journal of the American Medical
Association, 273*, 942–947.

Soininen, H., Partanen, K., Pitkanen, A., Hallikainen, M., Hanninen, T., Helisalmi, S., Mannermaa,
A., Ryynanen, M., Koivisto, K., & Riekkinen, P. (1995). Decreased hippocampal volume asymmetry on MRIs in nondemented elderly subjects carrying the apolipoprotein E ε4 allele. *Neurology, 45*, 391.

Sparks, D. L., Liu, H., Gross, D. R., & Scheff, S. W. (1995). Increased density of cortical apolipoprotein E immunoreactive neurons in rabbit brain after dietary administration of cholesterol.
Neuroscience Letters, 187, 142–144.

Summary of the Second Report of the National Cholesterol Education Program (NCEP) Expert
Panel on Detection, Evaluation, and Treatment of High Blood Cholesterol in Adults (Adult
Treatment Panel II). (1993). *Journal of the American Medical Association, 269*, 3015–3023.

Swan, G. E., LaRue, A., Carmelli, D., Reed, T. E., & Fabsitz, R. R. (1992). Decline in cognitive performance in aging twins, heritability and biobehavioral predictors from the National Heart,
Lung, and Blood Institute Twin Study. *Archives of Neurology, 49*, 476–481.

Talbot, C., Lendon, C., Craddock, N., Shears, S., Morris, J. C., & Goate, A. (1994). Protection against
Alzheimer's disease with ApoE e2. *The Lancet, 343*, 1432–1433.

Tang, M. X., Stern, Y., Marder, K., Bell, K., Gurland, B., Lantigua, R., Andrews, H., Fen, L., Tycko, B.,
& Mayeux, R. (1998). The APOE-ε4 allele and the risk of Alzheimer's disease among African
Americans, Whites, and Hispanics. *Journal of the American Medical Association, 279*, 751–755.

Wada, T., Matsubayashi, K., Okumiya, K., Kimura, S., Osaka, Y., Doi, Y., & Ozawa, T. (1997). Lower
serum cholesterol level and later decline in cognitive function in older people living in the community, Japan. *Journal of the American Geriatrics Society, 45*, 1411–1412.

Wada, T., Matsubayashi, K., Okumiya, K., Osaki, Y., & Doi, Y. (1997). Serum cholesterol levels and
cognitive function assessed by P300 latencies in an older population living in the community.
Journal of the American Geriatrics Society, 45, 122–123.

Weisgraber, K. H., Innerarity, T. L., & Mahley, R. W. (1982). Abnormal lipoprotein receptor-binding
activity of the human E apoprotein due to cysteine–arginine interchange at a single site. *Journal
of Biological Chemistry, 257*, 2518–2521.

Wieringa, G. E., Burlinson, S., Rafferty, J. A., Gowland, E., & Burns, A. (1997). Apolipoprotein E
genotypes and serum lipid levels in Alzheimer's disease and multi-infarct dementia. *International
Journal of Geriatric Psychiatry, 12*, 359–362.

Wilson, B. A. (1993). Ecological validity of neuropsychological assessment: Do neuropsychological
indexes predict performance in everyday activities? *Applied and Preventive Psychology, 2*, 209-215.

Wilson, P. W. F., Hoeg, J. M., D'Agostino, R. B., Silbershatz, H., Belanger, A. M., Poehlmann, H.,
O'Leary, D., & Wolf, P. A. (1997). Cumulative effects of high cholesterol levels, high blood
pressure, and cigarette smoking on carotid stenosis. *New England Journal of Medicine, 337*, 516–
522.

Wing, R. R., Vazquez, J. A., & Ryan, C. M. (1995). Cognitive effects of ketogenic weight-reducing diets. *International Journal of Obesity, 19,* 811–816.

Yaffe, K., Cauley, J., Sands, L., & Browner, W. (1997). Apolipoprotein E phenotype and cognitive decline in a prospective study of elderly community women. *Archives of Neurology, 54,* 1110-1114.

Zanchetti, A., Bond, M. G., Hennig, M., Neiss, A., Mancia, G., Dal Palu, C., Hansson, L., Magnani, B., Rahn, K.-H., Reid, J., Rodicio, J., Safar, M., Eckes, L., & Ravinetto, R. (1998). Risk factors associated with alterations in carotid intima-media thickness in hypertension: Baseline data from the European Lacidipine Study on Atherosclerosis. *Journal of Hypertension, 16,* 949–961.

CHAPTER FOUR

Diabetes-Associated Cognitive Dysfunction

CHRISTOPHER M. RYAN
University of Pittsburgh School of Medicine

Diabetes mellitus and cardiovascular (CV) disorders are closely intertwined. Adults with diabetes have rates of hypertension, dyslipidemia, heart disease, and stroke that are at least twice as high as those reported in adults without diabetes, whereas individuals with hypertension, obesity, and dyslipidemia have a greatly increased risk of subsequently developing diabetes and/or macrovascular disease. Like patients with CV disorders, adults (and children) with diabetes may also show evidence of brain dysfunction when evaluated with formal neuropsychological tests or with neurophysiological and neuroimaging measures.

More than 75 years of research have demonstrated a link between diabetes and cognitive dysfunction. To help organize that extensive literature, I have adopted a schema that postulates that both the nature and the extent of cognitive dysfunction, as well as the biomedical factors associated with that dysfunction, vary as a consequence of type of diabetes, age at diagnosis, age at assessment, and presence of intercurrent medical or psychological disorders. In general, the magnitude of diabetes-associated cognitive impairment is modest and restricted to only certain subgroups of diabetic patients. Delineating the phenomenology of impairment, identifying the biomedical variables associated with individual differences in susceptibility to brain dysfunction, and examining possible pathophysiological mechanisms comprise the three broad goals of this chapter.

EPIDEMIOLOGY AND ETIOLOGY OF DIABETES MELLITUS

Type 1 Diabetes

Diabetes mellitus refers to a family of metabolic disorders, all of which are characterized by chronically high blood glucose levels (hyperglycemia) that result from defects in insulin secretion and/or insulin action. *Type 1 diabetes*—formerly known as *insulin-dependent* or *juvenile-onset* diabetes—has been the most carefully studied form of diabetes and is thought to affect approximately 1 million Americans. This type of diabetes is usually diagnosed in childhood or adolescence and is characterized by a complete inability to secrete insulin because of autoimmune destruction of the pancreatic islet beta cells. Insulin acts to lower blood glucose levels by suppressing hepatic glucose production and by stimulating uptake of glucose in skeletal muscle and adipose tissue. In the absence of endogenous insulin, individuals are unable to metabolize carbohydrates efficiently and may experience dangerously high blood glucose levels several hours after a meal unless that hormone is supplied exogenously. Because of their complete inability to synthesize and release insulin endogenously, patients with Type 1 diabetes must inject themselves several times a day with exogenous insulin and regulate both diet and exercise patterns to "normalize" carbohydrate metabolism. Too much insulin, or a failure to balance self-administered insulin with food intake and activity level, can lead to extremely low blood glucose levels (hypoglycemia). If hypoglycemia is left untreated, blood glucose levels continue to fall and lead to seizure or loss of consciousness and a greatly increased risk of permanent brain damage or death.

In contrast, blood glucose levels may become abnormally high (> 300 mg/dl) when carbohydrate consumption is high or exogenous insulin doses are inadequate. Chronic hyperglycemia leads to the development of clinically significant diabetes-related biomedical complications that are associated with damage to both small and large blood vessels as well as to nerves in the autonomic and peripheral nervous systems. Macrovascular disease, which tends to develop somewhat later in the course of Type 1 diabetes, results in a greatly increased risk of heart attacks, stroke, and peripheral vascular disease, particularly in patients who also have a history of hypertension, hypercholesterolemia, or smoking.

When treating Type 1 diabetes, the primary therapeutic goal is to maintain good metabolic control by avoiding excessively high or low blood glucose levels. The diabetic patient's degree of metabolic control over the past 2 to 3 months can now be estimated by measuring various glycosylated fractions of hemoglobin—also known as hemoglobin A_1 or A_{1c} (HbA_1, HbA_{1c}). The greater the degree and duration of chronic hyperglycemia, the higher this percentage, and the more "out of control" the patient. To avoid the vascular complications of diabetes, most clinicians now advise their patients to maintain tight control and keep blood glucose levels as close to the normal range (< 7%) as possible by taking multiple daily injections of insulin, frequently monitoring blood glucose levels, and adjusting insulin dosages accordingly.

Type 2 Diabetes

This form of diabetes—previously known as *non-insulin–dependent* or *maturity onset* diabetes—differs dramatically from Type 1 diabetes in pathophysiology, etiology, and prevalence. Onset is rarely signaled by a clinically obvious medical crisis, as ordinarily occurs with Type 1 diabetes. Rather, it sneaks up on the individual over a number of years and may be diagnosed formally only after certain medical complications appear. Two different metabolic events underlie the occurrence of this disorder: the development of insulin resistance, followed by progressive impairment of beta cell function. Both changes effectively reduce the bioavailability of insulin and ultimately lead to chronic hyperglycemia and its associated micro- and macrovascular complications. Insulin resistance is a loss of sensitivity to the glucose-lowering effects of insulin at peripheral cell receptor sites in muscle and the liver. The pancreas initially compensates for the resulting increase in blood glucose levels by releasing more insulin. Over time, however, there develops a gradual deterioration in beta cell function and a corresponding decline in insulin secretion that ultimately results in higher circulating blood glucose levels. Obesity, inactivity, and smoking are known to trigger insulin resistance in genetically susceptible individuals, although the exact physiological mechanisms underlying this process remain incompletely understood.

Because pancreatic beta cells continue to release moderate amounts of insulin, many patients with Type 2 diabetes can control their blood glucose levels by losing weight, modifying their diet, or taking drugs that stimulate insulin secretion (e.g., sulfonylureas) or enhance insulin action in muscle and the liver (e.g., metformin). Daily insulin injections are usually recommended only when metabolic control is extremely poor or diet and oral medication regimens have failed. Poor metabolic control has the same effect in Type 2 patients as was previously described for those with Type 1 diabetes: a greatly increased risk of stroke, heart attacks, kidney disease, blindness, neuropathy, and foot problems as a consequence of micro- and macroangiopathy secondary to chronic hyperglycemia. Mortality data indicate that the life expectancy of adults with type 2 diabetes is reduced, on average, by 5 to 10 years, with coronary heart disease (CHD) being the primary cause of death.

Type 2 diabetes is predominantly a disease of middle-aged and elderly adults who are overweight. The average age at onset is 60 years, and although few cases were previously diagnosed in individuals under 30 years of age, there is now evidence that subgroups of highly susceptible individuals exist (e.g., Pima Indians) who may develop this disease as young adults or even as adolescents (*maturity onset diabetes of the young*). Approximately 7 million Americans have been diagnosed with Type 2 diabetes, and it is estimated that for every one who has been diagnosed there is an additional individual who would meet criteria for the disorder but remains undiagnosed largely because hyperglycemia develops gradually, and—at least early on—complications are subclinical. More detailed information on the pathophysiology and epidemiology of both forms of diabetes can be found elsewhere (National Diabetes Data Group, 1995; Pickup & Williams, 1997).

NEUROPSYCHOLOGICAL DYSFUNCTION ASSOCIATED WITH TYPE 1 DIABETES

The view that diabetes mellitus may disrupt cognition is not new. Just prior to the discovery of insulin, Miles and Root (1922) conducted what may be the first formal medical neuropsychology study. Seeking to document their patients' complaints of memory loss and difficulty concentrating, they administered several tests of mental efficiency to diabetic and nondiabetic individuals and found modest between-group differences in mental efficiency—15% to 20%, on average. Diabetic individuals had shorter immediate memory spans, and their performance was slower, but no less accurate, than healthy comparison individuals on tasks requiring sustained attention. On the other hand, they performed as well as control participants on highly overlearned tasks such as rapid addition of strings of single digits.

This early work suggested that diabetes may have a significant impact on cognitive function. Subsequent research—particularly that conducted in the past 15 years—has not only identified discrete patterns of cognitive impairment in different diabetic subgroups but also has attributed those patterns to specific biomedical and psychosocial variables associated with diabetes and its treatment.

Cognitive Dysfunction, Early Onset of Diabetes, and Hypoglycemia in Children and Adolescents

Type 1 diabetes is quite different from most of the other disorders described in this book: It is a disease that affects children as well as adults. From a scientific perspective, studies of children with diabetes can provide a clearer picture of the linkages between disease-related variables and patterns of cognitive dysfunction because these children are relatively unaffected by the micro- and macrovascular biomedical complications that ordinarily appear only after many years of diabetes.

Children who develop diabetes early in life have a greatly elevated risk of manifesting neuropsychological impairments (for a critical review, see Ryan, 1989). Younger school-aged children (6 to 14 years old) who developed diabetes before 4 years of age showed decrements in performance that were limited largely to visuospatial tasks, with girls more affected than boys (Rovet, Ehrlich, & Hoppe, 1987). By early adolescence, those diagnosed before 5 years of age manifested impairments on a broader array of cognitive domains, with both boys and girls showing performance decrements on tests of attention, learning and memory, visuospatial ability, mental and motor speed, and intelligence (Ryan, Vega, & Drash, 1985). Application of criteria to identify "clinically significant" impairment revealed that nearly 25% of the adolescents diagnosed before 5 years of age were clinically impaired, in contrast to 6% of adolescents diagnosed after age 5 and 6% of a demographically similar nondiabetic comparison group. Subsequent studies have attempted to identify specific cognitive operations that are most frequently affected and, although there is no evidence of differences in short-term memory rehearsal strategies (Wolters, Brouwers, Moss, & Pizzo, 1995), children and adolescents with an earlier onset of diabetes have more trouble than either later onset diabetic subjects or healthy comparison subjects in focusing attention (Hagen et al., 1990) and in accurately selecting among several very similar alternatives on a complex visual attention test (Rovet & Alverez, 1997).

Cognitive decline associated with an early onset of diabetes is now believed to occur relatively rapidly. Data from a large-scale prospective study of newly diagnosed diabetic children indicates that, over a 2-year period, those with a disease onset before 5 years of age manifested developmental delays insofar as their scores on both the Wechsler Intelligence Scale for Children Vocabulary and Block Design subtests improved less over time relative to either later onset diabetic children or community control children (Northam et al., 1998). Whether similar delays will appear on more traditional neuropsychological tests cannot yet be determined, given the very young age of these children (5 to 7 years old) at this second assessment as well as the absence of psychometrically sound tests that are sensitive to subtle neuropsychological deficits in children younger than 8 years.

If onset of diabetes in the first 4 to 6 years of life is the primary risk factor for developing cognitive dysfunction in children and adolescents, what is the pathophysiological mechanism? Converging data from metabolic, behavioral, and neurophysiological studies all point to the potentially deleterious effects of hypoglycemia on still-developing neural systems in the immature brain. Exactly how this occurs remains controversial, because several different neurochemical changes, reflecting cerebral energy failure, are known to be triggered by hypoglycemia-associated neuroglycopenia. Both intracellular calcium toxicity and excitotoxic cellular damage secondary to synaptic release of glutamate or aspartate are now considered to be two important mechanisms, although numerous other metabolic changes associated with hypoglycemia could certainly contribute to the brain dysfunction associated with an early onset of diabetes (McCall, 1992).

Earlier onset of diabetes is associated with a greatly increased risk of hypoglycemia, as was revealed by a retrospective review of the medical records of children (Rovet & Alverez, 1997) and adolescents (Ryan, Vega, & Drash, 1985) who developed diabetes in the first 4 to 6 years of life. To some extent, this may be due to differences in the efficiency with which younger children metabolize insulin (Ternand, Go, Gerich, & Haymond, 1982) and perhaps to differences in children's ability to communicate that blood glucose levels are low. If younger children are unable to clearly verbalize that their blood sugar levels have dropped, they may not be treated in a timely fashion, leading to either a deeper hypoglycemic event and/or a longer event. Animal studies have demonstrated that both depth and duration of hypoglycemia play critical roles in the development of neuronal necrosis (e.g., Siesjö & Bengtsson, 1989).

Evidence that hypoglycemia per se may disrupt cognitive function comes from studies comparing diabetic children with and without a prior history of severe hypoglycemia. Despite the difficulty in ascertaining severe hypoglycemia in a reliable manner, recent data from several small studies suggest that severe hypoglycemia (as indicated by seizure or loss of consciousness) is associated with greater performance decrements on measures of attention (Rovet & Alverez, 1997), psychomotor efficiency (Bjørgaas, Gimse, Vik, & Sand, 1997), and memory (Hershey, Bhargava, Sadler, White, & Craft, 1999; Rovet & Ehrlich, 1999). Repeated episodes of even mild hypoglycemia in younger diabetic individuals may have an adverse effect on cognitive functioning, particularly on visuospatial tasks (Golden et al., 1989). These neuropsychological findings are consistent with electroencephalographic (EEG) data showing that nonspecific EEG abnormalities are more common in diabetic children who have had one or more previous episodes of severe hypoglycemia (Bjørgaas, Sand, & Gimse, 1996; Eeg-Olofsson & Petersen, 1966; Haumont, Dorchy, & Pelc, 1979), and children diagnosed before 5 years of age have a far greater likelihood of EEG abnormalities than those diagnosed after that age (Gilhaus, Daweke, Lülsdorf, Sachsse, & Sachsse, 1973; Soltész & Acsádi, 1989).

Perhaps the most compelling, albeit indirect, support for a link among early onset of diabetes, severe hypoglycemia, and brain dysfunction is provided by studies of children and adolescents who develop diabetes later in life. These individuals typically do not manifest deficits on standard neuropsychological tests and show no evidence of clinically significant cognitive impairment when compared with demographically similar children drawn from the community (Ryan, Vega, & Drash, 1985). The only deficits noted routinely in later onset children is their tendency to earn somewhat lower scores on measures of verbal intelligence and academic achievement (Hagen et al., 1990; Holmes, Dunlap, Chen, & Cornwell, 1992; Rovet & Alverez, 1997; Ryan, Vega, Longstreet, & Drash, 1984). One plausible hypothesis offered to explain this pattern of results is psychosocial: Diabetic children, for a variety of reasons, may miss more school and hence have fewer exposures to the type of information ordinarily imparted in the classroom and evaluated on formal tests of academic achievement. Such an explanation is consistent with data reported in both cross-sectional (Holmes et al., 1992; Ryan, Longstreet, & Morrow, 1985) and longitudinal studies (Kovacs, Goldston, & Iyengar, 1992; Rovet, Ehrlich, & Czuchta, 1990), as well as with the failure to identify any biomedical predictors of cognitive impairment or any pathognomonic signs in the neuropsychological test protocols. However, because there has never been a formal test of this "school absence" hypothesis, other possible psychosocial explanations (e.g., development of disruptive behavior problems secondary to management of demanding chronic illness) cannot yet be ruled out.

Chronic Hyperglycemia and Cognitive Dysfunction in Adults With Type 1 Diabetes

Chronically high blood glucose levels, as indexed by elevated glycosylated hemoglobin values, lead to the development of biomedical complications such as retinopathy and peripheral neuropathy. With the exception of one intriguing report (Northam, Anderson, Werther, Warne, & Andrewes, 1999), there is little compelling evidence that chronic hyperglycemia is associated with cognitive dysfunction in diabetic children and adolescents. Nevertheless, a growing neuropsychological and neuroimaging literature supports the view that elevated blood glucose levels may affect the central nervous system (CNS) of adults with Type 1 diabetes.

Early neuropathological studies revealed evidence of a "diabetic encephalopathy" in adults with a long history of poorly controlled diabetes accompanied by micro- and macrovascular disease (Reske-Nielsen, Lundbaek, & Rafaelsen, 1965). Although formal neuropsychological assessments were not conducted, neurological evaluations showed the presence of reflex abnormalities and evidence of mental impairment on bedside mental state examination. On autopsy, the most frequently found changes included diffusely distributed demyelination in the cranial nerves, optic chiasm, and white matter and extensive gliosis in grey matter, basal ganglia, brain stem, and cerebellum. Because vascular damage was also noted, it was impossible to determine whether the brain tissue abnormalities were due solely to ischemia or whether they also—or alternately—occurred as a direct effect of diabetes-associated metabolic abnormalities.

Most diabetic patients, particularly those currently treated in North America, do not ordinarily develop the profound neurologic abnormalities seen in the individuals studied by Reske-Nielsen et al. (1965). Do these more typical patients go on to develop a subclinical encephalopathy, characterized by mild to moderately severe neuropsychological deficits and perhaps abnormalities on some structural or neurophysiological measures of brain function? Increasing evidence suggests that is the case—at least in a subset of adults with Type 1 diabetes.

A series of behavioral studies, conducted between 1965 and 1990, concluded that poor metabolic control was associated with deficits on measures of complex problem solving skill (Rennick, Wilder, Sargent, & Ashley, 1968), mental flexibility and motor speed (Skenazy & Bigler, 1984), and memory for recently learned information (Franceschi et al., 1984), although there was not complete agreement (Lawson et al., 1984). All of these early studies have a number of methodological shortcomings (for a review, see Richardson, 1990; Ryan, 1988), including reliance on relatively small convenience samples of respondents who were heterogeneous in terms of age, duration of diabetes, extent of biomedical complications, and operational definition of poor metabolic control.

More recent research has resolved many of these problems by studying large numbers of young and middle-aged adults randomly selected from a childhood-onset cohort of patients with Type 1 diabetes. Compared to age-matched healthy comparison individuals, diabetic patients showed deficits on two cognitive domains: attention and psychomotor efficiency, and spatial information processing (Ryan, Williams, Orchard, & Finegold, 1992). Within the diabetic group, the best predictor of performance decrement was poor metabolic control, as indexed by a clinical diagnosis of peripheral neuropathy. Other microvascular complications—including advanced background or proliferative retinopathy or overt nephropathy—did not independently predict low scores. Because rates of macrovascular complications were relatively low in this young adult group (mean age = 33.5 years), no effort was made to examine their statistical association with neuropsychological test scores. It should be noted, however, that this is characteristic of virtually all cognitive research with Type 1 diabetic patients: The potential contribution of either hypertension or macrovascular disease to cognitive deficits has rarely been considered.

The magnitude of the cognitive deficits noted in our young adult subjects is modest, with effect sizes ranging from about .3 to .4 (between "small" and "medium," according to Cohen's [1988] terminology). Although I suspect that these are unlikely to adversely affect activities of daily living such as cooking, shopping, and managing a household, I have concerns—but no scientific evidence—that they could interfere with certain work-related activities, particularly those that require sustained concentration, attention to detail, and psychomotor coordination. It is surprising that investigators have made no effort to determine whether these diabetic patients with cognitive problems also have difficulty functioning in their places of employment. In large part this may reflect the general absence of assessment techniques that can collect such information in a reliable and unobtrusive manner, either from a supervisor, or—preferably—by direct observation of the diabetic individual. Most research has relied solely on respondents' self-reported work history and problems (Heaton et al., 1994), but this introduces its own set of biases and distortions (Schwarz, 1999).

The strong association between peripheral neuropathy and cognitive dysfunction reported by our group led to the conclusion that chronic hyperglycemia induces a "central neuropathy." According to this view, the same metabolic processes underlying the development of peripheral neuropathy—namely, alterations in sodium–potassium ATPase activity in nerve cell membranes and a corresponding reduction in myo-inositol and sorbitol metabolism (Greene, Sima, Stevens, Feldman, & Lattimer, 1992)—may initiate similar biochemical abnormalities in brain neurons and in that way interfere with the normal cellular transport of metabolites and substrates (Ryan et al., 1992). Direct support for that hypothesized mechanism will have to await more sophisticated physiological studies than those conducted to date. Nevertheless, results from a series of electrophysiological and neuroimaging studies provide some evidence of a connection between peripheral neuropathy and a putative central neuropathy. Middle-aged Type 1 diabetic patients with biomedical complications—most frequently, peripheral neuropathy—are far more likely to show significantly slower brainstem auditory evoked-potential latencies (Kurita, Mochio, & Isogai, 1995; Pozzessere et al., 1988), and both younger (Lunetta et al., 1994) and middle-aged diabetic adults (Araki et al., 1994; Dejgaard et al., 1991; Nakamura et al., 1991) are more likely to show abnormalities on magnetic resonance imaging.

More important from a public health perspective is the fact that these cognitive problems are potentially preventable. The Diabetes Control and Complications Trial (DCCT) has demonstrated unequivocally that the use of intensive insulin therapy to improve metabolic control is associated with a corresponding reduction in microvascular complications, including peripheral neuropathy (DCCT Research Group, 1993, 1995). As intensive insulin therapy begins to be implemented throughout the world, one might expect to find a corresponding decline in the prevalence of both distal symmetrical polyneuropathy and cognitive dysfunction over the next 5 to 10 years. Unfortunately, because this therapeutic regimen is also associated with a two- to three-fold increase in the rate of severe hypoglycemia (DCCT Research Group, 1997), and because severe hypoglycemia can produce permanent brain neurologic sequelae in adults (Auer, Hugh, Cosgrove, & Curry, 1989; Chalmers et al., 1991; Gold et al., 1994), a number of writers have expressed concern that efforts to prevent hyperglycemia-associated adverse outcomes may lead to a different set of adverse outcomes: those triggered by iatrogenic hypoglycemia (Hershey et al., 1999; Rovet & Ehrlich, 1999).

Recurrent Hypoglycemia and Cognitive Dysfunction in Adults With Type 1 Diabetes

If a single episode of profound hypoglycemia can trigger significant brain damage in children and adults, will repeated episodes of severe hypoglycemia contribute to the development of cognitive dysfunction in the diabetic adult? Cross-sectional research has concluded that diabetic adults with multiple episodes of severe hypoglycemia tend to perform more poorly than those without prior hypoglycemia (Gold, Deary, & Frier, 1993). Visuospatial deficits and psychomotor slowing are prominent in diabetic patients who have had five or more lifetime episodes of severe hypoglycemia (Wredling, Levander, Adamson, & Lins, 1990), as are performance decrements on tasks requiring rapid decision making and fluid intelligence (Langan, Deary, Hepburn, & Frier, 1991; Lincoln, Faleiro,

Kelly, Kirk, & Jeffcoate, 1996). Poor performance on measures of learning and memory is sometimes (Sachon et al., 1992), but not consistently (Hershey, Craft, Bhargava, & White, 1997; Langan et al., 1991), associated with repeated hypoglycemia. Neuroimaging support for a relationship between repeated hypoglycemia and brain dysfunction is equivocal. Magnetic resonance imaging studies have shown an increased risk of cortical atrophy in patients with recurrent hypoglycemia (Perros, Deary, Sellar, Best, & Frier, 1997), whereas neither both positron emission tomography (Chabriat et al., 1994) nor neurophysiological event-related potential (P300) studies (Kramer et al., 1998) have found evidence of brain dysfunction in adults who experienced a hypoglycemic coma.

All of the studies that have reported hypoglycemia-associated cognitive dysfunction were cross-sectional in design, sampled small numbers of participants, and relied on retrospective recall to estimate number of prior hypoglycemic events. Results from two large-scale longitudinal clinical trials have failed to find any relationship whatsoever between prospectively ascertained episodes of severe hypoglycemia and performance on extensive neuropsychological test batteries. The most compelling evidence that recurrent hypoglycemia does not increase the risk of cognitive dysfunction is provided by the DCCT, a clinical trial that studied 1,441 participants, 13 to 39 years of age, for an average of 6.5 years. Despite the very high rates of hypoglycemia experienced by participants in the intensive therapy treatment group, there was no evidence of either clinically significant cognitive impairment or statistically significant between-group differences on any of the neuropsychological measures (Austin & Deary, 1999; DCCT Research Group, 1996). A similar conclusion was reached by the Stockholm Diabetes Intervention Study group (Reichard, Berglund, Britz, Levander, & Rosenqvist, 1991; Reichard, Phil, Rosenqvist, & Sule, 1996).

It would be foolhardy to conclude from these extremely well-conducted clinical trials that severe hypoglycemia is entirely benign. Numerous case reports have indicated that a single episode of severe hypoglycemia can produce structural brain damage, with concomitant neurological and neuropsychological sequelae (Fujioka et al., 1997). Nevertheless, the clinical trial data suggest that although the rate of severe hypoglycemic-induced cognitive dysfunction is unknown, it must necessarily be relatively low in young and middle-aged adults with Type 1 diabetes. How can one explain this discrepancy between the negative results from the longitudinal studies and the more positive results that have emerged from case reports or cross-sectional studies? Although it is tempting to attribute the differences to better ascertainment of hypoglycemic events in the longitudinal studies, other—largely metabolic—factors may need to be taken into account. Although animal studies have suggested that the best predictor of hypoglycemia-induced structural brain damage is the duration of hypoglycemia (Auer, Kalimo, Olsson, & Siesjö, 1985), research on stroke now indicates that the co-occurrence of hyperglycemia also seems to increase the risk, and the magnitude, of CNS damage (Kushner et al., 1990; Pulsinelli, Levy, Sigsbee, Scherer, &

Plum, 1983; Sieber & Traystman, 1992; Weir, Murray, Dyker, & Lees, 1997). Given those observations, we cannot rule out the possibility that individuals who suffer the greatest hypoglycemia-associated cognitive impairments (and are most likely to be described in clinical case reports) may also have a long history of chronic hyperglycemia, as indexed by diabetes-related microvascular complications. Consistent with that view are data showing that recurrent hypoglycemia interacts with chronic hyperglycemia (indexed by peripheral neuropathy) to exaggerate or otherwise magnify the extent of cognitive dysfunction in Type 1 diabetic adults (Ryan, Williams, Finegold, & Orchard, 1993).

METABOLIC CONTROL AND COGNITIVE DYSFUNCTION IN OLDER ADULTS WITH TYPE 2 DIABETES

Research on the neuropsychological status of adults with Type 2 diabetes was motivated initially not by the findings, described previously, that Type 1 diabetes could affect cognitive function, but by the hypothesis, first articulated by Kent (1976), that diabetes is a form of accelerated aging. This view was based on the observation that many of the degenerative disorders associated with the normal aging process appear at a younger age in adults diagnosed with Type 2 diabetes. Because learning and memory skills show some of the earliest age-related performance declines, researchers specifically focused their attention on these cognitive processes.

Studies of Small Clinical Samples

More than 20 case control studies of cognitive function have now been conducted in older adults with Type 2 diabetes, and virtually all of them have found evidence of impairment. Learning and memory deficits appear most prominently and consistently (Perlmuter et al., 1984; Reaven, Thompson, Nahum, & Haskins, 1990; U'ren, Riddle, Lezak, & Bennington-Davis, 1990), but deficits may also occur on measures of attention, psychomotor speed, and problem solving (for review, see Strachan, Deary, Ewing, & Frier, 1997). When present, the magnitude of these learning and memory deficits tends to be moderate to large, with effect sizes (d) ranging from approximately 0.6 (Perlmuter et al., 1984) to 1.0 (Reaven et al., 1990). Chronic hyperglycemia, as indicated either by elevated glycosylated hemoglobin values or by the presence of diabetes-related complications, is the best, albeit imperfect, predictor of cognitive dysfunction.

Understanding exactly what factors predispose diabetic adults to develop cognitive problems has been hampered by a variety of methodological and conceptual problems. All but one of the studies alluded to in the previous paragraph have been cross-sectional (cf. Robertson-Tchabo, Arenberg, Tobin, & Plotz, 1986) and, with a few exceptions (e.g., Perlmuter et al., 1984), sample sizes have been small. Especially problematic has been the failure of investigators to take into account more than two or three of the many common disorders that accompany diabetes and normal aging and that may affect cognitive functioning, including alcohol use, cerebrovascular disease, depression, ischemic heart disease, impaired vision, hyperlipidemia, hypertension, neuropathy, renal disease, and a variety of surgical procedures (e.g., cardiopulmonary bypass grafting), drug regimens, and recurrent hypoglycemia (Strachan et al., 1997). That is not to say that the cognitive dysfunction seen in these individuals is necessarily a consequence of these various comorbid conditions. Case control studies that have evaluated relatively healthy, high-functioning diabetic adults have also reported evidence of significant memory dysfunction, which was best predicted by glycosylated hemoglobin levels (Reaven et al., 1990).

One important question that remains unanswered is whether all Type 2 diabetic patients have an equal vulnerability to developing cognitive problems. Our preliminary work suggests that age may be a critical factor, with younger patients having a substantially lower risk. Virtually all previous studies that reported significant cognitive dysfunction associated with Type 2 diabetes were restricted to patients who were 60 or more years of age (Strachan et al., 1997). On the other hand, when Ryan and Geckle (1999) compared adults (mean age = 49 years) with and without Type 2 diabetes, they found little evidence of learning or memory impairments in a sample of middle-aged Type 2 adults. Why only, or primarily, elderly adults with Type 2 diabetes are likely to manifest cognitive problems remains unclear.

One of the few studies to examine the relationship between Type 2 diabetes and brain morphology has reported an interaction with age as well as with hypertension. Using computerized tomography techniques to estimate degree of brain atrophy in 416 medical patients, Pirttilä and associates (Pirttilä, Jarvenpaa, Laippala, & Frey, 1992) found that age, diabetes, hypertension, chronic cerebrovascular disorders, and number of medications were all associated, to some extent, with brain atrophy. Only 12% of the patients under age 65 showed cortical atrophy in the absence of both diabetes or hypertension, whereas atrophy was present in 27% of those with hypertension only, in 40% of those with diabetes only, and in 36% of those with both disorders. Rates of cortical atrophy were nearly doubled in patients 65 to 75 years of age: Of those with neither disorder, 42% showed atrophy, compared to 71% of those with both disorders. Whether the same pattern of results would be noted on cognitive tests remains to be established. To the best of my knowledge, only one neuroimaging study of older diabetic adults incorporated a cognitive assessment. Cortical atrophy was found to be associated with diabetes as well as with fasting blood glucose levels, but there was no relationship between degree of atrophy and cognition (Soininen, Puranen, Helkala, Laakso, & Riekkinen, 1992); these null results may be a consequence of the very small sample size or the limited neuropsychological assessment included in that study.

Preliminary evidence from several small treatment intervention studies now suggests that Type 2 diabetes-associated cognitive deficits may be reversible. If cognitive dysfunction arises in patients with Type 2 diabetes largely because of their poor metabolic control, then one would expect that any intervention that improves control and reduces glycosylated hemoglobin levels should be associated with a parallel improvement in cognitive function. Weak support for that prediction has now been provided by three studies (Gradman, Laws, Thompson, & Reaven, 1993; Meneilly, Cheung, Tessier, Yakura, & Tuokko, 1993; Naor, Steingruber, Westhoff, Schottenfeld-Naor, & Gries, 1997). In each, older adults with Type 2 diabetes completed a series of cognitive tests before receiving an oral hypoglycemic agent, with a follow-up evaluation 6 months later. Treatment was associated with improved metabolic control as well as with a corresponding improvement on measures of learning, memory, and attention. Not all cognitive changes were statistically significant, but that may have been a consequence of limited statistical power associated with relatively small sample sizes.

Large-Scale Epidemiologic Studies

Diabetes-related comorbid disorders (e.g., hypertension, dyslipidemia, CV disease) and their treatment (e.g., antihypertensive medication, cholesterol-lowering drugs, very low calorie diets) have, in general, not been implicated in the etiology of the cognitive problems reported in case control studies of elderly diabetic adults. Nevertheless, those null results do not necessarily mean that there are no relationships. In virtually all instances, the aforementioned case control studies have rarely included sufficient numbers of patients with a variety of scrupulously ascertained medical problems to permit investigators to uncover statistically reliable associations between cognitive dysfunction and CV disorders. Those methodologic shortcomings have now been obviated to some extent by several studies that explicitly measured diabetes-associated biomedical variables in very large population cohorts.

Consistent with results from small case control studies, these larger community-based investigations again demonstrate that diabetes is associated with a greatly increased risk of cognitive dysfunction. Analyses of a stroke-free cohort of 249 older adults (mean age = 71 years) showed that diabetes was a significant independent predictor of deficits on measures of abstract reasoning and visuospatial functioning, whereas hypercholesterolemia was the best predictor of memory dysfunction (Desmond, Tatemichi, Paik, & Stern, 1993). Assessment of more than 1,300 community-dwelling individuals, 24 to 81 years of age, also revealed a strong relationship between diabetes and cognitive functioning (van Boxtel et al., 1998). It is important that when the effects of Type 1 and Type 2 diabetes were examined separately, both were found to be associated with poorer memory, slower sensorimotor performance, and lower scores on measures of cognitive flexibility and psychomotor efficiency. On the other hand, there was no relationship between measures of cognitive function and CV disorders. An even larger study of nearly 4,000 older community-dwelling adults also showed a relationship between diabetes and cognitive performance as measured by the Mini-Mental State Examination (Launer, Dinkgreve, Jonker, Hooijer, & Lindeboom, 1993). In each of these cross-sectional studies, diabetes was obviously not the sole predictor of cognitive dysfunction, but it was certainly associated with a statistically significant increased risk of impairment, even after a variety of other biomedical, psychosocial, and demographic variables were taken into account.

Prospective cohort studies provide the strongest evidence of a causal relationship between diabetes and cognitive dysfunction. Recent analyses of data from a subsample of 1,811 participants (mean age = 67 years) in the Framingham Heart Study now demonstrate that diabetes and hypertension have both independent and synergistically interactive effects on cognitive functioning (Elias et al., 1997). One advantage of this study over all other studies of adults with Type 2 diabetes is its use of a prospective design with a 28- to 30-year follow-up period. Inclusion of detailed biennial medical examinations made it possible to determine with a high degree of accuracy just when participants developed Type 2 diabetes (as well as other disorders, such as hypertension). In addition, Framingham participants were evaluated with a relatively extensive neuropsychological test battery (e.g., eight subtests from the Wechsler Adult Intelligence Scale, Wechsler Memory Scale). After adjusting statistically for a variety of demographic and behavioral covariates as well as several important disease-related variables, analyses revealed five general findings. First, individuals who were hypertensive, but not diabetic, showed poorer performance on verbal memory tests, compared to those who had neither medical condition. Second, diagnosis of Type 2 diabetes at any time before the neuropsychological assessment was associated with poorer performance on verbal memory measures. Insulin-treated diabetic patients tended to perform worse than those treated with diet or oral medications, but that may reflect the fact that patients with more severe Type 2 diabetes tend to be treated with insulin. Third, duration of diabetes was associated with significantly poorer performance on verbal memory and abstract reasoning tests. Fourth, individuals who also had elevated diastolic blood pressure performed poorest on a composite cognitive test score as well as on visuospatial measures. Finally, these relationships were not influenced by the presence of pre-existing CV disease (i.e., myocardial infarction, angina pectoris, intermittent claudication).

The pathophysiological mechanism underlying the link between Type 2 diabetes and cognitive dysfunction remains poorly understood, but most researchers would now argue that it is more likely a direct consequence of one or more metabolic aberrations, as compared to the secondary effects of comorbid CV disorders. Chronic hyperglycemia could affect the CNS (and other systems throughout the body) by triggering the development of advanced glycosylated end products, largely because these oxidation products have been found in the senile plaques and neurofibrillary tangles that are characteristic of Alzheimer's disease (AD; Stewart & Liolitsa, 1999). This hypothetical pathophysiological mechanism remains controversial, however (Finch & Cohen, 1997). Although results from a large historical population cohort demonstrate that individuals with adult-onset diabetes mellitus have a greatly increased risk of dementia, including AD (Leibson et al., 1997), most clinical studies have failed to find evidence of either elevated rates of Type 2 diabetes in patients with AD (Nielson et al., 1996), or a greater degree of Alzheimer-type brain pathology (e.g., neurofibrillary tangles, senile plaques) in autopsy specimens from diabetic as compared to nondiabetic adults (Heitner & Dickson, 1997). Hyperglycemia could also produce CNS damage by means of several other possible pathways, including increases in aldose reductase activity (with a corresponding accumulation of sorbitol, depletion of neural myoinositol, and alterations of Na-K ATPase activity), as well as increases in protein kinase C activity (with analogous changes in brain microvasculature that affect transport of nutrients and hormones into neurons; Porte & Schwartz, 1996). This possibility must necessarily be quite a bit more speculative, because at this time our understanding of these alternate pathways is based almost entirely on preclinical animal or in vitro studies.

Attention has been focused on chronic hyperglycemia largely because elevated glucose levels are the defining characteristic of Type 2 diabetes. Nevertheless, because most patients with that disorder are also hyperinsulinemic, several investigators have begun to examine the possibility that excessive insulin levels may adversely affect the CNS and be responsible for impairments in cognitive function. We now know that elevated insulin levels—which ordinarily rise with increasing age—are a particularly potent predictor of poorer performance on a variety of cognitive measures. Results from the Zutphen Elderly Study showed that elderly men without diabetes who were in the highest insulin quartile made 25% more errors on the Mini-Mental State Examination as compared to participants in the lowest insulin quartile (Kalmijn, Feskens, Launer, Stijnen, & Kromhout, 1995). Age and insulinemia appeared to interact insofar as hyperinsulinemic men over 75 years of age tended to make more errors than younger men with similar insulin levels. The Rotterdam study also found an association between hyperinsulinemia and cognitive dysfunction, but this effect was limited to women without diabetes or dementia (Stolk et al., 1997). Differences in measurement of insulin across the two studies could account for these inconsistent findings. Hyperinsulinemia is also associated with poorer cognitive performance in nondiabetic men with hypertension (Kuusisto et al., 1993). Normotensive and normoinsulinemic hypertensive older men (mean age = 73) enrolled in the Kuopio cohort performed comparably on an extensive battery of cognitive tests; in contrast, hyperinsulinemic hypertensive participants performed significantly worse on 16 of the 19 neuropsychological outcome variables. A subsequent analysis of the Kuopio cohort demonstrated that in nondiabetic participants, hyperinsulinemia was associated with a greatly increased risk for AD (Kuusisto et al., 1997).

How could high levels of circulating insulin disrupt brain function and adversely affect cognitive functioning? Insulin is now known to cross the blood–brain barrier and enter the brain by means of a receptor-mediated active transport system (Baskin, Figlewicz, Woods, Porte, & Dorsa, 1987). Insulin receptors have also been identified in specific brain regions—particularly the hypothalamus and the limbic system—and researchers have found that insulin modulates synaptic activity, perhaps by inhibiting the firing of neurons in those brain regions or by regulating the synthesis of specific neurotransmitter reuptake transporters for dopamine and norepinephrine (for a review, see McCall & Figlewicz, 1997). Although preclinical studies demonstrate that insulin can affect brain activity, researchers remain far from understanding just how hyperinsulinemia disrupts complex cognitive processes.

SOME FINAL THOUGHTS

Diabetes mellitus and CV disorders may be closely intertwined biomedically, but there is little evidence to support the widely held view that the cognitive impairments associated with diabetes—especially those found in adults—are largely a consequence of comorbid CV disease. In children, the occurrence of clinically significant cognitive deficits is generally limited to those who developed diabetes in the first 4 to 6 years of life and who also experienced one or more moderately severe hypoglycemic episodes. Most diabetic children, especially those diagnosed after 6 years of age, perform normally on standard neuropsychological tests, although there is a tendency for them to earn somewhat lower scores than their peers on measures of academic achievement. Adults with Type 1 diabetes show relatively subtle cognitive impairment, if they show any impairment at all, and these are best predicted by the presence of hyperglycemia-associated complications such as peripheral neuropathy or by profound or recurrent hypoglycemia. CV disorders have been associated with brain dysfunction only infrequently in adults with Type 1 diabetes. On the other hand, older adults with Type 2 diabetes are far more likely to show clinically significant cognitive impairments—particularly on measures of learning and memory—and are also more likely to have pronounced CV disease. Nevertheless, both small case control studies and very large cohort studies have repeatedly demonstrated that diabetes per se has an effect on cognition that is independent of that associated with CV disease.

What mediates the link between diabetes and cognitive dysfunction? Hypoglycemia, chronic hyperglycemia, and hyperinsulinemia are now considered to be the most reasonable candidate biomedical variables. Investigators are not yet in a position to identify the underlying metabolic and hormonal pathophysiological processes that are associated with those biomedical variables and that are ultimately responsible for cognitive dysfunction. Nevertheless, it is becoming increasingly clear that the risk of cognitive impairment for any given individual is likely to be determined by interactions among multiple variables—including CV variables, such as blood pressure. To further elucidate these complex inter-relationships, large-scale studies are needed that not only incorporate extensive and appropriate cognitive assessment measures but also scrupulously ascertain medical and metabolic status, as well as mood state, and recruit participants across a wider age range. To date, no truly comprehensive assessment of diabetic adults has yet been conducted.

In addition to natural history studies, however, we also need to begin to conduct large-scale clinical treatment trials that are explicitly focused on improving cognitive function by treating diabetes and its metabolic and biomedical complications. According to most recent estimates, nearly 14 million Americans have Type 2 diabetes, and many of these individuals are now experiencing changes in memory and other cognitive processes. With adequate treatment, this cognitive dysfunction is potentially reversible, preventable, or both. Identification of which treatments are most effective, with which patients, and for what reasons, needs to be the goal of the next wave of clinical research on the neuropsychological correlates and consequences of diabetes mellitus.

ACKNOWLEDGMENT

Preparation of this chapter was supported in part by Grant DK 39629 from the National Institute of Diabetes, Digestive, and Kidney Disease.

REFERENCES

Araki, Y., Nomura, M., Tanaka, H., Yamamoto, H., Yamamoto, T., Tsukaguchi, I., & Nakamura, H. (1994). MRI of the brain in diabetes mellitus. *Neuroradiology, 36,* 101–103.

Auer, R. N., Hugh, J., Cosgrove, E., & Curry, B. (1989). Neuropathologic findings in three cases of profound hypoglycemia. *Clinical Neuropathology, 8,* 63–68.

Auer, R. N., Kalimo, H., Olsson, Y., & Siesjö, B. K. (1985). The temporal evolution of hypoglycemic brain damage. *Acta Neuropathologica, 67,* 13–24.

Austin, E. J., & Deary, I. J. (1999). Effects of repeated hypoglycemia on cognitive function. *Diabetes Care, 22,* 1273–1277.

Baskin, D. G., Figlewicz, D. P., Woods, S. C., Porte, D., & Dorsa, D. M. (1987). Insulin in the brain. *Annual Review of Physiology, 49,* 335–347.

Bjørgaas, M., Gimse, R., Vik, T., & Sand, T. (1997). Cognitive function in Type 1 diabetic children with and without episodes of hypoglycaemia. *Acta Paediatrica, 86,* 148–153.

Bjørgaas, M., Sand, T., & Gimse, R. (1996). Quantitative EEG in Type 1 diabetic children with and without episodes of severe hypoglycemia: A controlled, blind study. *Acta Neurologica Scandinavica, 93,* 398–402.

Chabriat, H., Sachon, C., Levasseur, M., Grimaldi, A., Pappata, S., Rougemont, D., Masure, M. C., De Rocondo, A., & Samson, Y. (1994). Brain metabolism after recurrent insulin-induced hypoglycemic episodes: A PET study. *Journal of Neurology, Neurosurgery, and Psychiatry, 57*, 1360–1365.

Chalmers, J., Risk, M. T. A., Kean, D. M., Grant, R., Ashworth, B., & Campbell, I. W. (1991). Severe amnesia after hypoglycemia. *Diabetes Care, 14*, 922–925.

Cohen, J. (1988). *Statistical power analysis for the behavioral sciences* (2nd ed.). Hillsdale, NJ: Lawrence Erlbaum Associates.

Dejgaard, A., Gade, A., Larsson, H., Balle, V., Parving, A., & Parving, H. (1991). Evidence for diabetic encephalopathy. *Diabetic Medicine, 8*, 162–167.

Desmond, D. W., Tatemichi, T. K., Paik, M., & Stern, Y. (1993). Risk factors for cerebrovascular disease as correlates of cognitive function in a stroke-free cohort. *Archives of Neurology, 50*, 162–166.

Diabetes Control and Complications Trial Research Group. (1993). The effect of intensive treatment on the development and progression of long-term complications in insulin-dependent diabetes mellitus. *New England Journal of Medicine, 329*, 977–986.

Diabetes Control and Complications Trial Research Group. (1995). The effect of intensive diabetes therapy on the development and progression of neuropathy. *Annals of Internal Medicine, 122*, 561–568.

Diabetes Control and Complications Trial Research Group. (1996). Effects of intensive diabetes therapy on neuropsychological function in adults in the Diabetes Control and Complications Trial. *Annals of Internal Medicine, 124*, 379–388.

Diabetes Control and Complications Trial Research Group. (1997). Hypoglycemia in the Diabetes Control and Complications Trial. *Diabetes, 46*, 271–286.

Eeg-Olofsson, O., & Petersen, I. (1966). Childhood diabetic neuropathy: A clinical and neurophysiological study. *Acta Paediatrica Scandinavica, 55*, 163–176.

Elias, P. K., Elias, M. F., D'Agostino, R. B., Cupples, L. A., Wilson, P. W., Silbershatz, H., & Wolf, P. A. (1997). NIDDM and blood pressure as risk factors for poor cognitive performance. *Diabetes Care, 20*, 1388–1395.

Finch, C. E., & Cohen, D. M. (1997). Aging, metabolism, and Alzheimer disease: Review and hypotheses. *Experimental Neurology, 143*, 82–102.

Franceschi, M., Cecchetto, R., Minicucci, F., Smizne, S., Baio, G., & Canal, N. (1984). Cognitive processes in insulin-dependent diabetes. *Diabetes Care, 7*, 228–231.

Fujioka, M., Okuchi, K., Hiramatsu, K., Sakaki, T., Sakaguchi, S., & Ishii, Y. (1997). Specific changes in human brain after hypoglycemic injury. *Stroke, 28*, 584–587.

Gilhaus, K. H., Daweke, H., Lülsdorf, H. G., Sachsse, R., & Sachsse, B. (1973). EEG–Veränderungen bei diabetischen Kindern. [EEG changes in diabetic children.] *Deutsche Medizinische Wochenschrift, 98*, 1449–1454.

Gold, A. E., Deary, I. J., & Frier, B. M. (1993). Recurrent severe hypoglycaemia and cognitive function in Type 1 diabetes. *Diabetic Medicine, 10*, 503–508.

Gold, A. E., Deary, I. J., Jones, R. W., O'Hare, J. P., Reckless, J. P. D., & Frier, B. M. (1994). Severe deterioration in cognitive function and personality in five patients with long-standing diabetes: A complication of diabetes or a consequence of treatment? *Diabetic Medicine, 11*, 499–505.

Golden, M. P., Ingersoll, G. M., Brack, C. J., Russell, B. A., Wright, J. C., & Huberty, T. J. (1989). Longitudinal relationship of asymptomatic hypoglycemia to cognitive function in IDDM. *Diabetes Care, 12*, 89–93.

Gradman, T. J., Laws, A., Thompson, L. W., & Reaven, G. M. (1993). Verbal learning and/or memory improves with glycemic control in older subjects with non-insulin-dependent diabetes mellitus. *Journal of the American Geriatric Society, 41*, 1305–1312.

Greene, D. A., Sima, A. A. F., Stevens, M. J., Feldman, E. L., & Lattimer, S. A. (1992). Complications: Neuropathy, pathogenetic considerations. *Diabetes Care, 15*, 1902–1925.

Hagen, J. W., Barclay, C. R., Anderson, B. J., Feeman, D. J., Segal, S. S., Bacon, G., & Goldstein, G. W.

(1990). Intellective functioning and strategy use in children with insulin-dependent diabetes mellitus. *Child Development, 61*, 1714–1727.

Haumont, D., Dorchy, H., & Pelc, S. (1979). EEG abnormalities in diabetic children: Influence of hypoglycemia and vascular complications. *Clinical Pediatrics, 18*, 750–753.

Heaton, R. K., Velin, R. A., McCutchan, J. A., Gulevich, S. J., Atkinson, J. H., Wallace, M. R., Godfrey, H. P. D., Kirson, D. A., Grant, I., & the HNRC Group. (1994). Neuropsychological impairment in human immunodeficiency virus-infection: Implications for employment. *Psychosomatic Medicine, 56*, 8–17.

Heitner, J., & Dickson, D. (1997). Diabetics do not have increased Alzheimer-type pathology compared with age-matched control subjects. *Neurology, 49*, 1306–1311.

Hershey, T., Bhargava, N., Sadler, M., White, N. H., & Craft, S. (1999). Conventional vs. intensive diabetes therapy in children with Type 1 diabetes: Effects on memory and motor speed. *Diabetes Care, 22*, 1318–1324.

Hershey, T., Craft, S., Bhargava, N., & White, N. H. (1997). Memory and insulin dependent diabetes mellitus (IDDM): Effects of childhood onset and severe hypoglycemia. *Journal of the International Neuropsychological Society, 3*, 509–520.

Holmes, C. S., Dunlap, W. P., Chen, R. S., & Cornwell, J. M. (1992). Gender differences in the learning status of diabetic children. *Journal of Consulting and Clinical Psychology, 60*, 698–704.

Kalmijn, S., Feskens, E. J. M., Launer, L. J., Stijnen, T., & Kromhout, D. (1995). Glucose intolerance, hyperinsulinaemia, and cognitive function in a general population of elderly men. *Diabetologia, 38*, 1096–1102.

Kent, S. (1976). Is diabetes a form of accelerated aging? *Geriatrics, 31*, 140–154.

Kovacs, M., Goldston, D., & Iyengar, S. (1992). Intellectual development and academic performance of children with insulin-dependent diabetes mellitus: A longitudinal study. *Developmental Psychology, 28*, 676–684.

Kramer, L., Fasching, P., Madl, C., Schneider, B., Damjancic, P., Waldhäusl, W., Irsigler, K., & Grimm, G. (1998). Previous episodes of hypoglycemic coma are not associated with permanent cognitive brain dysfunction in IDDM patients on intensive insulin treatment. *Diabetes, 47*, 1909–1914.

Kurita, A., Mochio, S., & Isogai, Y. (1995). Changes in auditory P300 event-related potentials and brainstem evoked potentials in diabetes mellitus. *Acta Neurologica Scandinavica, 92*, 319–323.

Kushner, M., Nencini, P., Reivich, M., Rango, M., Jamieson, D., Fazekas, F., Zimmerman, R., Chawluk, J., Alavi, A., & Alves, W. (1990). Relation of hyperglycemia early in ischemic brain infarction to cerebral anatomy, metabolism, and clinical outcome. *Annals of Neurology, 28*, 129–135.

Kuusisto, J., Koivisto, K., Mykkänen, L., Helkala, E.-L., Vanhanen, M., Hänninen, T., Kervinen, K., Kesäniemi, Y. A., Riekkinen, P. J., & Laakso, M. (1997). Association between features of the insulin resistance syndrome and Alzheimer's disease independently of apolipoprotein E4 phenotype: Cross sectional population based study. *British Medical Journal, 315*, 1045–1049.

Kuusisto, J., Koivisto, K., Mykkänen, L., Helkala, E.-L., Vanhanen, M., Hänninen, T., Pyörälä, P., & Laakso, M. (1993). Essential hypertension and cognitive function: The role of hyperinsulinemia. *Hypertension, 22*, 771–779.

Langan, S., Deary, I., Hepburn, D., & Frier, B. (1991). Cumulative cognitive impairment following recurrent severe hypoglycaemia in adult patients wtih insulin-treated diabetes mellitus. *Diabetologia, 34*, 337–344.

Launer, L. J., Dinkgreve, M. A. H. M., Jonker, C., Hooijer, C., & Lindeboom, J. (1993). Are age and education independent correlates of the Mini-Mental State Exam performance of community-dwelling elderly? *Journal of Gerontology, 48*, P271-P277.

Lawson, J. S., Erdahl, D. L. W., Monga, T. N., Bird, C. E., Donald, M. W., Surridge, D. H. C., & Letemendia, F. J. J. (1984). Neuropsychological function in diabetic patients with neuropathy. *British Journal of Psychiatry, 145*, 263–268.

Leibson, C. L., Rocca, W. A., Hanson, V. A., Cha, R., Kokmen, E., O'Brien, P. C., & Palumbo, P. J. (1997). Risk of dementia among persons with diabetes mellitus: A population-based cohort study. *American Journal of Epidemiology, 145,* 301–308.

Lincoln, N. B., Faleiro, R. M., Kelly, C., Kirk, B. A., & Jeffcoate, W. J. (1996). Effect of long-term glycemic control on cognitive function. *Diabetes Care, 19,* 656–658.

Lunetta, M., Damanti, A. R., Fabbri, G., Lombardo, M., Di Mauro, M., & Mughini, L. (1994). Evidence by magnetic resonance imaging of cerebral alterations of atrophy type in young insulin-dependent diabetic patients. *Journal of Endocrinological Investigation, 17,* 241–245.

McCall, A. L. (1992). The impact of diabetes on the CNS. *Diabetes, 41,* 557–570.

McCall, A. L., & Figlewicz, D. P. (1997). How does diabetes mellitus produce brain dysfunction? *Diabetes Spectrum, 10,* 25–32.

Meneilly, G. S., Cheung, E., Tessier, D., Yakura, C., & Tuokko, H. (1993). The effect of improved glycemic control on cognitive functions in the elderly patient with diabetes. *Journal of Gerontology: Medical Sciences, 48,* M117–M121.

Miles, W. R., & Root, H. F. (1922). Psychologic tests applied to diabetic patients. *Archives of Internal Medicine, 30,* 767–777.

Nakamura, Y., Takahashi, M., Kitaguti, M., Imaoka, H., Kono, N., & Tarui, S. (1991). Abnormal brainstem evoked potentials in diabetes mellitus: Evoked potential testings and magnetic resonance imaging. *Electromyography and Clinical Neurophysiology, 31,* 243–249.

Naor, M., Steingruber, H. J., Westhoff, K., Schottenfeld-Naor, Y., & Gries, A. F. (1997). Cognitive function in elderly non-insulin-dependent diabetic patients before and after inpatient treatment for metabolic control. *Journal of Diabetes and Its Complications, 11,* 40–46.

National Diabetes Data Group. (1995). *Diabetes in America* (2nd ed.). Bethesda, MD: National Institutes of Health.

Nielson, K. A., Nolan, J., Berchtold, N. C., Sandman, C. A., Mulnard, R. A., & Cotman, C. W. (1996). Apolipoprotein-E genotyping of diabetic dementia patients: Is diabetes rare in Alzheimer's disease? *Journal of the American Geriatric Society, 44,* 897–904.

Northam, E. A., Anderson, P. J., Werther, G. A., Warne, G. L., Adler, R. G., & Andrewes, D. (1998). Neuropsychological complications of IDDM in children 2 years after disease onset. *Diabetes Care, 21,* 379–384.

Northam, E. A., Anderson, P. J., Werther, G. A., Warne, G. L., & Andrewes, D. (1999). Predictors of change in the neuropsychological profiles of children with insulin dependent diabetes mellitus two years after disease onset. *Diabetes Care, 22,* 1438–1444.

Perlmuter, L. C., Hakami, M. K., Hodgson-Harrington, C., Gingsberg, J., Katz, J., Singer, D. E., & Nathan, D. M. (1984). Decreased cognitive function in aging non-insulin-dependent diabetic patients. *American Journal of Medicine, 77,* 1043–1048.

Perros, P., Deary, I. J., Sellar, R. J., Best, J. J. K., & Frier, B. M. (1997). Brain abnormalities demonstrated by magnetic resonance imaging in adult IDDM patients with and without a history of recurrent severe hypoglycemia. *Diabetes Care, 20,* 1013–1018.

Pickup, J. C., & Williams, G. (Eds.). (1997). *Textbook of diabetes* (2nd ed.). Oxford, England: Blackwell Science.

Pirttilä, T., Järvenpää, R., Laippala, P., & Frey, H. (1992). Brain atrophy on computerized axial tomography scans: Interaction of age, diabetes, and general morbidity. *Gerontology, 38,* 285–291.

Porte, D., & Schwartz, M. W. (1996, May 3). Diabetes complications: Why is glucose potentially toxic? *Science, 272,* 699–700.

Pozzessere, G., Rizzo, P. A., Valle, E., Mollica, M. A., Meccia, A., Morano, S., Di Mario, U., Andreani, D., & Morocutti, C. (1988). Early detection of neurological involvement in IDDM and NIDDM: Multimodal evoked potentials versus metabolic control. *Diabetes Care, 11,* 473–480.

Pulsinelli, W. A., Levy, D. E., Sigsbee, B., Scherer, P., & Plum, F. (1983). Increased damage after ischemic stroke in patients with hyperglycemia with or without established diabetes mellitus. *American Journal of Medicine, 74,* 540–544.

Reaven, G. M., Thompson, L. W., Nahum, D., & Haskins, E. (1990). Relationship between hyperglycemia and cognitive function in older NIDDM patients. *Diabetes Care, 13,* 16–21.

Reichard, P., Berglund, B., Britz, A., Levander, S., & Rosenqvist, U. (1991). Hypoglycemic episodes during intensified insulin treatment: Increased frequency but no effect on cognitive function. *Journal of Internal Medicine, 229,* 9–16.

Reichard, P., Phil, M., Rosenqvist, U., & Sule, J. (1996). Complications in IDDM are caused by elevated blood glucose level: The Stockholm Diabetes Intervention Study (SDIS) at 10-year follow up. *Diabetologia, 39,* 1483–1486.

Rennick, P. M., Wilder, R. M., Sargent, J., & Ashley, B. J., Jr. (1968, August–September). *Retinopathy as an indicator of cognitive-perceptual-motor impairment in diabetic adults.* Paper presented at the 76th Annual Convention of the American Psychological Association, San Francisco.

Reske-Nielsen, E., Lundbaek, K., & Rafaelsen, O. J. (1965). Pathological changes in the central and peripheral nervous system of young long-term diabetics. *Diabetologia, 1,* 232–241.

Richardson, J. T. E. (1990). Cognitive function in diabetes mellitus. *Neuroscience and Biobehavioral Review, 14,* 385–388.

Robertson-Tchabo, E. A., Arenberg, D., Tobin, J. D., & Plotz, J. B. (1986). A longitudinal study of cognitive performance in noninsulin dependent (Type II) diabetic men. *Experimental Gerontology, 21,* 459–467.

Rovet, J., & Alverez, M. (1997). Attentional functioning in children and adolescents with IDDM. *Diabetes Care, 20,* 803–810.

Rovet, J. F., & Ehrlich, R. M. (1999). The effect of hypoglycemic seizures on cognitive function in children with diabetes: A 7-year prospective study. *Journal of Pediatrics, 134,* 503–506.

Rovet, J., Ehrlich, R., & Czuchta, D. (1990). Intellectual characteristics of diabetic children at diagnosis and one year later. *Journal of Pediatric Psychology, 15,* 775–788.

Rovet, J. F., Ehrlich, R. M., & Hoppe, M. G. (1987). Intellectual deficits associated with the early onset of insulin-dependent diabetes mellitus in children. *Diabetes Care, 10,* 510–515.

Ryan, C. M. (1988). Neurobehavioral complications of Type 1 diabetes: Examination of possible risk factors. *Diabetes Care, 11,* 86–93.

Ryan, C. (1989). Neuropsychological consequences and correlates of diabetes in childhood. In C. S. Holmes (Ed.), *Neuropsychological and behavioral aspects of diabetes* (pp. 58–84). New York: Springer-Verlag.

Ryan, C. M., & Geckle, M. (1999). Effects of Type 2 diabetes on learning and memory skills in middle-aged adults. *Diabetes, 48*(Suppl. 1), A9–A10.

Ryan, C., Longstreet, C., & Morrow, L. A. (1985). The effects of diabetes mellitus on the school attendance and school achievement of adolescents. *Child: Care, Health, and Development, 11,* 229–240.

Ryan, C., Vega, A., & Drash, A. (1985). Cognitive deficits in adolescents who developed diabetes early in life. *Pediatrics, 75,* 921–927.

Ryan, C., Vega, A., Longstreet, C., & Drash, L. (1984). Neuropsychological changes in adolescents with insulin-dependent diabetes mellitus. *Journal of Consulting and Clinical Psychology, 52,* 335–342.

Ryan, C. M., Williams, T. M., Finegold, D. N., & Orchard, T. J. (1993). Cognitive dysfunction in adults with Type 1 (insulin-dependent) diabetes mellitus of long duration: Effects of recurrent hypoglycaemia and other chronic complications. *Diabetologia, 36,* 329–334.

Ryan, C. M., Williams, T. M., Orchard, T. J., & Finegold, D. N. (1992). Psychomotor slowing is associated with distal symmetrical polyneuropathy in adults with diabetes mellitus. *Diabetes, 41,* 107–113.

Sachon, C., Grimaldi, A., Digy, J. P., Pillon, B., Dubois, B., & Thervet, F. (1992). Cognitive function, insulin-dependent diabetes and hypoglycaemia. *Journal of Internal Medicine, 231,* 471–475.

Schwarz, N. (1999). Self-reports: How the questions shape the answers. *American Psychologist, 54,* 93–105.

Sieber, F. E., & Traystman, R. J. (1992). Special issues: Glucose and the brain. *Critical Care Medicine, 20,* 104–114.

Siesjö, B. K., & Bengtsson, F. (1989). Calcium fluxes, calcium antagonists, and calcium-related pathology in brain ischemia, hypoglycemia, and spreading depression: A unifying hypothesis. *Journal of Cerebral Blood Flow and Metabolism, 9,* 127–140.

Skenazy, J. A., & Bigler, E. D. (1984). Neuropsychological findings in diabetes mellitus. *Journal of Clinical Psychology, 40,* 246–258.

Soininen, H., Puranen, M., Helkala, E.-L., Laakso, M., & Riekkinen, P. J. (1992). Diabetes mellitus and brain atrophy: A computed tomography study in an elderly population. *Neurobiology of Aging, 13,* 717–721.

Soltész, G., & Acsádi, G. (1989). Association between diabetes, severe hypoglycemia, and electroencephalographic abnormalities. *Archives of Disease in Childhood, 64,* 992–996.

Stewart, R. J., & Liolitsa, D. (1999). Type 2 diabetes mellitus, cognitive impairment and dementia. *Diabetic Medicine, 16,* 93–112.

Stolk, R. P., Breteler, M. M. B., Ott, A., Pols, H. A. P., Lamberts, S. W. J., Grobbee, D. E., & Hofman, A. (1997). Insulin and cognitive function in an elderly population. *Diabetes Care, 20,* 792–795.

Strachan, M. W. J., Deary, I. J., Ewing, F. M. E., & Frier, B. M. (1997). Is Type 2 (non-insulin dependent) diabetes mellitus associated with an increased risk of cognitive dysfunction? *Diabetes Care, 20,* 438–445.

Ternand, C., Go, V. L. W., Gerich, J. E., & Haymond, M. W. (1982). Endocrine pancreatic response of children with onset of insulin-requiring diabetes before age 3 and after age 5. *Journal of Pediatrics, 101,* 36–39.

U'ren, R. C., Riddle, M. C., Lezak, M. D., & Bennington-Davis, M. (1990). The mental efficiency of the elderly person with Type II diabetes mellitus. *Journal of the American Geriatric Society, 38,* 505–510.

van Boxtel, M. P. J., Buntinx, F., Houx, P. J., Metsemakers, J. F. M., Knottnerus, A., & Jolles, J. (1998). The relationship between morbidity and cognitive performance in a normal aging population. *Journal of Gerontology, 53A,* M147–M154.

Weir, C. J., Murray, G. D., Dyker, A. G., & Lees, K. R. (1997). Is hyperglycaemia an independent predictor of poor outcome after acute stroke? Results of a long term follow up study. *British Medical Journal, 314,* 1303–1306.

Wolters, P. L., Brouwers, P., Moss, H. A., & Pizzo, P. A. (1995). Differential receptive and expressive language functioning of children with symptomatic HIV disease and relation to CT scan brain abnormalities. *Pediatrics, 95,* 112–119.

Wredling, R., Levander, S., Adamson, U., & Lins, P. E. (1990). Permanent neuropsychological impairment after recurrent episodes of severe hypoglycaemia in man. *Diabetologia, 33,* 152–157.

CHAPTER FIVE

Cardiovascular Risk Factors and Cognitive Functioning: An Epidemiological Perspective

MERRILL F. ELIAS
Boston University

PENELOPE K. ELIAS
Boston University

MICHAEL A. ROBBINS
University of Maine

PHILIP A. WOLF
Boston University School of Medicine

RALPH B. D'AGOSTINO
Boston University

The relationship between common cardiovascular (CV) risk factors and cognitive functioning in adults has received increasing scrutiny in recent decades. Most research has focused on hypertension and diabetes, where adverse effects on cognitive functioning are clearly established. Other major risk factors, such as obesity, cigarette smoking, and cholesterol, have received less attention. Researchers are just now beginning to focus on risk factors such as high total plasma homocysteine and low levels of vitamin B12, vitamin B6, and folate. One major objective of this chapter is to review the literature with respect to the cumulative impact of major risk factors for CV disease (CVD) on cognitive functioning. A second major objective is to consider the epidemiological significance of associations between CV risk factors and cognitive functioning. In other words, we are interested in the importance of these relationships with respect to large populations and public health.

Previous chapters in this book address three major risk factors for CVD: hypertension (chap. 2), diabetes (chap. 3), and high and low levels of serum cholesterol (chap. 4). Consequently, we address these topics briefly with a unique emphasis on the epidemiological significance of the findings. Several topics that have not been a central focus in other chapters are given more attention: cigarette smoking, alcohol consumption, obesity, total serum homocysteine (tHcy) levels, vitamin B12, vitamin B6, and folate.

The outcome measure of concern in this book is cognitive performance across a wide range of abilities, or within generally normal limits, as opposed to dementia. Because in this chapter we take an epidemiological perspective, there is an emphasis on studies using large community-based populations rather than clinical studies featuring case control methods. Because so few studies of multiple risk factors have been conducted with large community-based populations, a substantial portion of this chapter deals with data from the Framingham Heart Study.

We begin by defining the term *risk factor*. We then provide some brief illustrations of the epidemiological significance of relations between individual CV risk factors and cognitive functioning. These sections are followed by a discussion of studies of multiple risk factors and a presentation of our own research with the Framingham Heart Study cohort. Finally, we discuss possible mechanisms underlying relationships among risk factors and cognitive functioning and promising new directions for research.

WHAT IS A RISK FACTOR?

It is clear that the distinction between a risk factor for CVD and disease itself is academic. CVDs are risk factors for other diseases. Clinically defined hypertension is a good example. Several overlapping definitions of the term *risk factor* emerged early in the course of the Framingham Heart Study (Kannel, Dawber, Kagan, Revotski, & Stokes, 1961; Kannel & Sytkowski, 1987): (a) a correlate of CVD, (b) a characteristic of an individual that *predisposes* that individual to CVD, (c) a factor that emerges as a *cause* of a CVD. Because associations between risk and CVD are more easily demonstrated than causal relationships, the first and second definitions have been used more frequently in the literature dealing with vascular risk factors for cognitive decline.

Fortunately, there seems to be much agreement that the major biological risk factors for CVD include blood pressure (BP) level and hypertension, diabetes, cigarette smoking, cholesterol (total cholesterol, low-density lipoprotein [LDL] cholesterol, high-density lipoprotein [HDL] cholesterol), and age (Fowler, 1998; Lawrence & Cruickshank, 1998; Mann, 1998; Neil, 1998). Obesity, left ventricular hypertrophy, and family history of premature coronary heart disease (CHD) are also considered to be risk factors for CVD, and estrogen replacement therapy may reduce risk (Expert Panel, 1994). However, it has been argued that these latter factors, to a major extent, "work through" the major risk factors (Wilson et al., 1998). In this chapter we focus on the major risk factors.

EPIDEMIOLOGICAL SIGNIFICANCE

A number of studies reviewed in this chapter use odds ratios (ORs) to express the importance of relationships between risk factors and cognitive functioning. A brief description of the method will be helpful to behavioral and social scientists who do not use logistic regression analysis. Unlike linear regression methods, which use continuous-outcome variables, logistic regression analysis uses discrete or binary outcome measures (dependent variables). In logistic regression analyses ORs are estimated from the regression coefficients and used as indexes of relative risk or of how much more likely (or unlikely) it is that an outcome will occur among people for whom a characteristic is present (e.g., a risk factor or disease) than among persons for whom that characteristic is absent (Hosmer & Lemeshow, 1989). An OR of 1.00 would signify no additional risk. An OR of 2.00 would signify a doubling of risk. If, for example, an OR relating the presence of hypertension to the presence or absence of cognitive impairment were 1.90, people with hypertension would have an increased risk of cognitive impairment of 90%. An OR of 1.14 associated with each ten-mm Hg increase in BP would indicate a 14% increase in risk (relative to no increased risk) of cognitive impairment for every 10-mm Hg increase in diastolic BP. The outcome variable is expressed as a category of outcomes arranged in an ordinal fashion or, most often, as a binary outcome; for example, presence or absence of stroke. As is true for linear regression analysis, logistic regression analysis can include models with multiple predictors and covariates (statistical control variables). In this chapter we use the term *multivariate analysis* to describe analyses with multiple predictor variables.

With respect to test scores, often a binary outcome must be created by rescaling a continuously distributed dependent variable into a dichotomous variable on the basis of some relatively arbitrary criterion for performance; for example, poor performance defined as performance at or below the 25th percentile of the total distribution of scores. Although this can sometimes be undesirable in terms of the sensitivity of the analysis, it has heuristic value when one wishes to express the importance of an association between a CV risk factor or disease and cognitive functioning in terms of its epidemiological significance.

CV RISK FACTORS

There have been a number of studies in which risk factors for CVD have been related to neuropsychological test performance (chaps. 2–4), but there have been relatively few studies relating multiple CVD risk factors to neuropsychological test performance despite the fact that the relationship between cumulative CV risks and CVD has been a major focus in contemporary epidemiology (Gordon & Kannel, 1982; Wilson, Castelli, & Kannel, 1987; Wolf, D'Agostino, Belanger, & Kannel, 1991). Where cognitive functioning is concerned, selection of such risk factors for consideration in a multivariate context must take into account (a) a plausible biological link between the CV risk factor and cognitive functioning and (b) empirical evidence of a relationship between the risk factor and cognitive functioning. It is clear from chapters 2, 3, and 4 that hypertension and diabetes are strong candidates for inclusion in a multivariate risk factor scale.

Hypertension

With a few exceptions, the results of an overwhelming number of studies (see chap. 2) indicate that hypertension has a negative impact on cognitive functioning at all ages. Most importantly, there is a dose–response relationship between BP level (mm Hg) and cognitive functioning. As systolic and diastolic BP levels increase, level of cognitive functioning falls (M. F. Elias, Robbins, Schultz, & Pierce, 1990; Robbins, Elias, Croog, & Colton, 1994), and the rate of longitudinal decline in cognitive functioning becomes increasingly accelerated (M. F. Elias, Robbins, Elias, & Streeten, 1998a, 1998b; M. F. Elias, Robbins, & Elias, 1996). From an epidemiological perspective, it is important to note that three large-sample, community-based investigations have indicated that elevated BP may precede lowered neuropsychological test performance by as many as 14 to 30 years (M. F. Elias, Wolf, D'Agostino, Cobb, & White, 1993; Launer, Masaki, Petrovitch, Foley, & Havlick, 1995; Swan, Carmelli, & LaRue, 1996).

An illustration of the epidemiological significance of the impact of chronic hypertension on cognitive functioning comes from an investigation by P. K. Elias, D'Agostino, Elias, and Wolf (1995). The study population ($N = 1,695$) was free of stroke and 55 years to 88 years old at the time of neuropsychological testing. P. K. Elias et al. (1995) compared people who were chronically hypertensive on five biennial examinations 12 years to 14 years prior to neuropsychological assessment at Examinations 14 and 15 of the Framingham Study with people who were free from hypertension for this same time period.

The risk of obtaining a score below the 50th percentile (poorer performance) for the total distribution of scores, with statistical control for age, education, occupation, gender, alcohol consumption, and cigarette smoking, was estimated from logistic regression analyses. Independent of age, chronic hypertension was associated with significantly increased risk of poorer performance for the Logical Memory–Immediate Recall (OR = 1.44), Visual Reproductions (OR = 1.41), and Logical Memory–Delayed Recall tests (OR = 1.53) on the Wechsler Memory Scale. For these three neuropsychological tests similar results were obtained when lowered performance level was redefined as performance in the lower quartile of the distribution of test scores: ORs = 1.62, 1.29, and 1.41, respectively.

Diabetes

Chapter 3 indicates that lowered cognitive functioning in relation to Type 1 and Type 2 diabetes has been reported in many studies, although there have been failures to observe these relationships. Strachan, Deary, Ewing, and Frier (1997) pointed out that a number of studies, some with positive results and some with negative results, have involved small samples and have failed to control for potentially confounding factors, such as other risk factors. Clearly, more prospective studies using large community-based samples are needed (chap. 3 of this book; Strachan et al., 1997). In a recent prospective, community-based investigation, P. K. Elias et al. (1997) examined relationships between diabetes and cognitive functioning using data from stroke-free Framingham Heart Study participants. It is important to note that the P. K. Elias et al. study compared neuropsychological test performance for Type 2 diabetics ($n = 187$) and nondiabetics ($n = 1,624$) who were represented in the study in proportion to their representation in national samples. Poor performance was defined as performance at or below the 25th percentile of the total distribution of test scores. Diagnoses of diabetes were available at each of 15 biennial examinations (Examinations 1–15) conducted prior to, or concurrent with, neuropsychological assessment at Examinations 14 through 15. Measures of diastolic and systolic BP also were obtained at each biennial examination.

Thus, the P. K. Elias et al. study provides a good illustration of the epidemiological significance of associations between diabetes and cognitive functioning in the presence of increasing levels of BP. For example, when an overall composite of eight test scores, measuring verbal and visual–spatial memory, learning, and abstract reasoning was used in the statistical analysis, a statistically significant interaction between BP level and diabetes exposure was obtained. There was a twofold increased risk of poor performance for each 10-mm Hg increment in diastolic BP over the study period of 28 to 30 years for Type 2 diabetics ($n = 187$); that is, the OR associated with "poor performance" was 2.03. But the risk of poor performance was only 1.26 for people who remained nondiabetic at each of the 15 biennial examinations conducted over this 28–30-year period ($n = 1,624$). Conversely, every 5 years of exposure to diabetes was associated with an increased risk of 1.54 of poor performance for hypertensive individuals ($n = 576$), but the risk was only 1.03 (nonsignificant) for people who were normotensive ($n = 1,235$).

The general trend across all individual test scores making up the composite score was for the combination of diabetes and high BP to be associated with poor performance, although a statistically significant interaction was obtained only for the Visual Reproductions test (see descriptions of the neuropsychological tests in Table 5.1). Each 5 years of exposure to diabetes was associated with an increased risk of 33% (OR = 1.33) for hypertensive individuals. However, there was no significant increase in risk per 5-year exposure to diabetes for people who were free from hypertension during the study period (OR = 1.08). For non-diabetics, the increased risk associated with a 10-mm Hg increment in diastolic BP was only 13% and not statistically significant (OR = 1.13). For the diabetics, the increased risk of poor performance on the Visual Reproductions test for each 10-mm Hg increase in diastolic BP was 68% (OR = 1.68).

TABLE 5.1
Brief Summary of the Original Framingham Neuropsychological Test Battery,
Made Up of the Wechsler Adult Intelligence Scale (WAIS), the Wechsler
Memory Scale (WMS), and the Multilingual Aphasia Examination

Test	Summary
1. WMS Logical Memory–Immediate Recall	Learning and immediate recall for verbal material in the form of a story.
2. WMS Visual Reproductions	Learning and immediate recall of visual material in the form of designs.
3. WMS Paired Associate Learning	Learning and immediate recall for verbal material in the form of word pairs.
4. WMS Logical Memory–Delayed Recall	Delayed recall of the story learned with the Logical Memory–Immediate Recall test with interference from the tests intervening between Logical Memory–Immediate Recall and Logical Memory–Delayed Recall.
5. Controlled Oral Word Associations	Often referred to as the *Word Fluency test*. Taken from the Multilingual Aphasia Examination, this test measures fluency of speech but is also a measure of memory and organizational strategy.
6. WAIS Similarities	Verbal concept formation and abstract reasoning. Correlates highly with general intelligence.
7. WAIS Digit Span Forward	Assesses primary memory, immediate memory span, and efficiency of auditory attention and concentration.
8. WAIS Digit Span Backward	Requires mental double tracking in which memory for digits and reversal of the original order must proceed simultaneously.
Logical Memory–Retained	A savings score derived from comparing material retained with the Logical Memory–Immediate versus the Logical Memory–Delayed Recall Tests.
Learning and memory score	A composite score composed of scores on Tests 1, 2, and 3, above.
WAIS Digit Span (or the Attention and Concentration Composite Score)	A composite score composed of scores on Tests 7 and 8.
Total composite score	An overall composite (average) score composed of scores on Tests 1 through 8.

Note. The Framingham Test Battery, or the Kaplan–Albert Neuropsychological Test Battery, is described in detail in Farmer, White, Kittner, et al. (1987) and M. F. Elias, Elias, Silbershatz, D'Agostino, and Wolf (1997).

An OR of 1.68 takes on clinical meaning when we consider the impact of a catastrophic event such as stroke on Visual Reproductions test scores. Unpublished data from this same sample of individuals indicated that the increased risk of performance in the lower 25% of the distribution of Visual Reproductions test scores for people with a history of stroke (prior to the neuropsychological assessment) was 1.97. Thus, for diabetic people, an increase of 10 mm Hg in diastolic BP carries with it only slightly less risk for lower cognitive functioning than stroke.

Cholesterol

Evidence linking cholesterol and cognitive functioning is meager. High cholesterol levels have been related both to higher and lower levels of cognitive functioning (chap. 4). In the Framingham Study of multiple risk factors and cognitive functioning (M. F. Elias, Elias, D'Agostino, Silbershatz, & Wolf, 1998), elevated total cholesterol was unrelated to neuropsychological test performance. ORs expressing the risk of poor performance (scores in the lower quartile) associated with high cholesterol (>200 mg/Dl) ranged from 0.99 to 1.00 for the eight neuropsychological test measures. From a theoretical perspective, this null finding is surprising, because a lowering of total and LDL cholesterol results in a reduction of CHD and regression of atherosclerotic plaques (Neil, 1998). As Matthew F. Muldoon, Janine D. Florey, and Christopher M. Ryan point out in Chapter 3, the relationships between lipids and lipid proteins are complex. More sophisticated studies of HDL cholesterol, LDL cholesterol, very low density lipid cholesterol, and triglycerides are needed before a definitive statement can be made about the impact of cholesterol on neuropsychological test performance.

Cigarette Smoking

Natalie A. Phillips' brief discussion of the literature on cigarettes in Chapter 7, which focuses on peripheral vascular disease, reveals both positive and negative findings and a surprising paucity of studies of cigarette smoking and cognitive functioning. From an epidemiological perspective it is important to note that longitudinal changes in measures of mental status (Launer, Feskens, Kalmijn, & Kromhout, 1996) and cognitive functioning (Letteneur et al., 1994) were unrelated to cigarette smoking in studies involving large community samples. In the Honolulu–Asia Study population, people who were smokers or recent quitters showed marginally lower performance on a mental status screening instrument than did those who did not smoke (Galanis, Petrovitch, Launer, et al., 1997).

In cross-sectional data from the Framingham (Farmer, White, Abbott, et al., 1987) and the East Boston (Scherr et al., 1988) Study populations, a few selected subtests from a larger neuropsychological test battery were related to smoking versus nonsmoking status at the time of testing. In a more recent study with the

Framingham Study population (M. F. Elias, Elias, et al., 1998), the risks of poor performance (performance in the lower quartile of the total distribution of scores) as a function of a smoking versus nonsmoking history were 1.44 for the Logical Memory–Delayed test, 1.38 for the Controlled Oral Word Associations test, and 1.44 for a Learning and Memory factor (Logical Memory–Immediate Recall + Visual Reproductions + Paired Associates Learning) score. These odds were adjusted for multiple demographic variables, alcohol consumption, cholesterol, diabetes, obesity, and hypertension.

It is possible that differential survival between smokers and nonsmokers may actually diminish the strength of associations between smoking and cognitive functioning. In fact, it has been argued that the unexpected protective effect of smoking with regard to Alzheimer's disease (AD) is related to the fact that smokers who survive to an age marked by higher prevalence and incidence of AD may represent a genetically select population (J. E. Riggs, 1993). On the other hand, cigarette smoking is notoriously difficult to quantify accurately. Many studies report only a dichotomous (yes–no) smoking variable. Self-reports of number of cigarettes consumed within specific time periods are constrained by both memory and differential willingness on the part of study participants to admit to potentially lethal levels of a harmful health habit. Despite mixed evidence that smoking is a risk factor for lowered cognitive functioning, it is a powerful risk factor for stroke (Wolf, 1993). By virtue of this relationship alone it must be considered in any investigations of the cumulative impact of multiple risk factors on cognitive functioning.

Obesity

The positive association between atherogenesis and obesity is well known (Kannel & Sytkowski, 1987). Thus it is surprising that obesity has been largely ignored as a risk factor in studies of cognitive functioning. Indeed, it may operate by modifying other risk factors. On the other hand, its association with hypertension, diabetes, and high LDL cholesterol earns it a place in the list of candidate risk factors for investigations of the impact of multiple risks on cognitive functioning.

Alcohol: Protection at Moderate Levels

The adverse effects of heavy drinking on cognitive functioning are well known. However, a relatively recent literature indicates that alcohol consumption in the range of one to five drinks per day reduces the risk of CHD by 40% to 60% (P. Anderson, 1998). Recent studies indicate that a U- or J-shaped curve describes the relationship between level of alcohol use and cognitive functioning (Hendrie, Gao, Hall, Hui, & Unverzagt, 1996). Older African American men and women ($N = 2070$) who drank fewer than four drinks per week performed at a higher level than abstainers on a global score measuring multiple cognitive domains and on a more specific measure of memory: the delayed-recall score from the East Boston Memory Test. Hendrie et al. (1996) studied a combined sample of men and women. It is important to stratify the sample by gender when examining associations between level of alcohol intake and cognitive performance, because women consume smaller amounts of alcohol and do so less frequently than men (Gordon & Kannel, 1983; Steptoe & Wardle, 1992).

Gender differences with respect to alcohol and cognitive functioning were addressed in a recent study using data obtained from the Epidemiology of Vascular Aging Study (Dufouil, Ducimetière, & Alpèrovitch, 1997). No significant associations between drinking and cognitive functioning were found for men ($n = 574$), but for women ($n = 815$) moderate alcohol consumption was associated with significantly better performance on the following tests: Mini-Mental State Examination, Word Fluency, Digit Symbol Substitution, Paced Auditory Serial Addition, Trail Making B, Auditory Verbal Learning Test, and Raven Progressive Matrices. A composite of all test measures showed a similar relationship. Although the underlying cognitive abilities measured in this study vary considerably from test to test, most require learning and executive functioning. These findings were recently confirmed in the Framingham Heart Study population (P. K. Elias, Elias, D'Agostino, Silbershatz, & Wolf, 1999). Self-report data of weekly alcohol intake for 733 men and 1,053 women were used to construct groups consisting of abstainers and very light, light, moderate, and heavy drinkers. These groups were compared with respect to performance on the neuropsychological test battery given at Examinations 14 through 15.

Women who consumed alcohol moderately (2–4 drinks per day), relative to abstainers, exhibited superior performance on the following measures: Logical Memory–Delayed Recall, Word Fluency (Controlled Oral Word Associations), Similarities, the Learning and Memory Factor Score, the Attention and Concentration Factor Score, and the Total Composite Score. A similar pattern was observed among the men, but moderate alcohol consumption was related significantly only to Logical Memory–Delayed Recall.

It is important to note that these analyses involved adjustment for age; education; occupation; diabetes; BP; cigarette smoking; body mass index; total cholesterol; and pre-existing CV diseases, including myocardial infarction, angina pectoris, intermittent claudication, coronary insufficiency, transient ischemic attack, and congestive heart failure. Individuals with dementia and definitely completed stroke were excluded from the study.

It has been suggested that the lower cognitive performance of abstainers may be related to the fact that many abstainers had given up drinking because they were unwell or were formerly heavy drinkers. However, this hypothesis has not been confirmed with respect to research on coronary artery disease (CAD) outcomes (P. Anderson, 1998), and it is not supported by the community-based studies we reported earlier (Dufouil et al., 1997; P. K. Elias et al., 1999). In fact, there appears to be a dose–response relationship favoring light and moderate drinking compared to very light drinking as well as abstention. In the P. K. Elias et al. (1999) study, very light drinking afforded no advantage for cognitive performance over abstention, and moderate drinkers performed significantly better than the very light drinkers. However, much more work is needed before a final conclusion regarding the facilitative effects of moderate drinking on cognitive functioning can be reached. Potential mechanisms linking moderate drinking to higher levels of cognitive functioning are discussed in the Mechanisms Underlying Risk-Related Cognitive Dysfunction section.

The social psychological factors that might lead to a positive relationship between moderate drinking and superior cognitive functioning have not been adequately explored. Furthermore, it is important to conduct multiple health impact studies in which the benefits of moderate drinking on cognitive functioning are considered in relation to adverse effects of moderate alcohol consumption on other health outcomes, such as cancer. Until these data are available, people who abstain or drink very lightly should carefully consider the merits of initiating a moderate alcohol consumption program for the purposes of enhancing CV health or cognitive ability.

One important limitation with respect to studies relating alcohol to cognitive functioning is the lack of adequate data with respect to consumption above 8 to 12 drinks per day for men and 4 to 8 drinks per day for women in large community-based samples. As exemplified by the Framingham Study (P. K. Elias et al., 1999), too few individuals self-report high levels of alcohol consumption for meaningful analyses.

MULTIPLE RISK FACTORS

There have been surprisingly few community-based studies in which risk factors have been examined in a multivariate context. Recently, Desmond, Tatemichi, Paik, and Stern (1993) examined the independent effects of hypertension, diabetes mellitus, myocardial infarction, angina pectoris, hypercholesterolemia, and cigarette smoking on measures of memory, language, visual–spatial ability, abstract reasoning, and attention in a relatively large ($N = 249$) cohort of elderly people (over 70 years of age). Statistical controls for medication and demographic variables were included in the regression model. Diabetes (fasting glucose > 140 mg/dL, >7.7 mmol/L) was significantly associated with poorer abstract reasoning (OR = 10.9) and visual–spatial ability (OR = 3.5). Hypercholesterolemia (total cholesterol >240 mg/dL, >6.20 mmol/L) was significantly associated with poorer memory test ability (OR = 3.5). Here, poor performance was defined as performance below the mean of the total distribution of scores. None of the risk factors were significantly associated with neuropsychological indexes of attention or verbal ability. Cigarette smoking (yes–no) and hypertension (largely self-report) were unrelated to any of the measures of cognitive functioning. One must take three features of this study and the analyses into consideration when interpreting these results. The sample consisted of individuals who were randomly selected from Medicare records (53%), volunteers from the community (29.7%), and spouses of stroke patients (17.3%). The risk factor data were, for the most part, collected by self-report and physician interview rather than physical examinations or diagnostic studies, although Desmond et al. noted that some laboratory data—for example, fasting glucose levels, to confirm diabetes—were used when available (percentage of participants not specified). The failure to find relationships between hypertension and cognitive functioning may have been due to the fact that ascertainment of hypertension was largely by self-report.

Using a sample of the Framingham study population, P. K. Elias et al. (1997) examined the relationships among multiple risk factors and neuropsychological test performance. Beginning in 1950, all participants were screened for CV risk factors and events every 2 years. All were free from a history of definite completed stroke and Type 1 diabetes. Participants ranged from 55 to 88 years of age at the time of neuropsychological testing.

Systolic and diastolic BP levels were assessed at biennial Examinations 4 through 15. Glucose status and diabetes were assessed from Examinations 1 through 15. A diagnosis of diabetes was positive if participants were more than 30 years of age when they met one of the following criteria: (a) treatment with insulin or oral hypoglycemic agents (b) a glucose tolerance test indicating a blood glucose concentration of >8.9 mmol/l at 1 hr after challenge and >7.8 mmol/l after 2 hr, (c) had two or more casual blood glucose levels of >8.3 mmol/l. Definite hypertension was defined as systolic BP >160 mm Hg or diastolic BP >95 mm Hg. Self-report data on number of cigarettes smoked per day was obtained at neuropsychological assessment. Covariates in the regression model included age, ounces of alcohol consumed per week, gender, lifetime occupation, education, treatment of hypertension, history of transient ischemic attack, and history of pre-existing CV disease (myocardial infarction, angina pectoris, intermittent claudication, and coronary insufficiency). Each predictor variable was controlled for each other predictor variable in the multivariate regression analyses.

To determine estimates of risk of "poor" neuropsychological test performance, each participant was assigned a score of 0 or 1 on each of the neuropsychological test scores depending on whether he or she performed at or below the 25th percentile (score = 1) or above the 25th percentile (score = 0) of the overall distribution of standardized (z) test scores.

We recalculated the ORs from the logistic regression coefficients presented by P. K. Elias et al. (1997) and created Table 5.2 in an effort to provide a general sense of the level of independent risk of lowered cognitive functioning associated with each risk factor. Table 5.2 shows ORs (estimates of risk) associated

TABLE 5.2

Adjusted Risk (Odds Ratios) of Performing At or Below the 25th Percentile
on the Framingham Neuropsychological Test Measures

Neuropsychological Test	Type 2 Diabetes[a]	DBP[b]	Cigarettes/ Day[c]	Age (Years)[a]
Composite Score	1.21**	1.30***	1.04	1.61****
Learning and Memory factor[d]	1.22**	1.25***	1.03	1.67****
Visual Reproductions[e]	1.17**	1.17*	1.06*	1.65****
Logical Memory–Immediate Recall[e]	1.24***	1.20**	1.07**	1.39****
Paired Associates Learning[e]	0.99	1.15	1.03	1.52****
Logical Memory–Delayed Recall[e]	1.19**	1.29***	1.09***	1.41****
Logical Memory–Retained	1.00	1.23***	1.00	1.31****
Controlled Oral Word Associations[e]	1.16*	1.23**	1.01	1.23****
Similarities[e]	1.19**	1.01	1.09**	1.44****
Attention and Concentration factor[f]	1.00	1.15	0.98	1.19****
Digit Span Forward[e]	1.06	1.11	1.00	1.18****
Digit Span Backward[e]	0.90	0.99	0.95	1.12***

Note. Covariates in the model included education, occupation, gender, alcohol consumption, previous history of cardiovascular disease, and antihypertensive treatment.

[a]5-year increments.   [b]10-mmHg increments.   [c]five-cigarette increments.   [d]Learning and Memory factor = (Visual Reproductions + Logical Memory–Immediate Recall + Paired Associates) /3.   [e]Measures used in composite score.   [f]Attention and Concentration factor = (Digit Span Forward + Digit Span Backward) /2.

*p < .10.   **p < .05.   ***p < .01.   ****p < .0001.

with performance below the 25th percentile. Risk is expressed, arbitrarily, as a function of 5-year increments in exposure to Type 2 diabetes, 10-mm Hg increments in diastolic BP, increments of 5 cigarettes per day, and 5-year increments in age. The data for age and cigarettes were calculated at the time of neuropsychological testing. BP was determined as the average of all diastolic BP measurements from Examinations 1 to 15. Duration of diabetes reflected the length of time the participant had been exposed to diabetes over the longitudinal study period (30 years). Clearly, for heuristic purposes, we are comparing "apples and oranges" with respect to the metrics and the time frame of the measurements. Yet it is clear that increasing chronological age was associated with lowered cognitive functioning for every dependent variable. Each 5-year increment in Type 2 diabetes was associated with increased risk for poorer performance with respect to Logical Memory–Immediate Recall, Logical Memory–Delayed Recall, Similarities, Visual Reproductions, the Learning and Memory Composite score, and the overall composite of test scores. Most importantly, the pattern of significant associations is very similar to that obtained when 10-mm Hg increments in diastolic BP was the predictor variable. Fewer significant associations were obtained for cigarette smoking, but smoking was associated with higher risk of poor cognitive performance for Logical Memory–Immediate Recall and Logical Memory–Delayed Recall scores.

Using Logical Memory–Immediate Recall as an example, it may be seen (Table 5.2) that for every 5 years of exposure to diabetes the risk of poor cognitive functioning was increased by 24% (OR = 1.24). For every 10-mm Hg increase in diastolic BP, the risk of poor cognitive performance was raised by 20%. Five cigarettes per day, at the time of neuropsychological testing, increased risk of poor performance by 7%. In contrast, every 5 years of age was related to a 39% increase in risk of poor cognitive performance.

As noted before, direct comparisons of the risk of poor performance associated with the various CV risk factors is made difficult by the fact that the scaling and the metric are different for each risk factor. However, examination of Table 5.2 reveals information with respect to the pattern of significant findings and conveys a sense of the importance of these findings in a large population. Although the risk of poor performance associated with each variable may appear very small, one must consider the increase in risk in terms of the wide range of values observed for the predictor variables (Table 5.2): diabetes exposure (0–30 years), diastolic BP (56–119 mm Hg), age (55–88 years), and number of cigarettes per day (0–60).

A RISK FACTOR SCALE

Previous studies of multiple CV risk factors and cognitive functioning have shown that the major risk factors (e.g., BP, diabetes, smoking) are related to poorer performance on many neuropsychological test measures (Desmond et al., 1993; P. K. Elias et al., 1997). These studies have included several risk factors in the same statistical model, and thus the independent contribution of each risk factor can be assessed while controlling for the other risk factors.

However, it also is important to evaluate the cumulative impact of multiple risk factors on various domains of cognitive functioning; that is, one must ask what the cumulative risk of poor cognitive performance is for persons with one, two, three, or more concurrent CV risk factors. M. F. Elias, Elias et al. (1998) addressed this question by using a simple scale that involved counting the number of risk factors. Four risk factors were selected for this analysis: hypertension, Type 2 diabetes, cigarette smoking, and obesity. Smoking was defined as self-report of smoking (yes–no), hypertension as systolic BP >140 mm Hg and/or a diastolic BP >90 mm Hg regardless of treatment, obesity as body mass index (weight/height) in excess of 29 kilograms per meter^2 (kg/m^2), and diabetes as use of an oral hypoglycemic agent or casual glucose level >200 mg/dL. Because total cholesterol level was unrelated to any of the neuropsychological test measures, and light and moderate levels of alcohol consumption were associated with higher levels of cognitive functioning for some measures, both were excluded as risk factors but included in the regression model as controls.

At each examination (4–15) participants received a score of 0, 1, 2, 3, or 4, depending on the number of risk factors present (0–4) from among the list of four target risk factors. From this scoring system two *independent* variables were derived: immediate risk and long-term risk. Immediate risk was determined by simply counting the number of risk factors present at the examination in which the neuropsychological test battery was completed (Examinations 14–15). Long-term risk was determined by calculating a mean risk factor score for each individual by dividing the number of risk factors per examination by the number of examinations. The *dependent* (outcome) variables were the test scores listed and defined in Table 5.1. The stroke- and dementia-free subsample of 55- to 88-year-old persons examined in the P. K. Elias et al. (1997) study were studied (*n* = 1,799). The risk factor surveillance period extended over 18 to 20 years prior to neuropsychological testing and included 11 biennial physical examinations. As in the previous study, statistical controls for pre-existing CV disease, alcohol consumption, age, education, occupation, and gender were used in the regression model.

A significant linear relationship between number of risk factors and lowering of performance level was observed when the full range of scores was used as the outcome measure: the number of risk factors and performance level were inversely related. M. F. Elias, Elias, et al. (1998) obtained estimates of risk of poor performance (ORs associated with performance in the lowest quartile) associated with each unit increase in the number of risk factors (i.e., 0–1, 1–2, 2–3, and 3–4), to evaluate the epidemiological importance of these findings. The relative risk of poor performance for each test measure for the long-term risk scale and the short-term scale is summarized in Table 5.3. It is clear (Table 5.3) that the relationships were stronger when the long-term risk scale was used. One cannot dismiss the relationships between cumulative risk and cognitive functioning as trivial. For example, for each increase in the number of risk factors the risk of performing in the lower quartile of the distribution of test scores for the Learning and Memory factor was increased by 39%.

Finally, the four risk factors were examined in the context of a multiple regression model in which each risk factor was entered separately into the model, along with the other covariates. Two findings emerged from this analysis: (a) the multivariate combination of CV risks, in contrast to the simple "counting scale," predicted only a small amount of additional variance in the neuropsychological test scores, and (b) the standardized weights assigned to each CV risk factor varied in relationship to the neuropsychological measure used. Table 5.4 shows a rank order of the CV risk factors in terms of their weights for each neuropsychological test measure. Diabetes was consistently assigned the highest weight, but hypertension received the second-highest weighting for most of the dependent variables.

TABLE 5.3
Adjusted Odds Ratios (ORs) and 95% Confidence Limits (95% CL) Associated
With Each Increment (0, 1, 2, 3, 4) in Number of Risk Factors

	At Testing[a]		Per Examination[b]	
Test	OR	95% CL	OR	95% CL
Composite score	1.23****	1.05–1.44	1.31****	1.08–1.58
Learning and Memory factor	1.32*****	1.15–1.53	1.39*****	1.16–1.68
Visual Reproductions	1.28*****	1.10–1.47	1.32*****	1.10–1.57
Logical Memory–Immediate	1.14	0.99–1.31	1.15	0.97–1.37
Paired Associate Learning	1.10	0.95–1.27	1.15	0.96–1.38
Logical Memory–Delayed	1.20**	1.05–1.38	1.29***	1.09–1.53
Controlled Oral Word Associations	1.11	0.95–1.27	1.23**	1.03–1.48
Similarities	1.11	0.95–1.29	1.13	0.93–1.48
Attention and Concentration factor	1.08	0.94–1.25	1.06	0.89–1.27

[a]Adjusted ORs and 95% CL associated with poor performance for each one-unit increment in the number of risk factors present at the neuropsychological examination (Examinations 14–15).
[b]Adjusted ORs and 95% CL associated with poor performance for each one-unit increment in the number of risk factors per examination (Examinations 1–15).
**$p < .05$. ***$p < .01$. ****$p < .001$. *****$p < .0001$.

TABLE 5.4
Rank Ordering by Standardized Regression Weights Assigned to the Four
Cardiovascular Risk Factors Based on Multiple Linear Regression Analyses

	Rank Order Highest (1) to Lowest (4) Weighting			
Test Score	1	2	3	4
Composite Score*	Diabetes	Hypertension	Obesity	Smoking
Learning and Memory Factor*	Diabetes	Hypertension	Obesity	Smoking
Visual Reproductions*	Diabetes	Hypertension	Smoking	Obesity
Logical Memory Immediate	Diabetes	Hypertension	Obesity	Smoking
Paired Associates Learning	Diabetes	Hypertension	Obesity	Smoking
Logical Memory Delayed*	Diabetes	Hypertension	Smoking	Obesity
Controlled Oral Word Associations*	Diabetes	Smoking	Obesity	Hypertension
Similarities	Smoking	Diabetes	Obesity	Hypertension
Attention and Concentration Factor	Diabetes	Hypertension	Smoking	Obesity

*Linear and logistic regression indicated statistically significant associations between the number of risk factors and cognitive functioning for this test measure.

MECHANISMS UNDERLYING
RISK-RELATED COGNITIVE DYSFUNCTION

It is clear from every chapter in this book that biological processes linking vascular risk factors to cognitive decline have not been identified directly, but many reasonable hypotheses have been advanced. For example, it has been argued that cognitive decline, in the presence of multiple risk factors, is mediated through the "mechanism of clinically silent stroke and may be the first sign of significant cerebrovascular disease" (Desmond et al., 1993, p. 162). However, mechanisms other than silent stroke must be considered. Models (M. F. Elias, 1998; M. F. Elias & Robbins, 1991; Waldstein, 1995; see also chap. 2 of this book) linking hypertension and lowered cognitive functioning have been proposed, including disturbed cerebral perfusion with impaired cerebral blood flow, impaired brain cell metabolism, cerebral infarction, cerebrovascular endothelial dysfunction, atherosclerotic vascular wall changes, and (in elderly adults) the presence of white matter lesions. Fluctuations in blood glucose and insulin levels, accompanied by subclinical electroencephalographic changes are potential mechanisms linking Type 2 diabetes to lowered cognitive functioning (Kalmijn, Feskens, Launer, Stijnen, & Kromhout, 1995). Increased carboxyhemoglobin and resultant tissue damage (Ganda, 1980) and nicotine-related vascular injury (Powell et al., 1997) may link cigarette smoking to lowered cognitive functioning. Cerebral lipid metabolism and atherogenic correlates of hypercholesterolemia are possible links between blood lipid levels and cognitive performance (see chap. 3). Generally, it seems likely that atherogenic mechanisms associated with vascular risk factors may play a significant role in lowering cognitive functioning for diabetes, hypertension, and cigarette smoking. Evidence in support of this hypothesis comes from studies (see chap. 7) indicating that peripheral vascular disease is related to lowered cognitive ability. Underlying mechanisms linking obesity with lowered levels of performance are less clear, although it is well known that obesity precipitates and exacerbates risk factors such as diabetes, hypercholesterolemia, and hypertension.

Some hypotheses with respect to the positive effect of moderate alcohol consumption on cognitive functioning are suggested by the literature on CHD. With respect to the reduction of CHD, several mechanisms have been identified in a recent review by P. Anderson (1998), including (a) increase in HDL levels in the blood and (b) antithrombotic effects, including decreased levels of platelet aggregation and plasma fibrinogen. Thus the protective effect on cognitive functioning may be mediated by means of reduction in the rate of atherogenesis. There is also some evidence that low levels of alcohol consumption may reduce the risk of nonhemorrhagic stroke (P. Anderson, 1998). However, the risk of hemorrhagic stroke may be increased even at low drinking levels (P. Anderson, 1998). As noted previously, more work is needed to identify psychosocial variables that may link moderate alcohol consumption with higher levels of cognitive functioning.

IMPORTANT AREAS FOR FUTURE RESEARCH

More attention has been paid to the adverse effects of high BP on cognitive functioning than to low BP. Relatively recent studies indicate that a fall in BP from previously higher levels results in decreased psychomotor speed (Swan, Carmelli, & Larue, 1998) and that low BP is associated with AD (Guo, Viitanen, Fratiglioni, & Winblad, 1996). It has been hypothesized that a positive association between lower BP and poorer performance exists by virtue of the fact that low systolic BP or a fall in systolic BP is associated with chronic diseases, including CHD (Guo, Winblad, & Vitanen, 1997; Swan et al., 1998). This is an important topic for further research given the negative consequences of a premature and erroneous conclusion that the current policy of aggressive lowering of systolic hypertension in the elderly has an adverse effect on cognitive functioning. Preliminary, unpublished analyses of our own data in the Maine–Syracuse longitudinal studies of hypertension and cognitive functioning indicate that treated individuals whose BP falls from previously high levels perform as well as normotensive individuals and do not exhibit hypertension-related comorbidity (Elias & Robbins, 1999).

In this chapter we have focused on major risk factors for CV disease, but other risk factors also have been the focus of studies relating CV risk to cognitive functioning. Low blood levels of folate and vitamin B12 and elevated homocysteine levels have been associated not only with AD (Clarke et al., 1998) but also with lowered cognitive performance in elderly individuals (K. M. Riggs, Spiro, Tucker, & Rush, 1996). More studies of the relationships between these risk factors and normal cognitive functioning are needed. Both for normal cognitive ability and the dementias, the major question is whether higher homocysteine levels and lower levels of folate and vitamin B12 are a cause or a consequence of lowered cognitive ability.

Rosenberg et al. (1985) have reported that female smokers who use oral contraceptives are at 20 times the risk of CHD than female nonsmokers who do not use oral contraceptives. We are unaware of any studies relating the cumulative risk of smoking and use of oral contraception to cognitive functioning.

Apolipoprotein ε4 (ApoE-ε4) allele is a risk factor not only for AD but also for cognitive decline within generally normal limits (Brayne et al., 1996; Budge et al., in press; Henderson et al., 1995; Reed et al., 1994) and in the absence of dementia (Small, Basun, & Bäckman, 1998). The need for studies that examine the impact of CV risk factors on cognitive functioning in the presence of the ApoE ε4 allele is particularly great. Recently, Haan, Shemanski, Jagust, Manolio, and Kuller (1999) reported a study in which they followed 5,888 Medicare-eligible individuals for 5 to 7 years retrospectively. Measures of subclinical cerebrovascu-lar risk factors were modest predictors of cognitive decline longitudinally. How-ever, individuals with the ApoE ε4 allele in combination with atherosclerosis, peripheral vascular disease, or diabetes mellitus were at substantially higher risk of cognitive decline compared to individuals who did not have the ApoE ε4 allele or who did not exhibit subclinical CAD. The measures of test performance were limited to the modified Mini-Mental State Examination and the Digit Sym-bol Substitution test. Although Haan et al. examined an impressively large sam-ple, further studies with more comprehensive neuropsychological test batteries should yield useful information with respect to which specific cognitive abilities are adversely affected by the simultaneous presence of the ApoE ε4 allele and one or more of the traditional CV risk factors.

It is now well known that hard-driving aggressiveness, hostility, depression, anxiety, anger, social isolation, low social support, low socioeconomic status, marital stress, and job stress (Muir, 1998) represent social psychological risk fac-tors for CV disease and that the lethal mechanisms include increases in BP, blood cholesterol (Muir, 1998), and sympathetic and CV responses (Suarez, Kuhn, Schanberg, Williams, & Zimmerman, 1998). We need a systematic series of studies that examine the cumulative impact of both biological–CV risk factors and psychosocial–CV risk factors on cognitive performance.

CLINICAL SIGNIFICANCE

The central theme in this chapter has been the epidemiological significance of the impact of CV risk factors on cognitive functioning. We addressed the fol-lowing question: What is the impact of the presence of one or multiple CV risk factors with respect to populations of individuals? We see from Tables 5.2 and 5.3 and from chapters 2, 3, and 4 that the risk for individuals most often is not as-sociated with the low levels of functioning seen, for example, among patients with vascular dementia or AD. This does not imply that the risk of poor cogni-tive performance will be trivial in all cases; neither does it suggest that even small changes in cognitive functioning will be meaningless to individual patients. Even modest changes in cognitive functioning have an adverse effect on quality of life in this highly competitive and technical society.

On the other hand, reduction of risk in large populations would make a sub-stantial impact on preservation of a valuable national resource: cognitive ability. For each risk factor present at neuropsychological testing (Table 5.3), the risk of a lower level of performance (performance at or below the 25th percentile) on the composite score increased by 23 percent. However, elimination, attenua-tion, or prevention of a single risk factor would have a major impact on preserv-ing cognitive functioning in a large population.

SUMMARY

It has become increasingly clear that hypertension, diabetes, and cigarette smoking are risk factors for lowered cognitive functioning. The roles of obesity and high cholesterol levels in lowered cognitive functioning are less clear, but initial findings support the need for more, and better, studies. Most importantly, the risk of lowered cognitive functioning is increased in direct relationship to the number of CV risk factors present—that is, more risk, more deficit. Risk factors such as diabetes and hypertension have adverse synergistic effects on cognitive ability. It is our experience that patients take losses of cognitive functioning, even minor losses, very seriously, which is a reasonable concern in this competitive society. Thus, physicians can offer yet another incentive for adherence to prescriptions for prevention and treatment: Reduce CV risk factors to preserve the highest possible level of cognitive functioning over the life span.

ACKNOWLEDGMENT

This research was supported, in part, by Research Grants 5R37 AG0355, 5R01 AG08122–09, and K01-AG00646–05 from the National Institute on Aging and the National Insitutes of Health (NIH), Research Grant NS17950–16 from NIH/NINDS, Research Grant R01 HL65177–01 from the National Heart, Lung and Blood Institute (NHLBI/NIH), and Research Contract NIH/NHKBU B01-HC 38038 from NIH.

We wish to express our appreciation to Dr. Marc Budge of Oxford University and Dr. Shari Waldstein of the University of Maryland for their constructive and helpful suggestions with respect to this chapter.

REFERENCES

Anderson, P. (1998). Alcohol. In M. Lawrence, A. Neil, D. Mant, & G. Fowler (Eds.), *Prevention of cardiovascular disease: An evidence based approach* (pp. 81–93). Oxford, England: Oxford University Press.

Brayne, C., Harrington, C. R., Wischik, C. M., Huppert, F. A., Chi, L. Y., Xuereb, J. H., O'Connor, D. W., & Paykel, E. S. (1996). Apolipoprotein E genotype in the prediction of cognitive decline and dementia in a prospectively studied elderly population. *Dementia, 7*, 169–174.

Budge, M., Johnston, E., Hogervorst, C., de Jager, E., Milwain, S. D., Iversen, L., Barnetson, L., King, E., & Smith, A. D. (in press). Plasma total homocysteine and cognitive performance in a volunteer elderly population. *Annals of the New York Academy of Science.*

Clarke, R., Smith, A. D., Jobst, K. A., Refsum, H., Sutton, L., & Ueland, P. M. (1998). Folate, vitamin B-12, and serum total homocysteine levels in confirmed Alzheimer disease. *Archives of Neurology, 55*, 1449–1455.

Desmond, D. W., Tatemichi, T. K., Paik, M., & Stern, Y. (1993). Risk factors for cerebrovascular disease as correlates of cognitive function in a stroke-free cohort. *Archives of Neurology, 50,* 162–166.

Dufouil, C., Ducimetière, P., & Alpèrovitch, A. (1997). Sex differences in the association between alcohol consumption and cognitive performance. *American Journal of Epidemiology, 146,* 405–412.

Elias, M. F. (1998). Effects of chronic hypertension on cognitive functioning. *Geriatrics, 53* (Suppl. 1), S49–S52.

Elias, M. F., Elias, P. K., D'Agostino, R. B., Silbershatz, H., & Wolf, P. A. (1998, November). *Cardiovascular risk impacts negatively on cognitive ability: More risk, more deficit: The Framingham Study.* Paper presented at the 71st Scientific Sessions of the American Heart Association, Dallas, TX. November 9, 1998. Abstract 492, *Circulation, 98* (Suppl.), I-97.

Elias, M. F., Elias, P. K., D'Agostino, R. B., Silbershatz, H., & Wolf, P. A. (1997). Role of age, education, and gender on cognitive performance in the Framingham Heart Study: Community-based norms. *Experimental Aging Research, 23,* 201–235.

Elias M. F., & Robbins, M. A. (1991). Cardiovascular disease, hypertension and cognitive function. In A. P. Shapiro & A. Baum (Eds.), *Perspectives in behavioral medicine* (pp. 249–285). Hillsdale, NJ: Lawrence Erlbaum Associates.

Elias, M. F., & Robbins, M. A. (1999). [Cognitive performance in relation to longitudinal fall in blood pressure]. Unpublished raw data.

Elias, M. F., Robbins, M. A., & Elias, P. K. (1996). A 15-year longitudinal study of Halstead–Reitan neuropsychological test performance. *Journal of Gerontology: Psychological Sciences, 51B,* P331–P334.

Elias, M. F., Robbins, M. A., Elias, P. K., & Streeten, D. H. P. (1998a, November). *Cognitive ability declines as a function of blood pressure level.* Paper presented at the 71st Scientific Sessions of the American Heart Association, Dallas, TX. November 11, 1998. Abstract 4512, *Circulation, 98* (Suppl.), I860.

Elias, M. F., Robbins, M. A., Elias, P. K., & Streeten, D. H. P. (1998b). A longitudinal study of blood pressure in relation to performance on the Wechsler Adult Intelligence Scale. *Health Psychology, 17,* 486–493.

Elias, M. F., Robbins, M. A., Schultz, N. R., Jr., & Pierce, T. W. (1990). Is blood pressure an important variable in research on aging and neuropsychological test performance? *Journal of Gerontology: Psychological Sciences, 45,* P128–P135.

Elias, M. F., Wolf, P. A., D'Agostino, R. B., Cobb, J., & White, L. R. (1993). Untreated blood pressure level is inversely related to cognitive functioning: The Framingham Study. *American Journal of Epidemiology, 138,* 353–364.

Elias, P. K., D'Agostino, R. B., Elias, M. F., & Wolf, P. A. (1995). Blood pressure, hypertension, and age as risk factors for poor cognitive performance. *Experimental Aging Research, 21,* 393–417.

Elias, P. K., Elias, M. F., D'Agostino, R. B., Cupples, L. A., Wilson, P. W., Silbershatz, H., & Wolf, P. A. (1997). NIDDM and blood pressure as risk factors for poor cognitive performance. *Diabetes Care, 20,* 1388–1395.

Elias, P. K., Elias, M. F., D'Agostino, R. B., Silbershatz, H., & Wolf, P. A. (1999). Alcohol consumption and cognitive performance in the Framingham Heart Study. *American Journal of Epidemiology, 150,* 580–589.

Expert Panel. (1994). National Cholesterol Education Program Second Report: The expert panel on detection, evaluation, and treatment of high blood cholesterol in adults (Adult Treatment Panel II). *Circulation, 89,* 1333–1445.

Farmer, M. E., White, L. R., Abbott, R. D., Kittner, S. J., Kaplan, E., Wolz, M. M., Brody, J. A., & Wolf, P. A. (1987). Blood pressure and cognitive performance: The Framingham Study. *American Journal of Epidemiology, 126,* 1103–1114.

Farmer, M. E., White, L. R., Kittner, S. J., Kaplan, E., Moes, E., McNamara, P., Wolz, M. M., Wolf, P. A., & Feinleib, M. (1987). Neuropsychological test performance in Framingham: A descriptive study. *Psychological Reports, 60,* 1023–1040.

Fowler, G. (1998). Smoking. In M. Lawrence, N. Andrew, D. Mant, & G. Fowler (Eds.), *Prevention of cardiovascular disease* (pp. 3–17). New York: Oxford University Press.

Galanis, D. J., Petrovitch, H., Launer, L. J., Harris, T. B., Foley, D. J., & White, L. R. (1997). Smoking history in middle age and subsequent cognitive performance in elderly Japanese-American men. *American Journal of Epidemiology, 145*, 507–515.

Ganda, O. P. (1980). Pathogenesis of macorvascular disease in human diabetics. *Diabetes, 29*, 931–932.

Gordon, T., & Kannel, W. B. (1982). Multiple risk functions for predicting coronary heart disease: The concept, accuracy, and application. *American Heart Journal, 103*, 1031–1039.

Gordon, T., & Kannel, W. B. (1983). Drinking and its relation to smoking, BP, blood lipids, and uric acid: The Framingham Study. *Archives of Internal Medicine, 143*, 1366–1374.

Guo, Z., Viitanen, M., Fratiglioni, L., & Winblad, B. (1996). Low blood pressure and dementia in elderly people: The Kungsholmen project. *British Medical Journal, 312*, 805–808.

Guo, Z,, Winblad, B., & Vitanen, M. (1997). Clinical correlates of low blood pressure in very old people: The importance of cognitive impairment. *Journal of the American Geriatric Society, 45*, 701–705.

Haan, M. N., Shemanski, L., Jagust, W. J., Manolio, T. A., & Kuller, L. (1999). The role of ApoE e4 in modulating effects of other risk factors for cognitive decline in elderly persons. *Journal of American Medical Association, 282*, 40–46.

Henderson, A. S., Easteal, S., Jorm, A. F., Mackinnon, A. J., Korten, A. E., Christensen, H., Croft, L., & Jacomb, P. A. (1995). Apolipoprotein E allele epsilon 4, dementia, and cognitive decline in a population sample. *The Lancet, 346*, 1387–1390.

Hendrie, H. C., Gao, S., Hall, K. S., Hui, S. L., & Unverzagt, F. W. (1996). The relationship between alcohol consumption, cognitive performance, and daily functioning in an urban sample of older Black Americans. *Journal of the American Geriatrics Society, 44*, 1158–1165.

Hosmer, D. W., & Lemeshow, S. L. (1989). *Applied logistic regression* (pp. 56–63). New York: Wiley.

Kalmijn, S., Feskens, E. J. M., Launer, L. J., Stijen, T., & Kromhout, D. (1995). Glucose intolerance, hyperinsulinemia and cognitive function in a general population of elderly men. *Diabetologia, 38*, 1096–1102.

Kannel, W. B., Dawber, T. R., Kagan, A., Revotski, N., & Stokes, J., III. (1961). Factors of risk in the development of coronary heart disease—Six-year follow-up experience: The Framingham Study. *Annals of Internal Medicine, 55*, 33–50.

Kannel, W. B., & Sytkowski, P. A. (1987). Atherosclerosis risk factors. *Pharmacology and Therapeutics, 32*, 207–235.

Launer, L. J., Feskens, E. J. M., Kalmijn, S., & Kromhout, D. (1996). Smoking, drinking, and thinking: The Zutphen Elderly Study. *American Journal of Epidemiology, 143*, 219–227.

Launer, L. J., Masaki, K., Petrovitch, H., Foley, D., & Havlick, R. J. (1995). The association between midlife blood pressure levels and late life cognitive functioning. *Journal of the American Medical Association, 274*, 1841–1851.

Lawrence, M., & Cruickshank, K. (1998). Hypertension. In M. Lawrence, A. Neil, D. Mant, & G. Fowler (Eds.), *Prevention of cardiovascular disease* (pp. 18–34). Oxford, England: Oxford University Press.

Letenneur, L., Dartigues, J. F., Commenges, D., Barberger-Gateau, P., Tessier, J. F., & Orgogozo, J. M. (1994). Tobacco consumption and cognitive impairment in elderly people: A population-based study. *Annals of Epidemiology, 4*, 449–454.

Mann, J. (1998). Diabetes. In M. Lawrence, A. Neil, D. Mant, & G. Fowler (Eds.), *Prevention of cardiovascular disease* (pp 105–119). Oxford, England: Oxford University Press.

Muir, J. (1998). Personality and psychological environment. In M. Lawrence, A. Neil, D. Mant, & G. Fowler (Eds.), *Prevention of cardiovascular disease* (pp. 93–105). Oxford, England: Oxford University Press.

Neil, A. (1998). Lipids and lipoproteins. In M. Lawrence, A. Neil, D. Mant, & G. Fowler (Eds.), *Prevention of cardiovascular disease* (pp. 35–53). Oxford, England: Oxford University Press.

Powell, L. T., Edwards, R. J., Worell, P. C., Franks, P. J., Greenhalgh, R. M., & Poulter, N. R. (1997). Risk factors associated with the development of peripheral vascular disease in smokers: A case control study. *Atherosclerosis, 129*, 41–48.

Reed, T., Carmelli, D., Swan, G. E., Breitner, J. C., Welsh, K. A., Jarvik, G. P., Deeb, S., & Auwerx, J. (1994). Lower cognitive performance in normal older adult male twins carrying the apolipoprotein E epsilon 4 allele. *Archives of Neurology, 51,* 1189–1192.

Riggs, J. E. (1993). Smoking and Alzheimer's disease: Protective effect or differential survival bias? *The Lancet, 342,* 793–794.

Riggs, K. M., Spiro, A., Tucker, K., & Rush, D. (1996). Relations of vitamin B-12, vitamin B-6, folate, and homocysteine to cognitive performance in the Normative Aging Study. *American Journal of Clinical Nutrition, 63,* 306–314.

Robbins, M. A., Elias, M. F., Croog, S. H., & Colton, T. (1994). Unmedicated blood pressure levels and quality of life in elderly hypertensive women. *Psychosomatic Medicine, 56,* 251–259.

Rosenberg, L., Kaufman, D. W., Helmrich, S. P., Miller, D. R., Stolley, P. D., & Shapiro, S. (1985). Myocardial infarction and cigarette smoking in women younger than 50 years of age. *Journal of the American Medical Association, 253,* 2965–2969.

Scherr, P. A., Albert, M. S., Funkenstein, H. H., Cook, N. R., Hennekens, C. H., Branch, L. G., White, L. R., Taylor, J. O., & Evans, D. A. (1988). Correlates of cognitive function in an elderly community population. *American Journal of Epidemiology, 128,* 1084–1101.

Small, B., Basun, H., & Bäckman, L. (1998). Three-year changes in cognitive performance as a function of Apolipoprotein E genotype: Evidence from very old adults without dementia. *Psychology and Aging, 13,* 80–87.

Steptoe, A., & Wardle, J. (1992). Cognitive predictors of health behaviour in contrasting regions of Europe. *British Journal of Clinical Psychology, 31,* 485–502.

Strachan, M. W. J., Deary, I. J., Ewing, F. M. E., & Frier, B. M. (1997). Is Type II diabetes associated with an increased risk of cognitive dysfunction? *Diabetes Care, 20,* 438–445.

Suarez, E. C., Kuhn, C. M., Schanberg, S. M., Williams, R. B., & Zimmerman, E. A. (1998). Neuroendocrine, cardiovascular and emotional responses of hostile men: The role of interpersonal challenge. *Psychosomatic Medicine, 60,* 78–88.

Swan, G. E., Carmelli, D., & LaRue, A. (1996). The relationship between blood pressure during middle age and cognitive impairment in old age: The Western Collaborative Group Study. *Aging, Neuropsychology, and Cognition, 3,* 1–11.

Swan, G. E., Carmelli, D., & LaRue, A. (1998). Systolic blood pressure tracking over 25 to 30 years and cognitive performance in older adults. *Stroke, 29,* 2334–2340.

Waldstein, S. (1995). Hypertension and neuropsychological function: A lifespan perspective. *Experimental Aging Research, 21,* 321–352.

Wilson, P. W. F., Castelli, W. P., & Kannel, W. B. (1987). Coronary risk prediction in adults: The Framingham Heart Study. *American Journal of Cardiology, 59,* 91–94.

Wilson, P. W. F., D'Agostino, R. B., Levy, D., Belanger, A. M., Silbershatz, H., & Kannel, W. B. (1998). Prediction of coronary heart disease using risk factor categories. *Circulation, 97,* 1837–1847.

Wolf, P. A. (1993). Lewis A. Connor lecture: Contributions of epidemiology to the prevention of stroke. *Circulation, 88,* 2471–2478.

Wolf, P. A., D'Agostino, R. B., Belanger, A. J., & Kannel, W. B. (1991). Probability of stroke: A risk factor profile from the Framingham Study. *Stroke, 22,* 312–318.

CHAPTER SIX

Atherosclerosis and Cognitive Functioning

SUSAN A. EVERSON
University of Michigan School of Public Health

EEVA-LIISA HELKALA
University of Kuopio, Kuopio, Finland

GEORGE A. KAPLAN
University of Michigan School of Public Health

JUKKA T. SALONEN
University of Kuopio, Kuopio, Finland

It is well recognized that the incidence and severity of cognitive impairment and dementia increase with age (Graham et al., 1997; Ritchie & Kildea, 1995). However, aging does not inevitably lead to cognitive decline, although subtle changes in cognitive function may occur with age (Rapp & Amaral, 1992). An expanding literature indicates that both subtle alterations in cognition and more severe deficits may be associated with hypertension, atherosclerosis, and other cardiovascular (CV) diseases or risk factors (Breteler, Claus, Grobbee, & Hofman, 1994; M. F. Elias, Wolf, D'Agostino, Cobb, & White, 1993; Haan, Shemanski, Jagust, Manolio, & Kuller, 1999; Launer, Feskens, Kalmijn, & Kromhout, 1996; Waldstein, Manuck, Ryan, & Muldoon, 1991). The purpose of this chapter is to review the available evidence linking atherosclerosis and cognitive impairment and decline.

This chapter is divided into five sections. We begin by briefly discussing the pathophysiology of atherosclerosis, including clinical manifestations of the disease and three hypotheses about the initiation of atherogenesis. Then we discuss some epidemiological aspects of atherosclerosis, including current statistics regarding prevalence of atherosclerosis and risk factors for atherosclerosis. Next, we discuss cross-sectional and longitudinal evidence for an association between atherosclerosis and poorer cognitive functioning. We proceed to a discussion of potential mechanisms underlying the associations between atherosclerosis and cognitive function, which is followed by a discussion of the clinical relevance of these associations. We conclude with an overall summary and suggestions for future research.

PATHOPHYSIOLOGY OF ATHEROSCLEROSIS

Atherosclerosis is a disease of the arteries in which the lumen of the artery becomes narrowed by fatty deposits and fibrous tissue that accumulate on the intimal layer of the vessel wall. Atherosclerotic lesions originate as fatty streaks, characterized by subendothelial accumulation of large foam cells that are derived from macrophages and consist of intracellular lipids. Fatty streaks typically develop early in life and can be found in the coronary arteries and aorta of most people by age 20. The more advanced atherosclerotic lesions, fibrous plaques, develop from the fatty streaks and often contain a necrotic core of degenerating foam cells, cholesterol crystals, and cellular debris separated from the arterial lumen by a fibrous cap of connective tissue. Fibrous plaques are found, in order of frequency, in the abdominal aorta, coronary arteries, popliteal arteries, descending thoracic aorta, internal carotid arteries, and the circle of Willis (Bhattacharyya & Libby, 1998). It is not uncommon for plaques to occur in multiple locations or at multiple arterial sites. In other words, atherosclerosis tends to co-occur in the coronary, carotid, cerebral, and peripheral arteries. Atherosclerotic plaques typically develop gradually and go unnoticed until clinical symptoms develop.

Clinical manifestations or complications of atherosclerosis may result from fibrous plaques in several ways. For example, fibrous plaques may become calcified, thereby increasing the rigidity of the blood vessel and making the blood vessel more fragile. In addition, fibrous plaques are prone to rupture or ulceration and thus may induce thrombosis that can occlude the vessel and lead to myocardial infarction or stroke. Hemorrhage into the plaque may occur if the fibrous cap or any of the capillaries that vascularize the plaque ruptures. The resulting hematoma may further narrow the lumen of the artery and obstruct blood flow. Emboli may occur at distal sites if atherosclerotic plaques become fragmented. Finally, vessel walls become weakened from plaque formation, thus increasing the likelihood of aneurysm formation and rupture. Complications of atherosclerosis include ischemia, angina pectoris, myocardial infarction, stroke, and claudication (Bhattacharyya & Libby, 1998).

The pathophysiologic characteristics of atherosclerosis have long been known, whereas the mechanisms by which atherosclerosis develops are less completely understood. Three important hypotheses about the core processes or mechanisms related to the initiation of atherogenesis have been postulated, and each has supporting evidence. Endothelial denudation, activation, or injury are considered the initiating event(s) in the *response-to-injury* hypothesis, oxidation of lipoproteins is thought to be the primary event in the *lipoprotein oxidation* hypothesis, and subendothelial retention of lipoproteins is considered the initiating event in the *response-to-retention* hypothesis. Regardless of the initiating event, it is recognized that several important steps or components are involved in atherogenesis, including involvement of the smooth-muscle cells and endothelial cells of the vessel wall, accumulation of lipoproteins, circulating platelets and monocytes, and cytokine mediation (Ross, 1993).

Several lines of evidence suggest that the primary event in atherogenesis is injury to the arterial endothelium and thus support the *response-to-injury* hypothesis (Ross, 1993; Ross & Glomset, 1976a, 1976b; Ross, Glomset, & Harker, 1977). Large shear stress gradients and fluid mechanical forces can induce morphological and functional changes in the endothelium (DePaola, Gimbrone, Davies, & Dewey, 1992; Dewey, Bussolari, Gimbrone, & Davies, 1981). Areas susceptible to flow turbulence and shear stress—for example, at arterial branch points such as the carotid bifurcation—are where most advanced atherosclerotic lesions occur (Asakura & Karino, 1990; DePaola et al., 1992). In addition, animal studies indicate that atheromatous lesions develop in response to injury to the endothelium (J. R. Kaplan, Pettersson, Manuck, & Olsson, 1991), and several known risk factors for atherosclerosis (e.g., cigarette smoking, high cholesterol, diabetes, and hypertension) are associated with endothelial dysfunction (Ross, 1993; Vogel, 1997). Research also has found a link between infectious agents such as cytomegalovirus, herpesvirus, and chlamydia pneumoniae and atherosclerosis, suggesting that the development of atherosclerotic lesions may be part of an infectious process that damages the endothelium (Nieto, 1998; Nieto et al., 1997). Further support for the role of infection in atherosclerosis comes from the observation that fatty streaks, the earliest type of atherosclerotic lesion seen in children and adolescents, consist only of T lymphocytes and monocyte-derived macrophages (Ross, 1999).

Oxidative modification of low-density lipoprotein (LDL) or other lipoproteins also is involved in the pathogenesis of atherosclerosis and is thought by some to be the primary or initiating event (Salonen et al., 1992; Witztum, 1994; Witztum & Steinberg, 1991). This is called the *lipoprotein oxidation hypothesis* of atherosclerosis. Oxidized LDL is necessary for cellular accumulation of cholesterol and uptake of macrophages (Berliner et al., 1995). Additionally, lipid peroxidation, which occurs primarily in the intimal layer of the arteries, generates a variety of biologically active substances that can have diverse biochemical, hormonal, and immunologic effects that are proatherogenic (Berliner et al., 1995; Witztum, 1994). Lipid peroxidation, mediated by free radicals, may induce endothelial injury or dysfunction, enhance platelet aggregation, and increase uptake of LDL into the arterial walls (Hennig & Chow, 1988).

It also has been argued that subendothelial retention of atherogenic lipoproteins is the primary pathogenic process in atherosclerosis and is both necessary and sufficient for the development of atherosclerotic lesions (Guyton & Klemp, 1996; Simionescu & Simionescu, 1993; Williams & Tabas, 1995). Support for this *response-to-retention* hypothesis derives largely from animal studies, which demonstrate substantial and rapid accumulation and retention of atherogenic lipoproteins within the arterial walls following induction of hypercholesterolemia and in prelesional focal arterial sites susceptible to atheromatous lesions (Nievelstein, Fogelman, Mottino, & Frank, 1991; Schwenke & Carew, 1989a, 1989b). Support also comes from the observation that the core of atherosclerotic plaques, which consists of extracellular lipids that are rich in free cholesterol—including oxidized LDL, proteins, and peptides—can be found in fatty streaks in the human aorta in the very early stages of lesion development and prior to formation of fibrous plaques (Guyton & Klemp, 1996).

EPIDEMIOLOGY OF ATHEROSCLEROSIS

CV diseases, including hypertension, coronary heart disease (CHD), stroke, atherosclerosis, congestive heart failure, rheumatic fever and rheumatic heart disease, congenital heart defects, and arrhythmias, are the leading causes of death for men and women in the United States and most westernized countries. In 1996 more than 959,000 deaths in the United States were attributed to one or more CV diseases, accounting for more than 41% of all deaths; of these, 50% were attributed to CHD and 2% were attributed to atherosclerosis (American Heart Association [AHA], 1998). It is critical to note, however, that atherosclerosis is the underlying disease process for the vast majority of CHD and thus can be considered the leading cause of death in the United States. The prevalence of CHD among American adults over the age of 20 is 7.2% for the general population (AHA, 1998), with an estimated 12 million Americans alive today who have a history of CHD or atherosclerosis.

Several risk factors for atherosclerosis or CHD have been identified. These include biological and disease-related factors, such as diabetes, hypertension, hypercholesterolemia, homocysteine, and Lp(a); demographic factors, such as older age and lower socioeconomic status; and behavioral and psychosocial factors, such as smoking, sedentary lifestyle, diet, obesity, and stress (Marmot & Elliott, 1992). Research shows that many of these risk factors are related to both the prevalence and incidence of atherosclerosis in the population as well as to accelerated progression of the disease over time. Moreover, the prevalence of certain risk factors—for example, physical inactivity and obesity—appears to be increasing and represents a growing threat to the health of populations (AHA, 1998).

LITERATURE REVIEW AND METHODOLOGIC CRITIQUE

Several recent studies have examined the impact of atherosclerosis or risk factors for atherosclerosis on cognitive performance and neuropsychological functioning. To date, much of the evidence for such an association comes from cross-sectional studies, although some prospective evidence is now available. The present lack of prospective or cohort studies is partly due to the fact that until relatively recently it was difficult to reliably assess the extent and severity of atherosclerosis without invasive procedures. However, advances in ultrasonography have allowed scientists and clinicians to noninvasively measure atherosclerosis in certain arterial beds and in the carotid arteries in particular. Indeed, much of the evidence reviewed next comes from studies in which atherosclerosis in the carotid arteries was measured noninvasively. It should be noted that research and clinical data have shown that carotid atherosclerosis is a reliable marker of the atherosclerotic process throughout the body, including the coronary arteries (Grobbee & Bots, 1994; Salonen & Salonen, 1991; Wong, Edelstein, Wollman, & Bond, 1993).

Cross-Sectional Findings

G. A. Kaplan, Everson, Koivisto, Salonen, and Salonen (1996) reported that mild to moderate carotid atherosclerosis is significantly related to poorer cognitive performance in a subset of more than 500 participants from the Kuopio Ischemic Heart Disease Risk Factor Study (Salonen, 1988), an ongoing epidemiologic investigation of risk factors for ischemic heart disease and associated morbidity and mortality in a population-based sample of middle-aged men. These men completed a series of five brief neuropsychological tests as part of a follow-up examination, and carotid atherosclerosis was assessed noninvasively using B-mode ultrasonography of the right and left common carotid arteries (CCA). Measures of carotid atherosclerosis included mean intimal–medial thickness (IMT) of the CCA, the mean of approximately 100 measurements in the right and left CCA, considered a measure of the overall atherosclerotic process in the carotid arteries, and maximal IMT, the average of the points of maximum thickness from the right and left CCA and indicative of the depth of intrusion of atherosclerotic thickening into the lumen in this part of the arteries.

Age-adjusted regression models revealed that mean and maximum atherosclerotic thickening were significantly associated with lower scores on the Mini Mental State Examination (MMSE; Folstein, Folstein, & McHugh, 1975), a measure of overall cognitive abilities; Russell's adaptation of the Visual Reproduction Test–Immediate Recall (Lezak, 1983), a test of nonverbal memory; the Trail Making Test, Form B (Trails B; Reitan, 1958), a measure of cognitive flexibility and frontal lobe functioning; a verbal fluency test on letters (Borkowski,

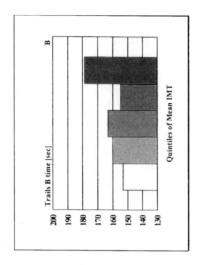

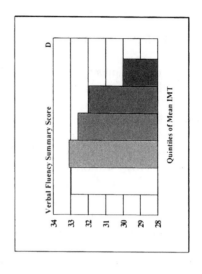

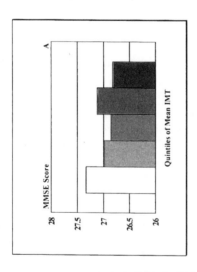

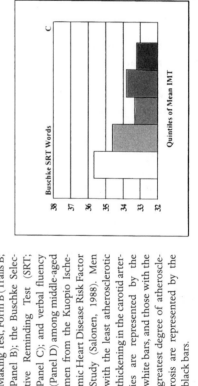

FIG. 6.1. Quintiles of atherosclerosis, assessed as intimal–
medial thickness (IMT) of the
common carotid arteries, and
age-adjusted performance on
the Mini-Mental State Exam
(MMSE; Panel A); the Trail
Making Test, Form B (Trails B;
Panel B); the Buschke Selective Reminding Test (SRT;
Panel C); and verbal fluency
(Panel D) among middle-aged
men from the Kuopio Ischemic Heart Disease Risk Factor
Study (Salonen, 1988). Men
with the least atherosclerotic
thickening in the carotid arteries are represented by the
white bars, and those with the
greatest degree of atherosclerosis are represented by the
black bars.

Benton, & Spreen, 1967); and the Buschke Selective Reminding Test (SRT; Buschke & Fuld, 1974), a measure of short- and long-term verbal memory. Results for the MMSE, Trails B, Buschke SRT, and verbal fluency test are shown in Fig. 6.1 (Panels A–D). Data are graphed by quintiles of mean IMT, and there is a clear pattern of worsening performance from individuals with the least disease (represented by the white bars) to those with the most atherosclerosis (represented by the black bars) across the four neuropsychological tests. The pattern of observed findings suggests an involvement of atherosclerotic processes in cognitive functioning, even at a relatively young age (the mean age of the participants in this study was 56.9 years).

Several other studies also provide cross-sectional evidence for an association between poorer cognitive function and atherosclerosis. Auperin et al. (1996) reported modest inverse associations between carotid atherosclerosis and poorer cognitive performance in a community sample of approximately 500 French men, ages 59 to 71. After adjusting for vascular risk factors, the prevalence of atherosclerotic plaques in the carotid arteries, assessed ultrasonographically, was inversely related to performance on the MMSE (Folstein et al., 1975) and the Digit Symbol Substitution test from the Wechsler Adult Intelligence Scale–Revised (WAIS–R; Wechsler, 1981), a measure of visual–motor speed and attention and concentration. In men with evidence of carotid plaques, poorer cognitive performance was modestly related to greater atherosclerotic thickening in the carotid arteries. However, no associations between atherosclerosis and cognitive performance were noted among the more than 700 female participants in this study. Auperin et al. reported that this study cohort was better educated and had higher cognitive scores than the general age-matched French population, and thus participation was probably selective. Nonetheless, the pattern of findings indicates consistent mild decrements in cognitive function in men with more numerous atherosclerotic plaques.

Similarly, a recent report from the Atherosclerosis Risk in Communities (ARIC) study found that the WAIS–R Digit Symbol Substitution test (Wechsler, 1981) was inversely related to ultrasonographically assessed IMT of the carotid arteries in a sample of nearly 14,000 middle-aged men and women without a history of stroke or transient ischemic attacks (Cerhan et al., 1998). Performance on the Digit Symbol test also was negatively related to fibrinogen level, smoking, and depressive symptoms in both sexes. In women, IMT also was related to performance on the Delayed Word Recall Test (Knopman & Ryberg, 1989), a measure of long-term memory, but the association became nonsignificant in the multivariate model. In this study the differences in performance on the tests of cognitive function between participants with the least carotid wall thickness (bottom quintile of the distribution) and those with the greatest carotid wall thickness (top quintile) were quite small (on average, between 0.1 and 0.2 SD) and thus, as the authors noted, may not necessarily lead to clinically meaningful deficits with age.

Additional, albeit indirect, evidence for the role of atherosclerosis in cognitive function comes from studies of peripheral vascular disease (PVD; for a review, see chap. 7). For example, Breteler and colleagues (1994) reported that participants in the Rotterdam Study with an ankle–brachial index of less than 0.90, an accepted clinical indicator of PVD, or those with ultrasonographically measured plaque in the internal carotid arteries, had worse cognitive performance, as assessed by the MMSE and after adjustment for age and education, than their counterparts without significant PVD. Breteler et al. importantly noted that although absolute differences in MMSE scores between groups were small and of unknown clinical significance, they reflected an overall shift in the population toward lower levels of cognitive functioning and thus resulted in a higher proportion of participants who met the criteria for dementia. In other words, these data demonstrate that atherosclerosis may account for a considerable proportion of cognitive impairment at the population level.

Another study of elderly patients with PVD but without a history of stroke or clinically evident cerebrovascular disease identified neuropsychological deficits consistent with mild vascular-related brain dysfunction (Phillips & Mate-Kole, 1997). This study compared 29 PVD patients with 29 age- and education-matched patients with documented atherothrombotic cerebral infarcts and 13 healthy elderly control participants, also matched on age and education. PVD patients performed significantly worse than controls on tests of executive function, learning and memory, attention and concentration, and visuospatial and constructional ability. Performance was worse with increasing severity of peripheral atherosclerosis and prevalent ischemic heart disease, suggesting that multiple manifestations of atherosclerosis contribute to greater risk of cognitive dysfunction. Despite a small sample size, this study importantly shows that PVD patients without evidence of prior stroke or neurological deficits, a group that clinically is generally assumed to have normal cognitive function, have a pattern of neuropsychological deficits that is similar to that seen in people with cerebrovascular disease.

Not all data support the hypothesis that atherosclerosis is related to poorer cognitive function, however. No associations between cognitive impairment, assessed by the Short Portable Mental Status Questionnaire (Pfeiffer, 1975), and coronary artery disease or other vascular disease, determined by medical records review, were noted in a sample of nearly 4,000 noninstitutionalized primary-care patients aged 60 and older (Callahan, Hendrie, & Tierney, 1995). Similarly, Ahto et al. (1999) found no differences in cognitive impairment, assessed by the MMSE, between CHD cases and controls in a community sample of noninstitutionalized men and women aged 64 or older. CHD cases were defined as having a medically confirmed history of myocardial infarction or chest pain on effort or ischemia during an electrocardiogram. Ahto et al. noted that several of the cross-sectional studies that have found positive associations between CHD and cognitive impairment have included more severely ill cardiac patients, and they suggested that more complicated forms of CHD, such as cardiac failure, may be related to cognitive dysfunction.

In sum, available cross-sectional data are suggestive, though not entirely consistent. More definitive tests of the hypothesis would come from longitudinal studies of the role of atherosclerosis in cognitive impairment. Although limited in scope, currently available longitudinal data are reviewed next.

Longitudinal Findings

A recent report from the Cardiovascular Health Study (Haan, Shemanski, Jagust, Manolio, & Kuller, 1999) found that baseline assessments of carotid artery atherosclerosis, systolic blood pressure (BP), ankle–arm BP, and prevalent diabetes were significantly related to 7-year declines in cognitive functioning, as measured by the modified MMSE (Teng & Chui, 1987) and the WAIS–R Digit Symbol Substitution test (Wechsler, 1981). Moreover, among participants in that study who had carotid atherosclerosis, diabetes, or PVD, those with at least one apolipoprotein E (ApoE; a plasma protein involved in cholesterol metabolism and transport) ε4 allele showed dramatically greater rates of cognitive decline than those without the ε4 allele.

Similarly, Slooter et al. (1998) found that among 838 Rotterdam Study participants who were nondemented at baseline, those who were ApoE ε4 carriers and who had at least two indicators of atherosclerosis at baseline (i.e., history of myocardial infarction, history of stroke, ultrasonographically assessed carotid artery atherosclerosis, or an ankle–arm index < 90), indicative of more severe disease, had a significantly lower MMSE score at follow-up nearly 3 years later compared to non-ApoE ε4 carriers without atherosclerosis. These effects were not confounded by age, education, sex, or family history of dementia. It is interesting that the main effects of ApoE ε4 and atherosclerosis on cognitive decline were small and nonsignificant, suggesting that the gene–environment interaction is critical in determining cognitive decline in the elderly.

To our knowledge, no other longitudinal studies directly measuring atherosclerosis and cognitive impairment have been published. Clearly, additional prospective investigations are needed to explicate the causal pathways linking atherosclerosis to decrements in cognitive functioning. Moreover, longitudinal findings will help establish or clarify the clinical significance of the generally mild cognitive impairments associated with atherosclerosis that have been identified to date and will provide important information regarding both treatment and prevention strategies.

UNDERLYING MECHANISMS

Atherosclerosis may adversely affect cognitive performance directly or indirectly, through a variety of mechanisms. As noted above, atherosclerotic plaques may induce clinical CV or cerebrovascular symptoms through calcification, rupture or ulceration, hemorrhage, fragmentation, weakening of the vessel wall and aneurysm, or some combination of these. Plaques that occur in the carotid or cerebral arteries thus could decrease or obstruct blood flow to the brain, thereby increasing the likelihood of cognitive dysfunction and impairments.

Alternatively, atherosclerotic lesions, cerebrovascular disease, and cognitive performance difficulties may result from or be influenced by a common genetic factor or by metabolic factors. For example, several studies have found that ApoE, and particularly the ε4 allele, is associated with declining cognitive function and increased risk of cognitive impairment (Feskens et al., 1994; see also chap. 3 of this book, for a review). Moreover, ApoE is related to greater prevalence of atherosclerosis and higher levels of total serum cholesterol and LDL cholesterol (Cattin et al., 1997; Kaprio, Ferrell, Kottke, Kamboh, & Sing, 1991).

Metabolic abnormalities that may influence cognitive function, atherosclerotic processes, and cerebrovascular disease included impaired insulin metabolism or insulin abnormalities, such as those seen in diabetes mellitus or hyperinsulinemia, and high levels of homocysteine, an amino acid that is a metabolic byproduct of methionine, an essential amino acid. High levels of homocysteine in the blood are related to poorer cognitive performance and increased risk of vascular dementias and Alzheimer's disease (Clarke et al., 1998; McCaddon, Davies, Hudson, Tandy, & Cattell, 1998) as well as atherosclerosis, thrombosis, and other CV and cerebrovascular diseases (den Heijer, Rosendaal, Blom, Gerrits, & Bos, 1998; Voutilainen, Alfthan, Nyyssonen, Salonen, & Salonen, 1998), although not all data are supportive (Evans, Shaten, Hempel, Cutler, & Kuller, 1997). Insulin abnormalities are related to increased risk of atherosclerosis, hypertension, and stroke (Folsom et al., 1997; Lukovits, Mazzone, & Gorelick, 1999; Salonen et al., 1998) and poorer cognitive functioning, including memory impairments, visuospatial dysfunction, and abstract-reasoning deficits (Helkala, Niskanen, Viinamäki, Partanen, & Uusitupa, 1995; Kalmijn, Feskens, Launer, Stijnen, & Kromhout, 1995; see also chap. 4 of this book). It is interesting that a recent report from the Framingham Study showed that individuals with non-insulin–dependent diabetes *and* hypertension had the poorest cognitive performance (P. K. Elias et al., 1997), demonstrating an important interaction between CV disease and impaired insulin metabolism in relation to cognition.

Taken together, the available literature suggests several metabolic, genetic, and hemodynamic mechanisms by which atherosclerosis may be linked to impaired cognitive performance. These mechanisms may have direct or indirect effects, and the effects may be additive or interactive, thereby markedly increasing the risk for atherosclerosis and cognitive impairments in susceptible individuals. For example, as noted above, high BP and insulin abnormalities appear to interact and lead to greater cognitive deficits than either disorder alone (P. K. Elias et al., 1997). Moreover, as discussed earlier in this chapter, two recent studies

(Haan et al., 1999; Slooter et al., 1998) reported greater cognitive deficits or declines in people with atherosclerosis who had at least one ApoE ε4 allele compared to people without the ε4 allele or to those with neither risk factor. Additional work is needed to further examine potential interactions among genetic, hemodynamic, and metabolic factors that may underlie the association between atherosclerosis and cognitive impairments.

CLINICAL RELEVANCE

Many deficits in cognitive abilities observed in relation to atherosclerosis are relatively small, and the clinical significance of minor cognitive decrements has yet to be determined. However, a recent study found that a 1-*SD* difference in performance on the WAIS–R Digit Symbol Substitution test (Wechsler, 1981) was associated with a significant 44% excess risk of mortality over 5 years in a sample of community-dwelling older men, after taking into account the effects of age, education, smoking, BP, total serum cholesterol, prevalent ischemic heart disease or history of myocardial infarction or stroke, or self-reported history of cancer (Swan, Carmelli, & LaRue, 1995). It is interesting that, in Swan et al.'s (1995) study, among men without a history of cancer those with the poorest survival rate were the ones who scored 30 or lower on the Digit Symbol test—a score that is still considered in the normal range. In other words, subclinical cognitive deficits were associated with greater mortality risk, suggesting that some of the mild decrements in cognitive performance seen with atherosclerosis may have important health effects. Alternatively, these deficits may be a marker of poorer overall health.

The clinical relevance of the data reviewed here is highlighted by the observation that declining cognitive function and atherosclerotic diseases show similar patterns of increasing frequency with increasing age. Work by Breteler and Hofman and their colleagues (Breteler et al., 1994; Hofman et al., 1997) suggests an overall downward shift in the elderly population toward lower levels of cognitive functioning with increasing age and greater atherosclerosis, indicating that a considerable proportion of cognitive decline in the elderly population may be vascular in origin. Research also suggests that subclinical vascular disease is a risk factor for poorer cognitive function. Taken together, these lines of evidence imply that interventions to delay or reduce atherosclerosis may delay onset of cognitive decline in elderly people.

Finally, both atherosclerosis and cognitive decline are associated with greater morbidity, including greater functional limitations. Several cross-sectional studies have demonstrated that cognitive impairment and atherosclerosis are associated with limitations in activities of daily living (ADL) in men and women age 65 and older (Bassett & Folstein, 1991; Boult, Kane, Louis, Boult, & McCaffrey, 1994; Institute of Medicine, 1991), and a recent longitudinal study found that lower levels of cognitive functioning predicted 3-year onset of new ADL limitations after controlling for history of chronic diseases and incident health problems (Moritz, Kasl, & Berkman, 1995). Decreases in cognitive abilities also significantly predicted dementia in the elderly (van Duijn, 1996).

SUMMARY AND FUTURE DIRECTIONS

The evidence reviewed in this chapter shows fairly consistent support for the hypothesis that atherosclerosis contributes to mild yet consistent deficits in cognitive performance in middle-aged and elderly men and women. However, to date most of this evidence comes from cross-sectional studies, with very few longitudinal studies of cognitive performance and atherosclerosis reported in the literature. As noted previously, prospective data are needed to assess the causal pathways and the underlying mechanisms by which atherosclerosis may contribute to cognitive declines, to determine the clinical significance of the generally mild decrements in cognitive abilities related to atherosclerotic vascular disease that have been reported and to inform treatment and prevention strategies.

Studies to date have used a variety of measures of cognitive function, some of which are useful as dementia screening tools (e.g., the MMSE) but may be less sensitive to mild decrements or changes in cognitive function thought to result from CHD or atherosclerosis. Future research could benefit from a standardized approach to assessing cognitive functioning, which would allow more reliable comparisons across studies or populations. Moreover, prior studies have varied in terms of the health status of the populations or samples studied. Some cross-sectional studies have found that more severely ill cardiac patients show cognitive deficits, whereas less sick patients do not. It also is plausible that more severe CHD or atherosclerosis contributes to cognitive declines over time, although data supporting this hypothesis are limited at present. Thus, to fully characterize the role that atherosclerosis plays in cognitive dysfunction it will be important to systematically examine the impact of atherosclerotic disease on cognitive abilities, independent of other diseases and risk factors, particularly those associated with aging. Research also is needed to determine if the effect of atherosclerosis on cognitive functioning is confounded or modified by other risk factors for atherosclerosis; for example, male sex, older age, or lower socioeconomic position.

Clearly, atherosclerosis and cognitive impairment can lead to significant loss of quality of life for middle-aged and elderly adults. The elderly are a growing proportion of the population, with an estimated 15% to 18% of the population expected to be age 65 or older by the year 2030 (U.S. Bureau of the Census, 1986). Therefore, atherosclerotic diseases, cognitive impairment, and their consequent effects on health and well-being are a major public health concern that will be increasing in the coming years.

ACKNOWLEDGMENT

Preparation of this chapter was supported in part by grants from the National Institutes of Health (HL44199 and AG13199) and the American Heart Association (9630054N) and by grants from the Academy of Finland and the Finnish Ministry of Education.

REFERENCES

Ahto, M., Isoaho, R., Puolijoki, H., Laippala, P., Sulkava, R., & Kivelä, S.-L. (1999). Cognitive impairment among elderly coronary heart disease patients. *Gerontology, 45,* 87–95.

American Heart Association. (1998). *1999 Heart and stroke statistical update.* Dallas, TX: Author.

Asakura, T., & Karino, T. (1990). Flow patterns and spatial distribution of atherosclerotic lesions in human coronary arteries. *Circulation Research, 66,* 1045–1066.

Auperin, A., Berr, C., Bonithon-Kopp, C., Touboul, P. J., Ruelland, I., Ducimetiere, P., & Alperovitch, A. (1996). Ultrasonographic assessment of carotid wall characteristics and cognitive functions in a community sample of 59- to 71-year-olds: The EVA Study Group. *Stroke, 27,* 1290–1295.

Bassett, S. S., & Folstein, M. F. (1991). Cognitive impairment and functional disability in the absence of psychiatric diagnosis. *Psychological Medicine, 21,* 77–84.

Berliner, J. A., Navab, M., Fogelman, A. M., Frank, J. S., Demer, L. L., Edwards, P. A., Watson, A. D., & Lusis, A. J. (1995). Atherosclerosis: Basic mechanisms: Oxidation, inflammation, and genetics. *Circulation, 91,* 2488–2496.

Bhattacharyya, G., & Libby, P. (1998). Atherosclerosis. In L. S. Lilly (Ed.), *Pathophysiology of heart disease* (2nd ed., pp. 101–118). Baltimore: Williams & Wilkins.

Borkowski, J. G., Benton, A. L., & Spreen, O. (1967). Word fluency and brain damage. *Neuropsychologia, 5,* 135–140.

Boult, C., Kane, R. L., Louis, T. A., Boult, L., & McCaffrey, D. (1994). Chronic conditions that lead to functional limitation in the elderly. *Journal of Gerontology, 49,* M28–M36.

Breteler, M. M. B., Claus, J. J., Grobbee, D. E., & Hofman, A. (1994). Cardiovascular disease and distribution of cognitive function in elderly people: The Rotterdam Study. *British Medical Journal, 308,* 1604–1608.

Buschke, H., & Fuld, P. S. (1974). Evaluating storage, retention, and retrieval in disordered memory and learning. *Neurology, 24,* 1019–1025.

Callahan, C. M., Hendrie, H. C., & Tierney, W. M. (1995). Documentation and evaluation of cognitive impairment in elderly primary care patients. *Annals of Internal Medicine, 122,* 422–429.

Cattin, L., Fisicaro, M., Tonizzo, M., Valenti, M., Danek, G. M., Fonda, M., Da Col, P. G., Casagrande, S., Pincetti, E., Bovenzi, M., & Baralle, F. (1997). Polymorphism of the apolipoprotein E gene and early carotid atherosclerosis defined by ultrasonography in asymptomatic adults. *Arteriosclerosis, Thrombosis, and Vascular Biology, 17,* 91–94.

Cerhan, J. R., Folsom, A. R., Mortimer, J. A., Shahar, E., Knopman, D. S., McGovern, P. G., Hays, M. A., Crum, L. D., & Heiss, G. (1998). Correlates of cognitive function in middle-aged adults: Atherosclerosis Risk in Communities (ARIC) study investigators. *Gerontology, 44,* 95–105.

Clarke, R., Smith, A. D., Jobst, K. A., Refsum, H., Sutton, L., & Ueland, P. M. (1998). Folate, vitamin B12, and serum total homocysteine levels in confirmed Alzheimer disease. *Archives of Neurology, 55,* 1449–1455.

den Heijer, M., Rosendaal, F. R., Blom, H. J., Gerrits, W. B., & Bos, G. M. (1998). Hyperhomocysteinemia and venous thrombosis: A meta-analysis. *Thrombosis and Haemostasis, 80,* 874–877.

DePaola, N., Gimbrone, M. A., Jr., Davies, P. F., & Dewey, C. F., Jr. (1992). Vascular endothelium responds to fluid shear stress gradients. *Arteriosclerosis & Thrombosis, 12,* 1254–1257.

Dewey, C. F., Jr., Bussolari, S. R., Gimbrone, M. A., Jr., & Davies, P. F. (1981). The dynamic response of vascular endothelial cells to fluid shear stress. *Journal of Biomechanical Engineering, 103,* 177–185.

Elias, M. F., Wolf, P. A., D'Agostino, R. B., Cobb, J., & White, L. R. (1993). Untreated blood pressure level is inversely related to cognitive functioning: The Framingham Study. *American Journal of Epidemiology, 138,* 353–364.

Elias, P. K., Elias, M. F., D'Agostino, R. B., Cupples, L. A., Wilson, P. W., Silbershatz, H., & Wolf, P. A. (1997). NIDDM and blood pressure as risk factors for poor cognitive performance: The Framingham Study. *Diabetes Care, 20,* 1388–1395.

Evans, R. W., Shaten, B. J., Hempel, J. D., Cutler, J. A., & Kuller, L. H. (1997). Homocyst(e)ine and risk of cardiovascular disease in the Multiple Risk Factor Intervention Trial. *Arteriosclerosis, Thrombosis, & Vascular Biology, 17,* 1947–1953.

Feskens, E. J. M., Havekes, L. M., Kalmijn, S., de Knijff, P., Launer, L. J., & Kromhout, D. (1994). Apolipoprotein e4 allele and cognitive decline in elderly men. *British Medical Journal, 309,* 1202–1206.

Folsom, A. R., Szklo, M., Stevens, J., Liao, F., Smith, R., & Eckfeldt, J. H. (1997). A prospective study of coronary heart disease in relation to fasting insulin, glucose, and diabetes: The Atherosclerosis Risk in Communities (ARIC) Study. *Diabetes Care, 20,* 935–942.

Folstein, M. F., Folstein, S. E., & McHugh, R. R. (1975). "Mini-Mental State": A practical method for grading the cognitive state of patients for the clinician. *Journal of Psychiatric Research, 12,* 189–198.

Graham, J. E., Rockwood, K., Beattie, B. L., Eastwood, R., Gauthier, S., Tuokko, H., & McDowell, I. (1997). Prevalence and severity of cognitive impairment with and without dementia in an elderly population. *The Lancet, 349,* 1793–1796.

Grobbee, D. E., & Bots, M. L. (1994). Carotid artery intima-media thickness as an indicator of generalized atherosclerosis. *Journal of Internal Medicine, 236,* 567–573.

Guyton, J. R., & Klemp, K. F. (1996). Development of the lipid-rich core in human atherosclerosis. *Arteriosclerosis, Thrombosis, & Vascular Biology, 16,* 4–11.

Haan, M. N., Shemanski, L., Jagust, W. J., Manolio, T. A., & Kuller, L. H. (1999). Predictors of cognitive change in the elderly: Does ApoE4 change the course of cognitive decline due to atherosclerosis or diabetes? *Journal of the American Medical Association, 282,* 40–46.

Helkala, E.-L., Niskanen, L., Viinamäki, H., Partanen, J., & Uusitupa, M. (1995). Short-term and long-term memory in elderly patients with NIDDM. *Diabetes Care, 18,* 681–685.

Hennig, B., & Chow, C. K. (1988). Lipid peroxidation and endothelial cell injury: Implications in atherosclerosis. *Free Radical Biology & Medicine, 4,* 99–106.

Hofman, A., Ott, A., Breteler, M. M. B., Bots, M. L., Slooter, A. J. C., van Harskamp, F., van Duijn, C. N., Van Broeckhoven, C., & Grobbee, D. E. (1997). Atherosclerosis, apolipoprotein E, and prevalence of dementia and Alzheimer's disease in the Rotterdam Study. *The Lancet, 349,* 151–154.

Institute of Medicine. (1991). *Disability in America: Toward a national agenda for prevention.* Washington, DC: National Academy Press.

Kalmijn, S., Feskens, E. J., Launer, L. J., Stijnen, T., & Kromhout, D. (1995). Glucose intolerance, hyperinsulinaemia and cognitive function in a general population of elderly men. *Diabetologia, 38,* 1096–1102.

Kaplan, G. A., Everson, S. A., Koivisto, K., Salonen, R., & Salonen, J. T. (1996). Cognitive function and carotid atherosclerosis in eastern Finnish men. *Annals of Behavioral Medicine, 18* (Suppl.), S47.

Kaplan, J. R., Pettersson, K., Manuck, S. B., & Olsson, G. (1991). Role of sympathoadrenal medullary activation in the initiation and progression of atherosclerosis. *Circulation, 84* (Suppl. 6), 23–32.

Kaprio, J., Ferrell, R. E., Kottke, B. A., Kamboh, M. I., & Sing, C. F. (1991). Effects of polymorphisms in apolipoproteins E, A-IV, and H on quantitative traits related to risk for cardiovascular disease. *Arteriosclerosis & Thrombosis, 11,* 1330–1348.

Knopman, D. S., & Ryberg, S. (1989). A verbal memory test with high predictive accuracy for dementia of the Alzheimer type. *Archives of Neurology, 46,* 141–145.

Launer, L. J., Feskens, E. J. M., Kalmijn, S., & Kromhout, D. (1996). Smoking, drinking, and thinking: The Zutphen Elderly Study. *American Journal of Epidemiology, 143,* 219–227.

Lezak, M. D. (Ed.). (1983). *Neuropsychological assessments* (2nd ed.). New York: Oxford University Press.

Lukovits, T. G., Mazzone, T. M., & Gorelick, T. M. (1999). Diabetes mellitus and cerebrovascular disease. *Neuroepidemiology, 18,* 1–14.

Marmot, M., & Elliott, P. (1992). *Coronary heart disease epidemiology: From aetiology to public health.* Oxford, England: Oxford University Press.

McCaddon, A., Davies, G., Hudson, P., Tandy, S., & Cattell, H. (1998). Total serum homocysteine in senile dementia of Alzheimer type. *International Journal of Geriatric Psychiatry, 13,* 235–239.

Moritz, D. J., Kasl, S. V., & Berkman, L. F. (1995). Cognitive functioning and the incidence of limitations in activities of daily living in an elderly community sample. *American Journal of Epidemiology, 141,* 41–49.

Nieto, F. J. (1998). Infections and atherosclerosis: New clues from an old hypothesis? *American Journal of Epidemiology, 148,* 937–948.

Nieto, F. J., Sorlie, P., Comstock, G. W., Wu, K., Adam, E., Melnick, J. L., & Szklo, M. (1997). Cytomegalovirus infection, lipoprotein(a), and hypercoagulability: An atherogenic link? *Arteriosclerosis, Thrombosis, & Vascular Biology, 17,* 1780–1785.

Nievelstein, P. F. E. M., Fogelman, A. M., Mottino, G., & Frank, J. S. (1991). Lipid accumulation in rabbit aortic intima 2 hours after bolus infusion of low density lipoprotein: A deep-etch and immunolocalization study of ultrarapidly frozen tissue. *Arteriosclerosis & Thrombosis, 11,* 1795–1805.

Pfeiffer, E. (1975). A short portable mental status questionnaire for the assessment of organic brain deficit in elderly patients. *Journal of the American Geriatrics Society, 23,* 433–441.

Phillips, N. A., & Mate-Kole, C. C. (1997). Cognitive deficits in peripheral vascular disease: A comparison of mild stroke patients and normal control subjects. *Stroke, 28,* 777–784.

Rapp, P. R., & Amaral, D. G. (1992). Individual differences in the cognitive and neurobiological consequences of normal aging. *Trends in Neurosciences, 15,* 340–345.

Reitan, R. M. (1958). Validity of the Trail Making Test as an indicator of organic brain damage. *Perceptual & Motor Skills, 8,* 271–276.

Ritchie, K., & Kildea, D. (1995). Is senile dementia "age-related" or "ageing-related"? Evidence from meta-analysis of dementia prevalence in the oldest old. *The Lancet, 346,* 931–934.

Ross, R. (1993). The pathogenesis of atherosclerosis: A perspective for the 1990s. *Nature, 362,* 801–809.

Ross, R. (1999). Atherosclerosis—An inflammatory process. *New England Journal of Medicine, 340,* 115–126.

Ross, R., & Glomset, J. A. (1976a). The pathogenesis of atherosclerosis (first of two parts). *New England Journal of Medicine, 295,* 369–377.

Ross, R., & Glomset, J. A. (1976b). The pathogenesis of atherosclerosis (second of two parts). *New England Journal of Medicine, 295,* 420–425.

Ross, R., Glomset, J., & Harker, L. (1977). Response to injury and atherogenesis. *American Journal of Pathology, 86,* 675–684.

Salonen, J. T. (1988). Is there a continuing need for longitudinal epidemiologic research? The Kuopio Ischemic Heart Disease Risk Factor Study. *Annals of Clinical Research, 20,* 46–50.

Salonen, J. T., Lakka, T. A., Lakka, H.-M., Valkonen, V-P., Everson, S. A., & Kaplan, G. A. (1998). Hyperinsulinemia is associated with the incidence of hypertension and dyslipidemia in middle-aged men. *Diabetes, 47,* 270–275.

Salonen, J. T., & Salonen, R. (1991). Ultrasonographically assessed carotid morphology and the risk of coronary heart disease. *Arteriosclerosis & Thrombosis, 11,* 1245–1249.

Salonen, J. T., Yla-Herttuala, S., Yamamoto, R., Butler, S., Korpela, H., Salonen, R., Nyyssonen, K.,

Palinski, W., & Witztum, J. L. (1992). Autoantibody against oxidised LDL and progression of carotid atherosclerosis. *The Lancet, 339,* 883–887.

Schwenke, D. C., & Carew, T. E. (1989a). Initiation of atherosclerotic lesions in cholesterol-fed rabbits. I: Focal increases in arterial LDL concentration precede deveopment of fatty streak lesions. *Arteriosclerosis, 9,* 895–907.

Schwenke, D. C., & Carew, T. E. (1989b). Initiation of atherosclerotic lesions in cholesterol-fed rabbits. II: Selective retention of LDL vs. selective increases in LDL permeability in susceptible sites of arteries. *Arteriosclerosis, 9,* 908–918.

Simionescu, M., & Simionescu, N. (1993). Proatherosclerotic events: pathobiochemical changes occurring in the arterial wall before monocyte migration. *FASEB Journal, 7,* 1359–1366.

Slooter, A. J., van Duijn, C. M., Bots, M. L., Ott, A., Breteler, M. B., De Voecht, J., Wehnert, A., de Knijff, P., Havekes, L. M., Grobbee, D. E., Van Broeckhoven, C., & Hofman, A. (1998). Apolipoprotein E genotype, atherosclerosis, and cognitive decline: The Rotterdam Study. *Journal of Neural Transmission, 53* (Suppl.), 17–29.

Swan, G. E., Carmelli, D., & LaRue, A. (1995). Performance on the Digit Symbol Substitution test and 5-year mortality in the Western Collaborative Group Study. *American Journal of Epidemiology, 141,* 32–40.

Teng, E. L., & Chui, H. C. (1987). The Modified Mini-Mental State (3MS) examination. *Journal of Clinical Psychiatry, 48,* 314–318.

U.S. Bureau of the Census. (1986). *Statistical abstract of the United States* (Ed. 107). Washington, DC: U.S. Government Printing Office.

van Duijn, C. M. (1996). Epidemiology of the dementias: Recent developments and new approaches. *Journal of Neurology, Neurosurgery, & Psychiatry, 60,* 478–488.

Vogel, R. A. (1997). Coronary risk factors, endothelial function, and atherosclerosis: A review. *Clinical Cardiology, 20,* 426–432.

Voutilainen, S., Alfthan, G., Nyyssonen, K., Salonen, R., & Salonen, J. T. (1998). Association between elevated plasma total homocysteine and increased common carotid artery wall thickness. *Annals of Medicine, 30,* 300–306.

Waldstein, S. R., Manuck, S. B., Ryan, C. M., & Muldoon, M.F. (1991). Neuropsychological correlates of hypertension: Review and methodologic considerations. *Psychological Bulletin, 110,* 451–468.

Wechsler, D. (1981). *Wechsler Adult Intelligence Scale–Revised.* New York: Psychological Corporation.

Williams, K. J., & Tabas, I. (1995). The response-to-retention hypothesis of early atherogenesis. *Arteriosclerosis, Thrombosis, & Vascular Biology, 15,* 551–561.

Witztum, J. L. (1994). The oxidation hypothesis of atherosclerosis. *The Lancet, 344,* 793–795.

Witztum, J. L., & Steinberg, D. (1991). Role of oxidized low density lipoprotein in atherogenesis. *Journal of Clinical Investigation, 88,* 1785–1792.

Wong, M., Edelstein, J., Wollman, J., & Bond, G. (1993). Ultrasonic-pathological comparison of the human arterial wall: Verification of intima-media thickness. *Arteriosclerosis & Thrombosis, 13,* 482–486.

CHAPTER SEVEN

Thinking On Your Feet: A Neuropsychological Review of Peripheral Vascular Disease

NATALIE A. PHILLIPS
Concordia University and
Sir Mortimer B. Davis–Jewish General Hospital

This chapter concerns neuropsychological function in patients with chronic atherosclerotic occlusive disease of the lower extremity arteries, which can be referred to more generally as *peripheral vascular disease* (PVD). In this chapter I review risk factors, pathophysiological mechanisms, and the clinical course of PVD. The association between atherosclerotic PVD and atherosclerotic cerebrovascular disease (CVD) is discussed. Studies documenting neuropsychological impairment in patients with PVD are reviewed, and methodological and clinical issues are highlighted. Finally, directions for future research are proposed.

ATHEROSCLEROSIS

All arteries typically undergo diffuse intimal thickening. This normal aging process is characterized by a thickening of the intimal area, loss of elasticity, increases in calcium content, and increases in diameter. These changes are believed to take place throughout the major arterial system (Fuster, Kottke, & Juergens, 1980). Diffuse intimal thickening is considered a physiologic rather than a pathologic process and is considered an essential element of the arterial system's response to hemodynamic stress (Lie, 1994). *Arteriosclerosis* is a generic term used to describe all varieties of structural changes that result in hardening and thickening of the arterial wall. *Atherosclerosis* is one form of arteriosclerosis. It is a pathological process characterized by the focal accumulation of lipids, carbohydrates, blood products, fibrous tissue, and calcium deposits (Fuster et al., 1980). Its major negative effect is the narrowing of the arterial lumen through stenosis and thrombosis and, consequently, ischemia of the end organ or tissue (Lie, 1994).

PVD

Chronic atherosclerotic occlusive disease of the extremities involves the aorta, its major branches to the limbs, and the arteries of the extremities. The majority of cases affect the lower extremities and are due to the atherosclerosis of the terminal portion of the abdominal aorta, the iliofemoral and popliteal arteries, or the arteries below the knees (Juergens & Bernatz, 1980). The clinical manifestation of peripheral atherosclerotic occlusive disease is often referred to as *atherosclerosis obliterans;* however, in this chapter I use the more general abbreviation PVD. The average annual incidence of PVD is likely underestimated, but data from the Framingham Study estimate that approximately 26 per 10,000 men and 12 per 10,000 women are affected (Kannel, Skinner, & Schwartz, 1970). Current European estimates indicate a cumulative 5-year incidence of intermittent claudication, an early symptom of PVD, to be 6% to 9% (Leng et al., 1996). The incidence rises sharply with age (Juergens & Bernatz, 1980).

Clinical Manifestations and Course of PVD

Intermittent claudication is pain or weakness in the legs elicited by exercise, including walking. It is a frequent early symptom of PVD that signifies an inadequate supply of arterial blood to contracting muscles (Fairbairn, 1980). By the time intermittent claudication is experienced there is an increased likelihood of morbidity and mortality from coronary disease and CVD (Juergens & Bernatz, 1980). Thus, it signals the presence of clinically significant and probably generalized atherosclerosis. Within 5 years approximately 24% of patients with intermittent claudication experience the onset of rest pain, which heralds the progression of the disease to the point of critical ischemia (Krajewski & Olin, 1991). Ischemic ulceration and gangrene are frequent complications of PVD. These necessitate revascularization surgery in approximately 10% to 20% of claudicants and, given sufficient severity, is the principal cause for amputation. Approximately 3% to 6% of PVD patients undergo amputation, with the rate being roughly seven times higher in patients with concomitant diabetes (Rockson & Cooke, 1998). In the United States, more than 50,000 major amputations were performed in 1985 on diabetic PVD patients alone (Levin, 1991). More than two thirds of amputations in people over the age of 50 years are necessitated by PVD (Schwartz & Hoaglund, 1989). The presence of PVD also places patients at a higher risk of dying of vascular-related causes. Criqui et al. (1992) showed that the relative 10-year mortality risk was six times greater in individuals with PVD, compared to those without PVD, for deaths from cardiovascular disease, including myocardial infarction, coronary artery bypass surgery, stroke, or stroke-related surgery. Approximately 50% of deaths in men with PVD result from myocardial infarction, 15% from stroke, and 10% from atherosclerosis in the abdomen (Krajewski & Olin, 1991).

Risk Factors for Atherosclerotic Development

In all arterial systems, the risk factors for the development of atherosclerosis are the same and include cigarette smoking (particularly in the case of PVD; Fuster et al., 1980), hyperlipidemia, diabetes mellitus (Fuster et al., 1980), hypertension (Lie, 1994), increasing age, and male sex (Juergens & Bernatz, 1980). Each of the medical risk factors has be shown to exert negative effects on cognitive function. Neurobehavioral effects have been shown reliably in patients with hypertension, diabetes mellitus (particularly in Type 2 diabetics) and, to a lesser extent, hyperlipidemia (Brown, Baird, Shatz, & Bornstein, 1996). Because the pathophysiological mechanisms and neuropsychological effects of these risk factors are dealt with extensively in other chapters of this book, they are not reviewed here. Suffice it to say that the fundamental atherogenic mechanisms are likely the same regardless of the arterial system involved (Juergens & Bernatz, 1980). Only cigarette smoking has not been dealt with elsewhere and is reviewed here briefly.

Cigarette smoking has long been considered the major risk factor for the development of PVD (Juergens, Barker, & Hines, 1960; Lord, 1965). Over 90% of symptomatic PVD patients have a history of long-term smoking (Powell et al., 1997). An increased cumulative pack-year history, nicotine absorption, hypertension, and increased levels of apolipoprotein B increase the risk of PVD development in smokers (Powell et al., 1997). Increased concentration of carboxyhemoglobin and consequent tissue hypoxia (Ganda, 1980) or vascular injury due to nicotine (Powell et al., 1997) are possible atherogenic mechanisms. Carboxyhemoglobin has been shown to impair hepatic metabolism of lipoprotein remnants, and carbon-monoxide–induced hypoxia likely results in increased endothelial permeability and in the proliferation of cultured human arterial smooth cells (Ganda, 1980). It is reasonable to suspect that smoking could interfere with brain and neuropsychological functioning. Carbon monoxide has a higher affinity for hemoglobin than does oxygen and displaces it, thereby interfering with oxygen transport to the brain and other organs (Royal College of Physicians, 1977).

Most studies that have investigated the effects of smoking on neuropsychological function have examined young subject samples, and their findings cannot necessarily be applied to aging samples at risk for stroke. Hill (1989) examined the effects of smoking on cognitive function in elderly adults screened for health and intellectual impairments. Seventy-six participants (mean age: 72 years) were administered a broad battery of neuropsychological tests. Smokers performed more poorly than nonsmokers on tests of psychomotor speed. Given that this was a sample of elderly smokers free from health complications, these individuals may have been a particularly hardy group of individuals who were resistant to the negative effects of smoking (Hill, 1989). It is possible that the effects of smoking on cognitive function in the elderly may not be evident until other signs of physical decline are manifested. Launer, Feskens, Kalmijn, and Kromhout (1996) examined the performance of a large cohort of elderly men on the Mini-Mental State Examination and found that current smokers, on average, made 20% more errors on the test than those who had never smoked. It is interesting that cognitive decline was most pronounced in men with CVD, diabetes, or both, who either never smoked or who currently smoked relative to those who had quit; however, the potential role of selection bias and unmeasured confounds make conclusions from this latter finding tentative.

In summary, atherosclerotic risk factors for PVD are associated with generally mild neuropsychological changes (hypertension, see chap. 2; hyperlipidemia, see chap. 3; diabetes, see chap. 4). Despite the presence of at least one of these risk factors in most PVD patients, it is shown later (Phillips & Mate-Kole, 1997) that the severity of PVD is an independent predictor of cognitive dysfunction.

Relationship Between PVD and CVD

The incidence of atherothrombotic brain infarction is substantially higher than other causes of stroke, such as intracerebral hemorrhage, subarachnoid hemorrhage, or cerebral embolism from cardiac sources. Nonatherosclerotic causes of cerebrovascular insufficiency likely account for no more than 10% of all deaths from stroke (Lie, 1994). The majority of stroke patients have significant stenosis or occlusion of the extracranial arteries (internal carotid and vertebral; Lie, 1994), with the sites of predilection for atherosclerosis including the carotid bifurcations, the origins of the internal cerebral arteries, the middle cerebral arteries, the origin and course of the vertebral arteries (Lie, 1994), the anterior and pericallosal arteries, and the posterior cerebral artery (Toole, 1994).

Thus, atherosclerosis is the most common cause of ischemia in the central nervous system (CNS; Lie, 1994; Siekert, Whisnant, & Sundt, 1980) and in the periphery (Juergens & Bernatz, 1980). Given this shared pathophysiological mechanism, an association between these two disease syndromes is reasonable. CVD is viewed as a consequence of long-term processes, and the association between it and atherosclerosis elsewhere in the body indicates that it is part of a generalized vascular disease (Kannel & Wolf, 1983). In fact, the histopathological changes of atherosclerotic lesions found in the periphery are identical to those of the cerebral arteries (Juergens & Bernatz, 1980).

Several studies demonstrate that PVD and CVD coexist and reflect a generalized pattern of vascular disease within an individual. PVD is a risk factor for minor ischemic strokes and transient ischemic attacks (TIAs; Dennis, Bamford, Sandercock, & Warlow, 1989). Its prevalence is significantly higher in patients with TIAs than in those without TIAs (Ostfeld, Shekelle, & Klawans, 1973). PVD is an adverse prognostic factor in TIA patients (Hankey, Slattery, & Warlow, 1992), and the mortality rate following stroke is significantly higher in patients with concomitant PVD than in those without (Tonelli et al., 1993). Two studies have examined the prevalence of asymptomatic carotid artery stenosis in PVD. Ellis, Franks, Cuming, Powell, and Greenhalgh (1992) found that 14% of PVD patients had a stenosis of over 50% in either of the common or internal carotid arteries. Alexandrova, Gibson, Norris, and Maggisano (1996) examined 373 patients referred to a peripheral vascular laboratory and found that 57% had carotid artery stenosis of greater than 30%, an incidence much higher than the 8% incidence found in the general population (O'Leary, Anderson, Wolf, Evans, & Poehlman, 1992). The majority of these PVD cases (68%) were considered asymptomatic on study inclusion (i.e., had no prior history of stroke or TIA), despite the fact that exactly half had significant carotid stenoses between 60% and 99%.

To summarize thus far, CVD and PVD arise from the same mechanism: atherosclerosis. Identical risk factors underlie the development of atherosclerosis in the peripheral, coronary, and cerebral arteries. There is widespread agreement in the medical literature that the factors that lead to atherosclerosis in the lower extremities are likely to produce similar lesions in other arteries and that atherosclerosis of the extremities is just one manifestation of similar pathology in the heart and brain (Juergens & Bernatz, 1980). Evidence of PVD in an individual patient should be considered a strong marker of generalized atherosclerosis (Tonelli et al., 1993) and should lead to an inquiry for ischemic manifestations in other major organs, particularly the brain and heart (Rockson & Cooke, 1998).

PVD AND COGNITIVE FUNCTION

Given the association between PVD and CVD, it is possible that patients with PVD also suffer from impairment in cognitive function as a result of concomitant CVD. However, until recently there has been little known about their neuropsychological function. Some studies have included PVD patients as control subjects when examining neuropsychological outcome after surgery; for example, following carotid endarterectomy (Hemmingsen et al., 1986; Kelly, Garron, & Javid, 1980; van den Burg et al., 1985) and coronary artery bypass surgery (Shaw et al., 1987; Vanninen et al., 1998) to control for the practice effects in postoperative performance.

Kelly et al. (1980) failed to find presurgical differences in cognitive function between in 35 carotid endarterectomy patients and 17 age- and education-matched surgical control PVD patients. TIA patients had angiography-confirmed carotid stenosis of 70% or greater or ulcerated carotid artery plaque; all PVD controls were free of neurological signs or symptoms at the time of recruitment into the study. Kelly et al. interpreted their null findings as reflecting an absence of impairment in the carotid endarterectomy patients. However, they did discuss the possibility that the result was due to comparing two groups of patients, both of which exhibited cognitive deficits. In the absence of a normal healthy elderly control group, this possibility could not be excluded.

Hemmingsen et al. (1986) examined cognitive function pre- and postoperatively in 31 TIA patients with atherosclerotic disease of the carotid arteries who underwent carotid endarterectomy and 11 PVD surgical control patients. Again, the PVD controls were considered asymptomatic for CVD on admission to the study. The mean preoperative performance of both TIA and PVD patient groups was below age-corrected norms on all the neuropsychological tests administered save one. The carotid endarterectomy patients improved postoperatively on 95% of neuropsychological tests, whereas no significant improvement was observed in the PVD group. The unexpected finding of poor cognitive function in the PVD controls was supported by neuroimaging, which indicated that 18% of the PVD patients had hypodense lesions on computed tomography and corresponding changes in regional cerebral blood flow; 64% showed evidence of cerebral atrophy.

Shaw et al. (1987) evaluated neuropsychological function in 312 patients prior to and after coronary artery bypass graft surgery. They studied 50 patients with PVD undergoing peripheral-bypass grafting as surgical controls and 20 nonsurgical normal controls. Evidence of mild neuropsychological dysfunction was found in the PVD control group. Thirty-one percent showed deterioration of postoperative test scores relative to preoperative levels on at least one neuropsychological measure, including tests of attention and learning and memory.

Thus, evidence of at least mild neuropsychological dysfunction has been coincidentally noted in PVD patients (e.g., Hemmingsen et al., 1986; Shaw et al., 1987). Unfortunately, those studies were not designed to assess this patient group per se, which limits the information that can be drawn. To date, only three studies have specifically evaluated cognitive function in patients with PVD, namely, Pinzur, Graham, and Osterman (1988); Phillips, Mate-Kole, and Kirby (1993); and Phillips and Mate-Kole (1997). Pinzur et al. (1988) examined a group of 60 amputee patients in whom amputation was secondary to PVD in 93% of the cases. Six (10%) of the patients had severe cognitive deficits, 8 (13%) had "covert psychiatric illness," and 3 (5%) had both severe cognitive deficits and psychiatric illness. Pinzur et al. described the deficits as including impairment in short-term memory, attention and concentration, orientation, and judgment. Unfortunately, this study had a number of methodological difficulties. First, test administration was not consistent across participants. Different tests were used when patients were above or below the age of 60 and, even within an age group, not all participants were administered the same tests. The study did not include a control group against which one could evaluate the patients' performance, and the method by which cognitive impairment was determined was not specified. Finally, means and standard deviations of the participants' performance were not presented, and no statistical analyses were reported, making it impossible to evaluate the reliability of these findings.

The issue of neuropsychological function in PVD remained largely unexplored until a series of studies conducted by Phillips and colleagues (Phillips, 1996; Phillips et al., 1993; Phillips & Mate-Kole, 1997). In the first study (Phillips et al., 1993), neuropsychological function was assessed in 14 patients with lower extremity amputations secondary to atherosclerotic PVD (mean age: 67.4 years; mean education: 10.3 years) and 14 age- and education-matched healthy controls. By virtue of having had an amputation, the PVD patients were considered to represent the severe end of the continuum of vascular disease. A broad range of neuropsychological functions were assessed, including learning and memory, language, visuoperceptual and constructional abilities, and problem-solving and abstract-reasoning abilities. PVD patients were recruited from inpatient and outpatient rehabilitation services and had been referred for prosthetic rehabilitation; patients had no history of diagnosed psychiatric or neurological disorder, including cerebrovascular accident. The Beck Depression Inventory (BDI) was administered to 7 of the 14 patients. The mean score was 8.9, indicating that these patients reported either no or minimal depressive symptoms. PVD amputees performed significantly more poorly than controls on the Digit Symbol subtest of the Wechsler Adult Intelligence Scale–Revised (WAIS–R) and obtained fewer categories on the Modified Card Sorting Test than did the controls. In addition, there were trends toward lower patient scores on a number of other neuropsychological tests, including the WAIS–R Vocabulary, Arithmetic, Similarities, and Picture Arrangement subtests; oral fluency; and the copy administration of the Rey–Osterrieth Complex Figure. Despite the fact that PVD amputees exhibited poorer neuropsychological function than healthy age-matched controls, several questions remained unanswered. First, it was not known whether the findings were specific only to amputee patients with PVD or would be representative of patients with peripheral atherosclerosis in general. Second, it could not be inferred that the poor performance was the result of underlying CVD, because the PVD patients were not compared with a group of patients with known CVD. Third, it was not clear if cognitive impairment was related to PVD *per se* or whether the deficits could be accounted for by the neurobehavioral effects of the atherosclerotic risk factors typically found in PVD patients.

Phillips and Mate-Kole (1997) examined neuropsychological function in patients with symptomatic PVD, patients with symptomatic CVD (i.e., stroke patients), and normal age- and education-matched control subjects. This study replicated and extended the finding that PVD is related to lower levels of cognitive functioning by including patients representing a range of peripheral atherosclerotic severity. The profiles of neuropsychological function in PVD patients and CVD patients were compared to determine if similar patterns of impairment exist. Atherosclerotic risk factors also were examined to determine whether these would be predictive of cognitive deficits in PVDs. Because this represents the largest and best controlled study to date, I describe it in some detail.

Sixteen nonamputee PVD patients (mean age: 62 years) were recruited from a noninvasive vascular diagnostic laboratory. The inclusion criterion was the positive identification of lower extremity atherosclerotic arterial insufficiency (i.e., ankle–brachial pressure index < .8). Patients were excluded if they had a confirmed history of cerebrovascular accident or any medical or psychiatric history that might negatively affect cognitive function. Thirteen patients with lower extremity amputations secondary to PVD (mean age: 68 years) were recruited from a rehabilitation hospital and were subject to the same exclusion criteria as the nonamputee PVDs. For all PVD patients the variables of diabetes, hypertension, and hyperlipidemia were characterized following standard guidelines (Rutherford et al., 1986). Cigarette smoking was quantified in pack years. PVD severity was categorized (range: 0–6) following standard criteria (Rutherford et al., 1986). Ten nonamputee patients exhibited mild ischemic symptoms (mild claudication, severity Category 1), 6 nonamputees fell into Category 2 (moderate claudication), and all amputees fell within Category 6 (severe disease, major tissue loss). Phillips and Mate-Kole (1997) also recruited 29 CVD patients (mean age: 66 years) with unilateral atherothrombotic brain infarctions involving the carotid or vertebral–basilar arterial systems; 15 patients had right-hemisphere infarcts and 14 had left-hemisphere infarcts. Thirty healthy elderly control subjects (mean age: 68 years) were recruited from community centers. Both the CVD and normal control groups matched the PVD patient groups in age and education.

All participants were administered a comprehensive neuropsychological battery that evaluated cognitive function across several domains, including executive–frontal lobe function, learning of and memory for verbal and nonverbal information, attention and concentration, language, visuospatial–constructional ability, and sensory and motor function. A Bonferroni correction was used to control for Type I error. Phillips and Mate-Kole (1997) found that PVD patients performed significantly more poorly than elderly controls in the areas of attention and psychomotor speed (Trail Making Test Part B, WAIS–R Digit Symbol), executive function (Wisconsin Card Sorting Test [WCST] perseverative errors, WCST conceptual responses, WAIS–R Picture Arrangement), visuospatial ability (WAIS–R Block Design, Rey–Osterrieth Complex Figure Copy), and visual memory (Rey–Osterrieth Figure Delayed Recall). No overall impairment for the PVD group was found for tests of language ability, verbal memory, or lateralizing tests of sensory–motor functioning.

The data were compelling when considered in terms of their potential clinical significance. For a number of measures of executive function (WCST perseverative errors), attention (Trail Making Test Parts A and B), and visuospatial ability (WAIS–R Block Design and the Rey–Osterrieth Figure Copy), approximately 30% to 50% of the total PVD sample had scores falling in the bottom 5% of the distribution of normal controls' scores, indicating that impaired performance on these tests was common. Moreover, with the exception of the WAIS–R Picture Arrangement and Digit Symbol subtests, the PVD and CVD groups both performed significantly more poorly than controls, but their means did not differ from each another. Fig. 7.1 depicts the pattern of performance of the three groups across different neuropsychological measures. Individual scores for all three groups were converted to z scores, as a function of the mean and standard deviation of the control group's test scores. Apart from the general difference in the magnitude of negative z scores between the PVD patients and CVD patients (i.e., CVD patients generally had slightly lower scores), the overall similarity between the performance pattern of the two patient groups is striking. It is premature to draw conclusions regarding the clinical significance of the magnitude of such differences or the lack thereof. It is impossible to conclude that, on some measures, the PVD subjects were *as impaired* as the CVD subjects as this would involve accepting the null hypothesis. Also, in the functional outcome study reviewed next, I (Phillips, 1996) did not obtain follow-up data on the CVD sample as I did for the PVD sample. Until such work is carried out, conclusions regarding the clinical significance of such group differences must remain guarded.

Affect and Its Relationship With Neuropsychological Function

Patients with PVD potentially face a number of experiences that could negatively affect their psychological adjustment. These include moderate loss of function due to intermittent claudication, fatigue and discomfort due to ischemic lesions and rest pain, and major life adjustment necessitated by lower limb amputation. Phillips and Mate-Kole (1997) assessed the potential impact of psychological adjustment in PVD patients on neuropsychological performance using the BDI and the Symptom Check List-90-Revised Global Symptom Index. Most measures of depression and global psychological distress did not differ between the groups. The exception was that of amputee PVDs' self-report on the Beck Depression Inventory relative to that of the normal control subjects. The mean score of the PVD amputees fell in the mild-depression range, a level of depressive symptomatology far below that which is reported in studies of the neurobehavioral effects of clinical depression (e.g., Boone et al., 1995; King, Cox, Lyness, & Caine, 1995; Richards & Ruff, 1989). Moreover, none of the depression measures correlated with overall neuropsychological performance on

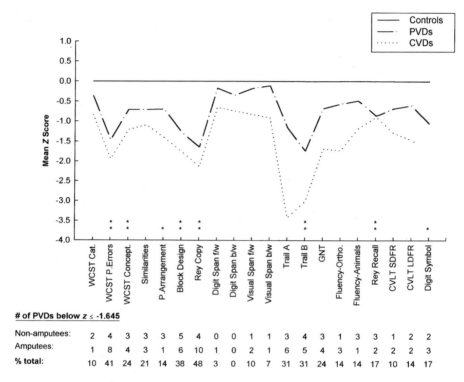

	WCST Cat.	WCST P.Errors	WCST Concept.	Similarities	P.Arrangement	Block Design	Rey Copy	Digit Span f/w	Digit Span b/w	Visual Span f/w	Visual Span b/w	Trail A	Trail B	GNT	Fluency-Ortho.	Fluency-Animals	Rey Recall	CVLT SDFR	CVLT LDFR	Digit Symbol
Non-amputees:	2	4	3	3	3	5	4	0	0	1	1	3	4	3	1	3	3	1	2	2
Amputees:	1	8	4	3	1	6	10	1	0	2	1	6	5	4	3	1	2	2	2	3
% total:	10	41	24	21	14	38	48	3	0	10	7	31	31	24	14	14	17	10	14	17

# of PVDs below $z \leq -1.645$

FIG. 7.1.   Mean z scores for normal control participants (——), participants with peripheral vascular disease (PVD; –·–·–), and participants with cerebrovascular disease (CVD; ······) for each neuropsychological test. Tests on which PVD participants differed from controls are indicated by an asterisk (*). Tests on which PVD and CVD participants differed from controls, but not from each other are indicated by a double asterisk (**). The number of amputee and non-amputee PVD participants (and total percentage of the PVD sample) falling in the bottom 5% of the distribution of normal control scores (i.e., $z \leq -1.645$) is indicated beneath each test. WCST = Wisconsin Card Sorting Test; Cat. = number of categories; P.Errors = perseverative errors; Concept. = conceptual responses; P.Arrangement = Wechsler Adult Intelligence Scale Picture Arrangement; Rey = Rey–Osterreith Complex Figure; f/w = forward; b/w = backward; Trail A = Trail Making Test, Part A; Trail B = Trail Making Test, Part B; GNT = Graded Naming Test; Ortho. = orthographic; CVLT = California Verbal Learning Test; SDFR = short delay, free recall; LDFR = long delay, free recall. From "Cognitive Deficits in Peripheral Vascular Disease: A Comparison With Mild Stroke Patients and Normal Controls," by N. A. Phillips and C. C. Mate-Kole, 1997, *Stroke, 28*, p. 781. Copyright 1997 by the American Heart Association. Reprinted with permission.

130

tests on which the PVD patients performed poorly, suggesting that level of depression did not influence cognitive performance.

Predictors of Cognitive Function

Using hierarchical multiple regression analyses, Phillips and Mate-Kole (1997) sought to identify medical variables that predicted cognitive function in PVD patients by assessing severity of PVD, self-reported history of TIA,[1] history/presence of ischemic heart disease, hypertension, smoking pack-years, diabetes, and hyperlipidemia. The severity of PVD and a history of ischemic heart disease were the two most consistent independent predictors of cognitive deficits. PVD severity was a significant negative predictor of performance on two measures of executive function (WCST perseverative errors and WCST conceptual responses) and on a test of attention (Trail Making Test Part B), accounting for approximately 14% of the variance in performance on these measures. In other words, the extent of PVD, a *peripheral* manifestation of atherosclerosis, was a significant predictor of neurocognitive deficits. This underscores the generalized pathological nature of the atherosclerotic process and suggests that the clinical effects of atherosclerosis in the major arterial systems may manifest themselves in a roughly parallel manner. The clinical implication is that patients with the most severe PVD, especially those with amputations, are at greatest risk for experiencing cognitive decline.

A history of ischemic heart disease was more frequently a significant predictor of cognitive function than was PVD severity. It was a negative predictor of performance on measures of executive function (WCST perseverative errors, WCST conceptual responses), attention (Trail Making Test Part B and WAIS–R Digit Symbol), and visuospatial–constructional ability (WAIS–R Block Design and Rey–Osterrieth Figure Copy). In fact, ischemic heart disease accounted for 20% to 30% of the variance on several of these measures. There are at least three possible explanations for these findings. First, ischemic heart disease is very strongly associated with atherosclerosis in the cerebral and peripheral arteries (Criqui et al., 1992; Juergens & Bernatz, 1980; Krajewski & Olin, 1991; Toole, 1994). Therefore, the presence of ischemic heart disease in some PVD patients may be yet another marker of the generalized and severe nature of their atherosclerotic disease. Second, ischemic heart disease can play a causative role in stroke, generally in the form of embolization from a thrombus (Adams & Victor, 1993). The third possibility relates to the fact that the most important

---

[1] All PVD participants were considered free of overt evidence of CVD as substantiated by a review of their medical records which, in many cases, included Doppler investigations of their carotid arteries. However, in some cases participants reported a past episode of possible TIA. All such cases had been investigated and judged by their physician to have no overt evidence of CVD. Nevertheless, a conservative approach was taken by including this self-report in the regression analyses. In no instance was it a significant predictor of cognitive function.

protective mechanism the brain has against cerebral infarction is the development of collateral circulation (Jack & Houser, 1994). In the presence of sufficient collateral circulation, infarction may not occur despite the stenosis of an artery. However, hypotension from reduced cardiac output can render these anastomotic channels ineffective (Adams & Victor, 1993) thereby functionally removing this protective collateral supply. It is possible that the presence of heart disease in PVD patients played such a role, although this remains to be determined by actually measuring cardiac function in PVD patients.

In general, there was no consistent relationship between any of the other medical–health variables examined (TIAs, hypertension, blood lipid abnormalities, smoking, and diabetes) and cognitive performance. Although there is evidence of negative neurobehavioral effects of the atherosclerotic risk factors, they were not significant predictors of cognitive function in Phillips and Mate-Kole's (1997) study when the effects of the clinical manifestations of atherosclerosis (i.e., PVD severity and ischemic heart disease) were considered. It has been suggested that the correlations between risk factors and neuropsychological function may ultimately be mediated through their association in the development of cerebral atherosclerosis (e.g., Light, 1978) and their expression in "end organ change" (Schultz, Elias, Robbins, Streeten, & Blakeman, 1989). This suggests that the negative effect of the risk factors may result from their role in the development of atherosclerosis (i.e., an indirect effect) rather than be due to the presence of those pathologies *per se* (i.e., a direct effect). This possibility is depicted in Fig. 7.2, which shows that athrosclerotic risk factors may have a direct but weak effect (dotted line) on cognitive function through hyperglycemia (diabetes), anoxia (smoking), and so on. However, these risk factors may have a stronger indirect effect through their role in the pathogenesis of atherosclerosis. According to this argument, more serious cognitive impairment may not be evident in patients with risk factors until atherosclerosis is manifested clinically. Phillips and Mate-Kole's results raise the interesting possibility that the presence of atherosclerotic symptoms such as PVD and ischemic heart disease should be examined more closely in future studies of the neurobehavioral effects of medical conditions such as diabetes and hypertension.

One important criticism of the evaluation of risk factors in Phillips and Mate-Kole's (1997) study is that, with the exception of smoking, the researchers rather crudely quantified risk factors as either present or absent or by using a somewhat arbitrary ordinal ranking system of severity, following the accepted standards in the PVD literature (Rutherford et al., 1986). Studies designed to evaluate the effects of atherosclerotic risk factors have often used more fine-grained methods to quantify the variable (e.g., by using continuous measures of glycemic control or hypertension; see Bornstein & Kelly, 1991). It is possible that Phillips and Mate-Kole's failure to observe any effects of the atherosclerotic risk factors on cognitive function was the result of artificially dichotomizing/categorizing these variables rather than looking at their full range of variation.

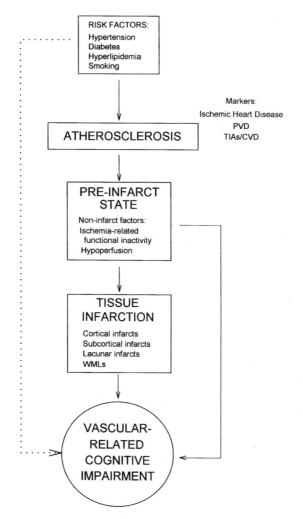

FIG. 7.2. A model of the distal and proximal causal effects on vascular-related cognitive impairment. PVD = peripheral vascular disease; TIA = transient ischemic attack; CVD = cerebrovascular disease; WML = white matter lesion.

Clinical Significance of Neuropsychological Function in PVD

Real-life functioning in populations with neuropsychological deficits is often poorly documented. Phillips (1996) followed the PVD patients studied by Phillips and Mate-Kole (1997) to determine whether neuropsychological performance predicted their level of everyday functioning after 1 year using the Functional Activities Questionnaire (FAQ; Pfeffer, Kuroaski, Harrah, Chance, & Filos, 1982). The FAQ was designed to measure adaptive functioning by assessing a range of activities in which older adults are typically engaged (e.g., shopping, balancing a cheque book), rather than more low-level activities that are appropriate for individuals in a institutional setting (Pfeffer et al., 1982). The FAQ has been shown to distinguish between normal elderly people and those with mild senile dementia (Pfeffer et al., 1982) and those with vascular dementia (Hershey, Jaffe, Greenough, & Yang, 1987). It is completed by a close lay informant and has been shown to correlate with measures of cognitive function in normal elderly people and in those with mild to moderate dementia living in the community (Pfeffer et al., 1982; Pfeffer, Kurosaki, Chance, Filos, & Bates, 1984). The total maximum score on the FAQ is 30 points, with higher scores indicating greater disability.

Approximately 1 year after their participation in Phillips and Mate-Kole's (1997) investigation, all PVD patients were invited by mail to participate in a follow-up study. Completed FAQs were received from informants for 10 amputee PVDs and 9 nonamputee PVDs, yielding a total return rate of 66%. There were no differences between responders and nonresponders in terms of age, education, or initial overall neuropsychological performance. The mean FAQ score of the patients rated by their lay informant was 3.4 ($SD = 5.2$, range = 0–20 points). Five patients were rated greater than or equal to the recommended normal cutoff score of 5 points (Pfeffer et al., 1982). Phillips (1996) tested the relationship between neuropsychological function and functional outcome by examining the correlation between FAQ scores and five neuropsychological domains. As shown in Fig. 7.3, poor performance on measures of attention, memory, and visuospatial function was significantly related to poorer functional outcome (i.e., higher FAQ scores) 1 year later; however, no such relationship was found for performance on tests of executive function and verbal ability. The influence of affect and psychological distress was also examined. Correlational analysis revealed that a higher level of depression as measured by the BDI was significantly related to poorer functional outcome in the PVD patients. Ideally, depression would have been considered together with the neuropsychological predictors; however, affective data were not available on all PVD patients, and not all patients participated in the follow-up study, resulting in a reduced number of cases that precluded the use of regression analyses.

To summarize, Phillips (1996) found that visuospatial, memory, and attentional processes predicted everyday adaptive functioning in PVD patients as

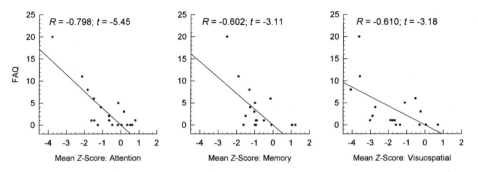

FIG. 7.3. Scatter plots of the significant relationship between functional outcome (Functional Assessment Questionnaire [FAQ]) of peripheral vascular disease patients and composite neuropsychological function (mean z score) measured 1 year earlier in three neuropsychological domains: attention, memory, and visuospatial.

rated by the participants' relatives 1 year later. These results are consistent with previous studies that found that impaired visuospatial ability (Jongbloed, 1986; Lehmann et al., 1975; Lorenze & Cancro, 1962; Richardson, Nadler, & Malloy, 1995) and memory function (Richardson et al., 1995) were prognostic indicators of poor function in stroke patients.

IMPLICATIONS OF COGNITIVE IMPAIRMENT IN PVD

The question remains as to whether PVD patients exhibit subtle but meaningful cognitive impairment or whether one is observing merely a lowered level of performance relative to age-matched controls that is statistically significant but functionally irrelevant. It is possible that in many PVD patients their impairment is either sufficiently subtle as to have gone unrecognized by the patient, family, and medical practitioner or, if subtle changes in cognitive function have been noted, they might be attributed only to the vagaries of aging. Nevertheless, several points argue that these changes do have clinical significance. First, as noted, Phillips and Mate-Kole (1997) found that on certain tests up to half of the PVD patients studied obtained *substantially* lowered scores (i.e., in the bottom 5% of the distribution of control scores). Second, Phillips (1996) observed a significant relationship between neuropsychological performance and functional level 1 year later, suggesting that there may be a real-life impact of lower levels of neuropsychological function.

There are several implications following from the demonstration of neuropsychological deficits in PVD patients. First, deficits in PVD amputees might present an impediment to prosthetic rehabilitation, resulting in prolonged or unsuccessful physical rehabilitation. Prosthetic rehabilitation is likely to be a multidetermined process, one dependent on perceptual and organizational–executive-function skills and learning and memory processes. It is not currently known if success in rehabilitation calls on some skills more heavily than others. Phillips (1996) indicated that specific neuropsychological deficits—namely, visuospatial, attention, and memory deficits—were related to poorer functional outcome at home. Future research should examine the predictive power of specific neuropsychological domains in relation to the rehabilitation process. Second, it is possible that neuropsychological assessment of PVD patients receiving rehabilitation services would lead to the early identification of patients in greatest need because of their cognitive deficits. This would facilitate the delivery of specialized rehabilitation services to these patients (e.g., more intensive training, more simplified and concrete instructions). The finding of a significant relationship between depression and functional outcome (Phillips, 1996) indicates that factors in addition to cognitive function may contribute to long-term functional outcome. It will be important to address these issues together in future research.

A third implication is that patients with PVD, especially those with evidence of generalized atherosclerosis (e.g., ischemic heart disease), severe atherosclerosis (e.g., those with amputations or who have had multiple reconstructive surgeries), or both, who are already showing evidence of neuropsychological compromise are at high risk for potentially more devastating strokes in the future. Many of the atherosclerotic risk factors (hypertension, diabetes, blood lipids, smoking) are amenable to treatment, and patients should be educated about these. Unfortunately, there is evidence that physicians do not treat atherosclerotic risk factors as aggressively in patients with PVD compared to patients with manifest cardiovascular disease (McDermott, Mehta, Ahn, & Greenland, 1997). Although it is likely that PVD patients have already received medical advice to control these factors (especially to quit smoking) in order to arrest or slow the progression of atherosclerotic disease in their legs (Krajewski & Olin, 1991; Playfer, 1983), it is possible that raising the spectre of potential stroke would provide further impetus for these patients to modify harmful lifestyle habits.

Fourth, the demonstration of cognitive deficits in PVD patients has implications for the studies that have evaluated neuropsychological outcome following vascular surgery, such as coronary artery bypass surgery (Shaw et al., 1987; Vanninen et al., 1998) and carotid endarterectomy (e.g., Hemmingsen et al., 1986; Kelly et al., 1980; van den Burg et al., 1985). These studies have used PVD patients as "normal" surgical controls with the assumption that they have intact cognitive function. Studies by me and my colleagues (Phillips, 1996; Phillips et al., 1993) demonstrated that this assumption is not correct, which may call into question some conclusions drawn from studies that used PVD controls. Studies that have observed postoperative improvement in cognitive function in carotid endarterectomy patients have attributed gains to the beneficial effects of surgery if postoperative improvement was not similarly observed in the control group (e.g., Hemmingsen et al., 1986). Conversely, failure to observe differences between carotid endarterectomy and PVD control groups preoperatively led one group of researchers to speculate that cognitive deficits may not exist in the target study group (e.g., Kelly et al., 1980). A recent review of the efficacy of cerebral revascularization has indicated mixed results. Baird (1991) argued that the literature does not strongly support the hypothesis that surgical revascularization procedures produce significant behavioural gains. However, the data from Phillips and colleagues suggest that the inclusion of PVD patients as control patients in previous studies of cerebral revascularization outcome may have contributed to the variability in the findings concerning efficacy.

PUTATIVE MECHANISMS
FOR NEUROPSYCHOLOGICAL DYSFUNCTION IN PVD

It is not yet known what accounts for the neuropsychologial deficits observed in patients with PVD. Are they in the early stages of multi-infarct dementia? Are there other vascular syndromes that could explain their deficits? One limitation to the series of studies conducted by Phillips and colleagues is that there was no structural information on the brains and cerebral arteries of the PVD patients. The patients were recruited to be free of an overt history of cerebrovascular accident, however, direct information about the integrity of cerebral arteries and brain matter would have been more definitive. It is probable that at least some of the patients tested had some degree of carotid stenosis. Currently, it is not known whether PVD severity and ischemic heart disease are predictors of cognitive function once the degree of carotid patency has been taken into consideration. Obtaining this information and relating it to neuropsychological function, rehabilitation, and functional outcome represents the next logical avenue of research in this area.

Some information regarding structural integrity can be gleaned from the literature. Hemmingsen et al. (1986) incidentally observed physiologic and structural evidence of brain abnormalities in PVD control patients. Bots et al. (1993) conducted a population-based study of magnetic resonance imaging scans of community-dwelling elderly people with and without cerebral white matter lesions (WMLs) to determine the relationship between WMLs and atherosclerosis in the cerebral, coronary, and peripheral arteries. Severity of peripheral insufficiency (using the ankle–brachial blood pressure ratio) was significantly related to the presence of WMLs, after controlling for sex and age. In fact, a 10% decrease in the ankle–brachial ratio was associated with a 20% increase in WML probability. The odds ratio of individuals with PVD having WMLs, after adjustment for sex and age, was 2.4. It is interesting that no decrease was observed in the magnitude of association between PVD and WMLs after additional adjustment of risk factors for cardiovascular disease (i.e., hypertension, hyperlipidemia, and smoking).

Fig. 7.2 presents a model of proposed distal and proximal causes of vascular-related cognitive impairment. This model elaborates some of the arguments of Emery and her colleagues (Emery, Gillie, & Ramdev, 1994; Emery & Oxman, 1994) and makes provision for the role of atherosclerotic risk factors (i.e., hypertension, diabetes, hyperlipidemia, smoking). In this model, tissue infarction is the most proximal direct cause of cognitive impairment. However, noninfarct factors, which include ischemia-related functional inactivity of neurons, can also have a direct deleterious effect on cognitive function. These factors may exert their power either prior to (the preinfarct state) or in the absence of actual tissue infarction (see also Sekhon, Morgan, Spence, & Weber, 1994). Last, atherosclerotic risk factors may themselves have a direct, albeit weak effect (see dotted line in Fig. 7.2) on cognitive function or a stronger, indirect effect through their role in atherogenesis.

It is not clear that the PVD participants in the studies reviewed in this chapter exhibited deficits that were sufficiently severe to warrant a diagnosis of vascular dementia, according to diagnostic criteria in the *Diagnostic and Statistical Manual of Mental Disorders* (4th ed., American Psychiatric Association, 1994), although some individual patients may have met these criteria. It is possible that the patients suffer from early or prodromal brain changes that may, for some, lead to dementia. This possibility is speculative and can be addressed only through longitudinal study. It also is important to replicate the relationship shown by Bots et al. (1993) between WMLs and peripheral atherosclerosis and to relate this directly to neuropsychological function in PVD patients.

DIRECTIONS FOR FUTURE RESEARCH

This chapter raises a number of questions that should be addressed in future research. First, it is not yet known whether cognitive impairments in PVD patients may affect their medical management (e.g., ability to follow instructions, take medications, etc.) or rehabilitation efforts. As one example, cognitive impairments in PVD amputees may impede their progress in rehabilitation and possibly require longer hospitalization, more intensive specialized training, or more follow-up care to maintain prosthetic competence in the home environment. An analysis of which cognitive domains relate to rehabilitation competence is also warranted. The results of Phillips (1996) and previous studies (e.g., Richardson et al., 1995) indicate that specific cognitive deficits (e.g., visuospatial, attention, and memory deficits) are strong predictors of everyday functions. Future studies should also include measures of affective functioning. By identifying specifically which factors pose an impediment to rehabilitation, steps can be taken to address and circumvent the deficits during rehabilitation training.

Previous research has indicated that atherosclerotic risk factors (hypertension, smoking, diabetes, hyperlipidemia) may have subtle negative effects on cognitive functioning. Studies of PVD patients may provide an alternate explanation. It has been shown that symptomatic manifestations of clinical atherosclerotic disease (PVD severity and heart disease) are better predictors of cognitive impairment than are the risk factors *per se*. This raises the interesting possibility that the presence of atherosclerotic symptoms such as PVD and ischemic heart disease, rather than being exclusionary factors, should be examined more closely in future studies of the neurobehavioral effects of medical conditions such as diabetes and hypertension. It is possible that the greatest impairments are found in patients with these risk factors who show clinical evidence of atherosclerosis.

Finally, the question remains as to whether in PVD patients a vascular dementia is being observed *in statu nascendi*. Subsequent research must determine the exact nature of the structural brain changes underlying cognitive decline (e.g., WMLs, cortical infarcts) and determine the predictive power of peripheral and coronary atherosclerosis and carotid integrity. Finally, the validity of the concept of a preinfarct state should be addressed further through animal models of noninfarctional cerebral ischemia and by studying the natural history of cognitive function in patients with atherosclerosis.

REFERENCES

Adams, R. D., & Victor, M. (1993). *Principles of neurology* (5th ed.). New York: McGraw-Hill.

Alexandrova, N. A., Gibson, W. C., Norris, J. W., & Maggisano, R. (1996). Carotid artery stenosis in peripheral vascular disease. *Journal of Vascular Surgery, 23,* 645–649.

American Psychiatric Association. (1994). *Diagnostic and statistical manual of mental disorders* (4th ed.). Washington, DC: Author.

Baird, A. D. (1991). Behavioral correlates of cerebral revascularization. In R. A. Bornstein & G. G. Brown (Eds.), *Neurobehavioral aspects of cerebrovascular disease* (pp. 297–313). New York: Oxford University Press.

Beck, A. T., & Speer, R. A. (1987). *Beck Depression Inventory: Manual.* San Antonio: The Psychological Corporation.

Boone, K. B., Lesser, I. M., Miller, B. L., Wohl, M., Berman, N., Lee, A., Palmer, B., & Back, C. (1995). Cognitive functioning in older depressed outpatients: Relationship of presence and severity of depression to neuropsychological test scores. *Neuropsychology, 9,* 390–398.

Bornstein, R. A., & Kelly, M. P. (1991). Risk factors for stroke and neuropsychological performance. In R. A. Bornstein & G. G. Brown (Eds.), *Neurobehavioral aspects of cerebrovascular disease* (pp. 182–201). New York: Oxford University Press.

Bots, M. L., van Swieten, J. C., Breteler, M. M. B., deJong, P. T. V. M., van Gijn, J., Hofman, A., & Grobbee, D. E. (1993). Cerebral white matter lesions and atherosclerosis in the Rotterdam Study. *The Lancet, 341,* 1232–1237.

Brown, G. G., Baird, A. D., Shatz, M. W., & Bornstein, R. A. (1996). The effects of cerebral vascular disease on neuropsychological functioning. In I. Grant & K. M. Adams (Eds.), *Neuropsychological assessment of neuropsychiatric disorders* (2nd ed., pp. 342–378). New York: Oxford University Press.

Criqui, M. H., Langer, R. D., Fronek, A., Feigelson, H. S., Klauber, M. R., McCann, T. J., & Browner, D. (1992). Mortality over a period of 10 years in patients with peripheral arterial disease. *New England Journal of Medicine, 326,* 381–386.

Dennis, M. S., Bamford, J. M., Sandercock, P. A. G., & Warlow, C. P. (1989). A comparison of risk factors and prognosis for transient ischemic attacks and minor ischemic strokes: The Oxfordshire Community Stroke Project. *Stroke, 20,* 1494–1499.

Derogatis, L. R. (1979). *SCL-90-R. Manual.* Towson, MD: Clinical Psychometric Research.

Ellis, M. R., Franks, P. J., Cuming, R., Powell, J. T., & Greenhalgh, R. M. (1992). Prevalence, progression, and natural history of asymptomatic carotid stenosis: Is there a place for carotid endarterectomy? *European Journal of Vascular Surgery, 6,* 172–177.

Emery, V. O. B., Gillie, E., & Ramdev, P. T. (1994). Vascular dementia redefined. In V. O. B. Emery & T. E. Oxman (Eds.), *Dementia: Presentations, differential diagnosis, and nosology* (pp. 162–194). Baltimore: Johns Hopkins University Press.

Emery, V. O. B., & Oxman, T. E. (1994). The spectra of dementia. In V. O. B. Emery & T. E. Oxman (Eds.), *Dementia: Presentations, differential diagnosis, and nosology* (pp. 384–407). Baltimore: Johns Hopkins University Press.

Fairbairn, J. F., II. (1980). Clinical manifestations of peripheral vascular disease. In J. L. Juergens, J. A. Spittell, Jr., & J. F. Fairbairn (Eds.), *Peripheral vascular diseases* (5th ed., pp. 3–49). Philadelphia: Saunders.

Folstein, M. F., Folstein, S. E., & McHugh, P. R. (1975). Mini-Mental State: A practical method for grading the cognitive state of patients for the clinician. *Journal of Psychiatric Research, 12,* 189–198.

Fuster, V., Kottke, B. A., & Juergens, J. L. (1980). Atherosclerosis. In J. L. Juergens, J. A. Spittell, Jr., & J. F. Fairbairn (Eds.), *Peripheral vascular diseases* (5th ed., pp. 219–235). Philadelphia: Saunders.

Ganda, O. P. (1980). Pathogenesis of macrovascular disease in the human diabetic. *Diabetes, 29,* 931–942.

Hankey, G. J., Slattery, J. M., & Warlow, C. P. (1992). Transient ischaemic attacks: Which patients are at high (and low) risk of serious vascular events? *Journal of Neurology, Neurosurgery, and Psychiatry, 55,* 640–652.

Hemmingsen, R., Mejsholm, B., Vorstrup, S., Lester, J., Engell, H. C., & Boysen, G. (1986). Carotid surgery, cognitive function, and cerebral blood flow in patients with transient ischemic attacks. *Annals of Neurology, 20,* 13–19.

Hershey, L. A., Jaffe, D. F., Greenough, P. G., & Yang, S.-L. (1987). Validation of cognitive and functional assessment instruments in vascular dementia. *International Journal of Psychiatry in Medicine, 17,* 183–192.

Hill, R. D. (1989). Residual effects of cigarette smoking on cognitive performance in normal aging. *Psychology and Aging, 4,* 251–254.

Jack, C. R., Jr., & Houser, O. W. (1994). Computed tomography and magnetic resonance imaging. In F. B. Meyer (Ed.), *Sundt's occlusive cerebrovascular disease* (pp. 154–178). Philadelphia: Saunders.

Jongbloed, L. (1986). Prediction of function after stroke: A critical review. *Stroke, 17,* 765–776.

Juergens, J. L., Barker, N. W., & Hines, E. A. (1960). Arteriosclerosis obliterans: Review of 520 cases with special reference to pathogenic and prognostic factors. *Circulation, 21,* 188–195.

Juergens, J. L., & Bernatz, P. E. (1980). Atherosclerosis of the extremities. In J. L. Juergens, J. A. Spittell, Jr., & J. F. Fairbairn (Eds.), *Peripheral vascular diseases* (5th ed., pp. 253–293). Philadelphia: Saunders.

Kannel, W. B., Skinner, J. J., Jr., & Schwartz, M. J. (1970). Intermittent claudication: Incidence in the Framingham study. *Circulation, 41,* 875–883.

Kannel, W. B., & Wolf, P. A. (1983). Epidemiology of cerebrovascular disease. In R. W. Ross Russell (Ed.), *Vascular disease of the central nervous system* (2nd ed., pp. 1–24). London: Churchill Livingstone.

Kelly, M. P., Garron, D. C., & Javid, H. (1980). Carotid artery disease, carotid endarterectomy, and behavior. *Archives of Neurology, 37,* 743–748.

King, D. A., Cox, C., Lyness, J. M., & Caine, E. D. (1995). Neuropsychological effects of depression and age in an elderly sample: A confirmatory study. *Neuropsychology, 9,* 399–408.

Krajewski, L. P., & Olin, J. W. (1991). Atherosclerosis of the aorta and lower extremity arteries. In J. R. Young, R. A. Graor, J. W. Olin, & J. R. Bartholomew (Eds.), *Peripheral vascular diseases* (pp. 179–200). St. Louis, MO: Mosby–Year Book.

Launer, L. J., Feskens, E. J. M., Kalmijn, S., & Kromhout, D. (1996). Smoking, drinking, and thinking: The Zutphen Elderly Study. *American Journal of Epidemiology, 143,* 219–227.

Lehmann, J. F., DeLateur, B. J., Fowler, R. S., Jr., Warren, C. G., Arnhold, R., Schertzer, G., Hurka, R., Whitmore, J. J., Masock, A. J., & Chambers, K. H. (1986). Stroke rehabilitation: Outcome and predictors. *Archives of Physical Medicine and Rehabilitation, 56,* 383–389.

Leng, G. C., Lee, A. J., Fowkes, F. G. R., Whiteman, M., Dunbar, J., Housley, E., & Ruckley, C. V. (1996). Incidence, natural history and cardiovascular events in symptomatic and asymptomatic peripheral arterial disease in the general population. *International Journal of Epidemiology, 25,* 1172–1180.

Levin, M. E. (1991). Diabetic foot lesions. In J. R. Young, R. A. Graor, J. W. Olin, & J. R. Bartholomew (Eds.), *Peripheral vascular diseases* (pp. 669–711). St. Louis, MO: Mosby–Year Book.

Lie, J. T. (1994). Pathology of occlusive disease of the extracranial arteries. In F. B. Meyer (Ed.), *Sundt's occlusive cerebrovascular disease* (2nd ed., pp. 25–44). Philadelphia: Saunders.

Light, K. C. (1978). Effects of mild cardiovascular and cerebrovascular disorders on serial reaction time performance. *Experimental Aging Research, 4,* 3–22.

Lord, J. W. (1965). Cigarette smoking and atherosclerosis occlusive disease. *Journal of the American Medical Association, 191,* 249–251.

Lorenze, E. J., & Cancro, R. (1962). Dysfunction in visual perception with hemiplegia: Its relation to activities of daily living. *Archives of Physical Medicine and Rehabilitation, 43,* 514–517.

McDermott, M. M., Mehta, S., Ahn, H., & Greenland, P. (1997). Atherosclerotic risk factors are less intensively treated in patients with peripheral arterial disease than in patients with coronary artery disease. *Journal of General Internal Medicine, 12,* 209–215.

Nelson, H. E. (1976). A modified card sorting test sensitive to frontal lobe deficits. *Cortex, 12,* 313–324.

O'Leary, D. H., Anderson, K. M., Wolf, P. A., Evans, J. C., & Poehlman, H. W. (1992). Cholesterol and carotid atherosclerosis in older persons: The Framingham study. *Annals of Epidemiology, 2,* 147–153.

Ostfeld, A. M., Shekelle, R. B., & Klawans, H. L. (1973). Transient ischemic attacks and risk of stroke in an elderly poor population. *Stroke, 4,* 980–986.

Pfeffer, R. I., Kuroaski, T. T., Chance, J. M., Filos, S., & Bates, D. (1984). Use of the Mental Function Index in older adults: Reliability, validity, and measurement of change over time. *American Journal of Epidemiology, 120,* 922–935.

Pfeffer, R. I., Kuroaski, T. T., Harrah, C. H., Jr., Chance, J. M., & Filos, S. (1982). Measurement of functional activities in older adults in the community. *Journal of Gerontology, 37,* 323–329.

Phillips, N. A. (1996). *Neuropsychological function in patients with peripheral vascular disease.* Unpublished doctoral dissertation, Dalhousie University, Halifax, Nova Scotia, Canada.

Phillips, N. A. & Mate-Kole, C. C. (1997). Cognitive deficits in peripheral vascular disease: A comparison of mild stroke patients and normal control subjects. *Stroke, 28,* 777–784.

Phillips, N. A., Mate-Kole, C. C., & Kirby, R. L. (1993). Neuropsychological function in peripheral vascular amputees. *Archives of Physical Medicine and Rehabilitation, 74,* 1309–1314.

Pinzur, M. S., Graham, G., & Osterman, H. (1988). Psychologic testing in amputation rehabilitation. *Clinical Orthopedics, 229,* 236–240.

Playfer, J. R. (1983). The medical treatment of peripheral arterial disease. In S. T. McCarthy (Ed.), *Peripheral vascular disease in the elderly* (pp. 78–86). New York: Churchill Livingstone.

Powell, J. T., Edwards, R. J., Worrell, P. C., Franks, P. J., Greenhalgh, R. M., & Poulter, N. R. (1997). Risk factors associated with the development of peripheral arterial disease in smokers: A case-control study. *Atherosclerosis, 129,* 41–48.

Reitan, R. M., & Wolfson, D. (1985). *The Halstead-Reitan Neuropsychological Test*. Tuscon: Neuropsychology Press.

Rey, A. (1941). L'examen psychologique dans les cas d'encéphalopathie traumatique. *Archives de Psychologie, 28*, 286–340. Translated by J. Corwin & F. W. Bylsma, *The Clinical Neuropsychologist* (1993), 4–9.

Richards, P. M., & Ruff, R. M. (1989). Motivational effects on neuropsychological functioning: Comparison of depressed versus nondepressed individuals. *Journal of Consulting and Clinical Psychology, 57*, 396–402.

Richardson, E. D., Nadler, J. D., & Malloy, P. F. (1995). Neuropsychologic prediction of performance measures of daily living skills in geriatric patients. *Neuropsychology, 9*, 565–572.

Rockson, S. G., & Cooke, J. P. (1998). Peripheral arterial insufficiency: Mechanisms, natural history, and therapeutic options. *Advances in Internal Medicine, 43*, 253–277.

Royal College of Physicians. (1977). Pharmacology and toxicology of tobacco smoke. In *Smoking or health: A report of the Royal College of Physicians* (pp. 39–51).

Rutherford, R. B., Flanigan, D. P., Gupta, S. K., Johnston, K. W., Karmody, A., Whittemore, A. D., Baker, J. B., Ernst, C. B., Jamieson, C., & Mehta, S. (1986). Suggested standards for reports dealing with lower extremity ischemia. *Journal of Vascular Surgery, 4*, 80–94.

Schultz, N. R., Jr., Elias, M. F., Robbins, M. A., Streeten, D. H. P., & Blakeman, N. (1989). A longitudinal study of the performance of hypertensive and normotensive subjects on the Wechsler Adult Intelligence Scale. *Psychology and Aging, 4*, 496–499.

Schwartz, S. I., & Hoaglund, F. T. (1989). Amputations. In S. I. Schwartz, G. T. Shires, & F. C. Spencer (Eds.), *Principles of surgery* (Vol. 2, 5th ed., pp. 2021–2038). New York: McGraw-Hill.

Sekhon, L. H. S., Morgan, M. K., Spence, L., & Weber, N. C. (1994). Chronic cerebral hypoperfusion and impaired neuronal function in rats. *Stroke, 25*, 1022–1027.

Shaw, P. J., Bates, D., Cartlidge, N. E. F., French, J. M., Heaviside, D., Julian, D. G., & Shaw, D. A. (1987). Neurologic and neuropsychological morbidity following major surgery: Comparison of coronary artery bypass and peripheral vascular surgery. *Stroke, 18*, 700–707.

Siekert, R. G., Whisnant, J. P., & Sundt, T. M., Jr. (1980). Ischemic cerebrovascular disease. In J. L. Juergens, J. A. Spittell, Jr., & J. F. Fairbairn (Eds.), *Peripheral vascular diseases* (5th ed., pp. 351–379). Philadelphia: Saunders.

Tonelli, C., Finzi, G., Catamo, A., Silvestrini, C., Squeri, M., Mombelloni, A., & Ponari, O. (1993). Prevalence and prognostic value of peripheral arterial disease in stroke patients. *International Angiography, 12*, 342–343.

Toole, J. F. (1994). *Cerebrovascular disorders* (4th ed.). New York: Raven Press.

van den Burg, W., Saan, R. J., Van Zomeren, A. H., Boontje, A. H., Haaxma R., & Wichmann, T. E. (1985). Carotid endarterectomy: Does it improve cognitive or motor functioning? *Psychological Medicine, 15*, 341–346.

Vanninen, R., Äikiä, M., Könönen, M., Partanen, K., Tulla, H., Hartikainen, P., Partanen, J., Manninen, H., Enberg, P., & Hippeläinen, M. (1998). Subclinical cerebral complications after coronary artery bypass grafting. *Archives of Neurology, 55*, 618–627.

Wechsler, D. (1981). *Wechsler Adult Intelligence Scale–Revised. Manual*. New York: The Psychological Corporation.

CHAPTER EIGHT

Cognitive Consequences of Myocardial Infarction, Cardiac Arrhythmias, and Cardiac Arrest

GUY VINGERHOETS
Ghent University, Belgium

In contrast to the well-documented cognitive changes associated with early manifestations of cardiovascular (CV) disease, such as essential hypertension, and of therapeutic interventions, such as antihypertensive medications or cardiopulmonary bypass surgery, little systematic research exists on the cognitive consequences of cardiac dysfunction. Following a perilous cardiac event, it is only natural that the heart is the focus of medical attention. Especially in the absence of frank neurological comorbidity, mental impairment is not expected, and the patient's medical staff and family members may not notice (subtle) cognitive changes. In addition, patients are often anxious or depressed following a cardiac event, and reduced cognitive performance can be interpreted as a result of the psychological distress. Only recently have researchers become interested in cognitive disturbances that seem to be linked with later manifestations of CV disease. In this chapter I investigate the cognitive deficits that have been associated with myocardial infarction (MI), cardiac arrhythmias, and cardiac arrest. I also investigate the potential underlying mechanisms that are believed to disturb the cognitive integrity of patients suffering from heart disease.

MYOCARDIAL INFARCTION

Although the incidence of acute MI has fallen in the United States and in a number of European countries, it remains one of the most common causes of death in men over age 45 years and in women over age 65 years. Currently, more than

1 million MIs occur annually in the United States, and in approximately 500,000 patients these will be fatal (American Heart Association, 1993).

Ischemic heart disease is a condition of diverse etiologies all having in common an imbalance between oxygen supply and demand. The most common cause of myocardial ischemia is atherosclerotic disease of epicardial coronary arteries. Advanced atherosclerotic lesions may impede the flow of blood to the heart, giving rise to ischemia and the symptoms of (stable) angina. The coronary arteries may also undergo denuding injury with sloughing of their endothelial cap, causing dynamic obstruction with nonoccluding thrombosis resulting in unstable angina. The surface of an unstable plaque is covered by platelet-rich thrombus, and distal embolization of small clumps of platelets occurs, causing focal microscopic myocardial necrosis. Finally, the plaques may undergo deep fissuring with acute occlusion of coronary arteries and resulting regional MI. MI most commonly occurs with an abrupt decrease in coronary blood flow that follows a thrombotic occlusion of a coronary artery previously narrowed by atherosclerosis. Following infarction, the ventricular shape may undergo drastic changes. In the first 24 hr after the infarction the dead area may thin and stretch because of slipping and tearing of bundles of myocytes. When organization and repair by fibrosis occurs, the expanded shape of the infarct zone is retained permanently. Left ventricular cavity size is increased, and the residual surviving myocardium may also undergo compensatory hypertrophy. This ventricular remodeling has long-term deleterious effects on cardiac function.

Cognitive Changes Following MI

Several authors have reported a relationship between dementia and a history of MI. Volpe and Petito (1985) presented case reports of two patients with dementia who had suffered several MIs. Autopsy findings of these patients showed chronic bilateral medial temporal lobe ischemic damage that included the hippocampus, subiculum, and amygdala. The authors suggested that the relatively circumscribed cerebral injury might have resulted from one or more episodes of global hypoxic ischemia even though no specific episodes of hypotension or cardiac arrest were documented. Aronson et al. (1990) found a surprisingly high association between dementia and a history of MI in very old women compared to men. This interaction suggested to the authors that women might be particularly susceptible to the cognitive consequences of MI, perhaps because women generally experience cardiac events later in life, at a time of diminished brain reserve. Investigating the risk factors for multiple-infarct dementia (MID), Gorelick et al. (1993) compared 61 MID cases and 86 controls with multiple cerebral infarcts without evidence of dementia. The authors found that a history of MI was positively and independently associated with MID and concluded that CV disease risk factors may be modifiable predictors of dementia associated with cerebral infarction.

Neuropsychological research has also found a surprisingly high prevalence of unrecognized cognitive dysfunction in nondemented cardiac patients. Barclay, Weiss, Mattis, Bond, and Blass (1988) found multiple cognitive deficits in 40% of a group of 20 clinically stable patients who had undergone cardiac surgery ($n = 13$) or were recovering from MI ($n = 7$) and who were free of known stroke or dementia. The neuropsychological deficits included problems with fine motor coordination, memory impairment, and disorientation. An additional 30% showed milder cognitive impairments. Only 1 patient had normal neurological examination results, and 75% of the sample had multiple neurological abnormalities suggestive of multifocal brain disease. Patients with a history of MI only, cardiac surgery only, or both were not significantly different in age, neurological findings, neuropsychological deficits, or ability to self-medicate reliably. Barclay et al. (1988) suggested that the cognitive deficits in cardiac patients might be related to multiple infarcts, acute or chronic hypoxic damage secondary to arrhythmias, cardiac failure, or small-vessel disease of the brain. They proposed the term *circulatory dementia* to describe patients with vascular disease and non-Alzheimer's–type dementia. Vingerhoets, Van Nooten, and Jannes (1997) unexpectedly noted the poor cognitive performance of some cardiac patients on a presurgical neuropsychological assessment that was intended to be a baseline measure to detect cognitive impairment following cardiopulmonary bypass surgery. The authors investigated the preoperative data of 77 cardiac patients who did not suffer from carotid artery stenosis. Twenty-five patients (33%) had had one previous heart attack, and 4 patients (5%) had had two previous heart attacks. Compared to 37 normal controls (and corrected for the possible influence of presurgical anxiety and depressive symptomatology of the patients), the surgical candidates had significantly impaired word fluency, manual dexterity, verbal learning, and psychomotor speed. A stepwise multiple regression analysis to determine the factors that contributed to the cognitive impairment included several preoperative variables indicating a more precarious heart function such as cardiomegaly, increased blood urea nitrogen, and length of history of cardiac complaints.

Mechanisms Underlying Cognitive Impairment Following MI

From the few available studies, it appears that cognitive dysfunction is not all that uncommon in patients with ischemic heart disease, and it may be associated with cardiac pathology. Although a causal relationship between MI and cognitive dysfunction remains uncertain, several possible mechanisms could— alone or in combination—be involved and will be evaluated further. The mechanisms include (a) generalized systemic vascular disease that leads to cardiac ischemia but also contributes to cerebrovascular insufficiency, (b) multiple cerebrovascular infarcts due to cardiogenic emboli, (c) acute or chronic hypoxic brain damage due to impaired cardiac function with resulting cerebral hypoperfusion, and (d) an emotional reaction following a life-threatening MI characterized by depressive symptomatology that mimics cognitive impairment.

MI and Cognitive Dysfunction Are Both Symptoms of a Generalized Systemic Vascular Disease

Atherosclerosis is the underlying cause of MIs, cerebrovascular disease, and peripheral vascular disease. Traditionally, atherosclerosis develops slowly, over many years, in the innermost layer of large- and medium-sized arteries as a healing response to repeated vascular-wall injury. Well-defined risk factors (see chaps. 4 and 5) promote endothelial cell dysfunction that in turn activates a protective response. With the repeated rounds of injury and repair, atherosclerotic plaques are formed. The distribution of atherosclerosis is peculiarly consistent in that plaques occur in the origin of the larger arteries with a high pressure and at points of arterial branching and tortuosity, which are sites of hemodynamic stress on the arterial wall. The most common sites of atheroma include the origin of the major arteries from the aorta, the aortic arch itself, the bifurcation of the common carotid artery into the internal and external carotid arteries, the carotid siphon, the origin and termination of the vertebral arteries, the basilar artery, the circle of Willis, and the proximal portion of the three cerebral arteries.

There is ample evidence of a close relation between CV disease and cerebrovascular disease (Love, Grover-McKay, Biller, Rezai, & McKay, 1992). Because the underlying pathologic features of atherosclerosis in cerebral, cardiac, and peripheral circulation are virtually identical, it is not surprising that they share similar risk factors and that people with one clinical manifestation are at increased risk of the others. The major CV risk factors for MI are also contributors to brain infarction. Dominant stroke risk factors in the prospective epidemiological Framingham Study were hypertension, clinical manifestations of coronary heart disease (CHD), cardiac failure, atrial fibrillation, and compromised coronary circulation. CHD almost tripled the risk of stroke (Kannel, Wolf, & Verter, 1983). Conversely, Rokey, Rolak, Harati, Kutka, and Verani (1984) showed that 29 of 50 patients (58%) who had had a mild stroke or a transient ischemic attack (TIA) had coronary artery disease (CAD) compared to 7% prevalence of CAD in a control group of similar age. Di Pasquale et al. (1986) detected asymptomatic CAD in 28% of cerebrovascular patients. This prevalence is four times greater than that in a control group of healthy individuals, thus indicating that asymptomatic ischemic heart disease is often associated with cerebrovascular disease; cerebral ischemic attacks may therefore be a marker of CAD (Di Pasquale et al., 1986). In addition, there is an impressive CV mortality in patients suffering from cerebrovascular disease, particularly in advanced age (Cartlidge, Whisnant, & Elneback, 1977; Heyden, Heiss, & Heyman, 1980; Sacco, Wolf, & Kannel, 1982). This may in part reflect the less well-recognized finding that specific brain lesions associated with stroke may lead to cardiac muscle changes (myocytolisis), arrhythmias, and electrocardiographic changes (Caplan, 1994).

The association of atherosclerosis of coronary and cerebral arteries is a well-recognized entity. Sollberg et al. (1968) investigated the severity of atherosclerosis in the cerebral arteries, coronary arteries, and aortas of 1,042 autopsied corpses. The results indicated that, on a group basis, there was a close association between the number and degree of stenosing lesions among the arteries. On an individual basis, however, it seemed impossible to predict the amount of atherosclerosis in the cerebral arteries from the number of lesions in the aorta and the coronary arteries. Breteler, van Swieten, et al. (1994) related brain magnetic resonance imaging findings with CV risk factors and found that a history of stroke or MI was significantly and independently associated with the presence of white matter lesions in elderly people. The authors concluded that pathologic correlates of white matter lesions support the hypothesis that atherosclerosis plays an important role in their pathogenesis. Previous vascular events (MI or stroke), presence of plaques in the carotid arteries, and presence of peripheral arterial atherosclerotic disease were associated with lower levels of cognitive performance independent of the effects of age and education (Breteler, Claus, Grobbee, & Hofman, 1994).

Asymptomatic carotid bruits predict MI just as well as brain infarctions (Wolf, Kannel, Sorlie, & McNamara, 1981). However, the site of stroke was usually remote from the vessel with the carotid bruit. The mechanism of stroke was more frequently hemorrhage from aneurysm, lacunar infarction, and embolism from the heart than cerebral infarction in the carotid artery territory. This suggested to Wolf et al. (1981) a nonspecific influence of atherosclerotic CV disease in the genesis of stroke, MI, and death, the presence of which was signaled by a carotid bruit. Patients with asymptomatic carotid artery stenosis (ACAS) also show substantial deficits on tasks of mental speed, learning, visuospatial abilities, verbal processing, and deductive reasoning (Benke, Neussl, & Aichner, 1991). Benke et al. noticed that the amount of cognitive impairment in ACAS individuals was remarkable despite the fact that the observed carotid stenoses were moderate and that flow reduction was only unilateral in most patients. Because the cognitive profile of ACAS patients indicated nonspecific impairment, Benke et al. related the cognitive impairment to chronic diffuse or multifocal ischemic lesions (widespread cerebrovascular disease) and concluded that ACAS is possibly an indicator of systemic intracranial vascular disease. Naugle, Bridgers, and Delaney (1986) suggested that the subtle neuropsychological deficits of hemodynamically significant carotid stenosis, even asymptomatic, might be related to prolonged impeded carotid blood flow in some patients. Vingerhoets et al. (1997) pointed out that the preoperative cognitive impairment found in their candidates for cardiac surgery (who were free of carotid artery stenosis) was similar to the deficits found in patients with hemodynamically significant carotid stenosis, namely, a reduced performance on tasks of immediate recall and learning, psychomotor speed, and mental flexibility (Benke et al., 1991; Naugle et al., 1986). These investigations suggest that a similar underlying pathology could be responsible for the nonspecific cognitive impairments in both carotid artery disease and cardiac disease (Vingerhoets et al., 1997).

Patients with peripheral vascular disease also performed significantly more poorly than normal elderly control participants and similarly to mild stroke patients on measures of executive function, attention, and visuospatial function (Phillips & Mate-Kole, 1997). Phillips and Mate-Kole (1997) highlighted the coexistence of peripheral vascular disease and cerebrovascular disease and suggested that a common pathophysiologic mechanism may explain these cognitive deficits as being due to unrecognized concomitant cerebrovascular disease in patients with peripheral vascular disease.

It appears from these studies that the clinical manifestation of atherosclerosis in the cerebral, cardiac, or peripheral circulation may be a marker of a more general systemic vascular disease that inevitably compromises the cerebral vasculature, leading to cognitive impairment.

MI Is an Indication of an Atherosclerotic Heart Leading to Cardiogenic Brain Embolism

In many patients a cerebral infarct does not arise from in situ thrombosis of cerebral vessels but from thromboembolism from the heart or extracranial arteries (Blackwood, Hallpike, & Kocen, 1969; Lhermitte, Gauthier, & Derouesne, 1970). Although cardiogenic embolism is difficult to diagnose with certainty in individual patients, it is believed that 15% to 20% of all ischemic strokes are due to cardiogenic embolism (Caplan, 1994). Sources of cardiac embolism can be divided into three groups: (a) cardiac wall abnormalities—for example, cardiomyopathies, hypokinetic and akinetic ventricular regions after MI, atrial septal and ventricular aneurysms, cardiac tumors, septal defects, and patent foramen ovale; (b) valve disorders, especially rheumatic mitral and aortic disease; and (c) arrhythmias, especially atrial fibrillation (Bogousslavsky et al., 1991). Nonrheumatic atrial fibrillation is the most frequent substrate of cardiogenic brain embolism (50%), but emboli from left ventricular mural thrombi in acute MI still account for 15% of its prevalence (Bogousslavsky et al., 1991; Cerebral Embolism Task Force, 1989; Mandawat & Ross Lorimer, 1996).

About 3% to 5% of patients with acute MI experience ischemic stroke within 4 to 6 weeks. The stroke risk is highest within the first 2 weeks following MI. The embolic origin of the majority of these strokes is supported by their striking relationship to left ventricular thrombi; a minority are attributable to atrial thrombi or other causes. Most cardiogenic emboli to the brain lodge in the middle cerebral artery (MCA) or its branches, and infarcts involving the cortex are common (Cerebral Embolism Task Force, 1986). Retrospective studies found a clearly higher incidence of cardiac embolism in the left MCA (Berlit, Eckstein, & Krause, 1986; Oder, Siostrzonek, & Lang, 1991). According to some authors, recurrent cardiogenic embolism typically involves the previously affected vascular territory, rather than a different one (Gates, Barnett, & Silver, 1986; Oder et al., 1991). In contrast, Yasaka et al. (1993) found that 24 of 31 recurrent attacks in acute cardioembolic stroke occurred in a vascular territory different from that of the initial attack. The ophthalmic circulation, the main trunk and parietal and angular branches of the MCA, are reported as the most common sites for lodgment of cardiac emboli (Gates et al., 1986). About 20% of cardiogenic emboli go to the posterior circulation (vertebro–basilar and posterior cerebral artery infarctions; Caplan, 1994). In a recent study, Kaps, Seidel, and Berg (1995) measured microaggregates arising from prosthetic cardiac valves in 44 patients undergoing bilateral transcranial Doppler monitoring for 1 hr in both MCAs. They concluded that asymmetry of the craniocervical vessels branching from the aortic arch generally does not entail lateralized differences in microembolism. Nevertheless, preferential distribution of microparticles was obvious in some cases, suggesting distinct streaming patterns in the supra-aortal circulation in some individuals. This is in good agreement with animal experiments (Gacs, Merer, & Bodosi, 1982) and with clinically observed lodging preferences of recurrent cardiac embolism (Gates et al., 1986).

Cognitive Dysfunction Is a Consequence of (Acute or Chronic) Hypoxic Brain Damage Due to Impaired Cardiac Function

Whereas *anoxia* refers to a complete absence of available oxygen to the brain, during hypoxia oxygen availability is reduced. The brain, as one of the most metabolically active organs, has a constant requirement for oxygen and is highly vulnerable to the loss of an adequate blood supply. Under normal circumstances human cerebral blood flow is well protected against variations in blood pressure (BP). Cerebral blood flow is autoregulated by intracranial mechanisms to ensure a constant supply of blood to the brain between mean systemic blood pressures (BPs) of approximately 60 mm Hg and 160 mm Hg. Outside these limits cerebral blood flow follows perfusion pressure, and hypoxia occurs if the systemic BP falls below the autoregulative window. Acute cardiac failure can result in serious anoxic episodes with subsequent brain damage (see Cardiac Arrest section).

Lower levels of oxygen deprivation are also associated with brain damage if the hypoxic episodes continue or frequently recur (Gibson, Pulsinelli, Blass, & Duffy, 1981). In chronic heart failure with reduced cardiac output, compensatory mechanisms redistribute the blood to vital organs such as the heart and brain while circulation to the not-acutely-vital skin and kidneys is significantly reduced (Wade & Bishop, 1962). However, hypotensive patients with severe heart failure were found to have significantly decreased cerebral blood flow relative to normal controls even though the mean arterial pressure in the patient group was well above the lower autoregulation limit (Paulson, Jarden, Vorstrup, Holm, & Godtfredsen, 1986; Rajagopalan, Raine, Cooper, & Ledingham, 1984). Impaired autoregulation and failing compensatory mechanisms could give rise to chronic hypoxia characterized by mild but wide-ranging cognitive impairment (Grant et al., 1987; Prigatano & Levin, 1988).

The neuropathologic consequences of a reduction in the overall cerebral blood flow appear to depend on the rapidity with which and the extent to which the flow is reduced. Reduced cerebral blood flow associated with systemic hypotension of varying speed of onset, intensity, and duration can give rise to a spectrum of change ranging from regions confined to the "watersheds" (arterial boundary zones) of the cerebrum and cerebellum to a purely diffuse, or laminar (involving layers of the cortex) destruction of neurons throughout each. A more moderate but sustained reduction in cerebral blood flow can cause a concentration of ischemic neuronal destruction along the arterial boundary zones of the human brain and has been described as a consequence of systemic hypotension that is due to myocardial insufficiency (Adams, Brierley, Connor, & Treip, 1966). Visual disturbances are the most regular features following border zone ischemia in humans and are produced by ischemic lesions in the parieto–occipital region, the common border zone territory among all three cerebral arterial territories. Some patients show bibranchial sensorimotor impairment and a disturbance of volitional saccadic eye movements caused by more anteriorly placed ischemia in the border zone between the anterior cerebral artery and the MCA. Some show a temporary dyslexia–dysgraphia and memory defect related to bilateral parietotemporal lesions in the border zone between the MCA and the posterior cerebral artery (Howard, Trend, & Ross Russell, 1987).

Concurrent Depression Compromises the Cognitive Performance of Patients Who Have Suffered MI

Minor and major depressive disorders are a recognized comorbidity of MI and are certainly among the most commonly described emotional reactions in the vast literature on psychological distress in patients who have had an MI (Frasure-Smith, Lespérance, & Talajic, 1995; Schleifer et al., 1989). Schleifer et al. (1989) found that 8 to 10 days after infarction 45% of 283 patients met diagnostic criteria for minor or major depression, including 18% with major depressive syndromes. Depression was not associated with the severity of cardiac illness. Three to 4 months after infarction 33% of 171 patients met criteria for minor or major depression.

Depression may interfere with the normal expression of cognitive abilities in intact individuals. Slowed mental processing, mild attention deficits, impairments in short-term recall and in learning verbal and visuospatial material are frequently associated with this emotional disorder. In elderly people, depression can mimic or exacerbate symptoms of progressive dementing conditions (Lezak, 1995). It is important to differentiate the influence of clinical depression on cognitive function from the CV causes of cognitive dysfunction in patients who have suffered an MI.

CARDIAC ARRHYTHMIA

Cardiac arrhythmia describes an abnormality of cardiac rhythm of any type. A heart rate between 60 and 100 beats per minute is arbitrarily defined as a normal sinus rhythm, and any disturbance from this is, by definition, an arrhythmia. The spectrum of cardiac arrhythmia ranges from innocent extrasystoles to acute, life-threatening conditions such as asystole or ventricular fibrillation, and it is difficult to draw the line between normal or acceptable cardiac arrhythmias and arrhythmias that threaten cardiac and cerebral integrity. Arrhythmias are frequently associated with structural heart disease or external provocative factors but may also be present in the absence of cardiac disease. The mechanisms responsible for cardiac arrhythmias are generally divided into categories: disorders of impulse formation, disorders of impulse conduction, or a combination of both. Cardiac arrhythmias can also be characterized as supraventricular (atrial or junctional) and ventricular arrhythmias.

The most frequently investigated cardiac arrhythmia in neuropsychological studies is nonrheumatic atrial fibrillation. Atrial fibrillation is a rather common cardiac condition in elderly people with a prevalence of 2%–4% after 60 years of age. Atrial fibrillation occurs in chronic and paroxysmal forms. Paroxysmal attacks usually last hours or days. If the abnormal rhythm persists after a period of 2 to 3 weeks, atrial fibrillation is said to be chronic. Known causal factors are hypertensive heart disease, ischemic heart disease, cardiac failure, chronic obstructive pulmonary heart disease, and thyrotoxicosis.

Cognitive Changes Associated With Cardiac Arrhythmias

As with MI, studies have related cardiac arrhythmias with dementia. Ratcliffe and Wilcock (1985) studied a postmortem series of 48 demented elderly people to determine the relationship between cerebral infarction and CV disease in that population. They found that atrial fibrillation was strongly associated with cerebral infarction and concluded that the role of atrial fibrillation has been underestimated in the pathogenesis of cerebrovascular dementia. Sulkava and Erkinjuntti (1987) reported on six patients in whom dementia was clinically judged to be associated with cerebral hypoperfusion due to cardiac arrhythmias and systemic hypotension. The patients were included if they had an acute onset of dementia in temporal connection with cardiac arrhythmias and systemic arterial hypotension. Hypotension was associated with cardiac arrhythmias in all six cases. De Pedis, Hedner, Johansson, and Steen (1987) found an increased prevalence of atrial fibrillation, ventricular tachycardia, and gaps (R–R interval > 1.5 seconds) in a group of 36 elderly patients with organic dementia compared to a geriatric control group without dementia or current heart disease. Rockwood, Dobbs, Rule, Howlett, and Black (1992) also found that 3 of 19 elderly patients who were scheduled for pacemaker implantation for dysrhythmias met criteria for dementia. Neuropsychological testing prior to pacemaker implantation further revealed deficits in attention, learning, memory, and verbal fluency compared to controls who were matched for age, gender, and mental status score. These deficits appeared to be due primarily to the poor performance of patients with complete heart block. No significant change in cognitive test performance was found 6 to 12 months after pacemaker implantation. Moroney et al. (1996) prospectively followed 185 initially nondemented patients with ischemic stroke and concluded that the presence of hypoxic–ischemic disorders (such as cardiac arrhythmias) was a significant and independent risk factor for the development of new dementia after stroke. Kilander et al. (1998) studied a cohort of 952 elderly men and found an association between atrial fibrillation and low cognitive function (as determined by the Mini-Mental State Examination and the Trail Making Tests), independent of stroke, high BP, and diabetes. Men with atrial fibrillation who received pharmacological treatment performed markedly better than those without treatment.

Kennedy, Hofer, Cohen, Shindledecker, and Fisher (1987) noted that 14 (15.7%) of 88 patients with mild to severe cardiac arrhythmias could be described as cognitively impaired on the basis of their performance on a cognitive screening test. All 14 patients suffered from ventricular tachycardia or fibrillation. A statistically significant relationship was identified between cognitive impairment and mortality. Arrhythmia severity or treatment efficacy (programmed electrical stimulation) was not related to the cognitive screening score. Jabourian (1995) investigated 450 patients with cardiac arrhythmias 1 day before and 8 days after pacemaker implantation with a cognitive screening test and two visual memory tests. At the first examination abnormal cognitive test scores were five to six times more frequent in the patient group than in the general population of the same age. Eight days after pacemaker implantation the cognitive scores of the patients were significantly increased. In 63% of the patients the correction of the cardiac arrhythmias resulted in improved cognitive functioning, and 14% no longer showed a profile of dementia. Postoperatively, electroencephalographic (EEG) normalizations were found in 55% of the sample. Neuropsychological performance and EEG measures were significantly associated. Clinical observation suggested to Jabourian that cardiac arrhythmia had a particular importance in the development of cerebral dysfunction. Some of the patients who needed replacement of the stimulator complained of a recurrence of neuropsychiatric symptoms with the fading of the battery, followed by a cognitive and emotional improvement on implantation of the new stimulator. Patients in whom the cognitive–emotional complaints persisted 3 to 4 days after the operation improved when the cardiac frequency of the stimulator was adjusted.

Farina et al. (1997) assessed the preclinical effects on cognitive function of nonrheumatic atrial fibrillation in 37 patients without a known history of cerebrovascular disease. They compared chronic and paroxysmal atrial fibrillation patients with a matched number of control participants in sinus rhythm. Chronic patients with atrial fibrillation showed a greater neuropsychological impairment than patients with paroxysmal atrial fibrillation. This is in agreement with the high frequency of (clinically silent) cerebral infarction found in patients with chronic atrial fibrillation without a history of cerebrovascular disease relative to the low risk of such lesions in normal controls and patients with paroxysmal atrial fibrillation (Petersen & Godtfredsen, 1986; Petersen, Pedersen, et al., 1989). Compared to normal controls, chronic atrial fibrillation patients exhibited poor performance in attention and memory tasks. The paroxysmal atrial fibrillation group showed significantly lower scores than controls only in a long-term memory task.

Cardiac arrhythmias appear to be a strong and independent risk factor for cerebral infarction and hypoperfusion, cognitive impairment, and dementia. Some findings also suggest that medical treatment of the cardiac arrhythmias is able to ameliorate the cognitive performance of the patients.

Mechanisms Underlying Cognitive Impairment Following Cardiac Arrhythmia

Cardiac arrhythmias are often associated with cerebral thrombi (Busse, 1982). Atrial fibrillation is the most frequent substrate for cardiogenic brain embolism, and patients with this dysrhythmia have a fivefold increase in the risk of stroke (Cerebral Embolism Task Force, 1986; Halperin & Hart, 1988). A retrospective study of 150 atrial fibrillation patients' records showed that 46 (31%) had suffered a stroke or peripheral embolism, and most emboli (42) involved the cerebral circulation (Sherman et al., 1987). A similar study showed that 13% of patients with chronic atrial fibrillation who presented with symptomatic cerebral ischemia had had a previous asymptomatic infarction, significantly more frequently than people in normal sinus rhythm (Kempster, Gerraty, & Gates, 1988). Although these computer-tomography–defined infarcts are labeled *asymptomatic* or *silent*, it is believed that they take a subtle, but cumulative, toll on cognition, especially in elderly people (Halperin & Hart, 1988). Atrial fibrillation covers a spectrum of heart disease, so it remains unclear whether cardiogenic emboli in atrial fibrillation are a consequence of the dysrhythmia itself or the result of the underlying cardiac disease that serves as the actual source of thromboembolism and of which dysrhythmia is a marker. Identification of subgroups of atrial fibrillation patients who are at even greater risk of impending cerebral damage might be possible (Cerebral Embolism Task Force, 1986; Halperin & Hart, 1988).

The ischemic lesions that are due to microembolization may be responsible for the neurological signs and cognitive dysfunction observed in atrial fibrillation (Farina et al., 1997; Gordon, 1978). On the other hand, Farina and colleagues found that the number of magnetic resonance imgaging ischemic lesions was not correlated with the degree of neuropsychological impairment, suggesting the possible involvement of factors other than microembolization.

Lavy et al. (1980) showed that cerebral blood flow was reduced in patients with chronic atrial fibrillation compared to that of controls in normal sinus rhythm. Reduced cerebral blood flow may also contribute to the frequent cerebral complications in atrial fibrillation (Petersen, Kastrup, Videbaek, & Boysen, 1989). It has been suggested that the reduced cardiac output (of patients with complete heart block) leads to cerebral hypoperfusion, which is the main cause of the cognitive impairment (Rockwood et al., 1992). Other research has found that the reduced cerebral blood flow in (milder dysrhythmic) atrial fibrillation patients was unrelated to the cardiac output but could be significantly increased after electrical cardioversion therapy to sinus rhythm (Petersen, Kastrup, et al., 1989). Farina et al. (1997) suggested diffuse hypoxic brain damage or the development of multiple microlacunae due to a critical chronic or episodic reduction of cerebral perfusion as an alternative explanation for cognitive impairment. Cardiac arrhythmias often lower cardiac output so that cerebral blood flow is impaired beyond the brain's normal compensatory mechanism and, as a consequence, induce cerebral hypoperfusion. Chronic-fibrillation patients would be submitted to a long-standing cerebral hypoperfusion, whereas, in the case of paroxysmal atrial fibrillation patients, a permanent injury could take place in the course of the attacks of atrial fibrillation (Farina et al., 1997). According to Jabourian (1995), not only does the effect of cardiac arrhythmias involve cerebral hypoperfusion, but also paroxysms of variable severity and duration may influence the metabolic function of the brain, thus compromising cognitive integrity.

CARDIAC ARREST

Cardiac arrest denotes the functional cessation of the pumping action of the heart. Sudden cardiac arrest usually results from severe disturbances of cardiac impulse generation or conduction, which cause cardiac output to fall to levels that cannot sustain cerebral or cardiac function. The majority of cases (70%–75%) are related to ventricular tachyarrhythmias or to profound bradyarrhythmias (25%–30%), although there remains a large number of additional potential causes of sudden cardiac death. The initiation and perpetuation of a ventricular tachyarrhythmia is believed to involve three factors: (a) triggers, (b) a pathophysiologic substrate for arrhythmia, and (c) modulating factors. Premature ventricular beats almost invariably act as triggers. The pathophysiologic substrate may be acute (MI or ischemia) or chronic (healed MI, cardiomyopathy, ventricular hypertrophy). The modulating factors include changes in autonomic tone, hemodynamic abnormalities, myocardial ischemia, electrolyte imbalance, or drugs.

The chances of surviving an out-of-hospital cardiac arrest are dismal and depend on a number of factors, including the nature of the rhythmic disturbance and the ability of nonmedical witnesses or paramedical personnel to respond quickly and in an appropriate manner. Research suggests that for every 100 patients who experience an out-of-hospital cardiac arrest, only 15 survive and can be dismissed from the hospital. Five of them have worsened cardiac or neurologic status, and only 10 ever achieve their prehospital status (Osborn, 1996).

Cognitive Changes Following Cardiac Arrest

Although anoxic survivors of cardiac arrest show a diffuse pattern of cognitive deficits, memory impairment is the most frequently described cognitive dysfunction. Numerous case studies and small-sample studies have reported on a wide range of memory disorders, including (pure) amnesia (Beuret et al., 1993; Cummings, Tomiyasu, Read, & Benson, 1984; Kaschel, Zaiser-Kaschel, Shiel, & Mayer, 1995; McNeill, Tidmarsh, & Rostall, 1965; Parkin, Miller, & Vincent, 1987; Volpe & Hirst, 1983), persistent mild to moderate anterograde memory difficulties (Bertini et al., 1990; Beuret et al., 1993; Bigler & Alfano, 1988; Dougherty, 1994; Grubb, O'Carroll, Cobbe, Sirel, & Fox, 1996; Meltzer, 1983; Reich, Regestein, Murawski, DeSilva, & Lown, 1983; Roine, Kajaste, & Kaste, 1993; Sauve, Doolittle, Walker, Paul, & Scheinman, 1996; Wilson, 1996), and modality-specific semantic knowledge loss for unique items (Kartsounis & Shallice, 1996).

Descriptions of the amnesic patients in the studies mentioned in the preceding paragraph indicate that some were oriented and did not confabulate (Volpe & Hirst, 1983), whereas others were disoriented to time and place (Parkin et al., 1987) and confabulated readily (Cummings et al., 1984). Marked retrograde amnesia was present in some patients (Meltzer, 1983; Parkin et al., 1987; Wilson, 1996). Severity of the memory impairment correlated significantly with measures of the duration of the cardiac arrest but was not associated with patients' age, occupation, measures of comorbidity, social deprivation, anxiety or depression scores, or estimated premorbid intelligence (Grubb et al., 1996).

Volpe, Holtzman, and Hirst (1986) measured the rate of forgetting for both recall and recognition memory of verbal material in 6 patients with an amnesic syndrome following cardiac arrest. Their data showed that recall decayed significantly faster for the amnesic patients than for controls, whereas the rate of forgetting for recognition memory was comparable in both groups. Volpe et al. suggested that dissociation between recall and recognition performance is a feature of the amnesic syndrome after cardiac arrest. This was not confirmed by Wilson (1996), who found that none of the 4 patients with hypoxia following cardiac arrest scored above chance on a recognition memory test. Mecklinger, von Cramon, and Matthes von Cramon (1998) measured event-related potentials (ERPs) during the performance on a recognition memory task in 8 survivors of cardiac arrest and in 8 matched controls. Although the recognition performance of the patients was well above chance level, old–new effects (i.e., larger ERP waveforms for previously studied items than for unstudied items) were absent or even inverted in polarity in the patients. Mecklinger et al. suggested that recognition, based on the retrieval of an item's study episode, is degraded in survivors of cerebral hypoxia. Further research in larger groups appears necessary to evaluate the integrity of recognition memory following cardiac arrest.

Prospective evaluation of cognitive difficulties following cardiac arrest showed improvement of function over the course of a 3-month and 1-year follow-up assessment (Roine et al., 1993). Three months after cardiac arrest, 41 of 68 patients (60%) showed moderate to severe cognitive deficits. At 12 months, 26 of 54 long-term survivors (48%) still had moderate to severe deficits, of which impaired delayed memory was the most common neuropsychological dysfunction. Similar findings were reported by Sauve et al. (1996), who noted that 38 of 45 survivors (84%) showed mild to severe cognitive deficits during hospitalization. Six months after resuscitation these deficits persisted in 19 of 38 survivors (38%). Here, too, problems with delayed recall were most prominent. Presence and duration of unconsciousness after resuscitation (postanoxic coma) appears to be related to worse cognitive outcome (Bertini et al., 1990; Sauve et al., 1996), although other research did not find such a relation (de Vos, de Haes, Koster, & de Haan, 1999).

It can be concluded that the majority of the anoxic survivors of cardiac arrest have mild to severe anterograde memory problems with severely depressed free recall and (at least in some cases) less depressed recognition, together with a reasonably normal short-term memory (Beuret et al., 1993; Grubb et al., 1996; Kaschel et al., 1995; McNeill et al., 1965; Parkin et al., 1987; Reich et al., 1983; Volpe & Hirst, 1983; Wilson, 1996). A substantial minority also suffer from visuospatial and visuoperceptual problems (Dougherty, 1994; Meltzer, 1983; Roine et al., 1993; Wilson, 1996), executive function problems, or both (Wilson, 1996). Less frequently reported cognitive deficits include agnosia; impairments in reading, writing, calculation, and abstraction; dysphasia; disorientation; intellectual deterioration; ataxia; and myoclonus (Beuret et al., 1993; Parkin et al., 1987; Roine et al., 1993). In several cases personality changes were noted, including apathy; irritability; petulance; emotional disinhibition; and disturbances of impulse control, insight, empathy, judgment, and social perceptiveness (Reich et al., 1983). Depressive symptoms are frequent early after cardiac arrest and persist in 45% of patients 12 months after the arrest (Roine et al., 1993)

Mechanisms Underlying Cognitive Impairment Following Cardiac Arrest

During the acute phase of cardiac arrest, as cerebral blood flow drops to (nearly) zero, the oxygen available to the brain is depleted within a few seconds. The resultant condition is termed *ischemic anoxia*. During ischemic anoxia, normal brain chemistry and physiology undergo radical changes that can lead to irreversible brain damage (Vaagenes et al., 1996). The adverse effects of acute anoxia include edema (brain swelling) and widespread neuronal damage, particularly to the basal ganglia, cerebral white matter, and brainstem, with sites of lesions related to the degree and duration of the anoxia. Neuroradiological findings following anoxic encephalopathy revealed diffuse cortical atrophy and ventricular enlargement (Bigler & Alfano, 1988). The rates at which different areas become damaged vary considerably. The regions of the brain concerned with autonomic function seem most resistant to anoxic damage. Most vulnerable are the perfusion borders among the MCA, the anterior cerebral artery, and the posterior cerebral artery (the so-called *watershed* or *border zone* regions of the cortex) and the terminal supply areas of the deep-penetrator arteries. These distal fields are at risk when there is an abrupt, profound episode of hypotension (as in acute MI), although the fall in perfusion pressure is probably shorter and less severe than in a (no-flow) cardiopulmonary arrest. In cardiac arrest, when blood supply to the entire brain ceases, global ischemia ensues. Following resuscitation, it appears that only a select population of neurons die. These selectively vulnerable cells include neurons in the anterior thalamus, the hippocampal CA-1 and subiculum areas, and Purkinje cells in the cerebellum. After cardiac arrest, diffuse cortical injury is more severe in the frontal lobes than in the parietal or occipital lobes and especially affects the middle layers (3 and 5) of the cortex (Adams et al., 1966; Brierley, 1979; Collins, Dobkin, & Choi, 1989; Cummings et al., 1984). This selective neuronal damage impairs cognition, motor function, coordination, memory, emotion, and drive, which accounts for the poor functional outcome in survivors of a cardiac arrest (Collins et al., 1989). In particular, bilateral loss of the small hippocampal CA-1 zone alone can cause severe impairment in memory in humans (Zola-Morgan, Squire, & Amaral, 1986) and is probably the cause of the mild to amnesic memory disturbances of these patients. This mechanism was confirmed by animal research: Rats with ischemic hippocampal damage induced by bilateral carotid and vertebral occlusion demonstrated the morphologic and behavioral deficits observed in survivors of cardiac arrest; postischemic rats had extensive damage in the CA-1 region of the hippocampus and showed impaired learning and memory of new information that appeared to be permanent (Colombo, Davis, Simolke, Markley, & Volpe, 1988). A positron emission tomography study of regional brain glucose utilization in 12 patients 1 month after brain anoxia due to cardiac arrest revealed a 25% decrease in mean cerebral glucose metabolism in conscious survivors relative to normal controls (De Volder et al., 1994). De Volder et al. (1994) suggested that cerebral anoxia resulted in a global brain hypometabolism as well as in regional disturbances preferentially located in arterial boundary zones, especially in the parieto–occipital cortex.

When circulatory arrest is complete and abrupt, brain stem nuclei and the spinal cord may be damaged. When the cerebral damage is very severe, cytotoxic edema causes massive brain swelling, with cessation of blood flow, irreversible coma, and brain death (Caplan, 1994).

In summary, survivors of out-of-hospital cardiac arrest often present with diffuse and long-standing neuropsychological deficits. Mild to severe anterograde memory problems are reported most often. This neuropsychological profile can be explained as the result of cerebral anoxia causing selective neuronal damage in the perfusion borders among the major cerebral arteries and in the hippocampal region.

CONCLUSION

In contrast with the many indications of the effect of potentially detrimental cardiogenic mechanisms on brain function, few studies have documented the cognitive status of patients suffering from later manifestations of CV disease, such as cardiac arrhythmias and MI. From the available investigations it appears that cognitive dysfunction and even dementia are not uncommon in such patients. The possible organic etiological mechanisms include general systemic vascular disease, cardiogenic embolism, and cerebral hypoperfusion. Concurrent psychoemotional reactions that compromise the cognitive performance of these patients also should be acknowledged. Cognitive impairment following cardiac arrest is described in many small and selected patient population studies or case reports. The frequently reported anterograde amnesia in survivors of out-of-hospital cardiac arrest has been linked with the resulting cerebral anoxia that destroys vulnerable cells in the hippocampal region.

The available literature suggests that cognitive impairment can be associated with diseases of the heart and that several pathophysiologic mechanisms can be described to explain this relation. However, many of these studies suffer from fundamental methodological shortcomings that limit their persuasiveness (Waldstein, Snow, & Muldoon, 1998). The use of (very) small sample sizes; the inadequate assessment of and control for the potential confounding influences of sociodemographic, psychological, and medical factors; a retrospective design; and the lack of control groups represent the major drawbacks of many reports. Other disadvantages include the focus on end-state cognitive impairment (dementia), the use of cognitive screening tests instead of comprehensive neuropsychological batteries, and the indirect and vague evidence of the alleged pathophysiological mechanisms. In general, there is little systematic research documenting the epidemiological impact of the problem; investigating the exact nature of the cognitive profile associated with specific cardiac disease; and relating cognitive deficits to paraclinical data that evaluate cerebral (hypo)perfusion, degree and distribution of atherosclerosis, and evidence of cardiogenic embolism. Further research is necessary to describe the course and kind of cognitive decline and to determine the relative importance of risk factors for cognitive impairment (or dementia) associated with heart disease. Screening procedures should be developed that can identify patients who are at risk of progressive intellectual loss and that can evaluate a patient's capacity for compliance with medication and other aspects of self-care. Beneficial prophylactic therapies that prevent cardiogenic brain damage and reduce the incidence of preventable vascular dementias should be explored. The continuing medical progress in the treatment of heart disease should not be blind to the close vascular interaction between the heart and the brain and to the vulnerability of the latter to dysfunction of the former.

REFERENCES

Adams, J. H., Brierley, J. B., Connor, R. C. R., & Treip, C. S. (1966). The effects of systemic hypotension upon the human brain: Clinical and neuropathological observations in 11 cases. *Brain, 89,* 235–268.

American Heart Association. (1993). *Heart and stroke facts: 1994 statistical supplement.* Dallas, TX: Author.

Aronson, M. K., Ooi, W. L., Morgenstern, H., Hafner, A., Masur, D., Crystal, H., Frishman, W. H., Fisher, D., & Katzman, R. (1990). Women, myocardial infarction, and dementia in the very old. *Neurology, 40,* 1102–1106.

Barclay, L. L., Weiss, E. M., Mattis, S., Bond, O., & Blass, J. P. (1988). Unrecognized cognitive impairment in cardiac rehabilitation patients. *Journal of the American Geriatrics Society, 36,* 22–28.

Berlit, P., Eckstein, H., & Krause, K. H. (1986). Die Prognose der kardialen Hirnembolie [Prognosis of cardiogenic brain embolism]. *Fortschritte Neurologie Psychiatrie, 54,* 205–215.

Benke, T., Neussl, D., & Aichner, F. (1991). Neuropsychological deficits in asymptomatic carotid artery stenosis. *Acta Neurologica Scandinavica, 83,* 378–381.

Bertini, G., Giglioli, C., Giovannini, F., Bartoletti, A., Cricelli, F., Margheri, M., Russo, L., Taddei, T., & Taiti, A. (1990). Neuropsychological outcome of survivors of out-of-hospital cardiac arrest. *Journal of Emergency Medicine, 8,* 407–412.

Beuret, P., Feihl, F., Vogt, P., Perret, A., Romand, J.-A., & Perret, C. (1993). Cardiac arrest: Prognostic factors and outcome at one year. *Resuscitation, 25,* 171–179.

Bigler, E. D., & Alfano, M. (1988). Anoxic encephalopathy: Neuroradiological and neuropsychological findings. *Archives of Clinical Neuropsychology, 3,* 383–396.

Blackwood, W., Hallpike, J. F., & Kocen, R. S. (1969). Atheromatous disease of the carotid arterial system and embolism from the heart in cerebral infarction: A morbid anatomical study. *Brain, 92,* 897–910.

Bogousslavsky, J., Cachin, C., Regli, F., Despland, P. A., Van Melle, G., & Kappenberger, L. (1991). Cardiac sources of embolism and cerebral infarction—Clinical consequences and vascular concomitants: The Lausanne Stroke Registry. *Neurology, 41,* 855–859.

Breteler, M. M. B., Claus, J. J., Grobbee, D. E., & Hofman, A. (1994). Cardiovascular disease and distribution of cognitive function in elderly people: The Rotterdam Study. *British Medical Journal, 308,* 1604–1608.

Breteler, M. M. B., van Swieten, J. C., Bots, M. L., Grobbee, D. E., Claus, J. J., van den Hout, J. H. W., van Harskamp, F., Tanghe, H. L. J., de Jong, P. T. V. M., van Gijn, J., & Hofman, A. (1994). Cerebral white matter lesions, vascular risk factors, and cgnitive function in a population based study: The Rotterdam Study. *Neurology, 44,* 1246–1252.

Brierley, J. B. (1979). Ischemic necrosis along brain arterial boundary zones: Some aspects of its etiology. In S. Fahn, J. N. Davis, & J. P. Rowland (Eds.), *Advances in neurology* (Vol. 16, pp. 155–162). New York: Raven.

Busse, E. W. (1982). Cardiovascular disease and psychopathology in the elderly. *Psychiatric Clinics of North America, 5,* 159–169.

Caplan, L. R. (1994). Cerebrovascular disease and neurologic manifestations of heart disease. In R. C. Schlant & R. W. Alexander (Eds.), *The heart, arteries and veins* (8th ed., pp. 2141–2162). New York: McGraw-Hill.

Cartlidge, N. E. F., Whisnant, J. P., & Elneback, L. R. (1977). Carotid and vertebralbasilar transient cerebral ischemic attacks: A community study. *Proceedings of the Mayo Clinic, 52,* 117–120.

Cerebral Embolism Task Force. (1986). Cardiogenic brain embolism. *Archives of Neurology, 43,* 71–83.

Cerebral Embolism Task Force. (1989). Cardiogenic brain embolism: The second report of the Cerebral Task Force. *Archives of Neurology, 46,* 727–743.

Collins, R. C., Dobkin, B. H., & Choi, D. W. (1989). Selective vulnerability of the brain: New insights into the pathophysiology of stroke. *Annals of Internal Medicine, 110,* 992–1000.

Colombo, P. J., Davis, H. P., Simolke, N., Markley, F., & Volpe, B. T. (1988). Forebrain ischemia produces hippocampal damage and a persistent working memory in rats. *Bulletin of the Psychonomic Society, 26,* 375–377.

Cummings, J. L., Tomiyasu, U., Read, S., & Benson, D. F. (1984). Amnesia with hippocampal lesions after cardiopulmonary arrest. *Neurology, 34,* 679–681.

De Pedis, G., Hedner, K., Johansson, B. W., & Steen, B. (1987). Cardiac arrhythmia in geriatric patients with organic dementia. *Comprehensive Gerontology, 1,* 115–117.

De Volder, A. G., Michel, C., Geurit, J. M., Bol, A., Georges, B., de Barsy, T., Laterre, C. (1994). Brain glucose metabolism in postanoxic syndrome due to cardiac arrest. *Acta Neurologica Belgica, 94,* 183–189.

de Vos, R., de Haes, H. C., Koster, R. W., & de Haan, R. J. (1999). Quality of survival after cardiopulmonary survival. *Archives of Internal Medicine, 159,* 249–254.

Di Pasquale, G., Andreoli, A., Pinelli, G., Grazi, P., Manini, G., Tognetti, F., & Testa, C. (1986). Cerebral ischemia and asymptomatic coronary artery disease: A prospective study of 83 patients. *Stroke, 6,* 1098–1101.

Dougherty, C. M. (1994). Longitudinal recovery following sudden cardiac arrest and internal cardioverter defibrillator implantation: Survivors and their families. *American Journal of Critical Care, 3,* 145–154.

Farina, E., Magni, E., Ambrosini, F., Manfredini, R., Binda, A., Sina, C., & Mariani, C. (1997). Neuropsychological deficits in asymptomatic atrial fibrillation. *Acta Neurologica Scandinavica, 96,* 310–316.

Frasure-Smith, N., Lespérance, F., & Talajic, M. (1995). Depression and 18-month prognosis after myocardial infarction. *Circulation, 80,* 999–1005.

Gacs, G., Merer, F. T., & Bodosi, M. (1982). Balloon catheter as a model of cerebral emboli in humans. *Stroke, 13,* 39–42.

Gates, P. C., Barnett, H. J. M., & Silver, M. D. (1986). Cardiogenic stroke. In H. J. M. Barnett, H. P. Mohr, M. B. Stein, & F. M. Yatsu (Eds.), *Stroke: Pathophysiology, diagnosis, and management* (Vol. 2, pp. 1085–1109). New York: Churchill Livingstone.

Gibson, G. E., Pulsinelli, W., Blass, J. P., & Duffy, T. E. (1981). Brain dysfunction in mild to moderate hypoxia. *American Journal of Medicine, 70,* 1247–1254.

Gordon, M. (1978). Occult cardiac arrhythmias associated with falls and dizziness in the elderly: Detection by Holter monitoring. *Journal of the American Geriatrics Society, 26,* 418–423.

Gorelick, P. B., Brody, J., Cohen, D., Freels, S., Levy, P., Dollear, W., Forman, H., & Harris, Y. (1993). Risk factors for dementia associated with multiple cerebral infarcts. *Archives of Neurology, 50,* 714–720.

Grant, I., Prigatano, J. P., Heaton, R. K., McSweeny, A. J., Wright, E. C., & Adams, K. M. (1987). Progressive neuropsychologic impairment and hypoxemia: Relationship in chronic obstructive pulmonary disease. *Archives of General Psychiatry, 44,* 999–1006.

Grubb, N. R., O'Carroll, R., Cobbe, S. M., Sirel, J., & Fox, K. A. A. (1996). Chronic memory impairment after cardiac arrest outside hospital. *British Medical Journal, 313,* 143–146.

Halperin, J. L., & Hart, R. G. (1988). Atrial fibrillation and stroke: New ideas, persisting dilemmas. *Stroke, 19,* 937–941.

Heyden, S., Heiss, G., & Heyman, A. (1980). Cardiovascular mortality in transient ischemic attacks. *Stroke, 11,* 252–255.

Howard, R., Trend, P., & Ross Russell, R. W. (1987). Clinical features of ischemia in cerebral arterial border zones after periods of reduced cerebral blood flow. *Archives of Neurology, 44,* 934–940.

Jabourian, A. P. (1995). Fonctions cognitives, EEG et troubles de la marche dans les arytmies cardiaques, un jour avant et huit jours après l'implantation d'un stimulateur cardiaque [Cognitive function, EEG, and gait disorders in cardiac arrhythmias one day before and eight days after pacemaker implantation]. *Annales Médico-Psychologiques, 153,* 89–105.

Kannel, W. B., Wolf, P. A., & Verter, J. (1983). Manifestations of coronary disease predisposing to stroke: The Framingham study. *Journal of the American Medical Association, 250,* 2942–2946.

Kaps, M., Seidel, G., & Berg, J. (1995). Is there a hemispheric side preference of cardiac valvular emboli? *Ultrasound in Medicine and Biology, 6,* 753–756.

Kartsounis, L. D., & Shallice, T. (1996). Modality specific semantic knowledge loss for unique items. *Cortex, 32,* 109–119.

Kaschel, R., Zaiser-Kaschel, H., Shiel, A., & Mayer, K. (1995). Reality orientation training in an amnesic: A controlled single case study (*n* = 572 days). *Brain Injury, 9,* 619–633.

Kempster, P. A., Gerraty, R. P., & Gates, P. C. (1988). Asymptomatic cerebral infarction in patients with chronic atrial fibrillation. *Stroke, 19,* 955–957.

Kennedy, G. J., Hofer, M. A., Cohen, D., Shindledecker, R., & Fisher, J. D. (1987). Significance of depression and cognitive impairment in patients undergoing programed stimulation of cardiac arrhythmias. *Psychosomatic Medicine, 49,* 410–421.

Kilander, L., Andren, B., Nyman, H., Lind, L., Boberg, M., & Lithell, H. (1998). Atrial fibrillation is an independent determinant of low cognitive function: A cross-sectional study in elderly men. *Stroke, 29,* 1816–1820.

Lavy, S., Stern, S., Melamed, E., Cooper, G., Keren, A., & Levy, P. (1980). Effect of chronic atrial fibrillation on regional cerebral blood flow. *Stroke, 11,* 35–38.

Lezak, M. D. (1995). *Neuropsychological assessment* (3rd ed.). Oxford, England: Oxford University Press.

Lhermitte, F., Gauthier, J. C., & Derouesne, C. (1970). Nature of occlusions of the middle cerebral artery. *Neurology, 20,* 82–88.

Love, B. B., Grover-McKay, M., Biller, J., Rezai, K., & McKay, C. R. (1992). Coronary artery disease and cardiac events with asymptomatic and symptomatic cerebrovascular disease. *Stroke, 23,* 939–945.

Mandawat, M. K., & Ross Lorimer, A. (1996). The heart as a source of embolism. In J. E. Tooke & G. D. O. Lowe (Eds.), *A textbook of vascular medicine* (pp. 636–643). London: Arnold.

McNeill, D. L., Tidmarsh, D., & Rostall, M. L. (1965). A case of dysmnesic syndrome following cardiac arrest. *British Journal of Psychiatry, 111,* 697–699.

Mecklinger, A., von Cramon, D. Y., & Matthes von Cramon, G. (1998). Event-related potential evidence for a specific recognition memory deficit in adult survivors of cerebral hypoxia. *Brain, 121,* 1919–1935.

Meltzer, M. L. (1983). Poor memory: A case report. *Journal of Clinical Psychology, 39,* 3–10.

Moroney, J. T., Bagiella, E., Desmond, D. W., Paik, M. C., Stern, Y., & Tatemichi, T. K. (1996). Risk factors for incident dementia after stroke: Role of hypoxic and ischemic disorders. *Stroke, 27,* 1283–1289.

Naugle, R. I., Bridgers, S. L., & Delaney, R. C. (1986). Neuropsychological signs of asymptomatic carotid stenosis. *Archives of Clinical Neuropsychology, 1,* 25–30.

Oder, W., Siostrzonek, P., & Lang, W. (1991). Distribution of ischemic cerebrovascular events in cardiac embolism. *Klinische Wochenschrift, 69,* 757–762.

Osborn, M. J. (1996). Sudden cardiac death: A. Mechanisms, incidences, and prevention of sudden cardiac death. In E. R. Guiliani, B. J. Gersh, M. D. McGoon, D. L. Hayes, & H. V. Schaff (Eds.), *Mayo Clinic practice of cardiology* (3rd ed., pp. 862–894). St. Louis, MO: Mosby.

Parkin, A. J., Miller, J., & Vincent, R. (1987). Multiple neuropsychological deficits due to anoxic encephalopathy: A case study. *Cortex, 23,* 655–665.

Paulson, O. B., Jarden, J. O., Vorstrup, S., Holm, S., & Godtfredsen, J. (1986). Effect of captopril on the cerebral circulation in chronic heart failure. *European Journal of Clinical Investigation, 16,* 124–132.

Petersen, P., & Godtfredsen, J. (1986). Embolic complications in paroxysmal atrial fibrillation. *Stroke, 17,* 622–626.

Petersen, P., Kastrup, J., Videbaek, R., & Boysen, G. (1989). Cerebral blood flow before and after cardioversion of atrial fibrillation. *Journal of Cerebral Blood Flow and Metabolism, 9,* 422–425.

Petersen, P., Pedersen, F., Johnsen, A., Madsen, E. B., Brun, B., Boysen, G., & Godtfredsen, J. (1989). Cerebral computed tomography in paroxysmal atrial fibrillation. *Stroke, 79,* 482–486.

Phillips, N. A., & Mate-Kole, C. C. (1997). Cognitive deficits in peripheral vascular disease: A comparison of mild stroke patients and normal control subjects. *Stroke, 28,* 777–784.

Prigatano, G. P., & Levin, D. C. (1988). Pulmonary system. In R. E. Tarter, D. H. Van Thiel, & K. L. Edwards (Eds.), *Medical neuropsychology: The impact of disease on behavior* (pp. 11–26). New York: Plenum.

Rajagopalan, B., Raine, A. E., Cooper, R., & Ledingham, J. G. (1984). Changes in cerebral blood flow in patients with severe congestive cardiac failure before and after captopril treatment. *American Journal of Medicine, 76* (Suppl. 5B), 86–90.

Ratcliffe, P. J., & Wilcock, G. K. (1985). Cerebrovascular disease in dementia: The importance of atrial fibrillation. *Postgraduate Medical Journal, 61,* 201–204.

Reich, P., Regestein, Q. R., Murawski, B. J., DeSilva, R. A., & Lown, B. (1983). Unrecognized organic mental disorders in survivors of cardiac arrest. *American Journal of Psychiatry, 140,* 1194–1197.

Rockwood, K., Dobbs, A. R., Rule, B. G., Howlett, S. E., & Black, W. R. (1992). The impact of pacemaker implantation on cognitive functioning in elderly patients. *Journal of the American Geriatrics Society, 40,* 142–146.

Roine, R. O., Kajaste, S., & Kaste, M. (1993). Neuropsychological sequelae of cardiac arrest. *Journal of the American Medical Association, 269,* 237–242.

Rokey, R., Rolak, L. A., Harati, Y., Kutka, N., & Verani, M. S. (1984). Coronary artery disease in patients with cerebrovascular disease: A prospective study. *Annals of Neurology, 16,* 50–53.

Sacco, R. L., Wolf, P. A., & Kannel, W. B. (1982). Survival and recurrence following stroke: The Framingham Study. *Stroke, 13,* 290–295.

Sauve, M. J., Doolittle, N., Walker, J. A., Paul, S. M., Scheinman, M. M. (1996). Factors associated with cognitive recovery after cardiopulmonary resuscitation. *American Journal of Critical Care, 5,* 127–139.

Schleifer, S. J., Macari-Hinson, M. M., Coyle, D. A., Slater, W. R., Kahn, M., Gorlin, R., & Zucker, H. D. (1989). The nature and course of depression following myocardial infarction. *Archives of Internal Medicine, 149,* 1785–1789.

Sherman, D. G., Goldman, L., Whitting, R. B., Jurgensen, K., Kaste, M., & Easton, J. D. (1987). Cerebral and sytemic thromboembolism in patients with atrial fibrillation. *Acta Neurologica Scandinavica, 76,* 137.

Sollberg, L. A., McGarry, P. A., Moossy, J., Strong, J. P., Tejada, C., & Löken, A. C. (1968). Severity of atherosclerosis in cerebral arteries, coronary arteries, and aortas. *Annals of the New York Academy of Science, 149,* 956–973.

Sulkava, R., & Erkinjuntti, T. (1987). Vascular dementia due to cardiac arrhythmia's and systemic hypotension. *Acta Neurologica Scandinavica, 76,* 123–128.

Vaagenes, P., Ginsberg, M., Ebmeyer, U., Ernster, L., Fischer, M., Gisvold, S. E., Gurvitch, A., Hossmann, K. A., Nemoto, E. M., Radovsky, A., Severinghaus, J. W., Safar, P., Schlichtig, R., Sterz, F.,

Tonnessen, T., White, R. J., Xiao, F., & Zhou, Y. (1996). Cerebral resuscitation from cardiac arrest: pathophysiologic mechanisms. *Critical Care Medicine, 24,* S57–S68.

Vingerhoets, G., Van Nooten, G., & Jannes, C. (1997). Neuropsychological impairment in candidates for cardiac surgery. *Journal of the International Neuropsychological Society, 3,* 480–484.

Volpe, B. T., & Hirst, W. (1983). The characterization of an amnesic syndrome following hypoxic ischemic injury. *Archives of Neurology, 40,* 436–440.

Volpe, B. T., Holtzman, J. D., & Hirst, W. (1986). Further characterization of patients with amnesia after cardiac arrest: Preserved recognition memory. *Neurology, 36,* 408–411.

Volpe, B. T., & Petito, C. K. (1985). Dementia with bilateral medial temporal ischemia. *Neurology, 35,* 1793–1797.

Wade, O. L., & Bishop, J. M. (1962). *Cardiac output and regional blood flow.* Oxford, England: Blackwell.

Waldstein, S. R., Snow, J., & Muldoon, M. F. (1998). Applications of neuropsychological assessement to the study of cardiovascular disease. In D. S. Krantz & A. Baum (Eds.), *Technology and methods in behavioral medicine* (pp. 69–94). Mahwah, NJ: Lawrence Erlbaum Associates.

Wilson, B. A. (1996). Cognitive functioning of adult survivors of cerebral hypoxia. *Brain Injury, 10,* 863–874.

Wolf, P. A., Kannel, W. B., Sorlie, P., & McNamara, P. (1981). Asymptomatic carotid bruit and risk of stroke: The Framingham Study. *Journal of the American Medical Association, 245,* 1442–1445.

Yasaka, M., Yamaguchi, T., Oita, J., Sawada, T., Shichiri, M., & Omae, T. (1993). Clinical features of recurrent embolization in acute cardioembolic stroke. *Stroke, 24,* 1681–1685.

Zola-Morgan, S., Squire, L. R., & Amaral, D. G. (1986). Human amnesia and the medial temporal region: Enduring memory impairment following a bilateral lesion limited to field CA1 of the hippocampus. *Journal of Neuroscience, 6,* 2950–2967.

PART II

Treatment of Cardiovascular Disease and Neuropsychological Performance

CHAPTER NINE

Cognitive Consequences of Antihypertensive Medications

DEBORAH L. JONAS
Duke University

JAMES A. BLUMENTHAL
Duke University and Duke University Medical Center

DAVID J. MADDEN
Duke University Medical Center

MATT SERRA
Duke University

Hypertension is often thought of as a silent killer. Although elevated blood pressure (BP) is usually asymptomatic, increased diastolic blood pressure (DBP) is associated with increased risk of both stroke and coronary heart disease (CHD; MacMahon et al., 1990). Individuals with naturally occurring low BP are at the lowest risk for developing cardiovascular (CV) disease, and pharmacologically lowering BP has been shown to decrease the risk of future complications such as stroke and CHD (Collins et al., 1990). Over the last 20 years, the number of available treatments for hypertension has increased dramatically. For the purposes of lowering BP, physicians can prescribe beta adrenergic antagonists (beta blockers [BBs]), angiotensin converting enzyme (ACE) inhibitors, calcium antagonists (calcium channel blockers [CCBs]), peripheral adrenergic inhibitors, central alpha agonists, combined alpha and beta blocking agents, direct vasodilators, and diuretics. In the United States, diuretics remain the most frequently prescribed medications to treat hypertension, although with the advent of CCBs and ACE inhibitors, their use has been steadily decreasing (Kaplan, 1998).

Because there are numerous types of antihypertensive medications, some of which cross the blood–brain barrier, it is important to know how these drugs affect patients' mental health as well as their physical health. Once a decision is made to initiate drug therapy for hypertension, the potential psychosocial consequences of lowering BP need consideration. Changes in psychosocial functioning can have a significant impact on a patient's quality of life. In particular, negative changes may lead to noncompliance with medication regimens.

Neuropsychological functioning is one aspect of quality of life that represents the behavioral correlates of brain function. Patients with untreated hypertension often perform more poorly than normotensive individuals on neuropsychological tests, although the dysfunction typically does not reach a level of clinical significance (Elias, Robbins, Schultz, Streeten, & Elias, 1987). Research assessing unmedicated hypertensives indicates that hypertension is consistently associated with subtle decrements on tests of abstract reasoning, attention, and memory (Waldstein, Manuck, Ryan, & Muldoon, 1991; see also chap. 1, this book). The pharmacological treatment of hypertension also may affect cognitive functioning. Medications associated with decreased cognitive abilities that are also negatively influenced by hypertension may be of particular concern, because the potential additive effects can further affect daily living. Conversely, cognitive benefits associated with medication have the potential to minimize the cognitive decrements associated with untreated hypertension.

In this chapter we present an overview of research that assesses the relationship between antihypertensive medications and cognitive functioning. We first discuss methodological issues that influence the approach to integrating data and drawing conclusions from studies in this area. Next, we present a review of the available evidence assessing the cognitive impact of antihypertensive medications. We then provide an overview of the mechanisms through which medications may affect cognitive functioning, and we conclude with suggestions for future research in this area.

METHODOLOGICAL ISSUES

We selected studies for this review by conducting a literature search on MedLine and by including studies cited in previous reviews (e.g., Muldoon, Shapiro, Manuck, & Waldstein, 1991; Muldoon, Waldstein, & Jennings, 1995). The treatment of hypertension is typically long term, and the immediate influences of medication may dissipate as drug tolerance develops (Broadhurst, 1980). We therefore chose to include studies that evaluated performance of adults taking a single medication for a period of at least 1 week. We included studies that assessed both normotensive individuals and patients with mild to moderate hypertension; studies that assessed populations with known concurrent conditions were excluded.

Many of the studies we reviewed were part of larger clinical trials designed primarily to determine safety or efficacy of the drugs. In such situations, protocols assessing drug effects on cognitive function were largely ancillary studies in which convenience was a major consideration in study design. Furthermore, in situations in which investigators were not limited by the designs of clinical trials, study designs were constrained by ethical considerations associated with keeping hypertensive individuals off active medication for extended periods of time.

The most common experimental paradigm used in this literature is the *placebo run-in,* in which participants receive placebo pills for a set period of time, followed by randomization to one of a number of possible drugs. Neuropsychological assessments are performed while participants take placebos and at least once during active treatment. Study reports typically include comparisons of participants' performance while they are taking one drug to their performance while they are taking another drug. Such comparisons provide information about the relative influences of medications. Additional comparisons can be made between performance while participants are on active medication and performance while they are on the placebo (e.g., Croog et al., 1986; Gengo, Huntoon, & McHugh, 1987), although not all investigators report such comparisons (e.g., Deary, Capewell, Hajducka, & Muir, 1991; Frcka & Lader, 1988; Lasser, Nash, Lasser, Hamill, & Batey, 1989). The two most significant drawbacks of this type of design, however, are (a) the limited ability to assess the unique impact of the individual drugs on cognitive functioning compared to the absence of treatment and (b) the difficulties in distinguishing between changes that are associated with repeated testing (i.e., practice effects) and changes associated with medication use. This issue is particularly important when interpreting data from neuropsychological tests that tend to improve with repeated testing, such as the Trail Making Test (Reitan, 1958; e.g., Croog et al., 1986, 1990).

A number of other interpretive considerations are important to keep in mind when reviewing data from studies assessing the influences of antihypertensive medications. For example, different drugs within classes of antihypertensive medications (i.e., BBs, diuretics, CCBs, etc.) may differentially influence cognitive functioning because they each have unique chemical properties. Although the majority of studies do not attempt to distinguish between the effects of different drugs within a single class, some research has assessed these differences. For example, a number of studies have refuted the hypothesis that BBs that cross the blood–brain barrier with relative ease, such as propranolol, have a greater impact on cognitive and other central nervous system (CNS) functioning than those that do not, such as atenolol (e.g., Blumenthal et al., 1988; Gengo et al., 1987; Gengo, Fagan, de Padova, Miller, & Kinkel, 1988). In a review of psychosocial influences of CCBs, Fletcher and Bulpitt (1992) suggested that the relationship between psychosocial functioning and treatment with CCBs differs according to the subclass of drug. Specifically, they concluded that calcium antagonists in the dihydropyridine class, such as nifedipine, may have more negative effects on psychological well-being than nondihydropyridines, such as verapamil. In general, when considering the impact of antihypertensive medications on cognitive ability, it is important to recognize the potential for different drugs within the same class to have larger or different effects than others.

Dosage used in testing also varies across studies. Typically, when testing the effects of medication in hypertensives, drugs are titrated until patients achieve a predefined criterion for lowering BP (e.g., DBP lower than 90 mmHg). From an ethical perspective, this approach is necessary because the doses taken by each patient are needed to achieve adequate BP control. From a clinical perspective, the doses are likely to be similar to what patients would take if a physician prescribed the drug. However, from a research perspective, this practice fails to eliminate the possibility that different doses differentially influence cognitive functioning. It is therefore important to consider dosage when comparing data from various studies.

There are a number of other issues that are relevant to the study of antihypertensive medications on cognitive functioning that are not discussed in depth here. For example, questions regarding the potential differences that antihypertensive medications may have on neuropsychological functioning in people who differ in terms of ethnicity, age, gender, and socioeconomic background are largely unaddressed in the literature. Some studies have assessed neuropsychological test performance during treatment with antihypertensive treatment on specific populations, such as African Americans or older women (Croog et al., 1990, 1994). However, no direct comparisons between groups have been made with regard to cognitive functioning. Because treatment success of antihypertension varies as a function of age and ethnicity (Freis, 1988), neuropsychological consequences may also vary across populations. These issues are discussed further in the Directions for Future Research section.

COGNITIVE TESTING

A wide number of tests have been used to assess the impact of antihypertensive medications on cognitive functioning. The tests can be classified into broad cognitive domains, such as attention, memory, perception, construction, abstract reasoning, and general intelligence (Lezak, 1983, 1995). Neuropsychological tests within each domain assess a wide number of skills that may be subdivided further. Neuropsychological tests also may assess multiple cognitive functions, which may be classified differently by different investigators. For example, the Digit Symbol subtest of the Wechsler Adult Intelligence Scale–Revised (WAIS–R; Wechsler, 1981) requires the substitution of symbols associated with specific numbers within a specified time interval (i.e., 90 seconds). Successful performance requires perceptual–motor skills, visual scanning, vigilance, and short-term figural memory. Table 9.1 provides operational definitions of the cognitive domains discussed in this review, along with the tests used to measure performance in each domain.

TABLE 9.1
Operational Definitions of Cognitive Domains
and Corresponding Neuropsychological Tests

Cognitive Domain	Skills	Tests
Attention		
Sustained attention	Continuous identification of target stimuli from a consecutive display of target and nontarget items. Also thought of as *vigilance*.	Cancellation tests, proof-reading, paced auditory serial addition, stop-signal tests
Selective attention	Identification of target items from an array of both target and nontarget stimuli. Requires the ability to choose correct information and ignore distracting information during a single presentation.	Stroop (1935), choice reaction-time tests
Mental flexibility	Ability to track two or more stimuli or ideas either simultaneously, alternatively, or sequentially.	Digit Span Backward, Wechsler Adult Intelligence Scale (WAIS; Wechsler, 1955)
Complex attention	Integration of sustained attention, visual scanning, directed visual shifting, and motor skills.	Trail Making Test, Version B (Reitan, 1958), WAIS Digit Symbol Substitution
Memory		
Short term	Ability to recall or recognize information immediately following presentation. Tests assess various memory skills, including memory for order, verbal memory, nonverbal memory, cued recall, gist recall, and learning over time.	WAIS Forward Digit Span, sentence repetition, Buschke Selective Reminding (Buschke & Fuld, 1974), subtests of the Wechsler Memory Scale (WMS; Wechsler, 1974) and Russell's Version of the WMS (Russell, 1975)
Long term	Ability to recall or recognize information following a delay (e.g., 20 minutes). Tests assess various memory skills, including memory for order, verbal memory, nonverbal memory, cued recall, gist recall, and learning over time.	Sentence repetition, Buschke Selective Reminding, subtests of the WMS and Russell's version of the WMS
Perceptual skills		
Visual recognition threshold	Retinal sensitivity to light.	Flicker fusion frequency, two flash fusion
Psychomotor skills		
Simple	Speeded redundant movements, speeded responses, or strength.	Finger tapping, grip strength, simple reaction-time tests
Complex	Coordination of multiple movements.	

EFFECTS OF ANTIHYPERTENSIVE MEDICATION
ON COGNITIVE FUNCTIONING

BBs

BBs regulate BP by reducing cardiac output and reducing renin release. BBs can be divided into classes on the basis of their cardioselectivity and their degree of lipid solubility. Cardioselectivity reflects differing degrees of $beta_2$ receptor blockade, whereas lipid solubility helps determine the duration and constancy of action of medication and the degree to which the drugs cross the blood–brain barrier.

Attention

The impact of BBs on attention has been tested extensively. Typically, BBs have little impact on tests of mental flexibility (Croog et al., 1990; Herrick et al., 1989; Palac et al., 1990; Steiner, Friedhoff, Wilson, Wecker, & Santo, 1990), although one large placebo-controlled study reported BB treatment to be associated with a performance decrement (Ameling, de Korte, & Man in 't Veld, 1991). BBs may produce small, subclinical cognitive decrements in mental flexibility that may go undetected or may not be apparent when making relative comparisons among multiple drugs.

Studies that have tested the influence of BBs on tests of sustained attention have produced inconsistent results that are difficult to interpret. BBs have been associated with decrements (Frcka & Lader, 1988; Palac et al., 1990), improvements (Dimsdale & Newton, 1992), and no change (Applegate et al., 1994; Deary et al., 1991; Dimsdale & Newton, 1992; Herrick et al., 1989; McCorvey et al., 1993; Prince, Bird, Blizard, & Mann, 1996; Van Gelder, Alpert, & Tsui, 1985) in performance on a variety of sustained-attention tests. Because the majority of studies, including one very large placebo-controlled trial (Applegate et al., 1994), have found no change in performance, BB treatment is generally not considered to be associated with significant changes in cognitive performance.

Tests that measure selective attention also have yielded inconsistent results. Two trials found no relationship between treatment and performance on choice reaction time tests (Broadhurst, 1980; Palac et al., 1990). Data assessing BBs' relationship to performance on the Stroop color–word test have shown no influence of treatment on standard versions of the test (Harvey, Clayton, & Betts, 1977; Streufert, DePadova, McGlynn, Piasecki, & Pogash, 1989) and a performance decrement on a more difficult version (Gengo et al., 1987). As with mental flexibility, it is possible that BB treatment causes small decrements in selective attention that are difficult to detect experimentally.

Tests that measure complex attention abilities have associated BB treatment with performance improvements on a number of trials, although the gains are often less than those seen with other antihypertensives (Croog et al., 1986, 1990; Gengo et al., 1987; Palac et al., 1990). Two studies that used crossover designs showed that BB treatment attenuates the benefits of practice (Ameling et al., 1991; Gengo et al., 1988). Therefore, it is possible that BB treatment is associated with small decrements in complex attention abilities that may be masked by improvements due to practice effects.

Overall, it appears that BB treatment is associated with small decrements in many attention-related abilities. The null findings reported may result from experimental designs or tests that are not sensitive enough to detect small drug effects (i.e., inadequate power, imprecise instruments, etc.). It is also possible that particular BBs, such as metoprolol, have less impact on attention-related abilities than others. For example, Gengo and colleagues (1987, 1988) demonstrated that treatment with metoprolol is associated with fewer negative consequences than atenolol. As we repeatedly note in this chapter, the advantages of treatment with metoprolol over other BBs generalizes beyond attention abilities.

Memory

Research assessing the impact of BBs on memory has consistently found no impact of BB treatment on a variety of short-term memory tests (e.g., Croog et al., 1990; Herrick et al., 1989; Leonetti & Salvetti, 1994; Madden et al., 1986, 1988; McCorvey et al., 1993; Powell, Pickering, Wyke, & Goggin, 1993; Prince et al., 1996; Skinner et al., 1992; Steiner et al., 1990). An exception may be found in tests that require participants to overcome interference from previously learned stimuli. Two studies that used tests with strong interference components associated BB treatment with performance decrements (Lichter, Richardson, & Wyke, 1986; Steiner et al., 1990). Together, these data suggest that BBs might be associated with performance decrements on very specific short-term memory skills, such as the ability to overcome interference, but that more general short-term memory skills are unaffected by BB treatment.

Assessments of the impact of BBs on long-term memory generally show that BBs either improve performance (Dimsdale & Newton, 1992; Steiner et al., 1990) or have no effect on it (Herrick et al., 1989; Powell et al., 1993). The finding that BBs have no effect, or are associated with improvements on some aspects of memory functioning may be particularly meaningful because memory has consistently been shown to be impaired by untreated hypertension (Waldstein et al., 1991).

Perceptual Skills

Research that has assessed the impact of BB treatment suggests BBs are related to a decrement in performance on tests of perceptual discrimination. BBs have been associated with a decrement in placebo-controlled studies (Gengo et al., 1987, 1988), with greater impairment associated with atenolol than with metoprolol (Gengo et al., 1987). BBs seem to have similar effects on perceptual abilities as do other classes of antihypertensive agents, as studies that do not include a placebo control show no differences between participants' performance when taking BBs and performance when taking other antihypertensive medications (Deary et al., 1991; Frcka & Lader, 1988).

Psychomotor Skills

Research assessing the impact of BBs on tests of psychomotor skills typically suggests no association with changes in performance on tasks involving simple psychomotor skills (Blumenthal et al., 1988; Kostis & Rosen, 1987; McCorvey et al., 1993; Skinner et al., 1992). Although the majority of data support the conclusion that BB treatment is unrelated to psychomotor performance, two studies found that BB treatment was related to decreased psychomotor abilities (Frcka & Lader, 1988; Streufert, DePadova, McGlynn, Pogash, & Piasecki, 1988). Therefore, it should be recognized that treatment might be associated with small, often undetected, performance decrements.

Summary

Table 9.2 summarizes the effects of BBs on cognitive functioning. Chronic BB treatment is associated with performance decrements on a number of attention and perceptual abilities. The majority of short-term memory skills are unaffected by BBs, although there may be a relationship between BB treatment and

TABLE 9.2
The Effects of Antihypertensive Medications on Cognitive Functioning

Cognitive Domain	Beta Blockers	ACE Inhibitors	Diuretics	Calcium Channel Blockers[a]
Attention				
Sustained	0	0	0	0
Selective	~	X	0	0
Complex	−	0	−	−
Mental flexibility	−	0	0	0
Memory				
Short term	0	0	0	0
Long term	+	0	0	0
Perceptual skills:				
Flicker fusion threshold	−	~	X	X
Psychomotor skills				
Simple	~	~	0	X
Complex	~	X	X	X

Note. − = a negative change in performance; + = a positive change in performance; ~ = inconsistencies in the data; 0 = no change in performance; X = insufficient or no data available; ACE = angiotensin converting enzyme.
[a]These conclusions are based on extremely limited data.

decrements in specific memory abilities, such as the need to overcome interference. Long-term memory either improves or remains unaffected by treatment. Finally, there are inconsistent results from tests of psychomotor abilities, although the majority of studies suggest that BB treatment is not associated with decrements in psychomotor skills. By and large, the decrements associated with BBs are small, although they may be detected by neuropsychological tests, the clinical significance may be relatively trivial in most cases.

ACE Inhibitors

ACE inhibitors decrease concentrations of aldosterone, increase concentrations of bradykinin, and reduce the circulating levels of angiotensin II. Decreased concentrations of aldosterone reduce salt and water retention. Increased bradykinin and reductions in angiotensin II result in vasodilation. Although ACE inhibitor action occurs outside the CNS, angiotensin II has been shown to impair performance on various learning and memory paradigms in animals (Domeney, 1994; Sudilovsky et al., 1989). Therefore, the reduction of angiotensin II caused by ACE inhibitors may enhance cognitive performance, particularly on learning and memory tasks.

Attention

ACE inhibitors have been shown to improve performance on tests of sustained attention, complex attention, and mental flexibility (Croog et al., 1986, 1990, 1994; Frcka & Lader, 1988; Herrick et al., 1989; Steiner et al., 1990). A number of studies have shown that the performance gains associated with repeated testing are greater during treatment with ACE inhibitors than with BBs (Frcka & Lader, 1988; Herrick et al., 1989; Steiner et al., 1990). At least one randomized, placebo-controlled crossover study (McCorvey et al., 1993) reported that ACE inhibitors have no influence on attention abilities. ACE-inhibitor treatment clearly is not associated with negative consequences on attention abilities and actually may enhance performance.

Memory

Studies that have assessed the influence of ACE inhibitor treatment on memory performance have consistently shown no relationship between treatment with ACE inhibitors and performance on a variety of tests measuring nonverbal memory, logical memory, sentence repetition, list learning, and paired-associate learning (Applegate et al., 1994; Croog et al., 1990; Herrick et al., 1989; Leonetti & Salvetti, 1994; Lichter et al., 1986; McCorvey et al., 1993; Palac et al., 1990; Powell et al., 1993; Steiner et al., 1990). Although no changes in memory abilities have been associated with ACE inhibitor treatment in the majority of studies, studies that have assessed specific populations have yielded mixed results. One study of healthy participants found a negative relationship (Frcka & Lader,

1988), whereas one study with older hypertensive women found a positive relationship between ACE inhibitor treatment and memory (Croog et al., 1994).

Perceptual Skills

Two studies have assessed the effects of ACE inhibitors on perceptual abilities. One reported that patients taking captopril performed similarly to those taking atenolol (Deary et al., 1991). Because atenolol is consistently associated with decreased perceptual skills, it is possible that ACE inhibitors are related to similar decrements. The other study found no performance differences between active treatment and placebo (Frcka & Lader, 1988). Thus, although data are limited, ACE inhibitors do not appear to be associated with improvements in perceptual skills, but they may be associated with performance decrements.

Psychomotor Skills

Performance on tests of psychomotor skills has been assessed in two studies. One study assessed performance in normotensive individuals and suggested that ACE inhibitors improved performance (Olajide & Lader, 1985). Another study assessed performance in older adults and reported no change in performance (McCorvey et al., 1993). Because the two studies assessed performance in different populations, it is unclear how ACE inhibitors influence psychomotor abilities. Again, on the basis of limited data, ACE-inhibitor treatment does not appear to be associated with decrements in psychomotor skills, and it may improve them.

Summary

Table 9.2 summarizes the impact of ACE inhibitors on cognitive functioning. There are no consistent deficits associated with treatment with ACE inhibitors, although ACE inhibitors may be associated with performance decrements on perceptual abilities. ACE inhibitors do not appear to improve memory functioning, and they may improve attention and psychomotor abilities.

Diuretics

The majority of data produced by assessments of the relationship between performance on cognitive tests and treatment with diuretics come from trials conducted with older adults who were involved in studies with the Systolic Hypertension in the Elderly Program in the United States (Applegate et al., 1994; Cushman et al., 1991; Gurland et al., 1988) and the Medical Research Council trial in the United Kingdom (Prince et al., 1996). Although the following review integrates data from trials assessing the impact of diuretic treatment alone, it is important to note that diuretics are often added to existing treatment regimens when the target BP level is not achieved with monotherapy. Croog et al. (1986) showed that, in general, patients requiring the addition of a diuretic to achieve

optimal BP reductions showed larger overall reductions in cognitive performance relative to those who did not require the additional medication. Because of
such selection bias, it is unclear if such differences were directly associated with
drug treatment or if they were a function of the severity of hypertension. Furthermore, Goldstein et al. (1990) showed that cognitive functioning is differentially affected by combination therapy that includes diuretic treatment. Therefore, the data relevant to monotherapy with diuretics may not generalize to
combination therapy.

Attention

Most studies suggest that diuretics have no impact on a variety of attention
skills, including sustained- and complex-attention skills (Applegate et al., 1994;
Gurland et al., 1988; McCorvey et al., 1993; Prince et al., 1996). However, Gurland et al. (1988) found a longitudinal decline associated with diuretic treatment
on speed of performance on the Trail Making Test Part A, and McCorvey et al.
(1993) found that diuretic treatment was associated with more errors on the
Trail Making Test Part B relative to treatment with placebo. These negative effects of treatment on the Trail Making Test are particularly noteworthy, because
repeated testing typically results in practice-related improvements. Diuretics,
therefore, may be particularly detrimental to the integration of skills required
by the Trail Making Test (e.g., perceptual–motor speed, sequencing, shifting
cognitive set, visual scanning, etc.).

Memory

Evidence assessing the impact of diuretics on memory performance consistently shows that diuretic treatment is not associated with performance changes
on cognitive and neuropsychological memory tests (Applegate et al., 1994;
Cushman et al., 1991; McCorvey et al., 1993; Prince et al., 1996).

Perceptual Skills

To our knowledge, there exist no data from randomized trials that have assessed the impact of diuretic treatment on perceptual skills.

Psychomotor Skills

Two trials have assessed the relationship between diuretic treatment and
psychomotor-skills performance. Both studies found no measurable impact of
treatment on test of finger tapping speed (Cushman et al., 1991; McCorvey et
al., 1993).

Summary

As is summarized in Table 9.2, diuretic treatment is not consistently related
to changes in performance on the majority of cognitive abilities. One exception
is that diuretic treatment has been associated with decrements in performance
on tests of complex attention abilities.

Other Antihypertensive Agents

The following section reviews the limited data assessing the impact of centrally acting agents, CCBs, and alpha blockers on cognitive functioning. Because centrally acting agents such as methyldopa and clonidine act within the CNS, they may be expected to influence cognitive functioning directly. CCBs and alpha blockers are not known to directly effect the CNS; therefore, fewer CNS effects are expected.

Attention

Treatment with CCBs appears to be unrelated to performance on tests of sustained attention (Leonetti & Salvetti, 1994), selective attention (Skinner et al., 1992) or mental flexibility (Croog et al., 1990). However, Skinner et al. (1992) found that CCB treatment was associated with decreased performance on complex attention abilities. They also found no differences after repeated testing with the Trail Making Test Part B, suggesting that CCB treatment eliminated the practice effects typically found with this test. Overall, the data suggest that CCB treatment is not related to changes in mental flexibility, sustained attention, and selective-attention abilities but may be associated with small decrements in complex-attention abilities.

The impact of the central alpha agonist methyldopa and the alpha blocker prazosin on attention abilities also has been assessed. Methyldopa has been associated with performance decrements on tests of simple and complex attention (Bayliss & Duncan, 1975; Croog et al., 1986). No differences have been detected in the performances of participants taking prazosin on a variety of tests of attention abilities, including mental flexibility, selective attention, and complex attention (Lasser et al., 1989).

Memory

No drug-related effects have been found on memory tests assessing the influence of treatment with methyldopa, prazosin, and the CCBs nifedipine and nitrendipine. For example, methyldopa had no impact on the Visual Reproduction test from the Wechsler Memory Scale (WMS; Wechsler, 1974; see Croog et al., 1986; Sudilovsky et al., 1989). Lasser et al. (1989) found that prazosin had no effect on WAIS–R Digit Span performance or on the Verbal and Visual Memory tests from the WMS. Finally, neither nifedipine nor nitrendipine has been associated with performance changes on immediate or delayed verbal memory tests (Leonetti & Salvetti, 1994; Powell et al., 1993).

Summary

CCBs and the centrally acting agent methyldopa appear to impair attention abilities. Few other effects have been found for CCBs, centrally acting drugs, or alpha blocking agents, although there currently are no data available to determine how they affect many cognitive abilities. This is particularly unfortunate in the case of CCBs, as they are among the most common antihypertensive agents currently prescribed in the United States (Kaplan, 1998).

Relationship of Neuropsychological Tests to Everyday Functioning

Because the treatment of hypertension typically continues for an extended period of time, if not for a lifetime, it is important to understand the clinical relevance of changes in cognitive functioning and how the changes in performance seen on neuropsychological and cognitive tests translate to everyday functioning. One approach to assessing the clinical significance of decrements in cognitive functioning that result from drug therapy is to compare the results from neuropsychological tests with published norms. When such data are available, drug-related decrements tend to not fall in the range of clinical impairment (e.g., Palac et al., 1990). Therefore, the cognitive decrements associated with drug treatment are unlikely to have a significant impact on patients' quality of life.

Because untreated hypertension is associated with consistent deficits in some areas of cognitive functioning (see Waldstein et al., 1991, and chap. 1, this book, for a review), it is of both theoretical and clinical value to know how changes associated with drug therapy influence the relationship between hypertension and cognitive functioning. For example, negative effects of drug therapy may be additive, increasing the likelihood that such changes would be associated with decreased competence in everyday functioning. In addition, benefits associated with drug treatment may actually restore hypertensives to the same level of functioning as normotensive individuals. This not only is relevant to patients' quality of life, but it also suggests that changes associated with hypertension are functional and can be reversed (Miller, Shapiro, King, Ginchereau, & Hosutt, 1984). To answer these questions, the performance of hypertensives needs to be compared with that of normotensives before and during treatment (e.g., Schenk, Lang, & Anlauf, 1981; Streufert et al., 1989). The results of one randomized study in which this comparison was made suggest that treatment with the BB metoprolol improves performance on cognitive tests such that treated hypertensives perform similarly to untreated normotensive individuals (Streufert et al., 1989).

It also is important to understand whether the effects of antihypertensive medications on cognitive functioning have any influence on everyday activities. Unfortunately, most tests that measure the influences of medication on cognition do not assess whether the changes associated with antihypertensive medications have an impact on skills such as driving, reading, playing musical instruments, managing finances, doing crossword puzzles, playing cards, and so on. Furthermore, the relationship of neuropsychological test performance to everyday functioning is not clear.

A number of studies have assessed the influence of BB treatment on performance on everyday tasks (e.g., Betts et al., 1985; Donaldson, Grant-Thomson, Morwood, O'Connor, & Tippett, 1980; Streufert et al., 1988). However, the majority of these studies assessed performance in normotensive individuals after a single dose of medication, which may not be applicable to chronic treatment (see Muldoon et al., 1991, for a review of these data). Two studies used randomized, longitudinal methods to assess the influences of BB treatment on cognitive measures that have predictive validity for job success in terms of income at different ages, job level at different ages, number of employees supervised, and number of promotions during the previous 10 years (Streufert et al., 1988, 1989). Results from these studies associate metoprolol with improvements in strategic capacity and the ability to deal effectively with emergencies. It is therefore possible that treating hypertension with metoprolol improves everyday functioning.

POTENTIAL MECHANISMS

Although a number of hypotheses have been posed to explain the mechanisms by which antihypertensives affect cognitive functioning, data are limited, and hypotheses are generally unproven. The most direct route by which medications can affect cognitive functioning is by way of their chemical properties that affect the CNS. This may occur through direct penetration of the CNS or by affecting other systems that in turn influence the CNS. Because BBs and ACE inhibitors are the most widely tested medications, the following discussion of drug-specific effects focuses primarily on the information available regarding their proposed mechanisms.

BBs

Investigators involved in early work with BBs hypothesized that degree of lipid solubility would determine the extent of a drug's impact on CNS functioning. These investigators suggested that because highly lipid-soluble medications cross the blood–brain barrier more easily, more lipid-soluble medications, such as propranolol and metoprolol, would be more concentrated in the cerebral spinal fluid than those with less lipid solubility. The increased concentration could potentially lead to greater effects on functions associated specifically with the CNS. This hypothesis, however, does not appear to explain drug differences. Many studies have shown that degree of lipid solubility does not predict differences in CNS functioning (Blumenthal et al., 1988; Gengo et al., 1987, 1988; Palac et al., 1990). Further evidence against this hypothesis is that metoprolol, a highly lipid-soluble BB, is associated with more cognitive benefits than atenolol, which has low lipid solubility (e.g., Gengo et al., 1987, 1988; Streufert et al., 1988, 1989). If lipid solubility determines the degree of benefit from BBs, then propranolol, which also has high lipid solubility, would demonstrate similar benefits. However, there currently is no evidence to support the idea that propranolol is associated with significant cognitive benefits. It is possible that lipid solubility does not accurately predict the CNS uptake of BBs because passive diffusion of the medication may not be the only mechanism through which CNS uptake occurs (Gengo et al., 1987, 1988). However, it is clear that lipid solubility alone does not account for differences in the drug's effects on cognitive functioning.

Another possible route by which BBs affect the CNS is by binding with noncardiac beta$_2$ receptors. As with the question of lipid solubility, it is unclear whether cardioselectivity contributes to cognitive effects. If selectivity were the primary predictor of BBs' effects on cognition, atenolol and metoprolol would have similar effects, because they are both highly selective to beta$_1$ receptors. However, as we have pointed out, metoprolol has fewer negative effects on cognitive functioning than atenolol does, suggesting that cardioselectivity does not uniquely predict effects on cognitive functioning.

Indirect effects of BBs may also affect cognition by means of peripheral mechanisms. For example, Nielson and Jensen (1994) suggested that BBs attenuate the effects of catecholamines released during arousal, which may affect performance on cognitive tasks. Furthermore, Muldoon et al. (1991) suggested that BBs affect motor performance through reductions in regional muscle blood flow, or adrenergically mediated metabolic substrate release. Unfortunately, the specific mechanisms by which BBs affect cognitive functioning remain unclear.

ACE Inhibitors

Although the conclusions drawn in this review suggest that ACE inhibitors have no influence on most areas of cognitive functioning, the hypotheses put forth regarding the impact of ACE inhibitors on cognitive functioning assume a positive influence on cognition. In a review of the pharmacological and biochemical basis for improved quality of life resulting from ACE inhibitors, Govantes and Marín (1996) concluded that ACE inhibitors are likely to improve quality of life through their effects on the renin–angiotensin system. The reduction of the availability of angiotensin II in the brain caused by ACE inhibitors may facilitate cognitive processes (e.g., Barnes, Barnes, Costall, Horovitz, & Naylor, 1989; Sudilovsky et al., 1989) through a variety of actions. Reduced angiotensin II may play a role in CNS functioning by inhibiting the metabolism of peptides (Zubenko & Nixon, 1984), affecting noradrenergic regulation (Strittmatter, Lo, Javitch, & Snyder, 1984), and by affecting adrenocorticotrophic hormone secretion (Ramsay, Keil, Sharpe, & Shinsako, 1978).

Cognitive Consequences of Lowering BP

Antihypertensive medications also may affect cognitive functioning by lowering BP, particularly if the cognitive effects of untreated hypertension are functional and can be reversed (Miller et al., 1984). Preliminary support for this hypothesis came from a retrospective study conducted by Miller et al. (1984), which demonstrated that previously undiagnosed hypertensive individuals who were tested both prior to taking various antihypertensive medications and after 15 months of continuous treatment improved on a variety of cognitive tests. In addition, Starr et al. (1996) found that patients with mild dementia who experienced the greatest drug-induced BP reduction also experienced the greatest cognitive gain, regardless of whether they were randomized to the ACE group inhibitor or the diuretic group.

It is difficult to separate direct effects of drugs and those associated with BP reductions. Nonetheless, researchers interested in identifying the mechanisms through which antihypertensive medications affect CNS functioning need to be aware of the possibility that performance differences associated with treatment may be a function of BP changes, direct results of drug treatment, or both.

DIRECTIONS FOR FUTURE RESEARCH

A number of questions should be addressed regarding the relationship between antihypertensive medications and cognitive functioning. In general, the relationship between specific medications and cognitive functioning needs further clarification. Future research should focus on areas in the literature that have the most inconsistencies, such as research assessing the relation of antihypertensive medications to perceptual and psychomotor functioning. In addition, research should focus on CCBs and diuretic treatment (particularly in young adults). Both drug types are widely prescribed, yet only limited research has assessed their behavioral effects.

Individual Differences

A number of important questions may be posed regarding the cognitive impact of medication as a function of age, race, and gender. Future research should attempt to compare the effects of medication across different populations, particularly when there are theoretical reasons to believe such differences may exist.

Age

Although a number of studies have assessed the impact of treatment on either young adults or older adults, to our knowledge there are currently no studies that have directly tested whether the cognitive impact of medications differs across age groups. Because certain cognitive abilities change with age (Craik & Salthouse, 2000), and because older and younger adults' physiological responses to some antihypertensive treatments differ (Fries, 1988), it is reasonable to suspect that cognitive functioning may also be differentially affected. In addition, because the cognitive impact of untreated hypertension varies across age groups (e.g., Madden & Blumenthal, 1998; Waldstein et al., 1996), and because these differences may result from functional differences affecting the CNS, it is possible that the functional impact of pharmacologically lowering BP also varies as a function of age.

Gender

Gender differences related to antihypertensive medications have appeared in the literature yet remain unexplained. For example, Croog et al. (1990) found that the CCB verapamil improved performance in African American men, but not women. It is possible that medications differentially interact with hormones, thereby affecting cognitive functioning differently in men and women. By including adequate numbers of men and women in protocols it would be relatively easy to determine whether there are consistent gender differences with regard to cognitive functioning. The literature reviewed in this chapter includes proportional numbers of men and women in studies that have assessed performance in older adults. However, in studies that have assessed performance in young adults, men made up approximately 85% of the participants. If gender differences are identified, it would be important to determine the cause of such differences.

Race–Ethnicity

Future work should also address potential racial and ethnic differences related to drug treatment. BP reduction in African Americans tends to be more effective with monotherapy of diuretics and CCBs than other types of therapy, whereas this is not true of other populations (Joint National Committee on the Prevention, Detection, Evaluation, and Treatment of High Blood Pressure, 1997). This suggests that the nature of hypertension may differ across populations. Although data have been gathered regarding the behavioral impact of medications in African Americans (Croog et al., 1990), there are no data that compare different effects in different racial or ethnic groups. Because of the differential effectiveness of treatment in different populations, it seems important to test whether there are different cognitive consequences between populations both with regard to the disease and the treatment.

Mechanisms

The final suggestion for future research concerns understanding the mechanisms by which different medications affect cognitive functioning. Changes in cognitive functioning associated with antihypertensive medications are, at least in part, likely to be related to functional changes in the brain resulting from changes in BP. It is therefore necessary to determine the functional mechanisms that underlie the relationship between hypertension and cognitive functioning before a complete understanding of the mechanisms by which drug therapy affects cognition can be understood. Recent developments in neuroimaging techniques (e.g., positron emission tomography [PET]; functional magnetic resonance imaging, structural magnetic resonance) are providing new information regarding brain structure and function. Such studies may also be useful for understanding the neuropsychological changes associated with untreated hypertension and the effects of drug treatment. Mentis et al. (1994) used PET to assess cerebral metabolic rates (CMR) for glucose and demonstrated that long-term treated hypertension is associated with reduced CMR in the basal ganglia and the border zone between the middle and anterior cerebral arteries. Because no differences were found between the hypertensive group and the control group on a number of neuropsychological tests, it remains unclear whether these functional changes are related to changes in cognitive functioning. It is also unclear how drug treatment influenced brain functioning, because Mentis et al. tested hypertensives only after a 2-week medication washout period. A logical follow-up study would take additional assessments while patients are taking medications and determine whether there were additional changes associated with drug therapy. In general, however, the combination of neuroimaging and behavioral assessments is likely to help determine functional changes in the brain associated with both hypertension and drug treatment.

GENERAL CONCLUSIONS

Although some antihypertensive drug therapies are associated with negative effects on cognitive abilities, the effects are generally small and are unlikely to outweigh the widely known benefits that drug therapy provides in reducing morbidity and mortality related to CV disease. There are also individual differences in response to medications that may be obscured by group comparisons. Therefore, the clinical management of hypertension requires some degree of trial and error to find the medication that is most effective in reducing BP while minimizing side effects, including relatively subtle cognitive deficits. It is therefore important to understand the potential costs of drug therapy to cognitive functioning.

ACKNOWLEDGMENT

This chapter was supported in part by grants from the National Institute of Mental Health (MH 49679) and the National Heart, Lung, and Blood Institute (HL 43028 and HL 49672).

REFERENCES

Ameling, E. H., de Korte, D. F., & Man in 't Veld, A. J., (1991). Impact of diagnosis and treatment of hypertension on quality of life: A double-blind, randomized, placebo-controlled, cross-over study of betaxolol. *Journal of Cardiovascular Pharmacology, 18,* 752–760.

Applegate, W. B., Pressel, S., Wittes, J., Luhr, J., Shekelle, R. B., Camel, G. H., Greenlick, M. R., Hadley, E., Moye, L., Perry, H. M., Schron, E., & Wegener, V. (1994). Impact of the treatment of isolated systolic hypertension on behavioral variables. *Archives of Internal Medicine, 154,* 2154–2160.

Barnes, J. M., Barnes, N. M., Costall, B., Horovitz, Z. P., & Naylor, R. J. (1989). Angiotensin II inhibits the release of [3H]acetylcholine from rat entorhinal cortex in vitro. *Brain Research, 491,* 136–143.

Bayliss, P. F. C., & Duncan, S. M. (1975). The effects of atenolol (Tenormin) and methyldopa on simple tests of central nervous function. *British Journal of Clinical Pharmacology, 2,* 527–531.

Betts, T. A., Knight, R., Crowe, A., Blake, A., Harvey, P., & Mortiboy, D. (1985). Effect of beta-blockers on psychomotor performance in normal volunteers. *European Journal of Clinical Pharmacology, 28* (Suppl.), 39–49.

Blumenthal, J. A., Madden, D. J., Krantz, D. S., Light, K. C., McKee, D. C., Ekelund, L. G., & Simon, J. (1988). Short-term behavioral effects of beta-adrenergic medications in men with mild hypertension. *Clinical Pharmacology and Therapeutics, 43,* 429–435.

Broadhurst, A. D. (1980). The effect of propranolol on human psychomotor performance. *Aviation, Space, and Environmental Medicine, 51,* 176–179.

Buschke, H., & Fuld, P. A. (1974). Evaluating storage, retention, and retrieval in disordered memory and learning. *Neurology, 24,* 1019–1025.

Collins, R., Peto, R., MacMahon, S., Herbert, P., Fiebach, N. H., Eberlein, K. A., Godwin, J., Qizilbash, N., Taylor, J. O., & Hennekens, C. H. (1990). Blood pressure, stroke, and coronary artery disease. Part 2, short-term reductions in blood pressure: Overview of randomised drug trials in their epidemiological context. *The Lancet, 335,* 827–838.

Craik, F. I. M., & Salthouse, T. A. (2000). *Handbook of aging and cognition II.* Mahwah, NJ: Lawrence Erlbaum Associates.

Croog, S. H., Elias, M. F., Colton, T., Raume, R. M., Leiblum, S. R., Jenkins, C. D., Perry, H. M., & Hall, W. D. (1994). Effects of antihypertensive medications on quality of life in elderly hypertensive women. *American Journal of Hypertension, 7,* 329–339.

Croog, S. H., Kong, W., Levine, S., Weir, M. R., Baume, R. M., & Saunders, E. (1990). Hypertensive black men and women. *Archives of Internal Medicine, 150,* 1733–1741.

Croog, S. H., Levine, S., Testa, M. A., Brown, B., Bulpitt, C. J., Jenkins, C. D., Klerman, G. L., & William, G. H. (1986). The effects of antihypertensive therapy on the quality of life. *New England Journal of Medicine, 314,* 1657–1664.

Cushman, W. C., Khatri, I., Materson, B. J., Reda, D. J., Freis, E. D., Goldstein, G., Ramirez, E. A., Talmers, F. N., White, T. J., Nunn, S., Schnaper, H., Thomas, J. F., Henderson, W. G., & Fye, C. (1991). Treatment of hypertension in the elderly. Response of isolated systolic hypertension to various doses of hydrochlorothiazide: Results of a Department of Veterans Affairs cooperative study. *Archives of Internal Medicine, 151,* 1954–1960.

Deary, I. J., Capewell, S., Hajducka, C., & Muir, A. L. (1991). The effects of captopril vs atenolol on memory, information processing and mood: A double-blind crossover study. *British Journal of Clinical Pharmacology, 32,* 347–353.

Dimsdale, J. E., & Newton, R. P. (1992). Cognitive effects of beta blockers. *Journal of Psychosomatic Research, 36,* 229–236.

Domeney, A. M. (1994). Angiotensin converting enzyme inhibitors as potential cognitive enhancing agents. *Journal of Psychiatry and Neuroscience, 19,* 46–50.

Donaldson, E., Grant-Thomson, J., Morwood, P., O'Connor, N., & Tippett, R. (1980). Pilot study of the value of beta-blocking drug in initial helicopter training. *Aviation, Space, and Environmental Medicine, 51,* 926–929.

Elias, M. F., Robbins, M. A., Schultz, N. R., Streeten, D. H. P., & Elias, P. K. (1987). Clinical significance of cognitive performance by hypertensive patients. *Hypertension, 9,* 192–197.

Fletcher, A., & Bulpitt, C. (1992). Quality of life in the treatment of hypertension: The effects of calcium antagonists. *Drugs, 44,* 135–140.

Frcka, G., & Lader, M. (1988). Psychotropic effects of repeated doses of enalapril, propranolol, and atenolol in normal subjects. *British Journal of Clinical Pharmacology, 25,* 67–73.

Freis, E. D. (1988). Age and antihypertensive drugs (hydrochlorothiazide, bendroflumethiazide, nadolol, and captopril). *American Journal of Cardiology, 61,* 117–121.

Gengo, F. M., Fagan, S. C., de Padova, A., Miller, J. K., & Kinkel, P. R. (1988). The effects of beta-blockers on mental performance on older hypertensive patients. *Archives of Internal Medicine, 148,* 779–784.

Gengo, F. M., Huntoon, L., & McHugh, W. B. (1987). Lipid-soluble and water-soluble beta-blockers. *Archives of Internal Medicine, 147,* 39–43.

Goldstein, G., Materson, B. J., Cushman, W. C., Reda, D. J., Freis, E. D., Ramirez, E. A., Talmers, F. N., White, T. J., Nunn, S., Chapman, R. H., Khatri, I., Schnaper, H., Thomas, J. R., Henderson, W. G., & Fye, C. (1990). Treatment of hypertension in the elderly: II. Cognitive and behavioral function. Results of a Department of Veterans Affairs Cooperative Study. *Hypertension, 15,* 361–369.

Govantes, C., & Marín, J. (1996). Effect of angiotensin converting enzyme inhibitors on quality of life in hypertensive patients: Pharmacodynamic basis. *Fundamentals of Clinical Pharmacology, 10,* 400–405.

Gurland, B. J., Teresi, J., Smith, W. M., Black, D., Hughes, G., & Edlavitch, S. (1988). Effects of treatment for isolated systolic hypertension on cognitive status and depression in the elderly. *Journal of the American Geriatric Society, 36,* 1015–1022.

Harvey, P. G., Clayton, A. B., & Betts, T. A. (1977). The effects of four anithypertensive agents on the Stroop Colour–Word test in normal male volunteer subjects. *Psychopharmacology, 54,* 133–138.

Herrick, A. L., Waller, P. C., Berkin, K. E., Pringle, S. D., Callender, J. S., Robertson, M. P., Findlay, J. G., Murray, G. D., Reid, J. L., Lorimer, A. R., Weir, R. J., Carmichael, H. A., Robertson, J. I. S., Ball, S. G., & McInnes, G. T. (1989). Comparison of enalapril and atenolol in mild to moderate hypertension. *American Journal of Medicine, 86,* 421–426.

Joint National Committee on Prevention, Detection, Evaluation and Treatment of High Blood Pressure. (1997). The sixth report of the Joint National Committee on Prevention, Detection, Evaluation, and Treatment of High Blood Pressure. *Archives of Internal Medicine, 157,* 2413–2445.

Kaplan, N. M. (1998). *Clinical hypertension.* Baltimore: Williams & Wilkins.

Kostis, J. B., & Rosen, R. C. (1987). Central nervous system effects of beta-adrenergic blocking drugs: The role of ancillary properties. *Circulation, 75,* 204–212.

Lasser, N. L., Nash, J., Lasser, V. I., Hamill, S. J., & Batey, D. M. (1989). Effects of antihypertensive therapy on blood pressure control, cognition, and reactivity. *American Journal of Medicine, 86,* 98–103.

Leonetti, G., & Salvetti, A. (1994). Effects of cilazapril and ditrendipine on blood pressure, mood, sleep, and cognitive function in elderly hypertensive patients: An Italian multicenter study. *Journal of Cardiovascular Pharmacology, 24*(Suppl. 3), S73–S77.

Lezak, M. D. (1983). *Neuropsychological assessment* (2nd ed.). New York: Oxford University Press.

Lezak, M. D. (1995). *Neuropsychological assessment* (3rd ed.). New York: Oxford University Press.

Lichter, I., Richardson, P. J., & Wyke, M. A. (1986). Differential effects of atenolol and enalapril on memory during treatment for essential hypertension. *British Journal of Clinical Pharmacology, 21,* 641–645.

MacMahon, S., Peto, R., Cutler, J., Collins, R., Sorlie, P., Neaton, J., Abbott, R., Godwin, J., Dyer, A.,

& Stamler, J. (1990). Blood pressure, stroke, and coronary heart disease. Part I: Effects of prolonged differences in blood pressure: Evidence from nine prospective observational studies corrected for the regression dilution bias. *The Lancet, 335,* 765–774.

Madden, D. J., & Blumenthal, J. A. (1998). Interaction of hypertension and age in visual selective attention performance. *Health Psychology, 17,* 76–83.

Madden, D. J., Blumenthal, J. A., Ekelund, L. G., Krantz, D. S., Light, K. C., & McKee, D. C. (1986). Memory performance by mild hypertensives following beta-adrenergic blockade. *Psychopharmacology, 89,* 20–24.

McCorvey, E., Jr., Write, J. T., Culbert, J. P., McKenney, J. M., Proctor, J. D., & Annett, M. P. (1993). Effect of hydrochlorothiazide, enalapril, and propranolol on quality of life and cognitive and motor function in hypertensive patients. *Clinical Pharmacy, 12,* 300–305.

Mentis, M. J., Salerno, J., Horwitz, B., Grady, C., Schapiro, M. B., Murphy, D. G. M., & Rapoport, S. I. (1994). Reduction of functional neuronal connectivity in long-term treated hypertension. *Stroke, 25,* 601–607.

Miller, R. E., Shapiro, A. P., King, E., Ginchereau, E. H., & Hosutt, J. A. (1984). Effect of antihypertensive treatment on the behavioral consequences of elevated blood pressure. *Hypertension, 6,* 202–208.

Muldoon, M. F., Shapiro, A. P., Manuck, S. B., & Waldstein, S. R. (1991). Behavioral sequelae of antihypertensive therapy: A review. In A. P. Shapiro & A. Baum (Eds.), *Behavioral aspects of cardiovascular disease* (pp. 287–325). Hillsdale, NJ: Lawrence Erlbaum Associates.

Muldoon, M. F., Waldstein, S. R., & Jennings, J. R. (1995). Neuropsychological consequences of antihypertensive medication use. *Experimental Aging Research, 21,* 353–368.

Nielson, K. A., & Jensen, R. A. (1994). Beta-adrenergic receptor antagonist antihypertensive medications impair arousal-induced modulation of working memory in elderly humans. *Behavioral and Neural Biology, 62,* 190–200.

Olajide, D., & Lader, M. (1985). Psychotropic effects of enalapril maleate in normal volunteers. *Psychopharmacologia, 86,* 374–376.

Palac, D. M., Cornish, R. D., McDonald, W. J., Middaugh, D. A., Howieson, D., & Bagby, S. P. (1990). Cognitive function in hypertensives treated with atenolol or propranolol. *Journal of General Internal Medicine, 5,* 310–318.

Powell, J., Pickering, A., Wyke, M., & Goggin, T. (1993). The effects of anti-hypertensive medication on learning and memory. *British Journal of Clinical Pharmacology, 35,* 105–113.

Prince, M. J., Bird, A. S., Blizard, R. A., & Mann, A. H. (1996). Is the cognitive function of older patients affected by antihypertensive treatment? Results from 54 months of the Medical Research Council's treatment trial of hypertension in older adults. *British Medical Journal, 312,* 801–805.

Ramsay, D. J., Keil, L. C., Sharpe, M. C., & Shinsako, J. (1978). Angiotensin II infusion increases vasopressin, ACTH, and 11-hydroxycorticosteriod secretion. *American Journal of Physiology, 234,* R66–R71.

Reitan, R. M. (1958). Validity of the Trail Making Test as an indicator of organic brain damage. *Perceptual & Motor Skills, 8,* 271–276.

Russell, E. W. (1975). A multiple scoring method for the assessment of complex memory functions. *Journal of Consulting and Clinical Psychology, 43,* 800–809.

Schenk, G. K., Lang, E., & Anlauf, M. (1981). Beta-receptor blocking therapy in hypertensive patients—Effects on vigilance and behavior. *Aviation, Space, and Environmental Medicine, 52,* S35–S39.

Skinner, M. H., Futterman, A., Morrissette, D., Thompson, L. W., Hoffman, B. B., & Blaschke, T. F. (1992). Atenolol compared with nifedipine: Effect on cognitive function and mood in elderly hypertensive patients. *Annals of Internal Medicine, 116,* 615–623.

Steiner, S., Friedhoff, A. J., Wilson, B. L., Wecker, J. R., & Santo, J. P. (1990). Antihypertensive therapy and quality of life: A comparison of atenolol, captopril, enalapril, and propranolol. *Journal of Human Hypertension, 4,* 217–225.

Streufert, S., DePadova, A., McGlynn, T., Piasecki, M., & Pogash, R. (1989). Effects of beta blockade with metoprolol on simple and complex task performance. *Health Psychology, 8,* 143–158.

Streufert, S., DePadova, A., McGlynn, T., Pogash, R., & Piasecki, M. (1988). Impact of beta-blockade on complex cognitive functioning. *American Heart Journal, 116,* 311–314.

Strittmatter, S. M., Lo, M. M. S., Javitch, J. A., & Snyder, S. H. (1984). Autoradiographic visualization of angiotensin-converting enzyme in rat brain with [3H]captopril: Localization to a striatonigral pathway. *Proceedings of the National Academy of Sciences, 81,* 1599–1603.

Stroop, J. R. (1935). Studies of interference in serial verbal reactions. *Journal of Experimental Psychology, 18,* 643–662.

Sudilovsky, A., Croog, S., Crook, T., Turnbull, B., Testa, M., Levine, S., & Klerman, G. L. (1989). Differential effects of antihypertensive medications on cognitive functioning. *Psychopharmacology Bulletin, 25,* 133–138.

Van Gelder, P., Alpert, M., & Tsui, W. H. (1985). A comparison of the effects of atenolol and metoprolol on attention. *European Journal of Clinical Pharmacology, 28* (Suppl.), 101–103.

Waldstein, S. R., Jennings, J. R., Ryan, C. M., Muldoon, M. F., Shapiro, A. P., Polefrone, J. M., Fazzari, T. V., & Manuck, S. B. (1996). Hypertension and neuropsychological performance in men: Interactive effects of age. *Health Psychology, 15,* 102–109.

Waldstein, S. R., Manuck, S. B., Ryan, C. M., & Muldoon, M. F. (1991). Neuropsychological correlates of hypertension: Review and methodologic consideration. *Psychological Bulletin, 110,* 451–468.

Wechsler, D. (1955). *WAIS manual.* New York: Psychological Corporation.

Wechsler, D. (1974). *Wechsler Memory Scale manual.* San Antonio, TX: Psychological Corporation.

Wechsler, D. (1981). *WAIS–R manual.* New York: Psychological Corporation.

Zubenko, G. S., & Nixon, R. A. (1984). Mood-elevating effect of captopril in depressed patients. *American Journal of Psychiatry, 141,* 110–111.

CHAPTER TEN

Neuropsychological Consequences of Coronary Artery Bypass Surgery

STANTON NEWMAN
Associate Fellow of the British Psychological Society

JAN STYGALL
ROBERT KONG
Fellows of the Royal College of Anaesthetists

The development of the heart–lung machine, which enables surgery to be performed while the patient's heart is stopped, revolutionized cardiac surgery. This chapter traces the history of the development of cardiopulmonary bypass (CPB) and the dramatic increase in the number of cardiac surgical procedures performed. It specifically examines the impact that coronary artery bypass graft (CABG) surgery with CPB has on cognitive function. The potential mechanisms by which neuropsychological (NP) changes occur are explored, and techniques that have been studied to lessen the impact of this procedure on the brain are discussed.

SURGERY FOR ISCHEMIC HEART DISEASE

Pathophysiology of Coronary Artery Disease

Ischemic heart disease is most commonly the result of coronary artery disease (CAD). Although its most distinctive symptom is angina pectoris, the clinical presentation is extremely variable and very often asymptomatic. In CAD one or more of the heart's major arteries, which include the left anterior descending, circumflex, and right coronary arteries, become progressively occluded by atherosclerotic plaque. The more distal vessels are usually less overtly affected but may possess an abnormal tone, and the combination of this and the degree and distribution of plaques accounts for the limitation of myocardial blood flow in CAD. The pathophysiology of the disease reflects an imbalance of myocardial blood supply and demand; total arterial occlusion can rapidly lead to ischemia and death of heart muscle or myocardial infarction.

Origins of Cardiac and Coronary Artery Surgery

Cardiac surgery had its beginnings in the 19th century with experiments on animals to repair penetrating lesions of the heart. In 1897, at a time when many clinicians dismissed the notion of heart surgery as somewhat fanciful, Rehn, a general practitioner from Frankfurt, reported the first successful repair of a stab wound of the heart in a man (Acierno, 1994). The first half of the 20th century saw significant advances with innovative procedures for congenital lesions and valvular and ischemic heart disease. But the turning point of the specialty came in the 1950s. All types of surgery benefit from a still and bloodless field, and in 1953 John Gibbon showed that this could be achieved during cardiac surgery when he successfully repaired an atrial septal defect with the aid of CPB.

The earliest surgical treatments for ischemic heart disease were aimed at relieving the symptoms, but not the cause, of intractable angina. Attempts to operate directly on the coronary arteries began in earnest in the 1960s, and the first successful coronary artery bypass operation was done by Garrett in 1964. It was Favoloro at the Cleveland Clinic who, with the crucial support of pioneering coronary angiography, began his series 3 years later and went on to convince the cardiac surgical world that the procedure was both effective and associated with a relatively low mortality. Within a few years CABG combined with CPB had become established as the preferred surgical technique for myocardial revascularization (Favaloro, 1998).

CABG: Technique and Indications

CABG is a major surgical procedure performed under general anesthesia and takes on average from 3 to 5 hr. The heart is reached through a midline chest incision and, after the sternum is divided (sternotomy), vascular bypass grafts are fashioned during CPB. The left anterior descending artery is usually bypassed using the left internal mammary artery, a vessel that runs behind the chest wall, and segments of saphenous vein from the leg are used to bypass other coronary arteries. Some surgeons may also use the right internal mammary, radial, gastroepiploic, and epigastric arteries. Arterial grafts remain patent for longer; over 90% of internal mammary grafts are patent 5 to 12 years after surgery, but more than 50% of vein grafts are occluded by this time (Lytle et al., 1985).

The indications for CABG have become better defined over the years (see Table 10.1). Patients who are likely to benefit from surgery in terms of func-

TABLE 10.1
Principal Indications for Coronary Artery Bypass Grafting (CABG)

Three-vessel disease
Left main coronary artery disease
Selected cases of two-vessel disease
Failure of medical therapy (and unsuitability of patient for PTCA)
Failed PTCA
Recurrent symptoms postCABG
Congenital coronary artery abnormalities

Note. PTCA = percutaneous transluminal coronary angio-plasty.

tional improvement and survival can now be identified on the basis of their clinical and angiographic characteristics.

Although surgery is indicated for only about 20% of all patients with CAD, this has resulted in quite a significant caseload, and every year an increasing number of patients are undergoing revascularization procedures. In the United States, it has been estimated that 191,000 CABG were performed in 1983 and 318,000 were performed in 1994—an increase of 66% (Rutkow, 1997). Current estimates are that, worldwide, approximately 800,000 patients undergo CABG each year (Roach et al., 1996).

CPB

Blood flow through the heart (and therefore the lung) is bypassed by directing venous blood away from the right side of the heart through components of the CPB circuit and is returned to the patient's arterial circulation downstream from the left heart (see Fig. 10.1). The circuit includes a reservoir, an oxygenator to add oxygen and remove carbon dioxide from the blood, a heat exchanger to cool or warm the blood, one or more filters to prevent gaseous or particulate materials from entering the patient, and a pump to propel the blood back into the patient. Several combinations are possible for the location of the venous (e.g., right atrium or femoral vein) and arterial (e.g., ascending aorta or femoral artery) lines. Because blood will rapidly clot once it is in contact with any "foreign" material, a prerequisite of CPB is the administration of an anticoagulant, typically heparin, which is injected into the patient before the start of extracorporeal circulation; its effects are reversed on completion of CPB.

OTHER INTERVENTIONS FOR CAD

An alternative technique to restore coronary blood flow involves inserting and inflating a balloon in the affected coronary arteries. Percutaneous transluminal

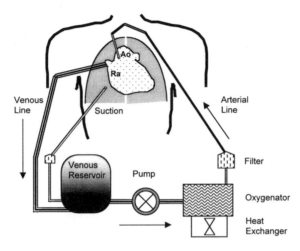

FIG. 10.1. Schematic diagram of cardiopulmonary bypass (see text). Venous blood is drained from the right atrium (Ra) and after oxygenation the arterialized blood is returned via the ascending aorta (Ao).

coronary angioplasty (PTCA) was introduced in 1977. Since then there has been a phenomenal increase in the number of patients treated. It has been estimated that by the late 1990s approximately 1 million patients had undergone this procedure worldwide (King, 1998). Initially directed at patients with single-vessel disease, for which it is the treatment of choice, PTCA is being used increasingly in multivessel disease. Cishek and Gershony (1996) summarized the clinical trials that have compared PTCA with CABG. They concluded that in-hospital complication was lower for PTCA but that long-term survival and rate of myocardial infarction after either procedure were similar. Patients were able to return to routine activity more quickly after PTCA, but functional status was similar for the two groups after 1 year. The most important drawback of PTCA is restenosis of the treated artery in about 50% of cases (King, 1998).

Several variations of the standard CABG operation were introduced in the 1990s and were labeled *minimally invasive*. These operations are performed through smaller incisions and with the aid of specially designed instruments. Compared with the standard approach, minimally invasive CABG may be associated with less trauma and morbidity, which will favor earlier hospital discharge and a shorter convalescence. Minimally invasive CABG techniques can be divided into to categories: (a) those in which surgery is performed on the beating heart, without the need for CPB, and (b) those that still require bypass but use an endovascular approach (Society of Thoracic Surgeons/American Association for Thoracic Surgery Committee on New Technology, 1998). Experience in minimally invasive CABG techniques has been acquired mostly with single-vessel grafting; consequently, meaningful outcome and safety comparisons with standard CABG cannot be made until these techniques find wider application in the treatment of multivessel disease.

NEUROLOGIC CONSEQUENCES OF CARDIAC SURGERY

Incidence

CABG is associated with a small but important risk of perioperative stroke. The incidence reported in the literature of 1.5% to 5.2% depends on the number and type of patients recruited, the design of the study, and the method of clinical assessment (McKhann et al., 1997). Stroke increases mortality, length of hospital stay, and the need for long-term care after cardiac surgery (Gardner et al., 1985; Roach et al., 1996). As the cardiac cause of death from cardiac surgery has declined, instances of death from neurologic causes have increased. Gardner et al. (1985) documented a decline in death attributed to cardiac causes from 85% to 54% in the 5 years from 1975 to 1982. During the same period neurologic factors as the cause of death increased from 4% to 18%.

Etiology

Neurologic complications of cardiac surgery are generally considered to be of two types: (a) hemodynamic changes with inadequate brain perfusion during surgery and (b) macroembolism. Although it is likely that the causes of stroke are multifactorial, the pathological evidence of fatalities in cardiac surgery indicates that strokes are ischemic rather than hypoxic, suggesting that macroemboli are the most important causal agent (Brierley, 1963). Harrison and Newman (2000) argued that stroke is more likely to be caused by macroembolic rather than hemodynamic factors; many strokes occur in the first 24 hr after surgery, when patients are hemodynamically stable. The risk is increased with factors known to be related to the generation of emboli, such as cardiac arrhythmia and aortic atheroma, and the appearance of infarcts on computerized tomography (CT) scans are not in the "watershed areas" (i.e., brain regions that fall between adjacent territories supplied by separate arteries), as would be expected as a result of hypoxia.

STUDIES DESIGNED TO DETERMINE THE INCIDENCE
OF NP DEFICITS FOLLOWING CARDIAC SURGERY

Rationale and Choice of NP Assessments

In the context of cardiac surgery NP assessment is designed to study the impact of surgery on cognition. It is customary to see the patient before and, at some time, after surgery. Unlike a chronic condition such as hypertension, or an acute event whose timing is uncontrollable, such as stroke, in cardiac surgery the potential insult can be anticipated, and measures can be taken before the event. The possibility of comparing data before and after the insult and evaluating the change in performance does, however, raise a whole series of methodological issues.

There are practical considerations as well. In most cardiac surgical environments patients are under tight time constraints, receiving investigations and preparations for surgery, and this often limits the time available for NP testing, realistically, to approximately 1 hr. Studies have used anywhere between 1 and 14 tests, but when more tests are used deficits are more likely to be detected. It is important to ensure that the assessment tools are sensitive to potentially diffuse brain injury. Early research used intelligence or screening tests such as the Mini Mental State Examination (Folstein, Folstein, & McHugh, 1975), but these have been replaced more recently by a wide variety of NP tests, many of which have been computerized to improve the standardization and ease of administration (S. Newman, 1993). Nonetheless, these tests vary in sensitivity and are thus likely to reveal a differing percentage of patients with NP deficits. Approximately 83 different NP tests have been applied in the study of cardiac surgery! When these tests are classified into the cognitive domain that they assess, it becomes apparent that the most frequently examined areas are memory and attention (see Table 10.2).

Incidence of NP Deficits

In this context, the incidence of NP deficits refers to the number of individuals rated as having postoperative deficits. The impact of these deficits on an individual's functioning in the world is highly variable and dependent on a number of factors, including the intellectual demands of his or her work. The timing of postoperative NP assessments has a profound effect on the incidence of deficits, which ranges from 18% to 70% in the early days after surgery (see Table 10.3). Early assessments may measure potential NP disturbance but are also likely to reflect general postoperative readjustment and recovery from anesthesia and surgery. Assessing NP performance some weeks or months after surgery produces lower levels of decline that appear to be more stable although are still quite variable (see Table 10.3).

TABLE 10.2
Domains Investigated in Incidence Studies

Study	No. and Type of Patient	Domain							
		Memory	Attention	Visuospatial	Numerical	Language	Visuomotor	Executive Function	Composite
Kolkka et al. (1980)	204 Combined	✓							
Fish et al. (1982)	20 CABG	✓	✓	✓					
Savageau et al. (1982a, 1982b)	245 Combined	✓	✓		✓				
Bethune (1982)	8 CABG 30 Valve	✓							
Jenkins et al. (1983)	318 CABG	✓	✓						
Raymond et al. (1984)	31 CABG	✓	✓	✓	✓	✓			✓
Aberg et al. (1984)	94 Combined			✓		✓	✓		
Freeman et al. (1985)	14 CABG								✓
Sontaniemi et al. (1986)	44 Valve	✓	✓	✓			✓		
Folks et al. (1986)	58 CABG	✓							✓
Calebrese et al. (1987)	59 CABG	✓	✓	✓		✓	✓		✓
S. Newman et al. (1987)	67 CABG	✓	✓						
Shaw et al. (1987a, 1987b)	298 CABG	✓	✓			✓			
Hammeke et al. (1988)	46 CABG	✓	✓			✓	✓	✓	
Jackson (1989)	57 Combined	✓	✓						
Townes et al. (1989)	78 Combined	✓	✓			✓			✓
Klonoff et al. (1989)	135 CABG	✓	✓					✓	
Nevin et al. (1989)	65 CABG	✓							✓

Continued

TABLE 10.2 (Continued)

Study	No. and Type of Patient	Domain							
		Memory	Attention	Visuospatial	Numerical	Language	Visuomotor	Executive Function	Composite
Stump et al. (1990)	27 CABG		✓				✓		
Mattler et al. (1988)	64 CABG	✓	✓	✓	✓	✓	✓		
Blumenthal et al. (1991)	31 Combined	✓	✓			✓			
D. O'Brien et al. (1992)	20 Combined	✓	✓						
Grote et al. (1992)	29 CABG	✓	✓	✓		✓			
Sellman et al. (1993)	54 CABG	✓	✓	✓		✓			
Toner et al. (1994)	15 CABG	✓	✓	✓		✓	✓		
Bruggemans et al. (1995)	63 CABG	✓	✓	✓		✓			
Mahanna et al. (1996)	232 CABG	✓							
Walzer et al. (1997)	70 CABG	✓		✓		✓		✓	
Vingerhoets et al. (1997)	109 Combined	✓	✓	✓		✓	✓		

Note. Combined = a combination of coronary artery bypass grafting (CABG) and valve patients.

Borowicz, Goldsborough, Selnes, and McKhann (1996) suggested that selective recruitment of patients may occur in studies of NP performance in CABG. They noted a refusal rate of 61% and found that patients who refused tended to have a higher rate of stroke and a higher mortality than participants in their study. In a recently completed two-center study, however, patients we recruited in England had a poorer mortality risk, as assessed by Parsonnet score (a commonly used clinical index of surgical risk), compared to nonstudy patients. Selective attrition of patients who perform poorly on baseline assessments also has

TABLE 10.3
Studies in Which Percentage Incidence of Decline
Has Been Specifically Reported

Study	No. and Type of Patient	Assessment Interval	Decline (%)
Walzer et al. (1997)	70 CABG	2 days	14
Freeman et al. (1985)	14 CABG	4 days	0
Mahanna et al. (1996)	232 CABG	6 days	66–15.3
Shaw et al. (1987)	298 CABG	7 days	79
Nevin et al. (1989)	65 CABG	7 days	33
Stump et al. (1989)	27 CABG	7 days	56
D. O'Brien et al. (1992)	20 Combined	7 days	25
Vingerhoets et al. (1997)	109 Combined	7 days	45
Bethune (1983)	8 CABG	8 days	12.5
S. Newman et al. (1987)	67 CABG	8 days	73
Savageau et al. (1982)	245 Combined	9 days	28
Jenkins et al. (1983)	318 CABG	9 days	30
Hammeke et al. (1988)	46 CABG	10 days	24
D. O'Brien et al. (1992)	20 Combined	4 weeks	10
Sellman et al. (1993)	54 CABG	4 weeks	17
Stump et al. (1990)	27 CABG	6 weeks	18.5
Mahanna et al. (1996)	232 CABG	6 weeks	34–1.1
Toner et al. (1994)	15 CABG	6–8 weeks	40
S. Newman et al. (1987)	67 CABG	8 weeks	37
Mattler et al. (1988)	64 CABG	8 weeks	0
Klonoff et al. (1989)	135 CABG	3 months	0
Savageau et al. (1982)	245 Combined	6 months	19
Jenkins et al. (1983)	318 CABG	6 months	5
Shaw et al. (1987)	259 CABG	6 months	57
Sellman et al. (1993)	54 CABG	6 months	7
Mahanna et al. (1996)	232 CABG	6 months	19.45–3.4
Vingerhoets et al. (1997)	91 Combined	6 months	12
Townes et al. (1989)	78 Combined	7 months	13
Mattler et al. (1988)	64 CABG	8 months	0
Klonoff et al. (1989)	135 CABG	12 months	0
Klonoff et al. (1989)	135 CABG	24 months	0

Note. Combined = a combination of coronary artery bypass grafting (CABG) and valve patients.

been observed by some investigators (Blumenthal et al., 1995; Borowicz et al., 1996), but again we have not found this pattern in our recent study. These transatlantic differences may reflect cultural differences in patients' willingness to participate in studies of this type but, more important, such findings emphasize the need to examine both participants and nonparticipants to ensure generalizablity of the results.

Defining NP Deficits

When research on the impact of cardiac surgery was in its infancy, there was a need to be able to make a clinical report on the number of patients with NP deficits. This was largely because of the need to persuade clinicians that a proportion of patients had a problem of brain function. The attempt to define criteria for incidence brought with it a number of attendant methodological problems. Foremost among these was the amount of change in NP scores that is considered sufficient to reflect a NP deficit (S. Newman, 1995). A number of different ways of computing the amount of change have been applied, but no consensus has been reached. One approach has been to calculate a standard deviation of the preoperative performance on each test and to consider a drop in performance equal to or greater than 1 SD as reflecting a deficit on that test (S. Newman et al., 1987). Others have considered a drop of 0.5 SD sufficient (Borowicz et al., 1996). It is also customary to consider a decline in at least two tests as indicative of a NP deficit. The drawback to using a fixed level of deterioration, irrespective of the absolute score before surgery, is that patients with low preoperative scores may be unable to deteriorate sufficiently to reach the 1-SD threshold (Mahana et al., 1996). An alternative approach, which considers a relative decline of 20% from baseline scores, also has been used (Stump, Newman, Coker, Phipps, & Miller, 1990). This approach suffers from the problem at the other end of the scale, where low preoperative scores may require only a small amount of change to be considered to reflect a deficit. This may be within the noise level of performance. Mahanna et al. (1996) highlighted the variability in techniques used to assess the incidence of NP deficits in cardiac surgery. Using five different criteria to define deficits, they found a sixfold difference in the incidence of deficits (3.4%–19.4%).

The need to move away from the crude measure of incidence of NP deficits has been recognized (S. Newman, 1993). Incidence measures were attractive in that they offered a technique to compare different units. Unfortunately, the problems outlined earlier make such comparisons difficult. Moreover, changes in cardiac surgical practice are also likely to have an impact on the incidence of NP deficits. In our own unit we have assessed approximately 1,200 patients undergoing routine CABG surgery, and the incidence of NP deficits has declined from approximately 33% in 1985 to 13% in 1992, when a similar test battery, method of calculating deficits, and follow-up times were used.

POTENTIAL AGENTS FOR NP DISTURBANCE
FOLLOWING CARDIAC SURGERY

Several factors may account for the NP disturbance suffered by a proportion of individuals who undergo cardiac surgery. Although these are often presented as competing hypotheses, it would not be surprising if the cause of NP decline were multifactorial.

Microemboli

The Retina

Blauth et al. (1993) and Blauth (1990) used fluorescein angiography to assess the microvasculature of the retina during surgery. They established that all patients undergoing CABG with bubble oxygenators developed retinal microvascular occlusions, findings that were confirmed in a dog model. The technique, however, offered only a snapshot view of the microvasculature.

Doppler Ultrasound

Doppler ultrasound had been widely used to measure blood flow velocity before it was applied to the detection of microemboli in surgery. Compared with the normal blood components (essentially the red blood cells), emboli produce much greater backscatter of ultrasound and consequently generate a characteristic signal that is easily distinguishable from that representing blood flow. These signals have been referred to as *high intensity signals* (HITS) and also as *microembolic events* (MEE). During cardiac surgery, insonation of the middle cerebral artery (by transcranial Doppler) or carotid arteries has detected the presence of HITS. Similar ultrasound signals could be reproduced in the laboratory by injection of microspheres into a model circulation (Padayachee et al., 1987; Pugsley, 1989; and Pugsley et al., 1990), which would suggest that MEE are produced by embolic material within the cerebral circulation during surgery. During the course of cardiac surgery the first appearance of MEE is likely to be associated with manipulations of the aorta and is usually observed during insertion of the aortic cannula. Most of the MEE then appear during CPB, and in coronary artery surgery the last are coincident with the removal of the aortic cannula at the end of bypass.

"Microembolic Load"

The total number of MEE recorded during surgery can range from almost none to a few thousand. Several factors may account for this: the nature of the emboli (gas or particulate), the extent of atheroma in the patient's aorta and cerebral arteries, technical considerations of cannulation and CPB, the type of Doppler equipment being used, and the site of insonation. It is important to note that the number of microemboli tends to increase as the length of time on CPB increases. This gives Doppler emboli detection a clear advantage over retinal fluorescein angiography in that it potentially offers the ability to measure the cumulative microembolic load during surgery.

What make up the microemboli? MEEs appear to be associated with surgical procedures (Stump, Rogers, Hammon, & Newman, 1996) presumably because at these times particulate material, such as atheroma in the vessel wall, is dislodged, or air is introduced into the arterial circulation. However, MEEs also appear during periods of surgical inactivity, and there is no good explanation as to why these occur. Besides air and atheroma, other potential candidates include antifoaming agents, platelet and fibrin aggregates, and other materials from damaged cells.

Great emphasis is being placed on the ability to discriminate between particulate and gaseous emboli. It is generally assumed, but largely unproven, that particulate emboli are more likely to cause harm, whereas gaseous ones are innocuous. At present the Doppler signals in CABG do not provide useful information on either the type or the size of microemboli. The physics would suggest that for emboli of similar size, gaseous material causes much greater backscatter than solid material (Markus & Brown, 1993; Markus & Tegeler, 1995), but a host of other factors that define the Doppler instrumentation are also likely to modify the signal characteristics. For investigators in this field, designing an instrument that can be used in the clinic to detect and differentiate emboli type is proving to be a difficult challenge.

Besides being limited in their ability to discriminate physical property, the techniques used to quantify the number of microemboli require scrutiny. Not only do different types of equipment produce different counts, but also there may not be a one-to-one relationship between embolus and signal. Continuous signals may be caused by a shower of emboli, and these are very difficult to resolve. Consequently, the counts of microemboli reflect only gross estimates of the microembolic load, hence the preference for referring to these signals as MEEs (Pugsley, 1989).

Relationship of Microemboli to NP Deficit

If microemboli can be implicated in NP deficits after cardiac surgery, then it would seem reasonable to assume that the numbers of microemboli should be related to the likelihood of having an NP deficit. A general relationship between microemboli as detected by transcranial Doppler monitoring and NP deficit assessed at 8 weeks on 10 NP tests was found in one study (Pugsley et al., 1994), but not in another (Arrowsmith et al., 1998).

Some of the factors that militate against finding a relationship between these two phenomena have been alluded to previously: the inexact counts of microemboli and their different types and sizes, which cannot be discriminated and which may have a differential impact on the brain. More important, areas of the brain are differentially sensitive to ischemia, and therefore the possibility of detecting an NP deficit would be critically dependent on where in the brain the microemboli ended up.

Hemodynamic Changes

Cerebral hypoperfusion has been implicated in the possible etiology of NP deficits, and the likely cause can be considered in terms of two physiological variables: (a) blood pressure (BP) and (b) cerebral blood flow. BP, which is monitored routinely in cardiac surgery, is presumed to reflect cerebral perfusion pressure (after subtracting intracranial pressure). The potential deleterious effects of hypotension have been established in an association between hypotensive episodes during cardiac surgery and concurrent loss of electroencephalographic signal (S. Newman et al., 1987). Significant or prolonged hypotension is not, however, a usual feature of routine clinical management, so it would be unlikely for hypotension per se to be an important cause of NP deterioration. Indeed, studies that have explored the relationship between hypotensive episodes and NP deficits have found no association (S. Newman et al., 1987; Roach et al., 1996; Venn et al., 1988).

During CPB the normal autoregulation of cerebral blood flow is preserved (Schell et al., 1993). Thus, over the clinically encountered range of BP and pump flow rate, cerebral blood flow should remain appropriate to metabolic needs (Henriksen, 1993). Venn et al. (1988) examined cerebral blood flow using xenon and confirmed that flow rates were related not to BP but to the method of blood gas management. In one approach, the increase in cerebral blood flow that can result may be detrimental to the brain through increased delivery of microemboli or the development of intracranial hypertension.

RELATIONSHIP BETWEEN NP DEFICIT AND OTHER MEASURES OF THE BRAIN

Brain Imaging

In one early study by Aberg et al. (1984), two patients were found to have abnormal CT scans after coronary artery surgery. Cognitive testing with three tests indicated deterioration in function in one case and a small increase in the other.

Magnetic resonance imaging (MRI) reveals evidence of new lesions after CABG in a proportion of patients. Toner et al. (1994) discovered new lesions in 30% of a small sample of patients. Simonetta et al. (2000), who studied 32 patients undergoing cardiac surgery (CABG and valve surgery), found 12.5% to have new lesions on MRI performed 5 to 7 days after surgery. All of these 4 patients, however, had undergone valve surgery. It is interesting that both studies found a significant proportion of patients to have abnormal scans before surgery and, in Toner et al.'s study, only those with abnormal MRI showed new postoperative abnormalities. In contrast, patients with normal MRI before surgery did not develop postoperative changes, suggesting that the presence of cerebrovascular disease may be an important factor in the development of new lesions. A relationship of a general nature has been found between MRI and NP assessment. Whereas Simonetta et al. observed that patients with abnormal MRIs were more likely to show NP deficits, Toner et al. found NP deficits in all individuals who developed new lesions.

Biological Markers of Brain Injury

There are a number of potential biochemical markers of brain injury (Johnsson, 1996). Of most recent interest, S-100β reflect glial injury, whereas neuron-specific enolase (NSE) assesses neuronal injury.

Increased blood concentrations of S-100β have been measured in patients during and after CABG, and the peak increase has been associated with high microemboli counts as detected by transcranial Doppler (Croughwell et al., 1997; Westaby et al., 1996). Problems remain in the interpretation of the mechanism of increased concentrations of S-100β (Grocott et al., 1998), and a good controlled study is needed to examine the relationship of S-100β changes with NP performance.

Isgro, Schmidt, Pohl, & Saggau (1997) studied NSE in 200 patients undergoing a range of cardiac procedures. Peripheral blood NSE concentration was measured immediately before and at 48 hr after surgery. The Mini-Mental State Examination was administered before and 48 hr and 72 hr after surgery. Although the authors found an association between deterioration on the Mini-Mental State Examination and NSE concentration, neither the timing nor the type of assessment is ideal for evaluating the relationship between NSE and NP deterioration.

Pathology

Moody, Bell, Challa, Johnston, and Prough (1990) proposed a putative pathological correlate of microemboli. They examined brain histology in patients who had died within days or weeks of cardiac surgery as well as dogs that had been subjected to CPB. Brain slices stained with alkaline phosphatase revealed the presence of capillary microaneurysms, which the investigators have called *SCADS* (small capillary and arteriolar dilatations). The highest numbers of SCADS were found in patients who had died within a couple of days of surgery, very few were found in patients who died within a couple of days of coronary angiography, and none were found at any time if the patients had undergone surgery that did not involve manipulation of the proximal aorta. The number of SCADS tended to decline with time, but the mechanism of this decline is unknown. In an experimental context, identical brain lesions were found when dogs were subjected to CPB or given a lipid mixture by injection into the carotid artery.

PATIENT FACTORS RELATED TO NP DETERIORATION

Age

Correlational analysis has shown that there is increasing risk of NP deterioration following CABG with increasing age (M. Newman et al., 1994; D. O'Brien et al., 1992; Sotaniemi, Mononen, & Hokkanen, 1986; Townes et al., 1989). Age may be a marker of other factors, such as the extent of CV disease. It also has been found that during surgery, older patients generate more microemboli (Stump, Tegeler, Newman, Wallenhaupt, & Roy, 1992) and are less able to maintain adequate cerebral blood flow autoregulation (M. Newman et al., 1994, 1995).

Sex

The differential outcomes for men and women on NP tests have been examined rarely, although it is known that women tend to have higher levels of morbidity and mortality following CABG (Edwards, Carey, Grover, Bero, & Hartz, 1998). As the number of women with CAD increases, this issue is likely to be an area of growing interest (Wenger, Speroff, & Packard, 1993).

Genetic Predisposition

The apolipoprotein E ε-4 allele, which has been implicated in dementia, was the subject of a study by M. Newman et al. (1995) of NP performance after CABG. They found an association between this genetic marker and decline in performance on NP tests after surgery. This suggests that individuals with this genotype, which may impair neuronal repair and maintenance, may be at particular risk of NP decline following cardiac surgery.

Other Features

Patients with more severe cardiac disease may also be at increased risk of NP decline following cardiac surgery (Lee, Brady, Rowe, & Miller, 1971; D. O'Brien et al., 1992; Savageau, Stanton, Jenkins, & Frater, 1982; Shaw et al., 1987). Cerebrovascular disease as evidenced on abnormalities on MRI also tends to predispose individuals to poor postoperative performance on NP tests (Simonetta et al., 2000; Toner et al., 1994).

STUDIES DESIGNED TO REDUCE THE IMPACT
OF CARDIAC SURGERY ON THE BRAIN

A number of different approaches to attempt to improve the outcome of CABG on cognitive function have been attempted and are discussed next. The first and most obvious intervention is to alter the equipment used in CABG. Studies of this type have examined the impact of using a filter in the bypass circuit and changing the method of oxygenating the blood. The nature of the anaesthetic regimen is another approach that has been used; these types of studies have examined the impact of using different temperatures and have compared continuous delivery of the blood with attempts to mimic heart action more closely by pulsing the blood into the patient and varying the pH of the blood. The final category of intervention is one directed at protecting the brain rather than attempting to reduce the cause of the problem. These studies involve the use of a putative pharmacological neuroprotective agent. To determine whether a particular intervention has an impact on NP changes following CABG it is necessary to consider how changes in NP are determined. This issue has been considered in some detail in the literature, and the different options are discussed next.

Data Analysis

Deficit Versus No Deficit

Studies designed to investigate techniques to reduce the impact of cardiac surgery on the brain have involved at least two groups of patients. Consequently, they should allow more sophisticated statistical analyses of the data. Unfortunately, in many studies the tendency has been to continue to use the conventionally determined measure of incidence. Although this approach enables a comparison to be made between the groups in terms of the number of individuals showing NP deficits, it remains crude, partly because statistical analysis is dependent on the distinction between two potential outcomes (deficit vs. no deficit). The analysis tends to compare the proportions of individuals in the intervention group and the control group who had a deficit. This approach, although it is intrinsically appealing to clinicians because it classifies individuals, ignores the richness of data available from the scores on the NP tests and the possibilities that they offer for a more sensitive and sophisticated analysis (S. Newman, 1995).

A binary classification also fails to account for the frequently observed improvements that occur with repetition on NP tests because it considers only deterioration in performance. The improvements observed on tests are considered an unwanted phenomenon, and tests are designed to reduce their occurrence, or corrections are made to account for such practice effects (Kneebone, Andrew, Baker, & Knight, 1998).

Relative Change in Performance

Analysis of the test scores offers a more sensitive technique for examining the performance of cardiac surgical patients and provides a way of looking at both improvement and deterioration in scores after surgery. This type of analysis can be performed in a number of different ways. Simple change scores can be calculated from before to after surgery, and an analysis can be performed on the change scores (see Pugsley et al., 1994). This provides a separate analysis of performance on each of the tests. One way to analyze individual test performance and also create a measure of overall NP change is to convert each patient's score into a standard score (z score) using the standard deviation of the preoperative performance of all patients in the study. From these standard scores a difference score can be calculated for each patient on each test by subtracting the postoperative standard score from the preoperative standard score to reflect the relative change in performance from before to after the surgery. The group's performance on each individual test can be examined and the z score differences combined to provide a composite NP score, which can be used to determine whether the groups were different (see Arrowsmth et al., 1998). Thus this approach, rather than treating learning as something that is unwanted, assumes that the ability to demonstrate learning is evidence of the retention of brain function in the face of cardiac surgery. It examines the overall postoperative change and takes into account potential preserved learning ability coupled with potential deterioration on the tests (see also Grieco, D'Hollosy, Culliford, & Jonas, 1996, for a similar approach).

A further development of this approach is to use a technique that takes into account the intercorrelation in test performance. The approach discussed in the preceding paragraph weights each test score as equivalent and ignores the possible interrelationship between tests. Given that some of the tests involve similar cognitive domains, it would be expected that the scores they generate would show some correlation. Statistical techniques that use this approach are available (see P. O'Brien, 1984) and are beginning to be applied to cardiac surgery.

CPB

The extent to which NP changes after cardiac surgery are attributable to the effects of CPB per se cannot be easily investigated. Currently, most patients undergoing coronary artery surgery without CPB, either through the usual incision or as a minimally invasive procedure, have single-vessel disease. In contrast, the standard CABG patients mostly require multiple-vessel surgery. Malheiros et al. (1995) compared 48 patients undergoing CABG with bypass and 33 without. The two groups differed in amount of time spent in surgery and number of grafts (patients in the CPB group had longer bypass times and more grafts). No differences in NP test performance were found at the only postoperative assessment, which was done within 1 week of surgery. Andrew, Baker, Kneebone, and Knight (1998) suggested that a greater proportion of patients undergoing standard CABG for multivessel surgery showed decline in postoperative NP performance compared to patients who underwent single-vessel grafting through a standard incision or as a minimally invasive procedure. Although one of the earliest studies of its type, there were few patients in the groups, and postoperative assessment, as in Malheiros et al.'s (1995) study, was performed too early.

Filters

Arterial line filters are an optional addition to the CPB circuit. Of varying pore size and material, the filters are used to prevent extraneous elements in the bypass circuit from entering the patient. Padayachee, Parsons, Gosling, and Deverall (1988) and Pugsley et al. (1988) found that the introduction of an arterial line filter significantly reduced the number of emboli detected at the middle cerebral artery during routine CABG, and therefore their use may be of benefit in preventing cerebral damage. Filters can increase the activation of platelets (Rinder et al., 1992), but we are not aware that this increases the occurrence of emboli.

Two early studies (Aris et al., 1986; Garvey et al., 1983) reported that arterial line filtration made no difference to NP outcome. Pugsley et al. (1994) found, however, that the use of a 40µ filter reduced the likelihood of NP deficit both at 8 days (46% filter vs. 71% nonfilter, $p = .05$) and 8 weeks (8% filter vs. 27% nonfilter, $p = 0.03$) after surgery (see Table 10.4). It is interesting that patients in the filtered group also showed fewer cerebral emboli as monitored by transcranial Doppler. The major weakness of the two earlier studies is the timing of postop-

TABLE 10.4
Filters Used in Various Studies

Study	N / Filter Type	Assessment Interval	Definition of Decline	Results
Garvey et al. (1983)	12 / Pall (40µm) filter 34 / AF-10 (25µm) filter 56 / No filter	7 days	Incidence, 1-SD drop from preop score	No difference
Aris et al. (1986)	50 / 20µm) filter 50 / No filter	10 days	Group comparisons and incidence, 1-SD drop on 1 or more tests	No difference
Pugsley et al. (1994)	50 / 40µm) filter 50 / No filter	8 days 8 weeks	Incidence, 1-SD drop on 2 or more tests, test scores	+ve In favor of filtration

Note. preop = preoperation.
+ve = positive effect of intervention.
Incidence as described in text.

TABLE 10.5
Oxygenators Used in Various Studies

Study	N / Oxygenator Type	Assessment Interval	Definition of Decline	Results
Carlson et al. (1973)	18 / Bubble oxygenators 26 / Membrane oxygenators	5 days	10% decline on tests using preop score – postop score × 100, preop score	+ve in favor of membrane oxygenators
Aberg et al. (1982)	17 / Galen Optiflo 1 29 / Galen Optiflo 2 24 / Bentley Bos 10	7 days	Score differences	No clear pattern
Smith et al. (1990)	50 / Membrane oxygenators 50 / Bubble oxygenators	8 days 8 weeks	Incidence, 1-SD drop on 2 or more tests, and test score comparison	Trend in favor of membrane oxyge-nators on test scores at 8 weeks

Note. preop = preoperation; postop = postoperation.
+ve = positive effect of intervention.
Incidence as described in text.

erative assessments (during in-hospital convalescent period), which may have masked any differences between the groups. Although Pugsley et al. (1994) were able to show a difference in NP deficits at this early assessment, the difference was even more apparent at 8 weeks.

Oxygenators

Oxygenators form part of the CPB circuit; their purpose is to act as the lungs by replacing the oxygen in the blood. They are of two basic types: bubble and membrane. Bubble oxygenators work on a principle of mixing blood with bubbles of oxygen. Oxygenated blood is stored in a reservoir designed in such a way that the larger bubbles float out of the reservoir. The membrane oxygenator consists of a microporous membrane that separates the blood from the gas and therefore prevents the larger bubbles from entering the system.

Oxygenators have been a major focus of development over the years, and NP techniques have been used to evaluate these (see Table 10.5). Aberg et al. (1982) reported a series of studies in which the NP outcomes of patients undergoing cardiac surgery were investigated. Three different types of bubble oxygenators were used. Although a lesser incidence of decline was suggested when one type of oxygenator was used, historical comparisons were made in the studies, making it difficult to disentangle the relative effects of the oxygenators that were examined.

Carlson et al. (1973) first suggested that patients undergoing cardiac surgery using membrane oxygenators had less NP deterioration compared to patients who had surgery in which bubble oxygenators were used. More recently, Smith et al. (1990) investigated 100 patients who were randomly assigned to CABG using either a bubble oxygenator or a membrane oxygenator. The patients were assessed preoperatively and at 8 days and 8 weeks postoperatively. At the 8-day assessment, no differences were found between the groups, but at 8 weeks the performance of the bubble oxygenator group was poorer on 9 of the 11 tests, although the results did not always reach significance. These findings indicate that the membrane oxygenator may be associated with less cognitive decline, but larger numbers are required to see if this trend reaches statistical significance.

Temperature

The use of hypothermia as a means of cerebral protection became established in the early days of cardiac surgery, when it was shown that hypothermia could prolong the safe period of circulatory arrest. Since then, *hypothermic perfusion*— actively cooling body temperature down to 28 to 32° C during CPB—has been favored by the majority of surgeons for both valve surgery and CABG. Many surgeons argue, however, that hypothermia is an unnecessary convention if systemic circulation is uninterrupted with the use of CPB and cerebral perfusion is assumed to be adequate. To date, neither clinical practice nor prospective randomized trials has produced any robust evidence to challenge the use of *normothermic perfusion*—a term that has been loosely applied to a policy of maintaining body temperature at around 37° C or, more commonly, allowing it to drift down without active cooling.

A few trials have indicated that hypothermic perfusion may be beneficial or that normothermic perfusion is potentially harmful. Martin et al. (1994) were the first to report an increased rate of postoperative stroke, both early and late, in CABG patients randomized to normothermic perfusion (actively warmed to 35° C or higher). These findings have been questioned, because the use of retrograde cardioplegia in these patients could have increased the risk of cerebral embolism. More patients with neurologic deficits were also found in the group randomized to normothermia by Mora et al. (1996), although NP testing did not support a difference in outcome between the two groups. Only one study so far has suggested an effect of temperature on NP performance. Regragui et al. (1996) studied 70 patients randomized to three temperature groups: 28° C, 32° C, and 37° C. Normothermia was found to result in worse NP performance than the other two groups. However, both the small numbers of patients and the method of analysis of NP deterioration in the study caution against accepting this finding.

Several studies have found no difference in neurological outcome, NP outcome, or both (Arom, Emery, & Northrup, 1995; Engelman et al., 1996; Heyer et al., 1997; McLean et al., 1994; Plourde et al., 1997). This has surprised many investigators given that even a small reduction in temperature is known to be powerfully neuroprotective. The failure to find any advantage of hypothermia in clinical trials should not negate the potential benefit of hypothermia in cardiac surgery. Both the observational and prospective studies can be criticized for their design, statistical analysis, timing of follow-up, and sample sizes (Kong & Smith, 2000). Moreover, whereas brain hypothermia is not guaranteed in all patients, there is the risk of brain hyperthermia, which may be detrimental in the presence of ischemic injury and may occur during rewarming.

Pulsatile Versus Nonpulsatile Flow

It might be supposed that the ideal pattern of blood flow during CPB should mimic the native circulation and be pulsatile. Studies that have attempted to show the benefits of pulsatile over nonpulsatile flow, however, have produced many conflicting results (Komer, 1991). In animal studies, there have been no advantages for pulsatile blood flow in terms of cerebral perfusion or metabolism during hypothermic or normothermic bypass (Hindman, Dexter, Ryu, Smith, & Cutkomp, 1994; Hindman, Dexter, Smith, & Cutkomp, 1995). In a large study, pulsatility was not found to have influenced neurologic and cognitive outcome in patients after CABG (Murkin, Martzke, Buchan, Bentley, & Wong, 1995). Recently, cerebral oxygenation was shown to be better using pulsatile rather than nonpulsatile flow (Mutch, Lefevre, Thiessen, Girling, & Warrian, 1998), but this was in a pig model, and it remains to be seen if similar results can be reproduced in humans.

pH Management

Monitoring arterial blood oxygen and carbon dioxide tension and pH is essential during anesthesia and CPB. Blood gas machines analyze blood samples for this purpose at $37°$ C, although the results are interpreted according to whether a correction is made for the patient's temperature at the time of sampling. Clinicians disagree about the correct strategy to follow. In *pH-stat management,* so called because of the aim to maintain a constant pH at all temperatures, the patient's temperature is factored in to derive temperature-corrected values. In *alpha-stat management* such a temperature correction is not deemed appropriate, because the optimal physiological conditions for cellular function may also vary with temperature. Addition of carbon dioxide, which tends to be required in pH-stat management, will impair cerebral autoregulation (Stephan et al., 1992) and increase cerebral blood flow with potentially undesirable cerebral effects (see preceding paragraph). Studies conducted by Murkin et al. (1995) and Patel et al. (1996) have shown that alpha-stat is associated with less NP deterioration compared to pH-stat management (see Table 10.6).

TABLE 10.6
pH Management in Various Studies

Study	N / Management Type	Assessment Interval	Definition of Decline	Results
Murkin et al. (1995)	158 / Alpha stat 158 / pH stat	7 days 2 months	Change score from normative control group—impaired performance in one or more of four domains assessed	+ve in favor of alpha stat
Patel et al. (1996)	35 / Alpha stat 35 / pH stat	6 weeks	Incidence, 1-SD drop on 2 or more tests	+ve in favor of alpha stat

Note. +ve = positive effect of intervention.
Incidence as described in text.

Pharmacological Interventions

Unlike other interventions, discussed earlier, which aim to prevent cerebral insult occurring during surgery, protecting the brain using pharmacological agents is principally concerned with the moderation of established injury. This strategy seems to be well founded on current concepts of the pathophysiology of ischemic neuronal injury. The cellular and biochemical steps leading to cell death have been elucidated in some detail, and experimental successes in a variety of animal models encourage the view that neuroprotection in man is imminently achievable. There is, however, a large gulf between the startling results in brain protection attained in the laboratory and that of clinical trials in cardiac surgery, which have appeared sporadically in the literature over the last decade.

An effective neuroprotective drug will be of enormous clinical and commercial interest because such a drug also may have applications to other areas of ischemic cerebral injury, such as cerebrovascular disease and traumatic head injury. Thiopental, one of the earliest and most investigated neuroprotective agents, is thought to act partly by suppressing cerebral metabolism, although other anesthetic agents that act similarly have no demonstrable neuroprotective property, even in animals. Despite its long history, there is no good evidence of its efficacy as a neuroprotectant in man. Although Nussmeier, Arlund, and Slogoff (1986) reported fewer patients with stroke in a group that received thiopental compared to a control group, Zaidan et al. (1991) were unable to show any benefit of thiopental. The contrasting findings of these two cardiac surgery studies may be explained by differences in surgical risk of stroke (valve vs. CABG), oxygenators (bubble vs. membrane), or temperature (normothermia vs. hypothermia) associated with each study. No significant difference between the thiopental group and the control group was found by Nussmeier et al. in terms of NP assessment. In the cardiac surgical literature, drugs that inhibit platelet aggregation (prostacyclin) or block calcium channels (nimodipine) or glutamate receptors (remacemide) have been examined (see Table 10.7). Neuroprotection research in cardiac surgery is flourishing, and the value of other agents soon will become evident. We are aware of studies, recently completed or in progress, assessing drugs that may modify the cellular consequences of cerebral ischemia in a variety of ways. Our group has evaluated clomethiazole (a gamma-aminobutrytic acid, GABA, receptor agonist) and aprotinin as potential neuroprotectants. Other investigators have targeted various anesthetic agents, sodium channel blockers, free-radical scavengers, and nitric oxide synthase inhibitors.

CONCLUSION

In NP studies on cardiac surgery the limited time available to perform assessments constrains the extent and duration of NP assessment. The ability to use a before-and-after design and examine change scores in the same individual does, however, provide the possibility of a robust design for these studies. Although the determination of the numbers of patients who show a significant NP decline

TABLE 10.7
Pharmacological Interventions to Protect the Brain During Cardiac Surgery

Study	Intervention	N / Group	Assessment Interval	Definition of Decline	Results
Slogoff et al. (1982)	Thiopental	110 / Thiopental 94 / Control	4 days	Abnormal test score combined with other measures	No difference
Nussmeier et al. (1986)	Thiopental	89 / Thiopental 93 / Control	5 days	Tests lacked specificity, discontinued use	No difference
Fish et al. (1987)	Prostacyclin	50 / Prostacyclin 50 / Control	7 days 2 months	Incidence and group comparisons on test score	−ve
Forsman et al. (1990)	Nimodipine	18 / Nimodipine 17 / Control	5 days 6 months	Group comparisons on test scores	Some advantages in nimodipine group
Grieco et al. (1996)	GM_1 Ganglioside	18 / GM_1 11 / Control	1 week 6 months	Several methods evaluated	No difference
Arrowsmith et al. (1998)	Remacemide	87 / Remacemide 84 / Control	8 weeks	Incidence, z-score change	No difference, Advantage to remacemide

Note. −ve = negative effect of intervention.
Incidence as described in text.

following CABG is fraught with methodological difficulties, it is clear that a significant number of individuals who undergo elective CABG do show cognitive deficits. How these deficits are brought about has been the subject of much research and, although the process is multifactorial, the occurrence of microemboli passing into the brain during surgery is well established, and their frequency of occurrence has been linked to the likelihood of NP deficits. That NP assessment has sufficient sensitivity to detect deficits has led to its use in evaluating the impact of different forms of equipment, anaesthetic techniques, and pharmacological neuroprotection.

Research findings suggest that it is possible to reduce the potential impact of microemboli and that some protection of the brain may be achieved. Although neuroprotective drugs have been applied, they have tended not to show significant effects. This may reflect the difficulty of generalizing results from animal models of cerebral injury, which do not mimic the problems encountered in CPB and the complexity of the mechanisms for brain ischemia, to humans.

REFERENCES

Aberg, T., Kihlgren, M., Jonsson, L., Stjernlöf, K., Lönn, U., Rystedt, T., Tydén, H., Westerholm, C. J., & Taube, A. (1982). Improved cerebral protection during open heart surgery: A psychometric investigation on 339 patients. In R. Becker (Ed.), *Psychopathological and neurological dysfunction following open heart surgery* (pp. 343–351). Heidelberg, Germany: Springer Verlag.

Aberg, T., Ronquist, G., Tydén, H., Brunnkvist, J., Hultman, J., Bergström, K., & Lilja, A. (1984). Adverse effects on the brain in cardiac operations as assessed by biochemical, psychometric and radiological methods. *Journal of Thoracic and Cardiovascular Surgery, 87,* 99–105.

Acierno, L. (1994). *Surgical modalities: The history of cardiology* (pp. 597–697). New York: Parthenon.

Andrew, M., Baker, R., Kneebone, A., & Knight, J. (1998). Neuropsychological dysfunction after minimally invasive direct coronary artery bypass grafting. *Annals of Thoracic Surgery, 66,* 1611–1617.

Aris, A., Solanes, H., Camara, M. L., Junque, C., Escartin, A., & Caralps, J. M. (1986). Arterial line filtration during cardiopulmonary bypass: Neurologic, neuropsychologic, and hematologic studies. *Journal of Thoracic and Cardiovascular Surgery, 91,* 526–533.

Arom, K. V., Emery, R. W., & Northrup, W. F. (1995). Warm heart surgery: A prospective comparison between normothermic and tepid temperature. *Journal of Cardiac Surgery, 10,* 221–226.

Arrowsmith, J., Harrison, M., Newman, S., Stygall, J., Timberlake, N., & Pugsley, W. (1998). Neuroprotection of the brain during cardiopulmonary bypass: A randomized trial of remacemide during coronary artery bypass in 171 patients. *Stroke, 29,* 2357–2362.

Bethune, D. (1982). Focal neurological lesions and diffuse organic brain damage in open-heart surgery patients. In R. Becker, J. Katz, M.-J. Polonius, & H. Spiedel (Eds.), *Psychopathological and neurological dysfunction following open-heart surgery* (pp. 300–306). Heidelberg: Springer-Verlag.

Blauth, C. (1993). Retinal flourescein angiography in the assessment of microembolism during cardiopulmonary bypass. In P. Smith & K. Taylor (Eds.), *Cardiac surgery and the brain* (pp. 165–181). London: Edward Arnold.

Blauth, C., Smith, P., Arnold, J., Jagoe, J., Wootton, R., & Taylor, K. (1990). Influence of oxygenator type on the prevalence and extent of microembolic retinal ischemia during cardiopulmonary bypass: Assessment by digital image analysis. *Journal of Thoracic and Cardiovascular Surgery, 99,* 61–69.

Blumenthal, J., Madden, D., Burker, E., Croughwell, N., Schniebolk, S., Smith, R., White, W., Hlatky, M., & Reves, J. (1991). A preliminary study of the effects of cardiac procedures on cognitive performance. *International Journal of Psychosomatics, 38*, 13–16.

Blumenthal, J., Mahanna, E., Madden, D., White, W., Croughwell, N., & Newman, M. (1995). Methodological issues in the assessment of neuropsychologic function after cardiac surgery. *Annals of Thoracic Surgery, 59*, 1345–1350.

Borowicz, J., Goldsborough, M., Selnes, O., & McKhann, G. (1996). Neuropsychologic change after cardiac surgery: A critical review. *Journal of Cardiothoracic and Vascular Anesthesia, 10*, 105–112.

Brierley, J. (1963). Neuropathological findings in patients dying after open-heart surgery. *Thorax, 18*, 291–304.

Bruggermans, E., Van Dijk, J., & Huysmans, H. (1995). Residual cognitive dysfunction at 6 months following coronary artery bypass graft surgery. *European Journal of Cardiothoracic Surgery, 9*, 636–643.

Calabrese, J. R., Skwerer, R. G., Gulledge, A. D., Gill, C., Mullen, J., Rodgers, D., Taylor, P., Golding, L., Lytle, B., Cosgrove, D., Bazarel, M., & Loop, F. (1987). Incidence of postoperative delirium following myocardial revascularization. A prospective study. *Cleveland Clinical Journal of Medicine, 54*, 29–32.

Carlson, R., Lande, A., Landis, B., Rogoz, B., Baxter, J., Patterson, R., Stenzel, K., & Lillehei, C. (1973). The Lande–Edwards membrane oxygenator during heart surgery: Oxygen transfer, microembolic counts, and Bender–Gestalt Visual Motor Test scores. *Journal of Thoracic and Cardiovascular Surgery, 66*, 894–905.

Cishek, M., & Gershony, G. (1996). Roles of percutaneous transluminal coronary angioplasty and bypass graft surgery for the treatment of coronary artery disease. *American Heart Journal, 131*, 1012–1017.

Croughwell, N., Lowry, E., White, W., Amory, D., Kirchner, J., Baldwin, B., Smith, P., Jones, R., Reves, G., & Newman, M. (1997). Impact of middle cerebral emboli on changes in S-100 levels during cardiac surgery. *Anesthesia and Analgesia, 84*, SCA12.

Edwards, F., Carey, J., Grover, F., Bero, J., & Hartz, R. (1998). Impact of gender on coronary artery bypass operative mortality. *Annals of Thoracic Surgery, 66*, 125–131.

Engelman, R., Pleet, A., Rousou, J., Flack, J. III, Deaton, D., Gregory, C., & Pekow, P. (1996). What is the best perfusion temperature for coronary revascularization? *Journal of Thoracic and Cardiovascular Surgery, 112*, 1622–1633.

Favaloro, R. (1998). Critical analysis of coronary artery bypass graft surgery: A 30-year journey. *Journal of the American College of Cardiology, 31*, 1B–63B.

Fish, K., Helms, K., Sarnquist, F., Tinklenberg, J., & Miller, D. (1982). Neuropsychological dysfunction after coronary artery surgery (abstract). *Anesthesiology, 57*, A55.

Folks, D., Franceschini, J., Sokol, R., Freeman III, A., & Folks, D. (1986). Coronary artery bypass surgery in older patients: Psychiatric morbidity. *Southern Medical Journal, 79*, 303–306.

Folstein, M. F., Folstein, S. E., & HcHugh, P. R. (1975). Mini-mental state. *Journal of Psychiatric Research. 12*, 189–198.

Forsman, M., Olsnes, B. T., Semb, G., & Steen, P. A. (1990). Effects of nimodipine on cerebral blood flow and neuropsychological outcome after cardiac surgery. *British Journal of Anaesthesia, 65*, 514–520.

Freeman, A., III, Folks, D., Sokol, R., Govier, A., Reves, J., Fleece, E., Hall, K., Zorn, G., & Karp, R. (1985). Cognitive function after coronary bypass surgery: Effect of decreased cerebral blood flow. *American Journal of Psychiatry, 142*, 110–112.

Gardner, T., Horneffer, P., Manolio, T., Pearson, T., Gott, V., Blaumgartner, W., Borkon, A., Watkins, L. Jr., & Reitz, B. (1985). Stroke following coronary artery bypass grafting: A ten year study. *Annals of Thoracic Surgery, 40*, 574–581.

Garvey, J., Willner, A., Wolpowitz, A., Caramonte, L., Rabiner, C., Weisz, D., & Wisoff, B. (1983). The effect of arterial filtration during open heart surgery on cerebral function. *Circulation, 68* (Suppl. 2), 125–128.

Grieco, G., D'Hollosy, M., Culliford, A., & Jonas, S. (1996). Evaluating neuroprotective agents for clinical anti-ischemic benefit using neurological and neuropsychological changes after cardiac surgery under cardiopulmonary bypass: Methodological strategies and results of a double-blind, placebo-controlled trial of GM1 ganglioside. *Stroke, 27*, 858–874.

Grocott, H., Croughwell, N., Amory, D., White, W., Kirchner, J., & Newman, M. (1998). Cerebral emboli and serum S100β during cardiac operations. *Annals of Thoracic Surgery, 65*, 1645–1650.

Grote, C., Shanahan, P., Salmon, P., Meyer, R., Barrett, C., & Lansing, A. (1992). Cognitive outcome after cardiac operations. Relationship to intraoperative computerized electroencephalographic data. *Journal of Thoracic and Cardiovascular Surgery, 104*, 1405–1409.

Hammeke, T. A., & Hastings, J. E. (1988). Neuropsychologic alterations after cardiac operation. *Journal of Thoracic and Cardiovascular Surgery, 96*, 326–331.

Harrison, M., & Newman, S. P. (2000). Impact of embolism in cardiac surgery. In S. Newman and M. Harrison (Eds.), *The brain and cardiac surgery* (pp. 173–184). Amsterdam: Harwood.

Henriksen, L. (1993). Cerebral blood flow before, during and after bypass. In P. Smith & K. Taylor (Eds.), *Cardiac surgery and the brain* (pp. 121–142). London: Edward Arnold.

Heyer, E., Adams, D., Delphin, E., McMahon, D., Steneck, S., Oz, M., Michler, R., & Rose, E. (1997). Cerebral dysfunction after coronary artery bypass grafting done with mild or moderate hypothermia. *Journal of Thoracic and Cardiovascular Surgery, 114*, 270–277.

Hindman, B. J., Dexter, F., Ryu, K. H., Smith, T., & Cutkomp, J. (1994). Pulsatile versus nonpulsatile cardiopulmonary bypass: No difference in brain blood flow or metabolism at 27 degrees C. *Anesthesiology, 80*, 1137–1147.

Hindman, B. J., Dexter, F., Smith, T., & Cutkomp, J. (1995). Pulsatile versus nonpulsatile flow: No difference in cerebral blood flow or metabolism during normothermic cardiopulmonary bypass in rabbits. *Anesthesiology, 82*, 241–250.

Isgro, F., Schmidt, C., Pohl., P., & Saggau, W. (1997). A predictive pattern in patients with brain related complications after cardiac surgery. *European Journal of Cardiothoracic Surgery, 11*, 640–644.

Jackson, M. (1989). Brain damage and open-heart surgery. *Lancet, 2*, 1096–1097.

Jenkins, C., Stanton, B., Savageau, J., Denlinger, P., & Klein, M. (1983). Coronary artery bypass surgery. Physical, psychological, social and economic outcomes six months later. *Journal of the American Medical Association, 250*, 782–788.

Johnsson, P. (1996). Markers of cerebral ischemia after cardiac surgery. *Journal of Cardiothoracic and Vascular Anesthesia, 10*, 120–126.

King, S. III. (1998). The development of interventional cardiology. *Journal of the American College of Cardiology, 31*(Suppl. B), 64B–88B.

Klonoff, H., Clark, C., Kavanagh-Gray, D., Mizgala, H., & Munro, I. (1989). Two-year follow-up study of coronary artery bypass surgery. Psychologic status, employment status, and quality of life. *Journal of Thoracic and Cardiovascular Surgery, 97*, 78–85.

Kneebone, A., Andrew, M., Baker, R., & Knight, J. (1998). Neuropsychologic changes after coronary artery bypass grafting: Use of reliable change indices. *Annals of Thoracic Surgery, 65*, 1320–1325.

Kolkka, R., & Hilberman, M. (1980). Neurologic dysfunction following cardiac operation with low flow, low pressure cardiopulmonary bypass. *Journal of Thoracic and Cardiovascular Surgery, 79*, 432–437.

Komer, C. (1991). Physiologic changes of cardiopulmonary bypass. In P. Casthely & D. Bregman (Eds.), *Cardiopulmonary bypass: Physiology, related complications, and pharmacology* (pp. 37–84). New York: Futura.

Kong, R., & Smith, P. (2000). Hypothermic and normothermic bypass. In S. Newman and M. Harrison (Eds.), *The brain and cardiac surgery* (pp. 209–229). Amsterdam: Harwood.

Lee, W. Jr., Brady, M., Rowe, J., & Miller, W. (1971). Effects of extracorporeal circulation upon behavior, personality, and brain function: Part II. Hemodynamic, metabolic, and psychometric correlations. *Annals of Surgery, 173*, 1013–1023.

Lytle, B., Loop, F. Cosgrove, D., Ratliff, N., Easly, K., & Taylor, P. (1985). Long-term (5 to 12 years) serial studies of internal mammary artery and saphenous vein coronary bypass grafts. *Journal of Thoracic and Cardiovascular Surgery, 89,* 248–258.

Mahanna, E., Blumenthal, J., White, W., Croughwell, N., Clancy, C., Smith, R., & Newman, M. (1996). Defining neuropsychological dysfunction after coronary artery bypass grafting. *Annals of Thoracic Surgery, 61,* 1342–1347.

Malheiros, S., Brucki, S., Gabbai, A., Bertolucci, P., Juliano, Y., Carvalho, A., & Buffolo, E. (1995). Neurological outcome in coronary artery surgery with and without cardiopulmonary bypass. *Acta Neurologica Scandinavica, 92,* 256–260.

Markus, H. S., & Brown, M. M. (1993). Differentiation between pathological cerebral embolic materials using transcranial Doppler in an *in vitro* model. *Stroke, 24,* 1–5.

Markus, H., & Tegeler, C. (1995). Experimental aspects of high intensity transient signals in the detection of emboli. *Journal of Clinical Ultrasound, 23,* 81–87.

Martin, T., D., Craver, J. M., Gott, J. P., Weintraub, W. S., Ramsay, J., Mora, C. T., & Guyton, R. A. (1994). Prospective, randomized trial of retrograde warm blood cardioplegia: Myocardial benefit and neurologic threat. *Annals of Thoracic Surgery, 57,* 298–302.

Mattler, C., Engblom, E., Vänttinen, E., & Knuts, L.-R. (1988). Neuropsychological findings and personality structure associated with coronary artery bypass surgery (CABS) (abstract). *Journal of Clinical and Experimental Neuropsychology, 10,* 329.

McKhann, G., Goldsborough, M., Borowicz, L. Jr., Mellits, E., Brookmeyer, R., Quaskey, S., Baumgartner, W., Cameron, D., Stuart, R., & Gardner, T. (1997). Predictors of stroke risk in coronary artery bypass patients. *Annals of Thoracic Surgery, 63,* 516–521.

McLean, R. F., Wong, B. I., Naylor, C. D., Snow, W. G., Harrington, E. M., Gawel, M., & Fremes, S. E. (1994). Cardiopulmonary bypass, temperature, and central nervous system dysfunction. *Circulation, 90*(Part 2), 250–255.

Moody, D., Bell, M., Challa, V., Johnston, W., & Prough, D. (1990). Brain microemboli during cardiac surgery or aortography. *Annals of Neurology, 28,* 477–486.

Mora, C. T., Henson, M. B., Weintraub, W. S., Murkin, J. M., Martin, T. D., Carver, J. M., Gott, J. P., & Guyton, R. A. (1996). The effect of temperature management during cardiopulmonary bypass on neurologic and neuropsychologic outcomes in patients undergoing coronary revascularization. *Journal of Thoracic and Cardiovascular Surgery, 112,* 514–522.

Murkin, J., Martzke, J., Buchan, A., Bentley, C., & Wong, C. (1995). A randomized study of the influence of perfusion technique and pH management strategy in 316 patients undergoing coronary artery bypass surgery: II. Neurologic and cognitive outcomes. *Journal of Thoracic and Cardiovascular Surgery, 110,* 349–362.

Mutch, W. A., Lefevre, G. R., Thiessen, D. B., Girling, L. G., & Warrian, R. K. (1998). Computer-controlled cardiopulmonary bypass increases jugular venous oxygen saturation during rewarming. *Annals of Thoracic Surgery, 65,* 59–65.

Nevin, M., Colchester, A. C., Adams, S., & Pepper, J. R. (1989). Prediction of neurological damage after cardiopulmonary bypass surgery. Use of the cerebral function analysing monitor. *Anaesthesia, 44,* 725–729.

Newman, M., Croughwell, N., Blumenthal, J., Lowry, E., White, W., Spillane, W., Davis, D., Glower, D., Smith, L., Mahanna, E., & Reves, J. (1995). Predictors of cognitive decline after cardiac operation. *Annals of Thoracic Surgery, 59,* 1326–1330.

Newman, M., Croughwell, N., Blumenthal, J., White, W., Lewis, J., Smith, L., Frasco, P., Towner, E., Schell, R., Hurwitz, B., & Reves, J. (1994). Effect of aging on cerebral autoregulation during cardiopulmonary bypass: Association with postoperative cognitive dysfunction. *Circulation, 90*(Part 2), 243–249.

Newman, S. (1993). Neuropsychological and psychological consequences of coronary artery bypass surgery. In P. Smith & K. Taylor (Eds.), *Cardiac surgery and the brain* (pp. 34–54). London: Edward Arnold.

Newman, S. (1995). Analysis and interpretation of neuropsychologic tests in cardiac surgery. *Annals of Thoracic Surgery, 59,* 1351–1355.

Newman, S., Smith, P., Treasure, T., Joseph, P., Ell, P., & Harrison, M. (1987). Acute neuropsychological consequences of coronary artery bypass surgery. *Current Psychological Research and Review, 6,* 115–124.

Nussmeier, N. A., Arlund, C., & Slogoff, S. (1986). Neuropsychiatric complications after cardiopulmonary bypass: Cerebral protection by a barbiturate. *Anesthesiology, 64,* 165–170.

O'Brien, D., Baurer, R., Yarandi, H., Knauf, D., Bramblett, P., & Alexander, J. (1992). Patient memory before and after cardiac operations. *Journal of Thoracic and Cardiovascular Surgery, 104,* 1116–1124.

O'Brien, P. (1984). Procedures for comparing samples with multiple endpoints. *Biometrics, 40,* 1079–1087.

Padayachee, T., Parsons, S., Gosling, T., & Deverall, P. (1988). The effect of arterial filtration on reduction of gaseous microemboli in the middle cerebral artery during cardiopulmonary bypass. *Annals of Thoracic Surgery, 45,* 647–649.

Padayachee, T. S., Parsons, S., Theobold, R., Linley, J., Gosling, R. G., & Deverall, P. B. (1987). The detection of microemboli in the middle cerebral artery during cardiopulmonary bypass: A transcranial Doppler ultrasound investigation using membrane and bubble oxygenators. *Annals of Thoracic Surgery, 44,* 298–302.

Patel, R. Turtle, M., Chambers, D., James, D., Newman, S., & Venn, G. (1996). Alpha-stat acid–base regulation during cardiopulmonary bypass improves neuropsychologic outcome in patients undergoing coronary artery bypass grafting. *Journal of Thoracic and Cardiovascular Surgery, 111,* 1267–1279.

Plourde, G., Leduc, A., Morin, J., De Varennes, B., Latter, D., Symes, J., Robbins, R., Fosset, N., Couture, L., & Ptito, A. (1997). Temperature during cardiopulmonary bypass for coronary artery operations does not influence postoperative cognitive function: A prospective randomized trial. *Journal of Thoracic and Cardiovascular Surgery, 114,* 123–128.

Pugsley, W. (1989). The use of Doppler ultrasound in the assessment of microemboli during cardiac surgery. *Perfusion, 4,* 115–122.

Pugsley, W. B., Klinger, L., Paschalis, C., Newman, S. N., Harrison, M., & Treasure, T. (1988). Does arterial line filtration affect the bypass related cerebral impairment observed in patients undergoing coronary artery surgery? *Clinical Sciences, 75* (Suppl. 19), 30–31.

Pugsley, W., Klinger, L., Paschalis, C., Treasure, T., Harrison, M., & Newman, S. (1994). The impact of microemboli during cardiopulmonary bypass on neuropsychological functioning. *Stroke, 25,* 1393–1399.

Pugsley, W., Treasure, T., Klinger, L., Newman, S., Paschalis, C., & Harrison, M. (1990). Microemboli and cerebral impairment during cardiac surgery. *Vascular Surgery, 24,* 34–43.

Raymond, M., Conklin, C., Schaeffer, J., Newstadt, G., Matloff, J., & Gray, R. (1984). Coping with transient intellectual dysfunction after coronary artery bypass surgery. *Heart and Lung, 13,* 531–539.

Regragui, I., Birdi, I., Izzat, M., Black, A., Lopatatzidis, A., Day, C., Gardner, F., Bryan, A., & Angelini, G. (1996). The effects of cardiopulmonary bypass temperature on neuropsychologic outcome after coronary artery operations: A prospective randomized trial. *Journal of Thoracic and Cardiovascular Surgery, 112,* 1036–1045.

Rinder, C., Bonan, J., Rinder, H., Mathew, J., Hines, R., & Smith, B. (1992). Cardiopulmonary bypass induces leukocyte platelet adhesion. *Blood, 79,* 1201–1205.

Roach, G., Kanchuger, M., Mangano, C., Newman, M., Nussmeier, N., Wolman, R., Aggarwal, A., Marschall, K., Graham, S., Ley, C., Ozanne, G., & Mangano, D. (1996). Adverse cerebral outcome after coronary bypass surgery. *New England Journal of Medicine, 335,* 1857–1863.

Rutkow, I. (1997). Surgical operations in the United States: Then (1983) and now (1994). *Archives of Surgery, 132,* 983–990.

Savageau, J., Stanton, B., Jenkins, C., & Klein, M. (1982a). Neuropsychological dysfunction following elective cardiac operation. I. Early assessment. *Journal of Thoracic and Cardiovascular Surgery, 84,* 585–594.

Savageau, J., Stanton, B., Jenkins, C., & Frater, R. (1982b). Neuropsychological dysfunction following elective cardiac operation: II. A six-month reassessment. *Journal of Thoracic and Cardiovascular Surgery, 84,* 595–600.

Schell, R., Kern, F., Greeley, W., Schulman, S., Frasco, P., Croughwell, N., Newman, M., & Reves, J. (1993). Cerebral blood flow and metabolism during cardiopulmonary bypass. *Anesthesia and Analgesia, 76,* 849–865.

Sellman, M., Holm, L., Ivert, T., & Semb, B. (1993). A randomized study of neuropsychological function in patients undergoing coronary bypass surgery. *Thoracic and Cardiovascular Surgeon, 41,* 349–354.

Shaw, P. J., Bates, D., Cartlidge, N. E., French, J. M., Heaviside, D., Julian, D. G., & Shaw, D. A. (1987a). Neurologic and neuropsychological morbidity following major surgery: Comparison of coronary artery bypass and peripheral vascular surgery. *Stroke, 18,* 700–707.

Shaw, P. J., Bates, D., Cartlidge, N. E., French, J. M., Heaviside, D., Julian, D. G., & Shaw, D. A. (1987b). Long-term intellectual dysfunction following coronary artery bypass graft surgery: A six month follow-up study. *Quarterly Journal of Medicine, 62,* 259–268.

Simonetta, A., Moody, D., Reboussin, D., Stump, D., Legault, C., & Kon, N. (2000). Brain imaging and cardiac surgery. In S. Newman & M. Harrison (Eds.), *The brain and cardiac surgery* (pp. 71–86). Amsterdam: Harwood.

Smith, P., Blauth, C., Newman, S., Arnold, J., Siddons, F., & Taylor, K. (1990). Cerebral microembolism and neuropsychological outcome following coronary artery bypass surgery (CABS) with either a membrane or a bubble oxygenator. In A. Willner & G. Rodewald (Eds.), *Impact of cardiac surgery on the quality of life* (pp. 337–342). New York: Plenum.

Society of Thoracic Surgeons/American Association for Thoracic Surgery Committee on New Technology. (1998). Policy statement: Minimally invasive coronary artery bypass surgery. *Annals of Thoracic Surgery, 66,* 1848–1849.

Sotaniemi, K. A., Mononen, H., & Hokkanen, T. E. (1986). Long-term cerebral outcome after open-heart surgery: A five-year neuropsychological follow-up study. *Stroke, 17,* 410–416.

Stephan, H., Weyland, A., Kazmaier, S., Henze, T., Menck, S., & Sonntag, H. (1992). Acid–base management during hypothermic cardiopulmonary bypass does not affect cerebral metabolism but does affect blood flow and neurological outcome. *British Journal of Anaesthesia, 69,* 51–57.

Stump, D., Newman, S., Coker, L., Phipps, J., & Miller, R. (1990). Persistence of neuropsychological deficits following CABG. *Anesthesiology, 73,* A113.

Stump, D., Rogers, A., Hammon, J., & Newman, S. (1996). Cerebral emboli and cognitive outcome after cardiac surgery. *Journal of Cardiothoracic and Vascular Anesthesia, 10,* 113–119.

Stump, D., Tegeler, C., Newman, S., Wallenhaupt, S., & Roy, R. (1992). Older patients have more emboli during coronary artery bypass graft surgery. *Anesthesiology, 77,* A52.

Toner, I., Peden, C. J., Hamid, S. K., Newman, S., Taylor, K. M., & Smith, P. L. (1994). Magnetic resonance imaging and neuropsychological changes after coronary artery bypass graft surgery: Preliminary findings. *Journal of Neurosurgical Anesthesiology, 6,* 163–169.

Townes, B. D., Bashein, G., Hornbein, T. F., Coppel, D. B., Goldstein, D. E., Davis, K. B., Nessly, M. L., Bledsoe, S. W., Veith, R. C., Ivey, T. D., & Cohen, M. A. (1989). Neurobehavioral outcomes in cardiac operations: A prospective controlled study. *Journal of Thoracic and Cardiovascular Surgery, 98,* 774–782.

Venn, G. E., Sherry, K., Klinger, L., Newman, S., Treasure, T., Harrison, M., & Ell, P. J. (1988). Cerebral blood flow during cardiopulmonary bypass. *European Journal of Cardiothoracic Surgery, 2,* 360–363.

Vingerhoets, G., Van Nooten, G., Vermassen, F., De Soete, G., & Jannes, C. (1997). Short-term and long-term neuropsychological consequences of cardiac surgery with extracorporeal circulation. *European Journal of Cardiothoracic Surgery, 11,* 424–431.

Walzer, T., Herrmann, M., & Wallesch, C.-W. (1997). Neuropsychological disorders after coronary bypass surgery. *Journal of Neurology, Neurosurgery and Psychiatry, 62,* 644–648.

Wenger, N., Speroff, L., & Packard, B. (1993). Cardiovascular health and disease in women. *New England Journal of Medicine, 329,* 247–256.

Westaby, S., Johnsson, P., Parry, A. J., Blomqvist, S., Solem, J. O., Alling, C., Pillai, R., Taggart, D. P., Grebenik, C., & Stahl, E. (1996). Serum S100 protein: A potential marker for cerebral events during cardiopulmonary bypass. *Annals of Thoracic Surgery, 61,* 88–92.

Zaidan, J. R., Klochany, A., Martin, W. M., Ziegler, J. S., Harless, D. M., & Andrews, R. B. (1991). Effect of thiopental on neurologic outcome following coronary artery bypass grafting. *Anesthesiology, 74,* 406–411.

CHAPTER ELEVEN

Neuropsychological Function Before and After Heart Transplantation

ROBERT A. BORNSTEIN
Ohio State University

As demonstrated in the previous chapters in this book, as well as numerous previous studies, neuropsychological impairment has been demonstrated in patients with cardiovascular disease and in subgroups of these patients who have undergone open-heart surgery and cardiopulmonary bypass (Becker, Katz, Polonius, & Speidel, 1982; Sotaniemi, Juolasmaa, Eero, & Hokkanen, 1981; Willner & Rodewald, 1990). In contrast, relatively few studies have examined neuropsychological factors in patients with the most severe cardiac disease who are candidates for, or who have undergone cardiac transplantation. This is the case even though several early studies (Ang, Gillett, & Kaufmann, 1989; Montero & Martinez, 1986; Schober & Herman, 1973) have revealed a high incidence of organic neurological complications in cardiac transplant recipients early in the postoperative period. In one series (Ang et al., 1989) 94% of patients had neuropathological changes, of which cerebrovascular were the most common. There was a high prevalence of multiple infarcts and diffuse abnormalities.

Heart transplantation was first introduced approximately 30 years ago, and although it is performed with increasing regularity it is still restricted to the patients with the most severe cardiac disease. This is in part due to the scarcity of organ donors, which results in the death of a significant proportion of patients before a suitable organ is located. Although most heart transplantation procedures are done in adults, they are increasingly being done in children, whose long-term survival rates are similar to those of adults (Parisi et al., 1999). Similar to some other cardiac surgery, transplantation involves placement on cardiopulmonary bypass, although the duration on bypass, as well as the duration of the procedure, is somewhat longer than some other procedures (e.g., coronary artery bypass). This prolonged duration increases the risk for complications associated with mechanical perfusion (as discussed elsewhere in this book). After the surgical procedure, patients are maintained on immunosuppressive therapies to prevent tissue rejection. Improved treatments for heart disease at earlier stages of illness may reduce the demand for heart transplantation. In addition, alternate approaches to organ donation, such as mechanical devices or nonhuman organs, continue to be explored.

Studies of cognitive function in the context of heart transplantation are important for several reasons. The complexity of the issues surrounding organ transplantation require that patients are able to understand and participate in the decision-making process prior to surgery. In addition, cognitive function can clearly influence the ability to understand and comply with the complicated posttransplant treatment protocols. Furthermore, neurological or neuropsychological morbidity before, during, and after heart transplantation is not infrequent. Finally, the study of patients prior to and following transplantation provides an opportunity to gain insights into the mechanisms underlying neuropsychological dysfunction in patients with severe heart disease.

The importance of these issues is underscored by the increasing frequency of cardiac transplantation and the large number of patients who are evaluated as candidates for this procedure. More than 2,300 heart transplant operations are performed each year in the United States alone (Keck et al., 1997), with some patients receiving heart and lung transplants. Cardiomyopathy is the most frequently reported diagnosis in patients undergoing heart transplantation (47%). In the United States, transplant recipients were predominantly male (77%), Caucasian (82%), and older than 50 years of age (55%). Recent advances in posttransplantation management of tissue rejection have resulted in improved 1-year (84.8%) and 5-year (66.5%) survival rates. Ten-year survival rates of more than 45% are now being reported and are related in part to the advent of immunosuppressive medications (Fraund et al., 1999; Robbins et al., 1999).

Although there are increasing numbers of patients being evaluated for, or receiving, heart transplantation, these patients are difficult to study because of the limitations in their stamina, the severity of their medical condition, and their inability to withstand the demands of prolonged effort required by comprehensive neuropsychological evaluations. Nevertheless, several recent studies have examined preoperative cognitive function as well as postoperative changes following cardiac transplantation. In the sections that follow I review these studies with respect to the frequency and nature of cognitive dysfunction, the hemodynamic variables that have been associated with cognitive function in these patients, and the methodological issues entailed in these studies.

COGNITIVE STATUS IN CANDIDATES
FOR HEART TRANSPLANTATION

Studies of the cognitive status of candidates for heart transplantation are frequently reported from centers in which neuropsychological measures have been included in the routine evaluation of surgical candidacy. This has become somewhat more common with the increased realization of the potential importance of psychosocial factors in selection and outcome. As with other diseases, studies that are based on a consecutive and nonselected series of patients provide a better estimate of the nature and extent of cognitive deficits than studies that are based on patients who are referred because of clinical symptoms. Patients who are candidates for heart transplantation are similar in many ways to patients with similar but less severe degrees of illness. There have been very few comparisons of the neuropsychological status of transplantation candidates with patients undergoing other types of cardiac surgery (e.g., valve replacement or bypass procedures). Focusing on a restricted range of disease severity presents obstacles to evaluation of the relationship between cognitive function and markers of disease severity (see Relationship of Cognitive Function and Hemodynamc Factors section).

Presurgical Neuropsychological Status

Several studies have reported relatively large samples preoperatively and followed a subgroup after surgery. Schall, Petrucci, Brozena, Cavarocchi, and Jessup (1989) evaluated 54 patients with end-stage heart failure. On an extensive neuropsychological test battery they noted a high prevalence of impaired performance in memory, motor speed, and higher level information processing. There were no differences related to the etiology of cardiac failure, but patients over 50 years of age had slightly greater cognitive deficits. Bornstein and colleagues (Bornstein & Starling, 1998; Bornstein, Starling, Myerowitz, & Haas, 1995) examined 62 consecutive candidates for transplantation with a comprehensive neuropsychological test battery. Approximately 60% of the participants met criteria for impairment on a summary measure of performance, but in most cases the impairment was relatively mild. The most frequent areas of cognitive impairment were abstract reasoning, memory, mental flexibility, attention, and motor speed. Both studies (Bornstein et al., 1995; Schall et al., 1989) had sufficiently large samples to compare subgroups on the basis of the type of cardiac disease (i.e., ischemic vs. dilated cardiomyopathy). In both cases there were no differences between these disease subtypes in the nature, severity, or frequency of cognitive deficit. Bornstein & Starling (1998) also found that there was evidence of depression in a substantial proportion of the patients (37% had a score greater than 70 on the Minnesota Multiphasic Personality Inventory

[MMPI]), and depression was significantly related to overall neuropsychological performance.

Grimm et al. (1996) used cognitive evoked potentials (P300) as well as the Mini Mental State Examination (MMSE) and the Trail Making Test (TMT), Part A, with 55 nonhospitalized candidates for heart transplantation. Compared to an age- and sex-matched control sample, the patient group was significantly impaired on the TMT and P300 studies. Roman et al. (1997) examined 17 patients prior to surgery using an extensive neuropsychological test battery. The patients performed within normal limits in reference to published test norms in all areas except for the percent age-retention score on a verbal learning task (the Rey Auditory Verbal Learning Test). A subgroup also completed the MMPI, and all scale scores were within normal limits. The lack of an appropriate control group limits the interpretability of these data. Furthermore, one of the selection criteria for inclusion in this study was based on being a "successful" transplantation as determined by posttransplant cardiac studies at least 1 year postsurgery. Thus, it is possible that this criterion may have resulted in a biased sample.

Riether, Smith, Lewison, Cotsonis, & Epstein (1992) examined 51 heart and 61 liver transplant candidates using the Wisconsin Card Sorting Test (WCST), the TMT, the California Verbal Learning Test (CVLT), and the MMSE (Lezak, 1995). Both groups had mean scores in the impaired range on all measures, and there was evidence of mild depression. Improvements on all cognitive measures, as well as in depression, were observed at 6- and 12-month follow-up. There were relatively few differences between the two transplant groups at baseline or follow-up. Deshields, McDonough, Mannen, and Miller (1996) examined psychological and cognitive status in 191 candidates for heart transplantation using the TMT, MMSE, subtests of the Wechsler Memory Scale, and the Beck Depression Inventory. There was evidence of mildly impaired verbal memory at baseline, as well as a tendency toward depression and anxiety, but other areas of cognitive function were normal. Significant improvements in cognitive function and depression were observed in the 21 patients who were re-examined 1 year posttransplantation. Putzke, Williams, Rayburn, Kirklin, and Boll (1998) studied the relationship between demographic, personality, and hemodynamic factors and cognitive performance in 62 heart transplant candidates. Psychiatric history, as well as self-reported symptoms of depression and anxiety, were unrelated to cognitive performance.

In addition to these studies of adult transplantation candidates, some preliminary studies of children receiving heart transplantation have been conducted. Wray and colleagues (Wray, Pot-Mees, Zeitlin, Radley-Smith, & Yacoub, 1994; Wray, Radley-Smith, & Yacoub, 1992) examined 28 children who underwent heart or heart–lung transplantation and compared them with 28 normal children. Developmental and cognitive function was within the normal range, but the children receiving transplants had lower scores on several developmental measures. This was most apparent in the children younger than 4.5 years. In addition, there was a higher prevalence of behavior problems in the transplant patients.

The available data indicate a relative increase in the prevalence of cognitive deficits among candidates for heart transplantation. Verbal memory deficits were reported in all studies, regardless of the comparison standard (matched controls, published norms) or the type of test used (paragraph recall or list learning). Other areas of cognitive function that frequently are implicated include motor speed, abstract reasoning, and attention. Older age and depression appear to be associated with increased cognitive deficits among heart transplant candidates. The frequency or severity of neuropsychological impairment does not appear to be associated with the subtype of cardiac disease (ischemic vs. dilated cardiomyopathy).

Relationship of Cognitive Function and Hemodynamic Factors

The demonstration of cognitive deficit in patients who are candidates for, or who receive, heart transplantation raises questions about the mechanism(s) underlying these deficits. General malaise, depression, medication side effects, neurological complications, and a host of other factors could contribute to these deficits. The most frequently invoked mechanism relates to diminished cerebral oxygenation. The brain receives 15% of cardiac output and accounts for 20% of total oxygen consumption (Chien, 1985). Consequently, impaired cardiac output and the adverse impact on cerebral oxygen delivery could be an important component underlying cognitive dysfunction in patients with end-stage heart disease.

Several measures of cardiac output are often available in the evaluation of patients with severe heart disease. These measures are typically obtained from cardiac catheterization studies and include left ventricle ejection fraction; right atrial pressure; pulmonary capillary wedge pressure; and various derived measures such as the cardiac index and stroke / volume index. Several of the studies mentioned earlier have examined hemodynamic measures in relation to cognitive function. In addition, some other studies have specifically focused on this question.

Putzke et al. (1998) examined 62 patients with an extensive neuropsychological test battery within 1 day of undergoing heart catheterization. This temporal proximity between cognitive and cardiac studies, in addition to the large sample, are major methodological strengths that greatly enhance our understanding of these relationships. After controlling for the effects of age and education, increased pulmonary wedge pressure and right atrial pressure were associated with worse cognitive function in the areas of attention, speed of mental processing, and mental flexibility. The relationship with cardiac output and cardiac index was somewhat less, and left ventricle ejection fraction was not related to neuropsychological performance. Bornstein et al. (1995; Bornstein & Starling,

1998) also reported a significant relationship between increased right atrial pressure and overall neuropsychological impairment as well as with measures of motor speed, reasoning, and mental flexibility. On the other hand, stroke volume and cardiac index were associated with better cognitive function. Similar to Putzke et al.'s (1998) study, there was no relationship with left ventricle ejection fraction. In contrast, Nussbaum, Allender, and Copeland (1995) stratified 23 patients with end-stage heart disease on the basis of the left ventricle ejection fraction. On a verbal learning task (the CVLT), poor total learning across trials was associated with lower ejection fraction. In addition, the patients with the lowest ejection fraction had a decreased rate of learning and performed worse on both short- and long-term delayed recall.

These studies suggest that increased right atrial pressure is associated with greater neuropsychological impairment. This is consistent with a previous report (Unverferth et al., 1984) that right atrial pressure was the most important prognostic variable for mortality. Following transplantation, there were significant improvements of a number of measures, which was interpreted as being of limited practical significance. The data regarding the relationship of left ventricle ejection fraction and cognitive function are less clear. The two largest studies (Bornstein & Starling, 1998; Putzke et al., 1998) found no relationship. The difference between these data and Nussbaum et al.'s (1995) results could be due to sample size, patient selection, or the somewhat arbitrary grouping of participants in that study. It is also possible that the participants in Nussbaum et al.'s study may have differed with respect to disease severity. Other studies that have examined patients with less severe cardiac disease, such as cardiac rehabilitation patients (Moser et al., 1999), or elderly patients with mild to moderate heart failure (Zuccala et al., 1997), have found that decreased ejection fraction is associated with worse cognitive function. Thus there does appear to be some evidence from correlational studies that cardiac output does influence cognitive function in patients with end-stage heart disease. Further studies are needed to better understand this relationship. Longitudinal studies, as well as comparisons of changes in cognitive and cardiac function following transplantation, can also elucidate these relationships.

Cognitive Function Following Heart Transplantation

Several studies have examined cognitive function in small groups of patients after transplantation. Schall (1989) followed 20 of the 54 patients who were examined approximately 27 months after transplantation. Improvements were noted in IQ, auditory processing, and motor speed, although only the motor speed changes were significant. This study did not have an unoperated control group, which limits interpretability of the postoperative changes. Bornstein & Starling (1998) examined 7 transplant and 4 nontransplant patients approximately 25 months following surgery. The transplant patients demonstrated an average

11.6% improvement on a battery of cognitive tests, whereas the nontransplant patients were unchanged (0% change). The greatest difference in patterns of change were observed on measures of nonverbal memory, motor speed, and mental flexibility. In view of the small size of these groups, the data can be regarded as only preliminary. Roman et al. (1997) examined 17 patients after an average postsurgical interval of 22 months. These patients demonstrated a significant improvement in verbal memory (percentage retention on delayed recall), which was the only area in which they had demonstrated impairment prior to transplantation. Again, the lack of an appropriate control group makes it difficult to know whether this is a real effect or simply regression toward the mean.

Riether et al. (1992) examined their patients at 3-month intervals, up to one year posttransplant. Significant improvement was observed in neuropsychological performance as well as depression. Similar improvements were also observed in a group of patients who received liver transplants. Thus it is unclear whether these improvements were due to resolution of depression, nonspecific recovery from systemic illness, or medication reductions. Furthermore, the lack of an untreated control group raises the possibility that these changes could be due to practice effects. Augustine, Goldsborough, McKhann, Selnes, and Baumgartner (1994) followed 10 patients prior to, and approximately 1 month after, transplantation. There was a trend toward a decline in performance on a verbal memory task (the Rey Auditory Verbal Learning Test), on which 7 of 10 patients showed a decline. It is possible that a 1-month follow-up interval was insufficient for these patients to have completely recovered from the general effects of surgery. Grimm et al. (1996) examined changes in cognitive evoked potentials (P300) in patients at 4 and 12 months postsurgery. Patients were improved at the 4-month examination but were worse at the 1-year evaluation. The decrease in performance was related to cumulative cyclosporine dosage and was interpreted as reflecting accumulated neurotoxicity.

There are very limited data regarding the neuropsychological consequences of cardiac transplantation. The few studies completed thus far all suffer from a variety of methodological weaknesses, including small samples, lack of appropriate control groups, limited examinations, and lack of control for extraneous variables that could affect changes in performance (e.g., depression). Roman et al. (1997) did document improvements in cardiac output but did not examine the relationship of those changes with changes in cognitive function. However, none of the other follow-up studies included assessments of cardiac output. Thus there is no evidence to support the hypothesis that changes in cardiac function (and, secondarily, cerebral oxygenation) represent the basis for the presumptive improvement in cognitive function following transplantation. At the current level of understanding there is no compelling evidence that cardiac transplantation results in improved cognitive function or, if it does, which of the multitude of associated specific or nonspecific factors are the basis for this change.

Methodological Issues

The study of cognitive function in patients with end-stage cardiac disease entails a vast array of methodological issues. As indicated previously, there are numerous disease entities that may culminate in candidacy for heart transplantation. Although there are an increasing number of patients being evaluated for, and undergoing, transplantation, it is difficult to gather a sufficient sample size in any single center. Transplant candidates are severely ill, and frequently they do not have the stamina to maintain their attention for the several hours necessary to complete a comprehensive examination. Although briefer or more targeted examinations can be accomplished, this necessarily limits the ability to fully understand the scope of neuropsychological impairment in these patients. The available literature suggests that verbal memory, motor speed, attention, and mental flexibility are the areas on which research should focus.

In addition to general health considerations, patients undergoing heart transplantation are characteristically taking a large number of medications that could affect performance on cognitive tests. Medication effects are typically observed on measures of attention and motor speed, which are precisely some of the areas implicated in end-stage heart disease. The screening and selection of patients is an important consideration. Consecutive series of patients will provide a better estimate of the prevalence of cognitive dysfunction. However, many patients with end-stage cardiac disease also have a history of cerebrovascular disease. Although exclusion of patients with these symptoms may provide a clearer assessment of the cognitive dysfunction associated with cardiac disease, this may result in an underestimate of the severity of cognitive deficits that may be encountered in this patient population. Thus, patient selection criteria are fundamentally dictated by the question under study. Studies dedicated to understanding the mechanism underlying cognitive deficit in heart disease will emphasize samples that exclude patients with confounding neurological conditions. On the other hand, descriptive studies that aim to characterize the nature and extent of cognitive deficit in end-stage heart disease will be more inclusive.

Finally, studies will need to control for potential intraoperative complications, such as the effects of extracorporeal circulation. This has been a chronic problem in cardiac surgery and can be an independent source of neuropsychological deficit. A recent study (Vingerhoets, Van Nooten, Vermassen, De Soete, and Jannes, 1997) examined 109 patients 1 day before and 7 days after surgery requiring cardiopulmonary bypass and included a surgical control group. A large subgroup (91) were also examined 6 months following surgery. One week postsurgery the patients demonstrated greater impairment in verbal memory and visual attention. This decline in performance was associated with a lower presurgery ejection fraction. At a 6-month follow-up, most (88%) of the patients were improved in comparison with the presurgical evaluation. Persistent cognitive impairment was associated with increased age. This study documents the

importance of controlling for surgical complications and illustrates the importance of the timing of examinations in the documentation of cognitive performance.

REFERENCES

Ang, L. C., Gillett, J. M., & Kaufmann, J. C. E. (1989). Neuropathology of heart transplantation. *Canadian Journal of Neurological Sciences, 16,* 291–298.
Augustine, A. M., Goldsborough, M., McKhann, G. M., Selnes, O., & Baumgartner, W. A. (1994). Neurocognitive deficits pre and one month post transplantation. *Journal of Heart and Lung Transplantation, 13*(Suppl.), 44.
Becker, R., Katz, J., Polonius, M. J., & Speidel, H. (1982). *Psychopathological and neurological dysfunctions following open-heart surgery.* New York: Springer-Verlag.
Bornstein, R. A., & Starling, R. C. (1998). Neuropsychological function before and after heart transplantation. In W. Albert, A. Bittner, & R. Hetzer (Eds.), *Quality of life and psychosomatics in mechanical circulation and in heart transplantation* (pp. 61–67). New York: Springer.
Bornstein, R. A., Starling, R. C., Myerowitz, P. D., & Haas, G. J. (1995). Neuropsychological function in patients with end-stage heart failure before and after cardiac transplantation. *Acta Neurologica Scandinavica, 91,* 260–265.
Chien, S. (1985). The Microcirculatory Society Eugene M. Landis Award lecture. Role of blood cells in microcirculatory regulation. *Microvascular Research, 29,* 129–151.
Deshields, T. L., McDonough, E. M., Mannen, R. K., & Miller, L. W. (1996). Psychological and cognitive status before and after heart transplantation. *General Hospital Psychiatry, 18,* 62S–69S.
Fraund, S., Pethig, K., Franke, U., Wahlers, T., Harringer, W., Cremer, J., Fieguth, H. G., Oppelt, P., & Haverich, A. (1999). Ten year survival after heart transplantation: Palliative procedure or successful long term treatment? *Heart, 82,* 47–51.
Grimm, M., Yeganehfar, W., Laufer, G., Madl, C., Kramer, L., Eisenhuber, E., Simon, P., Kupilik, N., Schreiner, W., Pacher, R., Bunzel, B., Wolner, E., & Grimm, G. (1996). Cyclosporine may affect improvement of cognitive brain function after successful cardiac transplantation. *Circulation, 94,* 1339–1345.
Keck, B. M., Bennett, L. E., Fiol, B. S., Daily, O. P., Novick, R. J., & Hosenpud, J. D. (1997). Worldwide thoracic organ transplantation: A report from the UNOS/ISHLT international registry for thoracic organ transplantation. *Clinical Transplantation, 29*–43.
Lezak, M. D. (1995). *Neuropsychological assessment* (3rd ed.). New York: Oxford University Press.
Montero, C. G., & Martinez, A. J. (1986). Neuropathology of heart transplantation: 23 cases. *Neurology, 36,* 1149–1154.
Moser, D. J., Cohen, R. A., Clark, M. M., Aloia, M. S., Tate, B. A., Stefanik, S., Forman, D. E., & Tilkemeier, P. L. (1999). Neuropsychological functioning among cardiac rehabilitation patients. *Journal of Cardiopulmonary Rehabilitation, 19,* 91–97.
Nussbaum, P. D., Allender, J., & Copeland, J. (1995). Verbal learning in cardiac transplant candidates: A preliminary report. *International Journal of Rehabilitation and Health, 1,* 5–12.
Parisi, F., Squitieri, C., Carotti, A., Abbattista, A. D., Cicini, M. P., Esu, F., & Catena, G. (1999). Tenyear follow-up after pediatric transplantation. *Journal of Heart and Lung Transplantation, 18,* 275–277.
Putzke, J. D., Williams, M. A., Rayburn, B. K., Kirklin, J. K., & Boll, T. J. (1998). The relationship between cardiac function and neuropsychological status among heart transplant candidates. *Journal of Cardiac Failure, 4,* 295–303.
Riether, A. M., Smith, S. L., Lewison, B. J., Cotsonis, G. A., & Epstein, C. M. (1992). Quality-of-life changes and psychiatric and neurocognitive outcome after heart and liver transplantation. *Transplantation, 54,* 444–450.

Robbins, R. C., Barlow, C. W., Oyer, P. E., Hunt, S. A., Miller, J. L., Reitz, B. A., Stinson, E. B., & Shumway, N. E. (1999). Thirty years of cardiac transplantation at Stanford University. *Journal of Thoracic and Cardiovascular Surgery, 117*, 939–951.

Roman, D. D., Kubo, S. H., Ormaza, S., Francis, G. S., Bank, A. J., & Shumway, S. J. (1997). Memory improvement following cardiac transplantation. *Journal of Clinical and Experimental Neuropsychology, 19*, 692–697.

Schall, R. R., Petrucci, R. J., Brozena, S. C., Cavarocchi, N. C., & Jessup, M. (1989). Cognitive function in patients with symptomatic dilated cardiomyopathy before and after cardiac transplantation. *Journal of the American College of Cardiology 14*, 1666–1672.

Schober, R., & Herman, M. N. (1973). Neuropathology in cardiac transplantation: Survey of 31 cases. *The Lancet*, 1:7810, 962–997.

Sotaniemi, K. A., Juolasmaa, A., Eero, M. A., & Hokkanen, T. (1981). Neuropsychologic outcome after open-heart surgery. *Archives of Neurology, 38*, 2–8.

Unverferth, D. V., Magorien, R. D., Moeschberger, M. L., Baker, P. B., Fetters, J. K., & Leier, C. V. (1984). Factors influencing the one year mortality of dilated cardiomyopathy. *American Journal of Cardiology 54*, 147–152.

Vingerhoets, G., Van Nooten, G., Vermassen, F., De Soete, G., & Jannes, C. (1997). Short-term and long-term neuropsychological consequences of cardiac surgery with extracorporeal circulation. *European Journal of Cardiothoracic Surgery, 11*, 424–431.

Willner, A. E., & Rodewald, G. (1990). *Impact of cardiac surgery on the quality of life.* New York: Plenum.

Wray, J., Pot-Mees, C., Zeitlin, H., Radley-Smith, R., & Yacoub, M. (1994). Cognitive function and behavioural status in paediatric heart and heart–lung transplant recipients: The Harefield experience. *British Medical Journal, 309*, 837–841.

Wray, J., Radley-Smith, R., & Yacoub, M. (1992). Effect of cardiac or heart–lung transplantation on the quality of life of the paediatric patient. *Quality of Life Research, 1*, 41–46.

Zuccala, G., Cattel, C., Manes-Gravina, E., Di Niro, M. G., Cocchi, A., & Bernabei, R. (1997). Left ventricular dysfunction: A clue to cognitive impairment in older patients with heart failure. *Journal of Neurology, 63*, 509–12.

CHAPTER TWELVE

Tracking the Cognitive Effects of Carotid Endarterectomy

ANNE D. BAIRD
Henry Ford Health System

ELIZABETH M. PIEROTH
Schwab Rehabilitation Hospital

Carotid endarterectomy (CE) has been shown to reduce risk of stroke in selected patients. This surgery provides a rich opportunity for neuropsychologists to study patients who have cerebrovascular occlusive disease but have not yet had a major stroke. Well-controlled studies of sufficient power will elucidate the neuropsychological impact of surgical removal of major blockages in the blood flow to the brain.

Candidates for CE have significant narrowing in one or both internal carotid arteries. Individuals who undergo CE may have had no symptoms or may have experienced one or more transient ischemic attacks (TIAs) or mild strokes before surgery.

TIAs are episodes of focal neurological symptoms lasting less than 24 hr, whereas strokes are characterized by symptoms lasting a day or longer. Some clinicians and researchers also distinguish between reversible ischemic neurological deficits (RINDS), with symptoms lasting from a day to a week, and strokes, with symptoms lasting longer than 7 days (Dull et al., 1982.) Symptomatic episodes are not characterized as TIAs, RINDs, and strokes unless they are deemed to be the result of ischemia, an interruption of the blood supply to part of the brain.

Randomized trials showed definite stroke reduction following CE in two situations (Biller et al., 1998). First, CE was effective in reducing stroke risk in patients who had experienced focal neurological symptoms—usually aphasia or lateralized numbness or weakness—and who had narrowing of 70% to 99% of the internal diameter of the internal carotid artery. In one trial, patients who fit these criteria and received CE and medical treatment had an estimated 16.5% greater reduction in risk of stroke and death over 2 years compared to patients who received medical treatment only (North American Symptomatic Carotid Endarterectomy Trial Collaborators, 1991). Patients who were accepted for randomization included those with TIAs and those with mild strokes. Patients with strokes that had resulted in severe weakness or numbness on one side of the body were excluded.

Second, CE produced a smaller but significant reduction in stroke risk for individuals who had not yet experienced focal neurological symptoms but nonetheless had 60% to 99% narrowing or stenosis of an internal carotid artery (Biller et al., 1998). The stroke risk reduction in these patients was estimated to be about 1% per year compared to patients receiving only medical treatment (Perry, Szalai, & Norris, 1997). Other specific indications are under study, such as benefit from CE in symptomatic patients who have 50% to 70% stenosis (Biller et al., 1998).

The seven randomized controlled CE trials included a total of 2,107 patients who received CE (Stukenborg, 1997). Unfortunately, no trial has included neuropsychological data (Biller et al., 1998; Holloway et al., 1998; Stukenborg, 1997). Hence, we know less about the effects of CE on thinking and day-to-day function than we understand about the role of surgery in reducing risk of stroke.

Nonetheless, the 10 neuropsychological studies performed in the past decade are worth close scrutiny (Casey, Ferguson, Kimura, & Hachinski, 1989; Gaunt et al., 1994; Iddon, Sahakian, & Kirkpatrick, 1997; Incalzi et al., 1997; Kügler, Vlajic, Funk, Raithel, & Platt, 1995; Lind et al., 1993; Meyer et al., 1990; Mononen, Lepojärvi, & Kallanranta, 1990; Sirkka, Salenius, Portin, & Nummenmaa, 1992; Uclés, Almarcegui, Lorente, Romero, & Marco, 1997). In this chaper we examine these studies after a review of the CE procedure and the mechanisms by which it may affect cognition. The neuropsychological research reveals diverse and extensive comorbidity in CE candidates and a spectrum of outcomes after surgery. Past work suggests that CE as currently performed on average boosts thinking and memory to a very modest degree at best. However, these studies leave open the possibility that CE may produce marked gains in neuropsychological test scores in a few patients and exert an important protective effect on cognition in many.

DESCRIPTION OF THE CE PROCEDURE

CE is a surgical procedure in which patients undergo excision of an atherosclerotic blockage in the extracranial portion of the right or left internal carotid artery. Each internal carotid artery is the predominant blood supply to the anterior two thirds of the cerebral hemisphere on the same side, although the internal carotid arteries are connected to each other and to the vessels feeding the posterior third of the hemispheres (the vertebrobasilar system). *Side of surgery* refers to whether the right or left internal carotid artery is operated.

CE candidates first undergo four-vessel cerebral angiography to determine the degree of arterial blockage (Biller et al., 1998). In some settings it may be common to perform CE on symptomatic patients who do not fit the recommended risk–benefit ratio derived from the randomized trials (Matchar et al., 1997) or to exclude asymptomatic patients who do (Perry et al., 1997).

Local or generalized anesthesia may be used during surgery (Robertson, 1997). Medications to elevate blood pressure (BP) and to thin the blood help the patient tolerate the reduction of blood flow to the brain during surgery. In one common variation of the procedure, the surgeon makes incisions to expose and then clamp parts of the common, external, and internal carotid arteries and the superior thyroid artery. The surgeon usually must expose and protect the hypoglossal nerve to perform these maneuvers.

In many CEs, after cutting open the internal and common carotid arteries the surgeon inserts a shunt or internal bypass (Robertson, 1997). The shunt is a silicon tube usually inserted inside the opened internal carotid artery and common carotid artery and stabilized by surgical ties or tourniquets. Once in place, blood flows through the tube from the common carotid artery to the brain while the endarterectomy is completed. If no electroencephalographic (EEG) changes appear after the initial clamping of blood vessels during surgery, shunting may not be done, depending on the surgeon's judgment. Blood flow from the other internal carotid artery and the vertebrobasilar arterial system presumably provides a sufficient cerebral blood supply in these patients.

In the final stages of surgery the surgeon meticulously separates the atherosclerotic plaque from the artery walls and removes it. The internal and common carotid vessels, which had been temporarily closed during the endarterectomy, are flushed with heparin before shunt removal, final closure of incisions, and reopening of the clamped blood vessels (Robertson, 1997).

CE standards specify careful monitoring of BP, use of antiplatelet medication, and medical and behavioral treatment of stroke risk factors before, during, and after surgery. Control of perioperative morbidity and mortality is an important variable—it was estimated by one consensus group that the complication rate must be kept at 3% or less in order for the decreased risk of future stroke achieved by surgery to outweigh the greater risks of surgery compared to medical treatment alone (Biller et al., 1998). However, higher complication rates remain common. In a study of CE in academic medical centers the rate of major complications ranged from 2% to 11.1% across the 12 hospitals (Matchar et al., 1997).

The number of surgeries done per surgical center varies greatly. Perioperative morbidity and mortality also range widely among centers and correlate negatively with surgical experience (Karp, Flanders, Shipp, Taylor, & Martin,

232

1998). The total number of procedures is very large. Robertson (1997) estimated that 110,000 to 115,000 CEs are performed yearly in the United States.

POSSIBLE MECHANISMS OF COGNITIVE EFFECTS OF CE

Clinical experience and research suggest that, in individual patients, CE may lead to improvement, maintenance, or decline of cognitive function. In individuals being considered for CE and other surgeries to improve cerebral blood supply there is a significant correlation between the degree of impairment on neuropsychological tests and the severity of blockages in the arteries to and within the brain (Baird et al., 1985; Hamster & Diener, 1984). This correlation leads to the hypothesis that diminished stenosis in the internal carotid artery may result in gains on neuropsychological tests from baseline status in some patients. The proven benefit of CE in selected patients has been prevention of stroke. Thus, in patients selected for CE according to established criteria, stable rather than deteriorating or fluctuating cognitive function should follow CE. Finally, perioperative strokes, a major complication of CE, certainly would be expected to produce transient or permanent declines in cognitive functioning.

Gain

Cessation of Frequent Microembolic Showers

Fifteen years ago, researchers raised the possibility that improvements in neuropsychological test performance would follow CE in patients who experience frequent microembolic showers before surgery—in other words, it was hypothesized that CE permitted natural recovery from TIAs to occur. Microembolic showers were hypothesized episodes in which very small pieces of atherosclerosis frequently broke off from the blocked internal carotid and flew up into the smaller intracranial arteries, which were then temporarily blocked (Boysen et al., 1983). These events were believed to produce repeated TIAs rather than stroke. However, because of the frequency of these showers, continuous or near-continuous cognitive impairment was thought to result. In this scenario CE might lead to cognitive gains by ending or reducing the frequency of these microembolic events and allowing natural recovery to occur.

Although investigators have documented the occurrence of frequent microembolic cascades during the CE procedure itself (Gaunt et al., 1994; Smith et al., 1998), no neurobehavioral study or randomized control trial of CE efficacy in stroke prevention has identified CE candidates with definite repeated microembolic showers before surgery. There is no direct evidence supporting the hypothesis that CE can produce gains on neuropsychological tests compared to baseline performance by reducing or stopping microembolic showers.

Improved Cerebral Blood Flow to Ischemic But Viable Regions

Researchers have hypothesized that removing carotid blockage might improve cerebral blood flow (CBF) to areas that are dysfunctional because of marginally sufficient oxygenation for viability or survival of those particular neurons (Meyer et al., 1990). Presumably, the onset of borderline viability in these areas is heralded in many cases by a TIA or stroke. It was thought that improvement from the preoperative neuropsychological state might follow restoration of blood flow to these areas; however, some recent work indicates that most patients with carotid stenosis or occlusion have low regional CBF and low oxygenation extraction rates in the area supplied by the narrowed carotid (Frackowiak, 1997). Neurons survive sizable decreases in CBF for a short period of time. They continue to function, or at least survive, because of mechanisms that allow the brain cells to extract a greater percentage of oxygen when regional CBF falls. Thus, a low oxygenation rate with low CBF implies that some or all of the neurons in the region corresponding to the TIA or stroke have died and will not benefit from an increase in CBF.

Although nonsurvival of neurons in an ischemic area may be the rule, one study (Frackowiak, 1997) suggested that 10% to 15% of patients with carotid stenosis had low regional CBF and an increased oxygen extraction ratio indicative of high metabolic demand. This group may be particularly likely to benefit from CE as a protection against further erosion of scarce oxygen supplies in recurrent ischemic events. Some of these patients may show reversal of cognitive deficits after CE.

CE is not indicated for acute stroke patients (Biller et al., 1998) because of high risk of cerebral hemorrhage and carotid thrombosis. Therefore, it seems unlikely that improved CBF is likely to result in cognitive restitution for the average CE patient, who comes to surgery weeks to months after the first TIA or stroke. Nonetheless, concurrent pre- and postoperative neurobehavioral and neurophysiological measurements may identify a few CE candidates who experience postoperative improvement in cognitive status correlated with increased regional CBF after CE and consequent revived function of neurons. If there is only a small percentage of CE candidates with reversible neuronal dysfunction at the time of surgery, this paucity might explain the conflicting results of neuropsychological studies to date despite dramatic reports of recovery in single cases (Baird, 1991).

Protection and Stabilization

The most well-established benefit of CE is the reduction of stroke risk, a major neurobehavioral benefit (Biller et al., 1998). Follow-up studies typically have measured only perioperative strokes and postoperative TIAs and strokes on the side of surgery. Presumably the benefit arises from improvement in blood supply and removal of atherosclerotic plaque. Carotid atherosclerosis puts the patient at risk both for ischemia due to total occlusion of the affected carotid and for cerebral emboli due to fragmentation of the plaque. The cumulative and remote effects of TIA and stroke prevention deserve further study.

Additionally, it is conceivable that CE protects patients against extremely mild and gradually evolving cerebral ischemia. Such conditions might not produce frank episodes of neurological symptoms but nonetheless cause decline in cognitive, perceptual, or motor functioning.

Decline in Cognition Following CE

The most serious complications of CE include strokes due either to carotid thrombosis or to cerebral hemorrhage (Biller et al., 1998; Robertson, 1997; Sila, 1998). *Carotid thrombosis* refers to the formation of a blood clot in the internal carotid artery following the CE. Cerebral hemorrhage results from rupture of blood vessels within the brain, typically as a consequence of excessive blood flow into the brain after surgery. This condition, also known as *luxury perfusion,* is thought to stem from impairment in the ability of smaller arteries within the brain to adjust to the marked increase in flow of blood through the carotid after surgery. In normal brains, autoregulatory mechanisms to match blood supply to the metabolic demands of brain tissue include changing the diameter of the blood vessels within the brain (Chillon & Baumbach, 1997) as well as changing the ratio of oxygen extracted from the blood (Frackowiak, 1997). However, autoregulation fails in some CE patients, especially those with poor pre- and postoperative BP control, chronically low blood flow in the brain before surgery, and a high degree of arterial narrowing before CE (Biller et al., 1998). Excessive blood flow results.

Although they have not been the focus of a neuropsychological study to date, carotid thrombosis and cerebral hemorrhage after CE certainly would be expected to result in serious neuropsychological impairment in patients who survive the major strokes that typically result. In a study of 1,945 CE procedures performed on Medicare beneficiaries in Georgia in 1993, mild to severe stroke, including death related to stroke, occurred in 4.2% of patients within the first 30 days after surgery (Karp et al., 1998). Hence, marked decline in neuropsychological functioning after CE is likely an infrequent but not rare event.

More direct evidence has emerged in the last few years regarding subtler complications that produce milder cognitive decrements after CE. Embolic showers during surgical manipulation of the carotid have been linked with mild cognitive decrements thereafter (Gaunt et al., 1994; Smith et al., 1998). Earlier studies have suggested that reduced somatosensory evoked potentials during CE correlated with increased cognitive problems postoperatively (Brinkman, Braun, Ganji, Morrell, & Jacobs, 1984; Cushman, Brinkman, Ganji, & Jacobs, 1984). Because intraoperative estimates of emboli and evoked-potential measurements are not a standard part of the CE procedure, as yet we cannot estimate what proportion of CE patients are likely to experience cognitive decrements as a result of mild cerebral ischemia during surgery.

CONFOUNDS IN THE STUDY OF COGNITIVE CHANGE AFTER CE

Natural recovery, practice effects, and medical risk factor treatment are potential confounds in many of the neuropsychological studies of CE to date. Although the effect of each of these variables is small on average, the CE literature thus far suggests that any neuropsychological changes after surgery also are likely to be modest when measured over groups of patients. Hence, these variables deserve careful attention.

Natural Recovery

Natural recovery from stroke may continue as long as 1 year at a decelerating rate. Recovery continues longer for patients with more severe initial deficits (Post-Stroke Rehabilitation Guideline Panel, 1995). Stroke patients who undergo CE are thus especially likely to exhibit postoperative gains on neuropsychological tests as a result of recovery from the stroke. Patients with milder symptoms, ranging from TIAs to minor stroke, may manifest very mild improvement in cognition over time (Loeb, 1988). CE candidates with frequent ischemic episodes before surgery may experience fluctuating cognitive impairment that may not be detected on only a single preoperative neuropsychological assessment. In most studies to date, one cannot exclude natural recovery as a factor in improved neuropsychological scores.

Improved Medical Treatment and Risk Factor Control

BP control, blood glucose control, cholesterol reduction, a prudent diet, adequate exercise, weight control, and smoking cessation all deserve attention in comprehensive programs for individuals with cerebrovascular occlusive disease (Wolf, 1997). Programs incorporating these goals may boost cognitive performance as well as reduce stroke risk (Rowe & Kahn, 1998, pp. 66–142). Hence, CE candidates who receive improved medical treatment and monitoring of risk factors perioperatively or following surgery may show neurobehavioral benefits independent of the direct results of the operation. In most neuropsychological studies of CE to date, medical comorbidity and medical treatment of risk factors are given scant mention, especially in comparison groups not considered for CE. The importance of this confound therefore remains uncertain.

Practice Effects

Substantial gains occur when neuropsychological tests are readministered frequently or within a short period of time. Use of alternate forms reduces, but may not cancel, such effects. Randomized assignment, multiple baseline assessments, use of comparison groups with similar testing schedules and initial mental status, and use of norms for change (Sawrie, Chelune, Naugle, & Lüders, 1996) provide increased confidence that practice effects are not the central source of any gains observed after CE. Although randomized assignment may be possible only in large ongoing trials for CE indications not yet proven (such as stenosis less than 60%), it would seem reasonable at minimum to use a similar testing schedule for CE patients and comparison groups. Most neuropsychological studies to date have not met this criterion, however.

NEUROPSYCHOLOGICAL STUDIES OF THE PAST DECADE

Description

In contrast to the large studies that have demonstrated the efficacy of CE and aspirin therapy in preventing stroke in some patients with cerebrovascular occlusive disease, neuropsychological studies of CE patients have included only small samples. Eight of 10 neuropsychological studies in the last decade were conducted in Europe. This small set of studies encompasses a variety of emphases: postoperative quality of life, cognitive deterioration in the immediate postoperative period, psychophysiologic changes after CE, short-term neuropsychological changes following CE, and long-term neuropsychological effects of CE. Table 12.1 summarizes participant selection, design, and conclusions.

Postoperative Quality of Life

Sirkka et al.'s (1992) study provides quality-of-life and neuropsychological data for patients evaluated an average of 8 years after CE but not assessed before surgery. There were two comparison groups. The first comprised 18 patients considered for CE an average of 11 years earlier. Physicians reportedly made the decision not to proceed with surgery, but the criteria were not specified. This research group matched CE patients on age, sex, duration of illness, and lateralization of carotid stenosis. Reportedly, in the operated group angiographic findings were more severe, hypertension was more common, and medical treatment was more frequent. A second comparison group of 29 normal individuals matched the CE and nonoperated group on age, education, and gender.

Results did not show overall differences between the mean performance of the groups on the neuropsychological or quality-of-life summary measures. Most participants in all groups had test scores in the normal range and reported a reasonably high life quality. However, the operated group had more high and low scores on the neuropsychological summary measure. Sirkka et al. (1992) concluded that long-term follow-up showed good life quality and normal cognitive status in most CE patients as well as in most patients with carotid stenosis who did not undergo CE.

Cognitive Deterioration in the Immediate Postoperative Period

Iddon et al. (1997) tested patients less than 3 days after CE to maximize sensitivity to postoperative deficits. No intraoperative shunt was used. In addition to letter and semantic verbal fluency tests, participants were administered seven tests taken from the Cambridge Neuropsychological Test Automated Battery (CANTAB; Fray, Robbins, & Sahakian, 1996), which comprises computerized tests of attention and memory, with parallel versions for most. Before surgery, no patients fell in the range suggestive of dementia on the Mini-Mental State Exam (MMSE; Folstein, Folstein, & McHugh, 1975) or endorsed a high number of symptoms on a depression screen. At the preoperative testing the vascular patients did not differ from the comparison group on age, estimated premorbid verbal intelligence, or any of the nine dependent measures. Healthy volunteers from the community constituted the comparison group. At postoperative testing no significant change was found on any part of the battery in the CE group. This study suggests that in some centers cognitive stability after CE is the rule.

Gaunt et al. (1994) correlated the number of air and particulate emboli during CE with neurological and cognitive changes 5 to 7 days after surgery in 100 consecutive patients. Air emboli are gaseous bubbles introduced into the brain circulation after the carotid artery is opened. Particulate emboli are small pieces of atheroma dislodged from the walls of the carotid during surgery or tiny blood clots that form during surgery. This study and others suggested that particulate emboli pose a greater risk of cerebral ischemia, perhaps because the air emboli often are quickly reabsorbed into the bloodstream instead of going on to block one or more cerebral arteries (Barbut & Caplan, 1997). Gaunt et al. determined the probable type of emboli by using transcranial Doppler (TCD) monitoring during CE. This noninvasive technique analyzes the sounds emitted by the blood flowing through the middle cerebral artery (Barbut & Caplan, 1997).

Gaunt et al. (1994) reported that the TCD technique detected emboli during CE in 92% of the 91 patients who completed all measures. However, there was no association between deterioration on psychological tests and the total number of emboli. When the authors calculated correlations separately for each of seven stages of CE and for the two types of emboli, only one significant correlation emerged: There was a significant association between postoperative deterioration on at least one test and the presence of particulate emboli during dissection of the carotid, the first stage of surgery. Twenty-three of 91 patients had particulate emboli during this stage; 11 of these 23 sustained a significant decline on at least one psychological test. Twenty-six patients had a similar decline, for

TABLE 12.1
Description of Recent Studies

Study	No. CEs	Preoperative Symptoms	Comparison Group	Follow-Up	Cognitive Measures	Conclusions
Sirrka et al. (1992)	44	Not described	Pts. considered for CE but not selected; healthy controls	8 years after surgery or 11 years after CE considered	Summary score based on 15 neuropsychological tests	No difference among the three groups postop. No preop testing done.
Iddon et al. (1997)	30	TIAs	Baseline only: Healthy controls	48 to 72 hr postop	Two verbal fluency tests and 7 from CANTAB	No baseline differences between controls and CE pts. No postop changes in CE pts.
Gaunt et al. (1994)	94	TIAs and strokes with and without residual sxs	None	5 to 7 days postop	Mental status test and four Wechsler Memory Scale subtests	Twenty-six of 94 dropped at least 1 SD on at least one test. In 11 of 26, embolization during carotid dissection was found. No. pts. with cognitive gains not given.
Uclés et al. (1997)	28	TIAs, RINDs, 2 non-disabling strokes	Baseline only: Age-matched controls	Within 1 month postop	MMSE version and Set Test	Slight gains in overall scores. Gains correlated with qEEG improvement. EEG recordings improved in both hemispheres.
Kügler et al. (1995)	30	asx, TIAs, minor strokes	Peripheral vascular disease pts. who underwent surgery of like duration	1 to 2 weeks postop	MMSE and SKT	Pts. with cognitive abnormalities excluded from study. No postop change in VEPs and SKT. P300 potentials improved in both groups.
Mononen et al. (1990)	46	TIAs and mild and moderate strokes	None	2 weeks and 2 months postop	Word fluency, Stroop color, serial learning, digit span, facial and Cronholm recognition, visual memory	Although similar on preop testing, after CE TIA pts. gained more on cognitive tests than stroke pts. Gains in TIA pts. appeared partially related to side of surgery.

TABLE 12.1 (Continued)

Study	No. CEs	Preoperative Symptoms	Comparison Group	Follow-Up	Cognitive Measures	Conclusions
Casey et al. (1989)	24	TIAs and RINDs	Pts. with TIAs who did not have CE because of insignificant stenosis on side referable to sxs	2 months	WAIS, WMS, Modified Knox Cubes, Finger Tapping, Two-Point Discrimination, Visual Search	No difference in postop gains for right or left CE pts. compared to controls on 15 scores. Concluded that CE does not improve cognition in pts. with TIAs or RINDs.
Incalzi et al. (1997)	28	TIAs and RINDs	Orthopedic pts. undergoing surgery with same anesthesia protocol	7 days and 4 months postop	Mental Deterioration Battery score and 21 measures from seven cognitive domains	Short-term cognitive gains reported in CE pts. but not in controls. No differences in right and left CE pts. preop or postop. Limited 4-month follw-up suggested preserved gains.
Lind et al. (1993)	25	TIAs, RINDs, minor strokes	None	Immediately postop and 14 months postop	Verbal and numeric problem-solving, BVRT, Critical Flicker Fusion, visual and auditory reaction time	For seven variables, found statistically significant, small gains in two scores, decline in one, and no change in four. On two tests, saw greater gains in left than right CE pts.
Meyer et al. (1990)	8	Multi-infarct dementia	STA–MCA bypass; group randomly assigned to medical treatment only	Every 3 to 9 months postop for an average of 26 months	Cognitive Capacity Screening Examination	Stable cognitive performance in all 3 groups, all of whom had medical treatment and medical risk factor control.

Note. The format and headings are from Table 15–1 (pp. 360–365), "The Effects of Cerebral Vascular Disease On Neuropsychological Functioning," by G. G. Brown, A. D. Baird, M. W. Shatz, and R. A. Bornstein, 1996, in I. Grant and K. M. Adams (Eds.), *Neuropsychological Assessment of Neuropsychiatric Disorders* (pp. 342–378), New York: Oxford University Press. Copyright 1996 by Oxford University Press. Adapted with permission.

CE = carotid endarterectomy; Pts. = patients; postop = postoperation; preop = preoperation; TIA = transient ischemic attack; CANTAB = Cambridge Neuropsychological Test Automated Battery; sxs = symptoms; RINDS = reversible ischemic neurological deficits; MMSE = Mini-Mental State Examination; qEEG = quantitative electroencephalograph; asx = asymptomatic; VEP = visual evoked potential; WAIS = Wechsler Adult Intelligence Scale; WMS = Wechsler Memory Scale; BVRT = Benton Visual Retention Test; STA–MCA = superficial temporal artery–middle cerebral artery.

unexplained reasons. Gaunt et al. did not report the number of patients who improved after CE. The 3 patients with neurological deterioration after CE experienced particulate embolization during the last surgical stage (recovery). A more recent article (Smith et al., 1998) described reduced particulate embolization through changes in surgical techniques and routine TCD monitoring. Gaunt et al.'s study indicates that the presence of particulate emboli during the first or last stage of CE greatly increases the risk of cognitive impairment after surgery. However, the cognitive impairment correlated with particulate embolization may not be detected with neurological exam and observation alone.

Psychophysiologic Changes After CE

Two studies that placed greater emphasis on psychophysiologic than cognitive measures yielded no evidence of marked postoperative change in cognition (Uclés et al., 1997; Kügler et al., 1995).

Uclés et al. (1997) focused on quantitative EEG recordings and selected general neurobehavioral indicators as correlates, as well as a quality-of-life tool, the Barthel Index (Mahoney & Barthel, 1965). They used an age-matched sample that was tested only once, to set normal limits for the neurobehavioral measures.

In Uclés et al.'s (1997) study psychological and neurodiagnostic tests were more sensitive to preoperative cognitive deficits than neurological and narrowly defined functional measures were. Only 2 patients had neurological findings at the time of CE; only 3 patients had any limitations in activities of daily living according to the Barthel Index. In contrast, 12 patients reportedly had markedly below-average or marginal MMSE scores, and 9 exhibited focal slowing on the EEG, corresponding to computed tomography (CT) scan evidence of infarcts. On average, CE candidates had MMSE scores in the normal range at preoperative testing. On this Spanish version of the MMSE, patients could obtain up to 35 points; scores from 30 to 35 were said to be within normal range.

Although statistically significant rises were noted in both the MMSE and the Set Test, a measure of verbal fluency (Isaacs & Kennie, 1973), these small increments a month or less after surgery may reflect practice effects. For example, from the pre- to postoperative measurement the group mean on this MMSE version rose only from 31.63 (SD = 2.58) to 32.9. EEG mean frequency increased significantly in 11 of 16 areas measured. Changes were greater in patients who underwent left CE (Uclés et al., 1997).

Kügler et al. (1995) assessed cognitive dysfunction in patients with cerebral and peripheral arteriosclerosis and evaluated the short-term effects of CE. They excluded patients with baseline impairment on the cognitive measures used in the study. This restriction of range on baseline test scores likely reduced the sensitivity of their study in detecting neuropsychological test changes after CE. In addition to the MMSE, Kügler et al. used the SKT, a measure of memory and attention that comprises nine subtests, including counting, naming, recall, and recognition tasks (Erzigkeit, 1992). Event-related P300 potentials were the core dependent measures.

The group with peripheral arteriosclerosis underwent ultrasound screening to eliminate those with significant carotid stenosis (Kügler et al., 1995). Patients who underwent cognitive and psychophysiologic follow-up were selected on a nonrandom basis from larger samples of patients with carotid and peripheral arteriosclerosis, most of whom went on to have CEs or bypass surgery. Patients in the study groups did not differ from the larger samples on preoperative test performance, age, and gender. The larger samples of carotid and peripheral arteriosclerosis patients did not differ in terms of duration of surgery or incidence of major medical conditions related to arteriosclerosis. Age-matched healthy participants provided reference data for visual P300 and pattern reversal visual evoked-potential (PVEP) measurements.

As in Uclés et al.'s (1997) study, in which quantitative EEG recordings were used, neurophysiological measurements showed more variability before surgery and more change thereafter than the cognitive measures. MMSE and SKT scores for the carotid and peripheral arteriosclerosis groups did not differ before surgery and did not change significantly on assessment 1 to 2 weeks after CE or bypass (Kügler et al., 1995). Amplitude and latency measurements from the PVEP did not differ before surgery. At baseline assessment the carotid group showed greater and more numerous differences in P300 potentials from the normal controls than did the peripheral arteriosclerosis group. After surgery, P300 latencies and amplitudes improved in peripheral and carotid arteriosclerosis patients who had abnormal values before surgery (Kügler et al., 1995).

Short-Term Neuropsychological Changes Following CE

Two studies with multiple cognitive measures and similar follow-up intervals reported increments in cognitive, perceptual, and motor test scores after CE. However, in one study (Casey et al., 1989), these gains were attributed to practice effects, because similar changes were noted in a comparison group. It is hard to draw firm conclusions from the positive results of the second study (Mononen et al., 1990) because of design limitations.

Casey et al. (1989) studied 24 CE patients with TIAs and RINDs and 12 TIA patients with no stenosis on the side referable to symptoms. The authors obtained 15 neuropsychological scores at baseline and 2 months later. Five neuropsychological scores rose equally in the group that had undergone CE in the interim and the group that had not. None of the 15 measures on the cognitive–perceptual–motor battery showed a difference in change from pre- to postoperative measurement between the CE group and the comparison group of TIA patients tested at the same interval.

In their study of 46 CE patients, Mononen et al. (1990) sought to determine whether TIA patients and stroke patients differed in terms of cognitive gains following CE. Another goal of their study was to determine whether changes in neuropsychological functioning after surgery could be associated with the cerebral hemisphere supplied by the carotid that underwent endarterectomy. They therefore administered four verbal tests thought to reflect predominantly left-hemisphere functioning (word fluency, digit span, Stroop color test, and a serial word learning measure) and three nonverbal–visual tests believed to tap primarily right-hemisphere functioning (facial recognition, design recognition, and concrete picture recognition). They studied 30 patients with TIAs only and 16 patients with mild and moderate strokes. For each measure, Mononen et al. compared TIA group and stroke group scores at 2 weeks and 2 months after CE with preoperative values.

In the TIA group, follow-up scores at 2 weeks, 2 months, or both, rose significantly from the preoperative level for word fluency, Stroop color, word serial learning, and design recognition tests (Mononen et al., 1990). For the stroke group, increments in test performance were seen on one or both postoperative testings for the serial word learning, design recognition, and concrete picture recognition tests.

Mononen et al. (1990) examined the correspondence between improvement on verbal and nonverbal tests and the side of surgery in the TIA group. TIA patients who underwent left CE improved on three of the four verbal or left-hemisphere-sensitive measures at one or both follow-up assessments relative to preoperative performance. The same subgroup showed no significant increases at either postoperative assessment on the three nonverbal or right-hemisphere-sensitive measures. In contrast, TIA patients who underwent right CE improved on three of four verbal tests and two of three nonverbal tests.

Although Mononen et al.'s (1990) data clearly suggest postoperative improvement in CE patients and a correspondence between side of CE and the tests on which gains were observed, limitations in the study's design make it impossible to rule out practice effects and spontaneous recovery as the primary basis of the gains. The most important weaknesses are the failure to use alternate forms of the verbal and nonverbal tests and the lack of a comparison group undergoing testing at the same intervals without receiving CE.

Long-Term Neuropsychological Effects of CE

Only one of three studies with longer follow-up intervals reported convincing levels of improvement in CE patients from pre- to postoperative assessment (Incalzi et al., 1997; Lind et al., 1993; Meyer et al., 1990). Even in this study—Incalzi et al. (1997)—it is not clear that improved neuropsychological test performance on follow-up directly reflects effects of CE rather than associated factors.

Incalzi et al. (1997) studied 28 CE patients 2 days before surgery and 7 days afterward. Their aim was to evaluate changes in the CE group versus those in a comparison group of 30 patients tested 2 days before and 1 week after an orthopedic operation. Pre- and postoperative medical risk factor control was not specified in detail, but the authors indicated that factors that affect cognition were addressed before preoperative testing, presumably in both groups.

Incalzi et al. (1997) showed that a summary score and 13 of 21 individual test scores improved on the first postoperative testing in the CE group. The effect size was moderate for 5 of the 13 measures and small for the rest (Cohen, 1988). Patients who underwent right versus left CE did not differ significantly overall or on most individual tests before or after surgery. These results indicate that cognitive changes overall were small and generalized rather than related to the side of CE. The authors also reported a trend toward sustained gains or further improvement in an unspecified number of CE patients seen 4 months after surgery.

By contrast, in the orthopedic group the summary measure showed significant deterioration, and only 4 of 21 measures changed significantly after orthopedic surgery, all in the negative direction (Incalzi et al., 1997). No reason is apparent or offered for these unfavorable changes after orthopedic surgery, which did not differ from CE in terms of duration, anesthesiological technique, and postoperative analgesic use. This unexpected result suggests that follow-up of the orthopedic group did not provide an adequate standard for gauging practice effects and general factors associated with recovery from anesthesia and surgery.

Although Incalzi et al. determined that their results suggest cognitive benefit from CE, they offered two alternative explanations: (a) postoperative changes in lifestyle or medical risk factor control in the CE group only and (b) natural recovery from TIA and RIND in the CE patients. The most reasonable conclusion from this study seems to be that CE either results in no change or produces small generalized cognitive improvement in most patients.

In Germany, Lind et al. (1993) conducted neuropsychological studies on 25 CE patients 4 days before surgery and 7 days and 14 months thereafter. There was no comparison group. The authors looked at seven dependent measures derived from measures of verbal and nonverbal ability, the Benton Visual Retention Test (Sivan, 1992), auditory and visual reaction time, and critical flicker fusion frequency. Averaging across the two postoperative measurements, Lind et al. found improvement on two scores, a decline in one score, and no significant change in four others. Analyses of postoperative change for each dependent measure and for each of six subgroups did not reveal consistent change in scores after CE. Only 12 of these 42 analyses achieved statistical significance, with 7 favorable results and 5 unfavorable results noted. Lind et al.'s work allows one to conclude only that neuropsychological performance after CE was fairly stable over 4 months of follow-up. Small positive or negative changes in cognitive test performance cannot be ruled out on the basis of these results.

In the longest neuropsychological follow-up study in this decade and the only one with randomized assignment, Meyer et al. (1990) followed 8 patients an average of 26 months after CE. All patients had diagnoses of multi-infarct dementia and hence most likely would not fit standard selection criteria for CE (Biller et al., 1998). Patients were randomly assigned to medical treatment only or to medical treatment plus the appropriate surgical intervention (CE or superficial temporal artery to middle cerebral artery [STA–MCA] bypass). The authors emphasized maximal medical risk factor treatment in all participants. In addition to taking antiplatelet medication, patients received any appropriate treatment for heart disease, high BP, hyperlipidemia, and diabetes, as well as counseling for smoking and alcohol. Analysis of the results showed stable regional CBF and performance on the Cognitive Capacity Screening Exam (Jacobs et al., 1977) during follow-up for CE patients, as well as for 10 patients with STA–MCA bypass and 18 with medical treatment only (Meyer et al., 1990).

Although the patients in Meyer et al.'s (1990) study had unusually severe cognitive deficits for CE candidates, the results nonetheless are in line with other studies that have indicated that the average patient experiences no marked changes in neuropsychological functioning after CE. Furthermore, the results are consistent with other evidence suggesting that there is no lasting change in regional CBF after CE, even though the blood flow through the carotid has increased.

Summary of Findings of Past Neuropsychological Studies

Neuropsychological studies to date do not provide convincing evidence that CE results in improvement in neuropsychological test scores after surgery, but this work also does not permit one to exclude the possibility of small positive changes due to CE. The mixture of positive and negative results suggests that on average any increments or decrements in neurobehavioral scores as a result of CE are likely to be modest. Certainly, the failure to find decrements after surgery in most patients provides a basis for reassuring individuals who are facing this major neurosurgical procedure. The lack of strong evidence of a lasting increase in regional CBF after CE in most patients also makes it seem unlikely that marked postoperative improvement on neuropsychological tests is common under present selection criteria for CE. Past neuropsychological studies offer no information regarding the role of CE in protecting the brain from future ischemic events.

Pointers from Past Neuropsychological Studies of CE

A review of past studies suggests a number of desirable features for future work. The most effective improvements would be the enrollment of large samples and the use of randomized assignment to surgical treatment versus medical treatment. Unfortunately, these features often are ethically or practically impossible to incorporate. Other suggestions include conformity with current standards for selecting and treating CE patients, providing information regarding perioperative morbidity and mortality and postoperative neurological follow-up, and addressing medical comorbidity and medical treatment of risk factors for stroke. Additional desirable features are information about or controls for age,

TABLE 12.2
Patient and Treatment Variables in Recent Studies

Study	Stenosis ≥ 70% On Operated Side for Patients With Symptoms	No Patients With Major or Disabling Strokes	Perioperative Major Strokes and Mortality < 3%	Antiplatelet Medication if Indicated	Medical Risk Factor Control in All Patients
Sirrka et al. (1992)					No
Iddon et al. (1997)	Yes	Yes	Yes		
Gaunt et al. (1994)	Yes		Yes		
Uclés et al. (1997)	Yes[a]	Yes	Yes		
Kügler et al. (1995)		Yes			
Mononen et al. (1990)			Yes		
Casey et al. (1989)[b]		Yes		Yes[c]	
Incalzi et al. (1990)	Yes	Yes			Partial
Lind et al. (1993)	Yes[d]	Yes			
Meyer et al. (1990)			No	Yes	Yes

[a]24 of 28 patients met the criterion. [b]15 of 24 patients had stenosis > 90%. [c]All carotid endarterectomy patients and 75% of controls were taking medication. [d]19 of 25 patients met the criterion.

education, practice effects, and natural recovery and preoperative symptom fluctuation; implementation of batteries that are sensitive to both general and lateralized effects of CE on behavior; and reports of concurrent neurophysiological or neuroradiological measurements.

Table 12.2 lists the studies according to the degree to which they fit current recommendations for selection and treatment of CE candidates (Biller et al., 1998). If patients in these small neuropsychological studies fit proven indications for CE in terms of preoperative symptom severity and the degree of stenosis in the internal carotid artery, then one can have more confidence than otherwise in the generalizability of the study's findings to the large numbers of individuals now receiving CE. Optimal medical as well as surgical treatment of CE candidates also helps to ensure a powerful test of surgical efficacy and generalizability of the results to the large-sample CE trials and retrospective reports in the literature.

Table 12.3 contrasts recent studies in terms of design features that increase statistical or experimental control or enhance understanding of changes in neuropsychological test scores associated with CE.

Statistical Power

All 10 of the studies discussed in this chapter lacked sample sizes large enough to detect small to moderate changes after CE. Only one—Meyer et al. (1990)—featured randomized assignment to medical treatment or surgery.

TABLE 12.3
Desirable Design Features in Recent Studies

Study	General Design			Comparison Group Features					Correlates of Neuro. Tests	
	Some Use of Alternate Test Forms	Analysis by Side of CE	Multiple Postoperative Testings	Random Assignment	Tested at Same Intervals	Similar Age or Education	Similar Medical Comorbidity	Similar Base Mental Status	Neuro. Exam Repeated Postoperation	Neuro. Diagnostic Tests
Sirrka et al. (1992)		No	No	No	No	Yes		Yes	No	No
Iddon et al. (1997)	Yes	No	Yes	No	No	Yes		No	Yes	No
Gaunt et al. (1994)	No	No	No	No	No	No	No	No	Yes	Yes
Uclés et al. (1997)	Yes	No	No	No	No	Yes		Yes	No	Yes
Kügler et al. (1995)	Yes	No	No	No	Yes	Yes	Yes	No	Yes	Yes
Mononen et al. (1990)	No	Yes	Yes	No	No	No	No	No		No
Casey et al. (1989)	Yes	Yes	No	No	No	No		No	No	Yes
Incalzi et al. (1990)	Yes	Yes	Yes	No	Yes	Yes	Yes	Yes	No	No
Lind et al. (1993)		Yes	Yes	No	No	No	No	No		
Meyer et al. (1990)	No	No	Yes	Yes	Yes		Yes	Yes	No	Yes

Note. The format and headings are from Table 15–2 (p. 366), "The Effects of Cerebral Vascular Disease on Neuropsychological Functioning," by G. G. Brown, A. D. Baird, M. W. Shatz, and R. A. Bornstein, 1996, in I. Grant and K. M Adams (Eds.), *Neuropsychological Assessment of Neuropsychiatric Disorders* (pp. 342–378), New York: Oxford University Press. Copyright 1996 by Oxford University Press. Adapted with permission. CE = carotid endarterectomy; Neuro. = neuropsychological.

Because present indicators for CE and past neuropsychological studies suggest that postoperative cognitive gains or decrements are likely to be very modest on average, it is desirable for neuropsychological studies of CE to have the power to detect small effects at least 80% of the time, the convention used by Cohen (1988, p. 56). However, some of the neuropsychological studies conducted thus far lack the power to detect even a moderate effect with confidence.

Selection of CE Candidates

One of the current selection criteria is that CE candidates have histories of no more than mild strokes at worst (Biller et al., 1998). About half the neuropsychological studies of the last 10 years give enough specific data to indicate that all or most CE patients were free of residual effects of major stroke.

Another standard for selection of CE candidates is that patients who have had a TIA or stroke have at least 70% stenosis of the internal carotid artery on the side of surgery (Biller et al., 1998). About half the studies reviewed here provide enough information to be reasonably certain that the majority of patients in that study met this criterion.

Perioperative Morbidity and Mortality and Postoperative Neurological Follow-Up

Recent studies indicate that very low complication rates are necessary in order to achieve a modest net benefit from CE in terms of stroke risk reduction (Biller et al., 1998). Centers are known to vary markedly in morbidity and mortality rates after CE. One would expect that neurobehavioral benefits of CE also would most likely be seen in centers with low morbidity rates after CE. Nonetheless, less than half the neuropsychological studies specify the incidence of major complications of CE, such as postoperative hemorrhagic stroke and carotid thrombosis at the site of surgery. Only about half the studies indicate whether patients with postoperative complications were included in the analysis of neuropsychological changes after surgery. Given the small samples of patients available for these studies, inclusion of even one patient with major stroke after CE might have skewed the data dramatically for the group as a whole and camouflaged the trend in patients who did not experience new major ischemic events after CE.

In small-sample studies such as the ones discussed here, it also would be helpful to know how many patients sustained minor complications, such as TIAs and minor strokes, during postoperative follow-up. In addition to careful history taking, neurological exams at approximately the same intervals as neuropsychological testing enable researchers to separate patients who may have sustained mild cognitive decrements since surgery from those free of such complications. Three of the 10 recent studies specified that patients underwent neurological exams around the times of neuropsychological assessment (Gaunt et al., 1994; Mononen et al., 1990; Uclés et al., 1997).

*Medical Comorbidity in CE Candidates
and Treatment of Risk Factors*

Standards for CE require monitoring and medical control of hypertension and other risk factors for stroke (Biller et al., 1998). Use of antiplatelet aggregating agents in the peri- and postoperative periods is stressed in particular. One would expect that equally fastidious attention to these factors would be important to be assured of the best possible outcome of CE in terms of neuropsychological test score changes. However, only 20% of the studies covered in this chapter (Casey et al., 1989; Meyer et al., 1990) verified that all or most patients with cerebrovascular occlusive disease received antiplatelet aggregating agents in the peri- and postoperative periods. Moreover, although many of the 10 articles document the high incidence of medical conditions that may interact with CE to determine stroke risk, only 2 stated that a systematic effort at medical risk factor control was made pre- and postoperatively in CE patients and the comparison group (Incalzi et al., 1997; Meyer et al., 1990). In only 1 of these articles (Meyer et al., 1990) did the authors stipulate that programs addressing these factors were identical in both surgical and nonoperated groups. When it is not possible to ensure identical treatment of medical risk factors in comparison groups as well as surgically treated groups, it will be important at least to provide information about the incidence and treatment of major risk factors in all subject groups, as was done to some extent by Incalzi et al. (1997), Kügler et al. (1995), and Meyer et al. (1990).

Age, Education, and Practice Effects

Use of multiple preoperative baseline assessments and measure- and population-specific reliability-of-change indexes deserve consideration in future studies. As shown in Table 12.1, most recent studies have used comparison groups, often with comparable education and age constitution. Table 12.3 indicates that half the studies used alternate forms. Nonetheless, use of comparison groups and alternate forms only partially compensates for the measurement error inherent in neuropsychological study (Sawrie et al., 1996).

*Natural Recovery and Preoperative Variation
in Cerebrovascular Occlusive Disease*

Symptom and angiographic variability among CE candidates occurs along multiple dimensions: the degree of stenosis in the operated carotid; pattern of stenosis and collateral circulation elsewhere in the cerebrovasculature; the nature of symptoms (e.g., aphasia vs. monoparesis); and the total number, duration, frequency, and recency of symptomatic ischemic episodes. Although recent studies generally have described the diversity of CE candidates on these dimensions to some degree, as listed in Table 12.1, it is difficult to summarize this material comprehensively in published reports and thus to compare the preoperative status of patients from one study to the next.

Randomization to CE versus medical treatment well may be the best way to deal with the multiple sources of variability among patients in terms of symptoms and pattern of stenosis. However, randomization is not ethically or practically possible in most settings in which neuropsychologists work. As specialists in analyzing and describing behavior, neuropsychologists should consider developing global indexes of preoperative symptom severity across multiple dimensions for use in comparing patients across neurobehavioral studies. An index of severity of stenosis in the cerebrovasculature based on the cerebral angiogram also would be useful. Baird et al. (1985) used a rough angiographic index of cerebrovascular stenosis some years ago and determined that it correlated with indexes of impairment on neuropsychological tests.

Natural recovery from previous TIAs and strokes is an issue uniquely important to neuropsychological studies. In addition to allowing for assessment of practice effects, multiple baseline measurements on CE candidates and comparison groups will provide a way to estimate the degree to which patients may be experiencing recovery from TIAs and strokes sustained before CE. Because practice effects diminish and recovery from TIA and stroke slows over time, a finding of greater increases in neuropsychological test scores after CE would argue strongly for a beneficial effect of CE on cognition (Baird, 1991; Brown et al., 1996).

Neuropsychological Test Batteries Suitable for CE Studies

As yet there has been considerable variability in the adequacy and type of neuropsychological measures used to study CE. Ideally, batteries used for CE studies should be of proven sensitivity to the cognitive deficits noted in patients with mild cerebrovascular disease and of proven reliability. The battery should include well-studied summary indexes as well as indexes that reflect primarily behaviors subserved by the right and left cerebral hemispheres and that tap major ability domains. When a large number of univariate analyses are conducted relative to a small sample of patients without specific hypotheses, interpretation of results is unclear unless there is an overwhelming majority of positive or negative results.

Inclusion of measures of emotional and functional status and life quality will help ascertain whether any changes in neuropsychological test scores after CE are clinically as well as statistically significant. Such measures are especially important given the modest size of changes in neuropsychological test scores reported in most studies thus far. Very-long-term follow-up with quality-of-life and neuropsychological measures will permit assessment of the protective role of CE in preventing cognitive decline in the future.

Neurophysiological and Neuroradiological Correlates

Only three studies followed patients with physiological as well as cognitive measures (Kügler et al., 1995; Meyer et al., 1990; Uclés et al., 1997). However, these measures, teamed with neuropsychological testing, can elucidate the source and mechanism of changes in mental activity and ability after CE much better than follow-up with history taking and neurological exam alone.

Positron emission tomography (PET) and functional magnetic resonance imaging (fMRI) may clarify the relationship between CE and neuronal function in the ischemic penumbra, the region of dysfunctional or nonfunctional tissue surrounding dead or infarcted brain tissue seen on neuroimaging of some stroke and TIA patients (Frackowiak, 1997). PET and fMRI estimate utilization of glucose or oxygen in brain regions in response to mental activity using radioactively labeled water or induction of a large magnetic field, respectively (Raichle, 1997). Measures such as PET and fMRI scans also should allow one to determine whether increases in carotid blood flow after CE are followed by increased use of oxygen and glucose in brain regions supplied by the carotid. If patients who show improved scores on neuropsychological tests after CE are the same ones who show increased neuronal function on PET or fMRI after surgery, then one would have more confidence in attributing the increase in test scores directly to the CE procedure.

Neuroelectrophysiological measurements already have proved to be sensitive indicators of transient or lasting decreases in brain activity due to intraoperative embolism or decreased cerebral perfusion (Cushman et al., 1984; Robertson, 1997). As noted earlier, studies of CE can be improved by conducting separate analyses for patients experiencing complications of CE and for those without complications.

Finally, CT and standard MRI are more sensitive measures of the severity of ischemic episodes than patient report or neurological exam, because they may reveal evidence of infarct or neuronal death even though symptoms have resolved (Tietgen, 1997). When CT or MRI scans suggest infarction or neuronal cell death before or after surgery, one can be more confident that low scores on neuropsychological tests before surgery reflect cerebral ischemia rather than other factors such as poor motivation, medication effects, anxiety, and medical illness.

CONCLUSIONS

The most striking finding in this review was that none of seven large, randomized controlled studies of CE included neuropsychological data (Stukenborg, 1997). If neuropsychological testing had been performed during pre- and postoperative exams in one or more of these trials, we likely would know more about the possibility of reversal of neuronal dysfunction in cerebral ischemia. Large sample sizes would make it possible to identify relatively small changes in cognitive test scores after CE. Even modest improvement in neuropsychological functioning following CE is clinically noteworthy given the large number of candidates for CE. Large-sample studies also would provide the power to search for subgroups of CE candidates who experience marked cognitive benefits, as recounted in anecdotes and published case studies (Baird, 1991).

Perhaps equally important is that long-term neuropsychological follow-up in randomized large trials is critical to determining whether patients who receive CE are protected from a decline in cognitive functioning compared to patients who receive medical treatment alone. Because cerebrovascular ischemia may not always produce obvious stroke symptoms, it will be important to compare the long-term cognitive status of CE patients and medically treated patients who do not report TIAs and strokes in follow-up assessments as well as to compare neuropsychological test performance in those who experience obvious TIA or stroke. The very-long-term clinical significance of protection from major stroke is unknown. Follow-up assessments over a longer time period may reveal a more important role for CE in protecting cognitive functioning than has been appreciated thus far, especially if research continues to suggest that cerebrovascular disease potentiates the behavioral expression of Alzheimer's disease (Snowdon et al., 1997).

A role will remain for neuropsychological studies that focus on subgroups of well-defined CE candidates and incorporate neurophysiological measures and control of medical risk factors for stroke. For example, no neuropsychological study thus far has focused exclusively on CE candidates who have not yet had strokes or TIAs, even though members of this group with at least 60% carotid stenosis have been shown to benefit from CE in terms of stroke risk reduction (Biller et al., 1998). Although conducting multiple PET scans and extensive neuropsychological testing may be too expensive and cumbersome for large studies, intensive study of small groups may help make clear how removing a blockage in the carotid artery in the neck affects blood flow and neuronal function upstream. More generally, these studies may elucidate how the brain adjusts to sudden and gradual changes in blood supply.

We cannot answer these questions without neurobehavioral data more extensive than those supplied by patient history and neurological exam alone. Therefore, it is imperative that neuropsychologists step forth as collaborators in future studies of CE and in studies of other surgical treatments for mild cerebrovascular disease.

ACKNOWLEDGMENT

We are grateful to Mike Barton for his help in translation of one of the articles. Further, we appreciate Dr. Jack Rock's assistance in the description of the carotid endarterectomy procedure.

REFERENCES

Baird, A. D. (1991). Behavioral correlates of cerebral revascularization. In R. A. Bornstein & G. Brown (Eds.), *Neurobehavioral aspects of cerebrovascular disease* (pp. 297–313). New York: Oxford University Press.

Baird, A. D., Boulos, R., Mehta, B., Adams, K. M., Shatz, M. W., Ausman, J. I., Diaz, F. G., & Dujovny, M. (1985). Cerebral angiography and neuropsychological measurement: The twain may meet. *Surgical Neurology, 23*, 641–650.

Barbut, D., & Caplan, L. R. (1997). Cerebrovascular complications of cardiac surgery. In K. M. A. Welch, L. R. Caplan, D. J. Reis, B. K. Siesjö, & B. Weir (Eds.), *Primer on cerebrovascular diseases* (pp. 783–786). San Diego, CA: Academic Press.

Biller, J., Feinberg, W. M., Castaldo, J. E., Whittemore, A. D., Harbaugh, R. E., Dempsey, R. J., Caplan, L. R., Kresowik, T. F., Matchar, D. B., Toole, J. F., Easton, J. D., Adams, H. P., Brass, L. M., Hobson II, R. W., Brott, T. G., & Sternau, L. (1998). Guidelines for carotid endarterectomy: A statement for healthcare professionals from a special writing group of the Stroke Council, American Heart Association. *Circulation, 97*, 501–509.

Boysen, G., Hemmingsen, R., Mejsholm, B., Vorstrup, S., Lassen, N. A., Lester, J., & Engell, H. C. (1983). Cerebral blood flow and intellectual function before and after carotid endarterectomy. *Journal of Cerebral Blood Flow Metabolism, 3*(Suppl. 1), S272–S273.

Brinkman, S. D., Braun, P., Ganji, S., Morrell, R. M., & Jacobs, L. A. (1984). Neuropsychological performance one week after carotid endarterectomy reflects intraoperative ischemia. *Stroke, 15*, 497–503.

Brown, G. G., Baird, A. D., Shatz, M. W., & Bornstein, R. A. (1996). The effects of cerebral vascular disease on neuropsychological functioning. In I. Grant & K. M. Adams (Eds.), *Neuropsychological assessment of neuropsychiatric disorders* (2nd ed., pp. 342–378). New York: Oxford University Press.

Casey, J. E., Ferguson, G. G., Kimura, D., & Hachinski, V. C. (1989). Neuropsychological improvement versus practice effect following unilateral carotid endarterectomy in patients without stroke. *Journal of Clinical and Experimental Neuropsychology, 11*, 461–470.

Chillon, J., & Baumbach, G. L. (1997). Autoregulation of cerebral blood flow. In K. M. A. Welch, L. R. Caplan, D. J. Reis, B. K. Siesjö, & B. Weir (Eds.), *Primer on cerebrovascular diseases* (pp. 51–54). San Diego, CA: Academic Press.

Cohen, J. (1988). *Statistical power analysis for the behavioral sciences.* Hillsdale, NJ: Lawrence Erlbaum Associates.

Cushman, L., Brinkman, S. D., Ganji, S., & Jacobs, L. A. (1984). Neuropsychological impairment after carotid endarterectomy correlates with intraoperative ischemia. *Cortex, 20*, 403–412.

Dull, R. A., Brown, G. G., Adams, K. M., Shatz, M. W., Diaz, F. G., & Ausman, J. I. (1982). Preoperative neurobehavioral impairment in cerebral revascularization candidates. *Journal of Clinical Neuropsychology, 4*, 151–165.

Erzigkeit, H. (1992). *SKT: A short cognitive performance test for assessing memory and attention.* Weinheim: Belz Test GmbH.

Folstein, M. F., Folstein, S. E., & McHugh, P. R. (1975). Mini-Mental State. A practical method for grading the cognitive state of patients for the clinician. *Journal of Psychiatric Research, 12*, 189–198.

Frackowiak, R. (1997). PET CBF investigation of stroke. In K. M. A. Welch, L. R. Caplan, D. J. Reis, B. K. Siesjö, & B. Weir (Eds.), *Primer on cerebrovascular diseases* (pp. 636–640). San Diego, CA: Academic Press.

Fray, P. J., Robbins, T. W., Sahakian, B. J. (1996). Neuropsychiatric applications of CANTAB. *International Journal of Geriatric Psychiatry, 11*, 329–336.

Gaunt, M. E., Martin, P. J., Smith, J. L., Rimmer, T., Cherryman, G., Ratliff, D. A., Bell, B. F., & Naylor, A. R. (1994). Clinical relevance of intraoperative embolization detected by transcranial

Doppler ultrasonography during carotid endarterectomy: A prospective study of 100 patients. *British Journal of Surgery, 81,* 1435–1439.

Hamster, W., & Diener, H. C. (1984). Neuropsychological changes associated with stenoses or occlusions of the carotid arteries. *European Archives of Psychiatry and Neurological Sciences, 234,* 69–73.

Holloway, R. G., Witter, D. M., Mushlin, A. I., Lawton, K. B., McDermott, M. P., & Samsa, G. P. (1998). Carotid endarterectomy trends in the patterns and outcomes of care at academic medical centers, 1990 through 1995. *Archives of Neurology, 55,* 25–31.

Iddon, J. L., Sahakian, B. J., & Kirkpatrick, P. J. (1997). Uncomplicated carotid endarterectomy is not associated with neuropsychological impairment. *Pharmacology, Biochemistry and Behavior, 56,* 781–787.

Incalzi, R., Gemma, A., Landi, F., Pagano, F., Capparella, O., Snider, F., Manni, R., & Carbonin, P. (1997). Neuropsychological effects of carotid endarterectomy. *Journal of Clinical and Experimental Neuropsychology, 19,* 785–794.

Isaacs, B., & Kennie, A. T. (1973). The Set Test as an aid to the detection of dementia in old people. *British Journal of Psychiatry, 123,* 467–470.

Jacobs, J. W., Bernhard, M. R., Delgado, A., & Strain, J. J. (1977). Screening for organic mental syndromes in the medically ill. *Annals of Internal Medicine, 86,* 40–46.

Karp, H. R., Flanders, W. D., Shipp, C. C., Taylor, B., & Martin, D. (1998). Carotid endarterectomy among Medicare beneficiaries. *Stroke, 29,* 46–52.

Kügler, C. F. A., Vlajic, P., Funk, H., Raithel, D., & Platt, D. (1995). The event-related P300 potential approach to cognition functions of nondemented patients with cerebral and peripheral arteriosclerosis. *Journal of the American Geriatrics Society, 43,* 1228–1236.

Lind, C., Wimmer, A., Magomeschnigg, H., Havelec, L., Reichenauer, M., & Zeiler, K. (1993). Effects of carotid endarterectomy on various neuropsychological parameters: A neuropsychological longitudinal study. *Langenbecks Arch Chir, 378,* 345–352.

Loeb, C. (1988). Intellectual function, transient ischemic attacks, and vascular and multiinfarct dementia. In J. S. Meyer, H. Lechner, J. Marshall, & J. F. Toole (Eds.), *Vascular and multi-infarct dementia* (pp. 23–33). Mount Kisco, NY: Futura.

Mahoney, F. I., & Barthel, D. W. (1965). Functional evaluation: The Barthel Index. *Maryland State Medical Journal, 14,* 61–65.

Matchar, D. B., Oddone, E. Z., McCrory, D. C., Goldstein, L. B., Landsman, P. B., Samsa, G., Brook, R. H., Kamberg, C., Hilborne, L., Leape, L., Horner, R., & the Appropriateness Project Investigators of the Academic Medical Center Consortium. (1997). Influence of projected complication rates on estimated appropriate use rates for carotid endarterectomy. *Health Services Research, 32,* 325–342.

Meyer, J. S., Lotfi, J., Martinez, G., Caroselli, J. S., Mortel, K. F., & Thornby, J. I. (1990). Effects of medical and surgical treatment on cerebral perfusion and cognition in patients with chronic cerebral ischemia. *Surgical Neurology, 34,* 301–308.

Mononen, H., Lepojärvi, M., & Kallanranta, T. (1990). Early neuropsychological outcome after carotid endarterectomy. *European Neurology, 30,* 328–333.

North American Symptomatic Carotid Endarterectomy Trial Collaborators. (1991). Beneficial effect of carotid endarterectomy in symptomatic patients with high-grade carotid stenosis. *New England Journal of Medicine, 325,* 445–453.

Perry, J. R., Szalai, J. P., & Norris, J. W. (1997). Consensus against both endarterectomy and routine screening for asymptomatic carotid artery stenosis. *Archives of Neurology, 54,* 25–28.

Post-Stroke Rehabilitation Guideline Panel. (1995). *Post-stroke rehabilitation clinical practice guideline Number 16.* Rockville, MD: U.S. Department of Health and Human Services.

Raichle, M. E. (1997). Functional imaging in behavioral neurology and neuropsychology. In T. E. Feinberg & M. J. Farah (Eds.), *Behavioral neurology and neuropsychology* (pp. 83–100). New York: McGraw-Hill.

Robertson, J. T. (1997). Carotid endarterectomy. In K. M. A. Welch, L. R. Caplan, D. J. Reis, B. K. Siesjö, & B. Weir (Eds.), *Primer on cerebrovascular disease* (pp. 582–586). San Diego, CA: Academic Press.

Rowe, J. W., & Kahn, R. L. (1998). *Successful aging.* New York: Pantheon.

Sawrie, S. M., Chelune, G. J., Naugle, R. I., & Lüders, H. O. (1996). Empirical methods for assessing meaningful neuropsychological change following epilepsy surgery. *Journal of the International Neuropsychological Society, 2,* 556–564.

Sila, C. A. (1998). Neurologic complications of vascular surgery. *Neurologic Clinics of North America, 16,* 9–20.

Sirkka, A., Salenius, J.-P., Portin, R., & Nummenmaa, T. (1992). Quality of life and cognitive performance after carotid endartectomy during long-term follow-up. *Acta Neurologica Scandinavica, 85,* 58–62.

Sivan, A. B. (1992). *Benton Visual Retention Test* (5th ed.). San Antonio, TX: The Psychological Corporation.

Smith, J. L., Evans, D. H., Gaunt, M. E., London, N. J. M., Bell, P. R. F., & Naylor, A. R. (1998). Experience with transcranial Doppler monitoring reduces the incidence of particulate embolization during carotid endarterectomy. *British Journal of Surgery, 85,* 56–69.

Snowdon, D. A., Greiner, L. H., Mortimer, J. A., Riley, K. P., Greiner, P. A., & Markesbery, W. R. (1997). Brain infarction and the clinical expression of Alzheimer disease: The Nun Study. *Journal of the American Medical Association, 277,* 813–817.

Stukenborg, G. J. (1997). Comparison of carotid endarterectomy outcomes from randomized controlled trials and Medicare administrative databases. *Archives of Neurology, 54,* 826–832.

Tietgen, G. E. (1997). Transient focal neurologic events. In K. M. A. Welch, L. R. Caplan, D. J. Reis, B. K. Siesjö, & B. Weir (Eds.), *Primer on cerebrovascular disease* (pp. 358–361). San Diego, CA: Academic Press.

Uclés, P., Almarcegui, C., Lorente, S., Romero, F., & Marco, M. (1997). Evaluation of cerebral function after carotid endarterectomy. *Journal of Clinical Neurophysiology, 14,* 242–249.

Wolf, P. A. (1997). Epidemiology and risk factor management. In K. M. A. Welch, L. R. Caplan, D. J. Reis, B. K. Siesjö, & B. Weir (Eds.), *Primer on cerebrovascular disease* (pp. 751–756). San Diego, CA: Academic Press.

PART III

Cerebrovascular Disease and Neuropsychological Performance

CHAPTER THIRTEEN

Classification of Cerebrovascular Diseases

José Merino
Vladimir Hachinski
University of Western Ontario, London, Ontario, Canada

Among all neurological illnesses stroke is the most common cause of mortality, and it ranks third, after coronary heart disease (CHD) and cancer, as a leading cause of death in the United States. The American Heart Association estimated that in 1997 there were 500,000 new strokes and almost 4 million stroke survivors (American Heart Association, 1997). Broderick et al., (1998), taking into account the racial and ethnic heterogeneity in the United States, have estimated that 731,000 strokes occurred in 1996. Several community-based studies from Europe, Australia, Asia, and the United States have found a similar incidence (Sudlow & Warlow, 1997). In the United States the lifetime cost per person of first strokes (averaged for all stroke subtypes) is around $100,000, and the aggregate lifetime cost for first strokes in 1990 was $40.6 billion (Taylor et al., 1996). As the world population ages, the incidence of acute stroke and the prevalence of disabled stroke survivors is expected to increase. Greater understanding of the pathophysiology and etiology of stroke, as well as the development of preventive and therapeutic measures, should be a major focus of research in the years to come.

In this chapter we first discuss the classification of cerebrovascular disease and the characteristics of ischemic and hemorrhagic strokes. Given the diversity of events and pathologies that lead to ischemic infarction, the major pathogenic mechanisms for brain infarction are subsequently presented in greater detail. A third section of the chapter deals with the risk factors of stroke, with particular emphasis on the interaction between diseases of the heart and their effects on the brain. The chapter finishes with a discussion of strategies used to prevent and treat stroke.

CLASSIFICATION OF STROKE

The World Health Organization (WHO) defines a stroke as rapidly developing clinical signs of focal (or global) disturbance of cerebral function, with symptoms lasting 24 hr or longer or leading to death with no apparent cause other than of vascular origin (WHO MONICA Project, Principal Investigators, 1988). This classification is useful for epidemiological studies but excludes transient ischemic attacks (TIAs) and strokes that are a complication of other conditions. However, for the purposes of the present chapter the term *stroke* will be used to refer to any disturbance of nervous function that is related to alterations of cerebral flood flow, irrespective of duration or cause. Strokes can be divided into two major groups: ischemic and hemorrhagic. The former comprise approximately 70% of infarctions and the latter 30% (Foulkes, Wolf, Price, Mohr, & Hier, 1988) in Western societies.

Ischemic Infarction

Ischemic infarction results when cerebral blood flow fails to meet the oxygen requirements of the brain. With drops in perfusion pressure to around 20% of normal, cell death occurs. Areas where irreversible changes have occurred constitute the ischemic core of the infarct. Surrounding this area is a penumbra region where the reduction of blood flow is less severe and the viability of tissue is maintained for a limited period of time. Prompt restoration of blood flow to this penumbral region can lead to restoration of function and, as such, may be the focus of therapeutic interventions. If the arterial occlusion persists, preventing the reperfusion of the infarcted region, the ischemic infarct is referred to as a *bland* infarct. If reperfusion does take place, however, the damaged endothelium allows the diapedesis of red blood cells into the area of the infarction, giving rise to small foci of hemorrhage, predominantly at the borders of the bland infarct. In this case the ischemic infarct is said to have undergone *hemorrhagic transformation* (not to be confused with *hemorrhagic stroke;* see subsequent discussion). If the concentration of red blood cells is large enough, a high-density appearance can be detected on imaging studies (Sacco, Toni, & Mohr 1998). It is important to differentiate both types of ischemic stroke, because they have different prognostic and therapeutic implications.

Ischemic strokes can be classified on the basis of their temporal profile, location, pathologic pattern, or etiologic mechanism (Hachinski & Norris, 1985). Depending on their temporal profile, ischemic events may be divided into TIAs and completed strokes. A TIA is a short-lived (by definition, less than 24 hr but in most cases less than 15 to 20 minutes) episode of neurologic dysfunction that can be attributed to interruption of blood flow to a specific area of the brain. TIAs can involve any segment of the cerebral circulation. They are strong pre-

TABLE 13.1
Signs and Symptoms of Stroke

Location	Clinical Features
Either hemisphere	Contralateral hemiparesis
	Contralateral sensory loss
	Contralateral visual field defect
	Extinction to double simultaneous stimulation
	Dysarthria
	Abulia
Dominant hemisphere (cortical syndromes)	Aphasia
	Alexia
	Ideomotor apraxia
	Finger agnosia
	Acalculia
Nondominant hemisphere (cortical syndromes)	Anosognosia
	Motor neglect
	Constructional apraxia
	Amusia
	Aprosodia
Brain stem and cerebellum	Vertigo
	Ataxia
	Bilateral or unilateral motor and sensory deficits
	Diplopia
	Dysarthria
	Dysphagia

dictors of subsequent stroke. The risk of stroke after TIA ranges from 4% to 8% in the first month, to 12% in the first year, and 24% to 29% within 5 years. TIAs can precede atherothrombotic, embolic, and lacunar strokes. There is a greater risk of subsequent stroke when TIAs are hemispheric (i.e., when the brain hemispheres are not adequately irrigated, leading to the symptoms detailed in Table 13.1) rather than retinal (when only the blood flow to the retina is compromised, resulting in isolated visual abnormalities). The risk is highest for events of recent onset.

Strokes can occur anywhere in the central nervous system. The location determines the clinical characteristics and may aid in establishing the etiology. Table 13.1 lists some of the clinical features of stroke. Stenosis or occlusion of the carotid artery or its branches leads to infarctions of the frontal, parietal, or part of the temporal lobes. Infarcts can be limited to the cortex, the underlying white matter, or both. Centrecephalic infarcts involve the deep gray nuclei (the basal ganglia, supplied by the carotid system, and the thalamus, irrigated by the vertebrobasilar circulation). The cerebellum and the brain stem are affected with pathology involving the posterior circulation. Ischemic infarcts can be produced by several etiologic mechanisms, as detailed in Table 13.2. Large-artery

TABLE 13.2
Causes of Ischemic Strokes

Disease Group	Associated Disorders
Large-vessel disease	*Atherosclerosis*
	Nonatherosclerotic vasculopathies: Cervicocephalic arterial dissections, arterial trauma, radiation, moyamoya disease, Takayasu's disease, fibromuscular dysplasia, homocysteinuria, Fabry's disease, Marfan's syndrome, dolichoectasia, syphilis
Small-vessel disease	*Lipohyalinosis*
	Infectious vasculitides
	Necrotizing vasculitides: PAN, Wegener's granulomatosis, Churg–Strauss syndrome
	Collagen vascular disorders: Systemic lupus erythematosus, scleroderma, rheumathoid arthritis, Sjorgen's syndrome
	Systemic vasculitides: Behcet's disease, ulcerative colitis, sarcoidosis
	Other: CADASIL, cerebral amyloid angiopathy
Thromboembolism	*Artery-to-artery embolization:* Atherosclerosis.
	Cardiac disease: Coronary artery disease, atrial fibrillation, valvular heart disease, cardiomyopathy, structural heart abnormalities, sick sinus syndrome, endocarditis, atrial myxoma, cardiac surgery, catheterization.
Hematologic abnormalities	*Primary hypercoagulable states:* Deficencies of antithrombin III; proteins C and S, coagulation cascade factors (V, VII, VIII, IX, XII, and XIII), dysfibrinogenemia, antiphospholipid antibody syndrome
	Systemic hypercoagulable states: Malignancy, contraceptive pills, polycythemia, thrombocytopenia, leukemia, nephrotic syndrome, pregnancy, disseminated intravascular coagulation

Note. PAN = periodic acid-schiff; CADASIL = cerebral autosomal dominant arteriopathy with subcortical infarcts and leukoencephalopathy.

atherosclerosis is the presumed etiology when there is more than 50% stenosis of a major brain artery or a branch cortical artery. Large-artery atherosclerosis can produce ischemia by either leading to embolization of plaque fragments to intracranial vessels or by obstructing blood flow and thereby producing a low perfusion state. When the arterial occlusions are presumed to be due to emboli arising from the heart they are termed *cardioembolic*. Changes in the arteriolar wall (small-vessel disease) can produce small areas of infarction deep within the brain. Other, less frequent etiologies of infarction include vasculitic and hematological disorders. When two or more causes are identified, or when the evaluation has been incomplete or inconclusive, infarcts are categorized as of undetermined etiology, and when no cause is identified they are termed *cryptogenic*. Specifics about each of these subtypes are discussed in subsequent sections of this chapter.

Hemorrhagic Strokes

Hemorrhagic strokes develop when there is extravasation of blood into the surrounding tissues. On the basis of the site of primary hemorrhage they can be classified as epidural, subdural, subarachnoid (SAH), and intraparenchymal (ICH). The main mechanism for the production of ICHs is chronic hypertension leading to weakening of small penetrating vessels, as is described next. Other nonhypertensive causes include cerebral amyloid angiopathy (responsible for lobar hemorrhages in the elderly), vascular malformations, tumors, the use of thrombolytic agents (such as tissue plasminogen activator, streptokinase, and urokinase), anticoagulants and sympathomymetic agents (such as amphetamines and cocaine), and vasculitides (e.g., isolated central nervous system granulomatous angiitis, periarteritis nodosa, and systemic lupus erythematosus; Kase, 1995). SAH is due to rupture of an aneurysm (most often, a congenital saccular aneurysm located at branching points of the arteries of the circle of Willis) in 60% of cases. Arteriovenous malformations cause a small proportion of SAHs. In up to 30% of cases a source of bleeding is not identified despite an aggressive workup. Epidural and subdural hemorrhages are most often due to trauma. In the former a skull fracture can lead to rupture of superficial meningeal arteries and bleeding into the epidural space. In subdural hemorrhages, which are common in the elderly, there is tearing of, and bleeding from, bridging veins in the subdural space. Coagulation abnormalities predispose to all types of bleeds.

In several studies the incidence of the various types of stroke has been examined. Findings are sometimes divergent because of differences in the population studied, sampling errors, and use of different definitions and inclusion–exclusion criteria as well as advances in the technology that permit a more precise characterization of stroke subtype. Given that similar risk factors can lead to atherosclerosis of the cerebral and cardiovascular arteries and arterioles, it is common to find several putative causes for an infarct in an individual. It has been shown, for example, that recurrent strokes are often, but not always, due to the same mechanism as the initial one (Yamamoto & Bogousslavsky, 1998). Two recent large trials have looked at the incidence of stroke, among other things. The National Institute of Neurological Disorders and Stroke (NINDS) Stroke Data Bank (Foulkes et al., 1988) is a multicenter project that prospectively collects data on the clinical course and sequelae of stroke. The TOAST (Trial of Org 10172 in Acute Stroke Treatment) trial is a multicenter study (Adams et al., 1993) designed to assess the efficacy of the low molecular weight heparinoid Org 10172 in acute stroke. Strokes were classified into various subtypes on the basis of strict criteria at presentation and at 3 months. Patients with hemorrhage were excluded, as were those with very minor or devastating strokes (Adams et al., 1993). This may partly explain the differences in frequencies of stroke subtypes in both trials. The relative frequencies of the various etiologies of stroke are shown in Table 13.3.

TABLE 13.3
Stroke Subtypes According to NINDS Stroke Data Bank and TOAST Criteria

	NINDS Stroke Data Bank		TOAST	
Stroke Subtype	Total[a]	Percentage	Total[b]	Percentage
Infarct	1,273	73	479	100
Large artery	182	10	166	35
Stenosis/occlusion	113	6		
Artery–artery embolus	69	4		
Lacune	337	19	184	38
Cardioembolic	246	14	74	15
Cryptogenic	508	28	51	11
Hemorrhage	480	27		
Intracerebral	237	13		
Subarachnoid	243	13		
Other	52	3		

Note. These data are from Adams et al. (1993) and Foulkes et al. (1988).
NINDS = National Institute of Neurologic Disorders and Stroke; TOAST = Trail of Org 10172 in Acute Stroke Treatment.
[a]Out of 1,805.   [b]Out of 479.

PATHOPHYSIOLOGIC MECHANISMS OF STROKE

Large-Vessel Disease

Atherosclerosis is the most common pathology of the large vessels. It affects intra- and extracranial arteries. Atherosclerotic plaque is most commonly found at the origin of the common and internal carotid arteries extracranially and at the internal carotid siphon, the basilar artery and, less frequently, the middle and posterior cerebral arteries. It can manifest as large hemispheric, watershed, or vertebrobasilar strokes and is often associated with TIAs. The major risk factors associated with atherosclerosis are hypertension, diabetes, smoking, and hyperlipidemia. The presence of carotid atherosclerosis is a strong predictor of coronary artery disease (CAD).

Atherosclerotic plaque consists of a necrotic core composed of focal subendothelial deposits of lipids, cholesterol crystals, cellular debris, macrocyte-derived foam cells, and fibrin. This core is surrounded by a superficial fibrous cap of smooth-muscle cells, lymphocytes, and connective tissue (Schoen, 1994). Early atherosclerotic plaque is smooth, with an intact fibrous cap. When the plaque ruptures, either spontaneously or because of intraplaque hemorrhage, thrombogenic substances are exposed, and microemboli consisting of cholesterol crystals or atheromatous material are released into the bloodstream (Ogata, Masuda, & Yutani, 1990).

Thrombus formation, or enlargement of the atherosclerotic plaque, can lead to narrowing or occlusion of the parent vessel. When the process is gradual, collateral circulation develops, preventing the development of symptoms. Thrombotic occlusion is common in both carotid and vertebrobasilar circulations and can present as transient episodes or as cerebral infarction. Hemodynamic changes may act in concert with atherosclerotic mechanisms to produce brain infarction (Grubb, Derdeyn, & Fritsch, 1998). In the setting of moderate to severe atherosclerotic narrowing of an artery, small decreases in blood pressure (BP) can lead to ischemia of distal perfusion, or watershed, areas.

Artery-to-artery embolization is increasingly being recognized as a source of stroke. The mechanism can be inferred when a cortical syndrome develops but no cardioembolic sources are identified and the degree of carotid occlusion is less than 80%. It can also be suspected when angiographically proven occlusion of an intracranial vessel exists distal to the site of carotid stenosis (Garcia, Khang-Loon, & Pantoni, 1998). The most common source of artery-to-artery embolization is the carotid artery. With the advent of transesophageal echocardiography the proximal aorta has been recognized as an important source of emboli to the brain, particularly when the plaque is thick, ulcerated, or with superimposed thrombus (Jones & Donnan, 1995). Atherosclerosis of the large vessels can also lead to small-vessel occlusions, as is detailed in subsequent sections.

Carotid atherosclerosis can be asymptomatic. It may be detected by the presence of a cervical bruit without evidence of infarction on clinical or radiographic examination. Cervical or carotid bifurcation bruits are present in 4% to 5% of individuals over age 45. The incidence rate increases to 6% to 8% in individuals older than 75 (Wolf, Kannel, Sorlie, & McNamara, 1981). The annual stroke rate for asymptomatic patients with hemodynamically significant carotid artery stenosis ranges from 2% to 5% (Executive Committee for the Asymptomatic Carotid Atherosclerosis Study, 1995). The risk of stroke is dependent on the degree of stenosis (Norris, Zhu, Bornstein, & Chambers, 1991).

Other pathologic processes can affect large vessels, and they are sometimes responsible for strokes. These include fibromuscular dysplasia, aortic dissections, Takayasu's arteritis, moyamoya syndrome, Fabry's disease, and pseudoxanthoma elasticum.

Small-Vessel Disease

All small vessels are damaged by chronic disease. The hemodynamic effects of hypertension and the metabolic derangements of diabetes lead to endothelial injury and leakage of plasma components and hyaline deposition in the walls of arterioles (Schoen, 1994). In the brain this process is combined with atheromatous lipid deposition (lipohyalinosis). As a consequence, there is narrowing of the vessel lumen and weakening of the arteriolar wall, leading to the development of small aneurysms that are susceptible to rupture. This alteration is common in areas of the brain where lacunar infarctions and hypertensive hemorrhages occur: the caudate, putamen, thalamus, internal capsule, pons, and cerebellum (Garcia, Khang-Loon, & Pantoni, 1998).

Acute hypertensive changes damage small vessels in a process termed *fibrinoid necrosis,* which consists of concentric, lamellated thickening of the walls of arterioles due to deposition of a bright, eosinophilic, finely granular material in the tunica media accompanied by necrosis of the arteriolar walls. This widespread pathological change is responsible for the encephalopathy seen in malignant hypertension.

Atherosclerotic disease of the large vessels can cause occlusion of the origin of small perforators of the brain, leading to clinical syndromes typical of small-vessel disease. This is particularly common in the vertebrobasilar circulation.

C. Miller Fisher (1965, 1969) described a series of classical clinical lacunar syndromes that he attributed to single-penetrating arteriolar occlusions caused by local lipohyalinosis related to long-standing hypertension. In Table 13.4 the four classical *lacunar syndromes* are described. The term is currently used to refer to deep-lying infarcts that are due to small artery occlusions and that appear on computer tomography (CT) or magnetic resonance imaging (MRI) scans as a small (<1.5 cm) area limited to the territory of a deep perforator (Bogousslavsky, 1992). However, several pathologic processes—and not just lipohyalinosis—can give rise to the classical lacunar syndromes. Lipohyalinosis affects the smallest vessels (40–200 micrometers in diameter), whereas atherosclerosis and embolism can give rise to occlusion of vessels up to 850 micrometers. The atherosclerotic lesions can be at the origin of the small vessels or at the wall of a larger vessel, occluding the opening of the penetrator. The area of the infarct depends on the size of the occluded vessel. Embolism can be presumed when an intact healthy artery is detected at autopsy, the presumption being that the clot has

TABLE 13.4
Lacunar Syndromes

Lacunar Syndrome	Location of Lesion	Clinical Features
Pure motor hemiparesis	Internal capsule, corona radiata, cerebral peduncule, pons	Contralateral face, arm, and leg weakness
Pure sensory stroke	Thalamus, corona radiata	Contralateral numbness of face, arm, and leg
Dysarthria (clumsy-hand syndrome)	Pons, internal capsule	Severe dysarthria, mild hand weakness and clumsiness, facial weakness and dysphagia
Ataxic hemiparesis	Upper pons, internal capsule	Pure motor hemiparesis and ataxia

lysed (C. M. Fisher, 1991). There is controversy as to which of these mechanisms is most frequently responsible for clinically relevant lacunes (C. M. Fisher, 1991; Longstreth et al., 1998).

White matter ischemic disease leading to dementia has been associated with small-vessel pathology. It is associated with hypodensities or hyperintensities of the subcortical and periventricular white matter on CT and MRI scans, respectively. The process, known as *leuko-araiosis* (Hachinski, Potter, & Merskey, 1986), is associated with advanced age and vascular risk factors (history of stroke, hypertension and, to a lesser degree, diabetes, cardiac disease, and increased fibrinogen levels). Small-vessel arteriolosclerosis and pathologic changes of the cerebral white matter that consist mainly of loss of myelin and axons with astrocytic gliosis without necrosis or cavitation are found (Brun & Englund, 1986).

Certain arteriolopathies are not related to hypertension (van Gijn, 1998). They may lead to ischemia, demyelination, and dementia. In cerebral amyloid angiopathy there is deposition of amyloid material in the walls of subcortical arterioles. The vessel lumen is thus narrowed, and the wall becomes weak and susceptible to rupture. It is the major source of lobar hemorrages in the elderly. Cerebral autosomal dominant arteriopathy with subcortical infarcts and leuko-encephalopathy (CADASIL) is a recently described hereditary disorder associated with a gene abnormality (Notch-3 gene) on chromosome 19 (Joutel et al., 1997). In this condition arterioles have periodic acid-schiff (PAS) positive granular material within the media expanding into the adventitia (Rango et al., 1995).

Embolic Disease

Emboli to the brain can come from the heart or from the arteries. Causes and mechanisms of embolus formation and release have been discussed in previous sections. Most common embolic materials consist of mural thrombi or platelet aggregates, although calcium particles, cholesterol crystals, air, and fat can embolize to the brain. Embolic material tends to lodge at arterial or arteriolar bifurcations, and the size of the embolic particle determines the site where initial lodging takes place. However, emboli material tends to alter its shape and to fracture. Smaller fragments thus continue to travel farther down the arterial tree. Emboli are evanescent; the proportion found in angiograms drops from >75% in angiograms done within 8 hr of event to 40% after 48 hr.

Although the clinical differentiation of embolic and nonembolic ischemic infarction is difficult and at times not possible, some features are suggestive, but not pathognomonic, of an embolic mechanism (Martin & Bogousslavsky, 1995). These include a nonprogressive, acute onset of deficits; a diminished level of consciousness; the presence of hemianopia without hemiparesis or sensory loss; Wernicke's aphasia; or ideomotor apraxia. Emboli can go anywhere in the cerebral circulation, with a predilection for the middle cerebral artery (MCA). When infarcts involve the territories of the posterior division of the MCA, the anterior cerebral artery (ACA), the cerebellum, or multiple vessels, they are likely to be embolic. Embolic infarctions have been associated with a greater tendency to become hemorrhagic because of reperfusion of the ischemic area secondary to lysis or fragmentation of the embolus. However, the presence or absence of any of these features does not preclude the need for a thorough evaluation of every stroke patient to determine the possible etiology of the infarction.

RISK FACTORS FOR STROKE

Epidemiologic studies have identified several risk factors associated with stroke. Stroke and CAD share many risk factors, although their relative importance in each condition may be different. In addition, heart disease itself is a major risk factor for stroke. Risk factors can be categorized into those that are modifiable and those that are not (Sacco, 1997). In Table 13.5 these risk factors are enumerated. Modifiable risk factors are potential targets for primary prevention of stroke. Those that are not modifiable act as markers of risk.

Nonmodifiable Stroke Risk Factors

Age

Age is the single most important risk factor for stroke. For each decade over 55 years of age, the stroke rate doubles in men and women (Wolf & D'Agostino, 1988). The incidence of stroke is 1 to 2/1,000 in the 45-to-54–year group; it increases to 10/1,000 in people aged 65 to 74 and to 20/1,000 in people 75 to 84 years old.

Heredity

Heredity plays a role in the incidence of stroke. There is an increased risk in first-degree relatives even after adjusting for other risk factors. This may be due

TABLE 13.5
Major Risk Factors for Stroke

Modifiable Risk Factors	Nonmodifiable Risk Factors
Age	Hypertension
Heredity	Heart disease
Race	Diabetes
	Lipid abnormalities
	Smoking
	Alcohol
	Obesity

to a genetic tendency toward stroke, a genetic predisposition toward other risk factors (such as diabetes or hypertension), or a common familial exposure to risks. Men and women both have this increased risk (Kiely, Wolf, Cupples, Beiser, & Myers, 1993).

Race–Ethnicity

Some racial or ethnic groups have a higher susceptibility to stroke, although this may be partly explained by confounding factors other than race (such as socioeconomic, lifestyle, and nutritional differences). In the United States, African Americans have been found to have a disproportionately higher incidence of stroke (Sacco et al., 1997). The reasons for this are not clear, and it may be only partly explained by the higher prevalence of hypertension and diabetes in this group. Hispanics have also been found to have an increased incidence of stroke, and this may be partly explained by an increased prevalence of diabetes and hypercholesterolemia (Sacco et al., 1997). Hispanics have also been found to have an increased incidence of ICH compared to Caucasians (Frey, Jahnke, & Bulfinch, 1998). Studies conducted in Asia have shown high stroke incidence rates (He, Klang, Wu, & Whelton, 1995; Heiss et al., 1991). The pathologic changes in the extra- and intracranial vasculature are different among racial groups. African Americans, Asians, and Hispanics have a higher rate of hemorrhage than Caucasians do (Kase, Mohr, & Caplan, 1998). The influence of race decreases with increasing age (Otten, Teutsch, Williamson, & Marks, 1990).

Modifiable Risk Factors

Hypertension

Hypertension is the single most important modifiable risk factor for stroke and ICH. It predisposes individuals to atherothrombotic stroke and to heart disease, which in turn promotes cardiogenic stroke. In the Framingham Heart Study men and women with definite hypertension had a risk of 3.1 and 2.9, respectively, compared to individuals who had normal BP levels (Wolf & D'Agostino, 1998). The incidence of nonembolic stroke increases with increasing severity of hypertension in men and women and in all age categories from 45 to 84 years. However, even individuals with borderline hypertension have a 50% increased stroke risk. Systolic BP (SBP) and diastolic BP elevations have been associated with increased stroke risk (Prospective Studies Collaboration, 1995). The impact of hypertension, however, may decrease with age. In a population-based study conducted in Rochester, Minnesota, the odds ratio of stroke in hypertensives was 4 at age 50 but only 1 in 90-year-olds (Whisnant, 1996).

Treatment of hypertension has led to a decrease in the incidence of stroke. In a composite analysis of 17 treatment trials involving 48,000 patients there was a 38% reduction in the incidence of all types of stroke; nonfatal strokes decreased by 40% (Herbert, Moser, Mayer, & Glynn, 1993). The importance of treating mild hypertension became evident in the Framingham Heart Study, in which it was found that 30% of strokes occurred in individuals with SBP in the range of 140 to 159 mmHg and only 36% of strokes in men and 41% of strokes in women occurred in individuals with SBP greater than 160 mmHg (Wolf, 1998).

Heart Disease

Heart disease is common in patients with stroke. Patients with stroke are at high risk of death from CAD. In a subsequent section of this chapter we deal with the relationship of heart and stroke, and risk factors are discussed there.

Diabetes Mellitus

The risk of stroke in diabetics is about four times that found in normal individuals. Atherosclerosis accounts for 80% of mortality in diabetic patients (Garber, Vinik, & Crespin, 1992). In the Honolulu Heart Program, patients with diabetes mellitus had a stroke rate of 62.3/1,000 patients, whereas nondiabetics had a rate of 32.7/1,000 after 12 years of follow-up. The relative risk of stroke was 2 (Abbot, Donahue, MacMahon, Reed, & Yano, 1987). In the Framingham Study the adjusted relative risk of atherosclerotic brain infarction was more than doubled in men and women with diabetes mellitus compared to those without it (Kannel & McGee, 1979). Similarly, in the Third National Heart and Nutrition Examination Survey, diabetes was associated with an increased risk of stroke or myocardial infarction, whereas normoglycemia was not, after adjusting for differences in age, gender, race, education, presence of hypertension, cholesterol level, and history of smoking (Qureshi, Giles, & Croft, 1998).

Lipids

Abnormalities of serum lipids, triglycerides, cholesterol, low-density lipoproteins (LDL), and high density lipoproteins (HDL) are risk factors for the development of atherosclerosis (Expert Panel on Detection, Evaluation, and Treatment of High Blood Cholesterol in Adults, 1993; Qizilbash, Duffy, Warlos, & Mann, 1992). Hypercholesterolemia has been clearly identified as a risk factor for myocardial infarction. However, such a clear and direct link has not been found for stroke (Iso, Jacobs, Wentworth, Neaton, & Cohen, 1989). The role of lipids in stroke has been analyzed from several points of view: epidemiologic, structural, and therapeutic.

After 36 years, follow-up data from the Framingham Heart Study failed to show a clear relationship between levels of total cholesterol or LDL cholesterol and stroke, and no protective effect of HDL was seen (Wolf, 1998). Other studies, however, have shown different results. In the Honolulu Heart Study the level of cholesterol was correlated with later strokes (Benfante et al., 1994). In the Multiple Risk Factor Intervention Trial, the incidence of stroke death was higher in individuals who had been found to have a high cholesterol level 6 years earlier

(Iso et al., 1989). In a case-controlled study of 90 consecutive patients with stroke or TIA of atherothrombotic origin who were compared with community-matched controls, high levels of LDL cholesterol and triglycerides were found to be independent risk factors for stroke (Hachinski et al., 1996).

A positive correlation exists between total cholesterol and LDL cholesterol and the formation of extracranial carotid atherosclerosis detected by ultrasonography of the vessels in the neck (Heiss et al., 1991). LDL cholesterol and total serum cholesterol appear to increase the intimal–medial thickness of the carotid artery wall and to promote atheroma formation, whereas HDL cholesterol seems to have a protective effect (O'Leary et al., 1996). At the opposite end of the spectrum, low serum cholesterol (less than 160 mg/dL) has been associated with an increased incidence of ICH (Segal, Eggleston-Sexton, Beiser, & Greenberg, 1999).

Treatment with new cholesterol-lowering drugs (HMG-CoA reductase inhibitors or statins) has shown significant reductions in stroke incidence and cardiovascular mortality that accompany reductions in cholesterol levels (Herbert, Gaziano, Chan, & Hennecens, 1997).

Smoking

Smoking increases the relative risk of stroke nearly two times (1.5–2.9 times) with a dose–response relationship (Shinton & Beevers, 1989). The risk of stroke is related to the number of cigarettes smoked. It is twofold in heavy smokers (40 cigarettes per day) compared to people who smoke fewer than 10 a day. Both the Framingham Study (Wolf, D'Agostino, Kannel, Bonita, & Belanger, 1988), and the Nurse's Health Study (Kawachi et al., 1993) showed that cessation of smoking led to a prompt reduction in stroke risk. There was a major risk reduction within 2 to 4 years. The effect of smoking on the risk of stroke decreases with age. Smoking is also a risk factor for hemorrhagic stroke. A study of Hawaiian–Japanese male smokers revealed that smoking was an independent risk factor that increased the risk of hemorrhage by 2.5 (Abbot, Yin, Reed, & Yano, 1986).

Alcohol

Alcohol has dose-dependent effects on stroke (Camargo, 1989). Moderate alcohol consumption (defined as <60 g of ethanol a day) decreases stroke risk, whereas excessive consumption increases risk up to 4 times (Gorelick, 1989). There is a linear association between moderate alcohol consumption and risk of hemorrhagic stroke (Camargo, 1989).

Obesity

Obesity has also been linked to stroke by its effects on BP, glucose levels, and atherogenic lipids. However, independent of these risks obesity, particularly abdominal, has been found to be a risk factor in "young men and older women" (Wolf, 1998).

Other

Other potential risk factors for stroke are homocysteinemia, acute infection, and high levels of fibrinogen. An area of important research is the relationship between the presence of antiphospholipid antibodies and stroke (Tanne, Triplett, & Levine, 1998).

THE HEART AND STROKE

A significant relationship exists, in health and disease, between the heart and the brain, and with the use of increasingly sophisticated imaging technology it has become evident that the heart is a much more important cause of stroke than was previously thought. In the Framingham Heart Study it was found that only 13.6% of the patients with stroke were free of cardiac disease, whereas 80% had hypertension, 33% had CAD, 14% had chronic heart failure, and 15% had atrial fibrillation (Wolf, 1998). Coronary and cerebrovascular diseases share the same risk factors, and they often coexist. Albers et al. (1994), for example, showed that 15% to 35% of stroke patients with significant stenosis of the extracranial vasculature and 50% of patients with lacunes also had a cardiac source of embolism. Heart disease has been identified as the major cause of cryptogenic stroke in the young (Bevan, Sharma, & Bradley, 1990).

Atrial fibrillation is the most powerful and treatable cardiac precursor of stroke. In the Framingham Study, nonvalvular atrial fibrillation was associated with a three- to fivefold increase in the risk of stroke (Wolf, Abbot, & Kannel, 1987). In contrast to hypertension, CAD, and cardiac failure, the impact of atrial fibrillation as a risk factor for stroke increased with age. In individuals aged 80 to 89 it was associated with 36.2% of strokes. When atrial fibrillation was associated with rheumatic heart disease it had an 18-fold rise in stroke incidence (Wolf, Abbot, & Kannel, 1991).

In atrial fibrillation multiple areas of the atria depolarize independently, bombarding the atrioventricular (AV) node with up to 300 discharges every minute. Depending on the refractoriness of the node, the ventricular response is irregular. The atrial contractions are hemodynamically ineffective, leading to atrial stasis of blood with an increased potential for the formation of intracavitary thrombi. (In contrast, in atrial flutter, which is due to a re-entrant circuit, the heart rate is rapid but regular, and the hemodynamic consequences are less severe.) Atrial fibrillation exists in two forms—chronic and paroxysmal—and may be associated with other cardiac abnormalities. When it occurs in isolation (lone atrial fibrillation) in the young it is considered to constitute a low risk for stroke (Bogousslavsky, Adnet-Bonte, Regli, Van Melle, & Kappenberger, 1990). When it is accompanied by other cardiac abnormalities, such as hypertension and heart failure, the risk of stroke is higher (Whisnant, Wiebers, O'Fallon,

Sicks, & Frye, 1996). Shiveley, Gelgand, and Crawford (1996) showed that the risk is highest when atrial fibrillation is associated with left ventricular dilatation and with a decreased left atrial ejection fraction with atrial dilatation.

Atrial fibrillation increases the risk of stroke by promoting intracavitary blood stasis and clot formation (Shiveley, Gelgand, & Crawford, 1996). Sohara, Amitani, Kuroze, and Miyahara (1997) showed that atrial fibrillation may enhance platelet aggregation. There is controversy regarding when this effect is greatest. Some support the idea that it occurs 12 hr after the onset of the arrhythmia, theoretically making paroxysmal, rather than chronic, atrial fibrillation a more potent cardioembolic risk factor. However, epidemiological studies favor a higher risk in the chronic arrhythmia (Oppenheimer & Lima, 1998). It may be that the coagulation abnormalities in atrial fibrillation are enhanced by structural abnormalities, which are present more commonly in chronic cases. Atrial fibrillation is associated with more severe strokes, so it is postulated that the decrease in cardiac output leads to compromise of viable tissue in the penumbra of the stroke (Oppenheimer & Lima, 1998).

The embolic potential of other cardiac arrhythmias, including atrial flutter, has not yet been fully investigated. However cardiac output changes seen with other arrhythmias may lead to global ischemic encephalopathy or watershed infarction (Oppenheimer & Lima, 1998).

CHD can predispose to stroke. In the 2 weeks following an acute myocardial infarction (AMI), stroke occurs in 0.7% to 4.7% of patients (Loh et al., 1997). In a population-based model of risk factors for stroke, the odds ratio for stroke in patients with AMI was 1.9 (Whisnant, 1996). Stroke is most common following anterior wall myocardial infarction (seen in 2%–6% of cases; Wolf, 1998). A large myocardial infarction, a greater rise in the cardiac enzymes, apical or anterior infarction, low cardiac output state, left ventricular failure, atrial fibrillation, atrial flutter, older age, and a history of stroke have been identified as risk factors for systemic and cerebral embolism (Hess, D'Cruz, Adams, & Nichols, 1993).

Several mechanisms can explain the increased risk of stroke following AMI. Similar risk factors can lead to both conditions, and CHD is a marker for more severe intra- and extracranial atherosclerosis. Secondary pump failure resulting from arrhythmias can lead to hypoperfusion of watershed areas, and hypokinesis of the myocardial wall predisposes to embolus formation. Therapy for AMI can lead to brain hemorrhages (Cheung, 1997).

Valvular heart disease can lead to stroke through hemodynamic disturbances as well as by predisposing to embolus formation and infective endocarditis. Mitral valve disease (stenosis, regurgitation, or calcification) is most frequently associated with stroke. The most common valvular cause of thromboembolism is mitral valve stenosis with or without regurgitation that leads to progressive left atrial dilatation and enlargement of the atrial appendage, which acts as a nidus for thrombus formation due to blood stasis. It also predisposes to atrial fibrillation. The thromboembolic risk is related to the stasis of blood within the left atrium, low cardiac output, degree of left atrial enlargement, coexisting atrial fibrillation, and the patient's age (Cheung, 1997).

In contrast, mitral regurgitation is only rarely associated with intra-atrial thrombus formation despite the fact that there is also atrial dilatation and enlargement of the atrial appendage. This is because the regurgitating jet of blood into the atria prevents blood stasis (Oppenheimer & Lima, 1998). The risk of stroke actually increases after surgical repair of the valve when blood flow normalizes, but the atrium remains enlarged.

In the Framingham Study mitral annulus calcification was associated with a doubled rate of stroke after adjusting for traditional risk factors for stroke. If combined with atrial fibrillation the risk was increased further (Benjamin et al., 1992).

Atrial fibrillation and mitral valve disease both lead to left atrial enlargement, which is itself associated with an increased risk of stroke. In the Framingham Study it was found that the adjusted risk of stroke was doubled in men and women for every 10-mm increase of left atrial size. This risk persisted in men after multivariate adjustment (relative risk 2.4; Benjamin et al., 1992).

Structural heart abnormalities are associated with stroke, particularly in the young. With the advent of transesophageal echocardiography, patent foramen ovale (PFO) and atrial septal aneurysm (ASA) are increasingly detected. A significant relationship between the presence of a PFO and stroke in young people has been found in case controlled (Di Tullio, Sacco, Gopal, Mohr, & Homma, 1992; Lechat et al., 1988) and large prospective studies. Cabanes et al. (1993) found that ASA and PFO, but not mitral valve prolapse, were significantly associated with the diagnosis of cryptogenic stroke in patients less than 55 years old.

Endocarditis has been associated with ischemic and hemorrhagic stroke. Three forms of endocarditis predispose to embolism: infectious; marantic, or nonbacterial thrombotic endocarditis; and Libman–Sachs endocarditis (in systemic lupus erythematosus).

In infectious endocarditis there is colonization of an abnormal native valve or of a valvular prosthesis by an infectious agent that may be bacterial, fungal, or viral. The valvular vegetations may embolize to the brain, resulting in occlusion of a vessel and the development of a focal ischemic infarct or the formation of a mycotic aneurysm at the bifurcation of small distal branches. The aneurysm may rupture, leading to a hemorrhage. When several microemboli travel to the brain, an encephalopathy may develop secondary to multiple small infarcts (Oppenheimer, 1998). Neurological complications develop in 20% to 40% of patients with infective endocarditis, and they are the presenting feature in 16% to 23% of affected patients (Tunkel & Kaye, 1993). Neurologic complications usually present within 3 days of diagnosis and onset of antibiotic treatment (Davenport & Hart, 1990).

Nonbacterial thrombotic endocarditis occurs in debilitated patients, usually in the terminal stages of AIDS or cancer. It is due to a hypercoagulable state complicated by dehydration, metabolic abnormalities, and inactivity. Vegetations consist of platelet–fibrin thrombus on native valves (Oppenheimer, 1998). It most commonly presents as a diffuse encephalopathy and, rarely, as hemorrhage (Graus, Rogers, & Posner, 1985)

PREVENTION AND TREATMENT OF STROKE

Exciting new developments are taking place in the field of stroke therapeutics. The results of the NINDS rt-PA Stroke Study (The National Institute of Neurological Disorders and Stroke rt-PA Stroke Study Group, 1995) showed that certain types of stroke could be treated when intervention was started, shortly after the onset of symptoms. Although the treatment is not a panacea, it has increased public awareness of the importance of treating stroke as a "brain attack." Several new agents are being developed, tested, and marketed for the acute management of stroke. Among these are several thrombolytics (intravenous and intra-arterial) and neuroprotective agents (M. Fisher & Bogousslavsky, 1998). Despite these advances, the best treatment for stroke, however, is still prevention. Primary prevention—that is, prevention of a new stroke—relies on identification and management of risk factors. Promotion of an active lifestyle; a balanced diet; avoidance of tobacco products; and the control of hypertension, diabetes, and hypercholesterolemia, as well as the judicious use of anticoagulants in heart disease, have led to reduced incidence of cardiovascular and cerebrovascular disease (Bronner, Kanter, & Manson, 1995). The prevention of recurrences in patients who have had strokes is termed *secondary prevention*. The value of antiplatelet agents, anticoagulants, and carotid endarterectomy has been well established in large clinical trials (Barnett, Eliasziw, & Meldrum, 1995). The choice of preventive measures to be used depends on the precise identification of the mechanism and etiology of stroke and the delineation of coexisting risk factors.

REFERENCES

Abbot, R. D., Donahue, R. P., MacMahon, S. W., Reed, D. M., & Yano, K. (1987). Diabetes and the risk of stroke: The Honolulu Heart Program. *Journal of the American Medical Association, 257,* 949–952.

Abbot, R. D., Yin, Y., Reed, D. H., & Yano, K. (1986). Risk of stroke in male cigarette smokers. *New England Journal of Medicine, 315,* 717–720.

Adams, H. J., Bendixen, B. H., Kappelle, L. J., Biller, J., Love, B. B., Gordon, D. L., & Marsh, E. E. III. (1993). Classification of subtype of acute ischemic stroke: Definitions for use in a multicenter clinical trial. *Stroke, 24,* 35–41.

Albers, G. W., Comess, K. A., DeRook, F. A., Bracci, P., Atwood, J. E., Bolger, A., & Hotson, J. (1994). Transesophageal echocardiographic findings in stroke subtypes. *Stroke, 25,* 23–28.

American Heart Association. (1997). *Heart and stroke facts and statistics: 1997 statistical supplement.* Dallas, TX: Author.

Barnett, H. J. M., Eliasziw, M., & Meldrum, H. E. (1995). Drugs and surgery in the prevention of ischemic stroke. *New England Journal of Medicine, 332,* 238–248.

Benfante, R., Yano, K., Hwang, L. J., Curb, J. D., Kagan, A., & Ross, W. (1994). Elevated serum cholesterol is a risk factor for both coronary heart disease and thromboembolic stroke in Hawaiian Japanese men. *Stroke, 25,* 814–820.

Benjamin, E. J., Plehn, J. F., D'Agostino, R. B., Belanger, A. J., Comai, K., Fuller, D. L., Wolf, P. A., & Levy, D. (1992). Mitral annular calcification and the risk of stroke in an elderly cohort. *New England Journal of Medicine, 327,* 374–379.

Bevan, H., Sharma, K., & Bradley, W. (1990). Stroke in young adults. *Stroke, 21,* 382–386.

Bogousslavsky, J. (1992). The plurality of subcortical infarction. *Stroke, 23,* 629–631.

Bogousslavsky, J., Adnet-Bonet, C., Regli, F., Van Melle, G., & Kappenberger, L. (1990). Lone atrial fibrillation and stroke. *Acta Neurologica Scandinavica, 82,* 143–146.

Broderick, J., Brott, T., Kohtari, R., Miller, R., Khoury, J., Pancioli, A., Gebel, J., Mills, D., Minneci, L., & Shukla, R. (1998). The Greater Cincinnati/Northern Kentucky Stroke Study: Preliminary first-ever and total incidence rates of stroke among Blacks. *Stroke, 29,* 415–421.

Bronner, L. L., Kanter, D. S., & Manson, J. E. (1995). Primary prevention of stroke. *New England Journal of Medicine, 333,* 1392–1400.

Brown, R. D., Whisnant, J. P., Sicks, R. D., O'Fallon, W. M., & Wiebers, D. O. (1996). Stroke incidence, prevalence and survival: Secular trends in Rochester, Minnesota, through 1989. *Stroke, 27,* 373–380.

Cabanes, L., Mas, J. L., Cohen, A., Amarenco, P., Cabanes, P. A., Oubary, P., Chedru, F., Guerin, F., Bousser, M. G., & de Recondo, J. (1993). Atrial septal aneurysm and patent foramen ovale as a risk factor for cryptogenic stroke in patients less than 55 years of age: A study using transesophageal echocardiography. *Stroke, 24,* 1865–1873.

Camargo C. A., Jr. (1989). Moderate alcohol consumption and stroke: The epidemiologic evidence. *Stroke, 20,* 1611–1626.

Cheung, R. T. F. (1997). Neurological complications of heart disease. *Baillières Clinical Neurology, 6,* 337–355.

Davenport, J., & Hart, R. G. (1990). Prosthetic valve endocarditis 1976–1987: Antibiotics, anticoagulation and stroke. *Stroke, 21,* 993–999.

Di Tullio, M., Sacco, R. L., Gopal, A., Mohr, J. P., & Homma, S. (1992). Patent foramen ovale as a risk factor for cryptogenic stroke. *Annals of Internal Medicine, 117,* 461–465.

Executive Committee for the Asymptomatic Carotid Atherosclerosis Study. (1995). Endarterectomy for asymptomatic carotid artery stenosis. *Journal of the American Medical Association, 273,* 1421–1428.

Expert Panel on Detection, Evaluation, and Treatment of High Blood Cholesterol in Adults. (1993). Summary of the second report of the National Cholesterol Education Program (NCEP) Adult Treatment Panel II report. *Journal of the American Medical Association, 269,* 3015–3023.

Fisher, C. M. (1965). Lacunes: Small, deep cerebral infarcts. *Neurology, 15,* 774–784.

Fisher, C. M. (1969). The arterial lesions underlying lacunes. *Acta Neuropathologica, 12,* 1–15.

Fisher, C. M. (1991). Lacunar infarcts—A review. *Cerebrovascular Diseases, 1,* 311–320.

Fisher, M., & Bogousslavsky, J. (1998). Further evolution toward effective therapy for acute ischemic stroke. *Journal of the American Medical Association, 279,* 1298–1303.

Foulkes, M. A., Wolf, P. A., Price, T. R., Mohr, J. P., & Hier, D. B. (1988). The Stroke Data Bank: Design, methods, and baseline characteristics. *Stroke, 19,* 547–554.

Frey, J. L., Jahnke, H. K., & Bulfinch, E. W. (1998). Differences in stroke between White, Hispanic, and Native American patients: The Barrow Neurological Institue Stroke Data Base. *Stroke, 29,* 29–33.

Garber, A. J., Vinik, A. I., & Crespin, S. R. (1992). Detection and management of lipid disorders in diabetic patients. *Diabetes Care, 15,* 1068–1074.

Garcia, J. H., Khang-Loon, H., & Pantoni, L. (1998). Pathology. In H. J. M. Barnett, J. P. Mohr, B. M.

Stein, & F. M. Yatsu (Eds.), *Stroke: Pathophysiology, diagnosis, and management* (3rd ed., pp. 139–158). Philadelphia: Churchill Livingstone.

Gorelick, P. B. (1989). The status of alcohol as a risk factor for stroke. *Stroke, 20,* 1607–1626.

Graus, F., Rogers, L. R., & Posner, J. B. (1985). Cerebrovascular complications in patients with cancer. *Medicine, 64,* 16–35.

Grubb, R. L., Derdeyn, C. P., & Fritsch, S. M. (1998). Importance of hemodynamic factors in the prognosis of symptomatic carotid occlusion. *Journal of the American Medical Association, 280,* 1055–1060.

Hachinski, V., Graffagnio, C., Bealdry, M., Bernier, G., Buck, C., Donner, A., Spence, J. D., Doig, G., & Wolfe, B. M. J. (1996). Lipids and stroke: A paradox resolved. *Archives of Neurology, 3,* 303–308.

Hachinski, V., & Norris, J. W. (1985). *The acute stroke.* Philadelphia: Davis.

Hachinski, V. C., Potter, P., & Merskey, H. (1986). Leuko-araiosis: An ancient term for a new problem. *Canadian Journal of Neurological Sciences, 13,* 533–534.

He, J., Klang, M. J., Wu, Z., & Whelton, P. K. (1995). Stroke in the People's Republic of China, I. Geographic variations in incidence and risk factors. *Stroke, 26,* 2222–2227.

Heiss, G., Sharrett, A. R., Barnes, R., Chambless, L. E., Szklo, M., & Alzola, C. (1991). Carotid atherosclerosis measured by B-mode ultrasound in populations: Association with cardiovascular risk factors in the ARIC study. *American Journal of Epidemiology, 134,* 250–256.

Herbert, P. R., Gazanio, M., Chan, K. S., & Hennecens, C. H. (1997). Cholesterol lowering with statin drugs, risk of stroke and total mortality. *Journal of the American Medical Association, 278,* 313–321.

Herbert, P. R., Moser, M., Mayer, J., & Glynn, R. J. (1993). Recent evidence of drug therapy of mild to moderate hypertension and decreased risk of coronary heart disease. *Archives of Internal Medicine, 153,* 578–581.

Hess, D. C., D'Cruz, I. A., Adams, R. J., & Nichols, F. T. III. (1993). Coronary artery disease, myocardial infarction, and brain embolism. *Neurologic Clinics, 11,* 399–417.

Iso, H., Jacobs, D. R. Jr., Wentworth, D., Neaton, J. D., & Cohen, J. D. (1989). Serum cholesterol levels and six year mortality from stroke in 350,977 men screened for the Multiple Risk Factor Intervention Trial. *New England Journal of Medicine, 320,* 904–910.

Jones, E., & Donnan, G. (1995). The proximal aorta: A source of stroke. *Baillières Clinical Neurology, 4,* 207–220.

Joutel, A., Vahedi, K., Corpechot, C., Troesch, A., Chabriat, H., Vayssiere, C., Cruaud, C., Maciazek, J., Weissenbach, J., Bousser, M. G., Bach, J. F., & Tournier-Lasserve, E. (1997). Strong clustering and stereotyped nature of Notch3 mutations in CADASIL patients. *The Lancet, 350,* 1511–1515.

Kannel, W. B., & McGee, D. L. (1979). Diabetes and cardiovascular disease: The Framingham Study. *Journal of the American Medical Association, 241,* 2035–2038.

Kase, C. S. (1995). Intracerebral hemorrhage. *Baillière's Clinical Neurology, 4,* 247–278.

Kase, C. S., Mohr, J. P., & Caplan, L. R. (1998). Intracerebral hemorrhage. In H. J. M. Barnett, J. P. Mohr, B. M. Stein, & F. M. Yatsu (Eds.), *Stroke: Pathophysiology, diagnosis, and management* (3rd ed., pp. 649–700). Philadelphia: Churchill Livingstone.

Kawachi, I., Colditz, G. A., Stampfer, M. J., Willet, W. C., Manson, J. E., Rosner, B., Speizer, F. E., & Hennekens, C. H. (1993). Smoking cessation and decreased risk of stroke in women. *Journal of the American Medical Association, 269,* 232–236.

Kiely, D. K., Wolf, P. A., Cupples, L. A., Beiser, A. S., & Myers, R. H. (1993). Familial aggregation of stroke: The Framingham Study. *Stroke, 24,* 1366–1371.

Lechat, P., Mas, J. L., Lascaut, G., Loron, P., Theard, M., Klimczac, M., Drobinski, G., Thomas, D., & Grosgogeat, Y. (1988). Prevalence of patent foramen ovale in patients with stroke. *New England Journal of Medicine, 318,* 1148–1152.

Loh, E., Sutton, M. S. J., Wun, C. C., Rouleau, J. L., Flaker, G. C., Gottlieb, S. S., Lamas, G. A., Moye, M. A., Goldhaber, S. Z., & Pfeffer, M. A. (1997). Ventricular dysfunction and the risk of stroke after myocardial infarction. *New England Journal of Medicine, 336,* 251–257.

Longstreth, W. T., Bernick, C., Manolio, T. A., Bryan, N., Jungreis, C. A., & Price, T. R. (1998). Lacunar infarcts defined by magnetic resonance imaging of 3660 elderly people: The Cardiovascular Health Study. *Archives of Neurology, 55,* 1217–1225.

Martin, R., & Bogousslavsky, J. (1995). Embolic versus nonembolic causes of ischemic stroke. *Cerebrovascular Diseases, 5,* 70–74.

The National Institute for Neurological Disorders and Stroke rt-PA Stroke Study Group. (1995). Tissue plasminogen activator for acute ischemic stroke. *New England Journal of Medicine, 333,* 1581–1587.

Norris, J. W., Zhu, C. Z., Bornstein, N. M., & Chambers, B. R. (1991). Vascular risks of asymptomatic carotid artery stenosis. *Stroke, 22,* 1485–1490.

Ogata, J., Masuda, J., & Yutani, C. (1990). Rupture of atheromatous plaque as a cause of thrombotic occlusion of stenotic carotid artery. *Stroke, 21,* 1740–1745.

O'Leary, D. H., Polak, J. F., Kronmal, R. A., Savage, P. J., Borhani, N. O., Kittner, S. J., Tracy, R., Gardin, J. N., Price, T. R., & Furberg, C. D. (1996). Thickening of the carotid wall: A marker for atherosclerosis in the elderly? *Stroke, 27,* 224–231.

Oppenheimer, S. M., & Lima, J. (1998). Neurology and the heart. *Journal of Neurology, Neurosurgery and Psychiatry, 64,* 289–297.

Otten, M. W. Jr., Teutsch, S. M., Williamson, D. F., & Marks, J. S. (1990). The effect of known risk factors on the excess mortality of Black adults in the United States. *Journal of the American Medical Association, 263,* 845–850.

Prospective Studies Collaboration. (1995). Cholesterol, diastolic blood pressure and stroke: 13,000 strokes in 450,000 people in 45 prospective cohorts. *The Lancet, 346,* 1647–1653.

Qizilbash, N., Duffy, S. W., Warlos, C., & Mann, J. (1992). Lipids are risk factors for ischemic stroke: Overview and review. *Cerebrovascular Diseases, 2,* 127–136.

Qureshi, A. I., Giles, W. H., & Croft, J. B. (1998). Impaired glucose tolerance and the likelihood of non fatal stroke and myocardial infarction: The Third National Health and Nutrition Examination Survey. *Stroke, 29,* 1329–1332.

Rango, M., Tournier-Lasserve, E., Fiori, M., Manca, A., Patrosso, M. C., Ferlini, A., Sirocchi, G., Trojano, L., Chabriat, H., & Salvi, F. (1995). An Italian kindred with cerebral autosomal dominant arteriopathy with subcortical infarcts and leukoencephalopathy (CADASIL). *Annals of Neurology, 38,* 231–236.

Sacco, R. L. (1997). Risk factors, outcomes, and stroke subtypes for ischemic stroke. *Neurology, 49*(Suppl. 4), S39–S44.

Sacco, R. L., Boden-Albala, B., Gan, R., Chen, X., Kargman, D. E., Shea, S., Paik, M. C., & Hauser, W. A. (1997). Stroke incidence among White, Black and Hispanic residents of an urban community: The Northern Manhattan Stroke Study. *American Journal of Epidemiology, 147,* 259–268.

Sacco, R. L., Toni, D., & Mohr, J. P. (1998). Classification of ischemic stroke. In H. J. M. Barnett, J. P. Mohr, B. M. Stein, & F. M. Yatsu (Eds.), *Stroke: Pathophysiology, diagnosis, and management* (3rd ed., pp. 341–354). Philadelphia: Churchill Livingstone.

Schoen, F. J. (1994). Blood vessels. In R. Cotran, V. Kumar, & S. L. Robbins (Eds.), *Robbins pathologic basis of disease* (5th ed., pp. 467–517). Philadelphia: Saunders.

Segal, A. Z., Eggleston-Sexton, P. M., Beiser, A., & Greenberg, S. M. (1999). Low cholesterol as a risk factor for primary intracerebral hemorrhage: A case-control study. *Neuroepidemiology, 18,* 185–193.

Shinton, R., & Beevers, G. (1989). Meta-analysis of relation between cigarette smoking and stroke. *British Medical Journal, 298,* 789–794.

Shiveley, B. K., Gelgand, E. A., & Crawford, M. H. (1996). Regional left atrial stasis during atrial fibrillation and flutter: Determinants and relation to stroke. *Journal of the American College of Cardiology, 27,* 1722–1729.

Sohara, H., Amitani, S., Kurose, M., & Miyahara, K. (1997). Atrial fibrillation activates platelets and coagulation in a time dependent manner: A study in patients with paroxismal atrial fibrillation. *Journal of the American College of Cardiology, 29,* 106–112.

Sudlow, C. L. M., & Warlow, C. P. (1997). Comparable studies of the incidence of stroke and its pathological types: Results from an international collaboration. *Stroke, 28,* 491–499.

Tanne, D., Triplett, D. A., & Levine, S. R. (1998). Antiphospholipid–protein antibodies and ischemic stroke: Not just cardiolipin anymore. *Stroke, 29,* 1755–1758.

Taylor, T. N., Davis, P. H., Torner, J. C., Holmes, J., Meyer, J. W., & Jacobson, M. F. (1996). Lifetime cost of stroke in the United States. *Stroke, 27,* 1459–1466.

Tunkel, A. R., & Kaye, D. (1993). Neurologic complications of infective endocarditis. *Neurologic Clinics, 11,* 419–440.

van Gijn, J. (1998). Leukoaraiosis and vascular dementia. *Neurology, 51* (Suppl. 3), S3–S8.

Whisnant, J. P. (1996). Effectiveness versus efficacy of treatment of hypertension for stroke prevention. *Neurology, 46,* 301–307.

Whisnant, J. P., Wiebers, D. O., O'Fallon, W. M., Sicks, J. D., & Frye, R. L. (1996). A population-based model of risk factors for ischemic stroke: Rochester, Minnesota. *Neurology, 47,* 1420–1428.

WHO MONICA Project, Principal Investigators. (1988). The World Health Organization MONICA Project (Monitoring Trends and Determinants in Cardiovascular Disease): A major international collaboration. *Journal of Clinical Epidemiology, 41,* 105–114.

Wolf, P. A., Abbot, R. D., & Kannel, W. B. (1987). Atrial fibrillation, a major contributor to stroke in the elderly: The Framingham Study. *Archives of Internal Medicine, 147,* 1561–1564.

Wolf, P. A., Abbot, R. D., & Kannel, W. B. (1991). Atrial fibrillation as an independent risk factor for stroke: The Framingham Study. *Stroke, 22,* 983–988.

Wolf, P. A., & D'Agostino, R. B. (1998). Epidemiology of stroke. In H. J. M. Barnett, J. P. Mohr, B. M. Stein, & F. M. Yatsu (Eds.), *Stroke: Pathophysiology, diagnosis, and management* (3rd ed., pp. 3–28). Philadelphia: Churchill Livingstone.

Wolf, P. A., D'Agostino, R. B., Kannel, W. B., Bonita, R., & Belanger, A. J. (1988). Cigarette smoking as a risk factor for stroke: The Framingham Study. *Journal of the American Medical Association, 259,* 1025–1029.

Wolf, P. A., Kannel, W. B., Sorlie, P., & McNamara, P. (1981). Asymptomatic carotid bruit and risk of stroke: The Framingham Study. *Journal of the American Medical Association, 245,* 1442–1445.

Yamamoto, H., & Bogousslavsky, J. (1998). Mechanisms of second and further strokes. *Journal of Neurology, Neurosurgery and Psychiatry, 64,* 771–776.

CHAPTER FOURTEEN

The Neuropsychology of Subcortical Ischemic Vascular Dementia

JOEL H. KRAMER
LADA A. KEMENOFF
University of California, San Francisco, Medical Center

HELENA C. CHUI
University of Southern California

Cerebrovascular disease takes many forms, and it adversely affects neuropsychological functioning in many ways. We are all familiar with the concept of stroke, which results from an occlusion of a large blood vessel in the brain, usually an artery. In fact, much of what is known about brain–behavior relationships has evolved from they study of stroke patients and observations of the patterns of behavioral changes associated with different focal lesions. Other forms of cerebrovascular disease produce more widespread pathology, however, and can produce global deficits in cognitive functioning. In this chapter we review the association between cerebrovascular disease and dementia, with a particular emphasis on the dementia caused by ischemia in small blood vessels in subcortical brain regions.

OVERVIEW OF VASCULAR DEMENTIA

Vascular dementia (VaD) is considered one of the most common types of dementia in the elderly. Beyond this somewhat general concept, however, there is much less agreement about the frequency with which VaD occurs and the mechanisms by which cerebrovascular disease produces a dementia syndrome

(Loeb & Meyer, 1996). In fact, given the heterogeneity of cerebrovascular disorders, it is not surprising that no clear consensus has emerged regarding causal
factors, underlying neuropathology, clinical symptoms, characteristic neuropsychological profiles, and developmental course.

Greater clarity in our understanding of VaD was achieved when investigators
began to differentiate between different types of cerebrovascular disease. First,
in a very broad sense, cerebrovascular disease can be either hemorrhagic or ischemic. Ischemia is the most common vascular mechanism leading to brain injury.
Ischemia occurs when blood flow is inadequate to provide the essential substrates (e.g., oxygen and glucose) to support cell metabolism. The relationship
between cerebral blood flow and cell dysfunction is not a simple one, however,
and is determined by the specific oxygen and glucose requirements of individual
cells, local cerebral blood flow, and duration of hypoperfusion. Of particular relevance to VaD is the fact that local cerebral blood flow is lowest in periventricular regions and deep white matter. These regions are perfused by long, small,
penetrating end-arterioles with no collaterals (de Reuck, 1971; Moody, Bell, &
Challa, 1990). Thus, the deep white matter is most susceptible to ischemia when
there is either a systemic drop in blood pressure (BP; acute hypotension) or widespread small-vessel arteriopathy (e.g., arteriolosclerois associated with chronic
hypertension; Pantoni & Garcia, 1997). When blood flow drops to approximately 17 ml/minute/100 gm, neuronal membranes depolarize, causing the
neurons to function abnormally (Sharbrough, Messick, & Sundt, 1973). If blood
flow is promptly restored, normal brain function may be restored, and the clinical diagnosis is a transient ischemic attack (TIA). When blood flow diminishes
below approximately 10 ml/minute/100 gm for more than 30 minutes, neuronal membranes degenerate, irreversibly causing neuronal death and cerebral
infarction (Heiss, 1983). Clinically, a completed stroke or cerebrovascular accident (CVA) has occurred. Focal ischemia results from occlusion of a single blood
vessel. More global ischemia follows systemic disturbances in circulation (e.g.,
cardiac arrest, hypovolemic shock). Here, the most vulnerable brain areas are
the border zones located at the far reaches of the major cerebral arteries and
the periventricular deep white matter where the long-penetrating arterioles end
(Bogousslavsky & Regli, 1986; Mounier-Vehier et al., 1994; Mull, Schwarz, &
Thron, 1997; Torvik, 1984).

Cummings (1994) and Loeb and Meyer (1996) have identified several different
dementia-producing vascular syndromes, such as multi-infarct dementia, Binswanger's disease, strategic infarcts, and subcortical ischemic disease. Neuropsychologists need to be aware of the differences among these syndromes, because
they entail different patterns of cognitive impairment. *Multi-infarct dementia* is
a term that was previously used quite broadly to refer to all types of VaD. It
now refers more specifically to large-vessel disease, usually occlusions of main
branches of the anterior, middle, and posterior cerebral arteries that produce
cortical lesions. These infarcts are typically caused by either atherosclerotic

plaques within the arterial walls, or they arise from emboli of cardiac origin. Resulting neurobehavioral symptoms vary greatly as a function of where and how large the cortical lesions are but can include aphasia, apraxia, agnosia, and inattention syndromes. The sudden onset and stepwise progression traditionally thought to be associated with cerebrovascular disease is probably specific to multi-infarct dementia and is less characteristic of the other vascular syndromes.

In 1894, Otto Binswanger described 8 patients with slowly progressive mental deterioration and pronounced white matter changes, with secondary dilatation of the ventricles. In *Binswanger's disease,* also known as *subcortical arteriosclerotic encephalopathy,* there is typically a history of persistent hypertension or systemic vascular disease. The clinical course may be insidious, with long plateaus and the accumulation of focal neurologic signs (Babikian & Ropper, 1987; Román, 1987). Slowly progressive dementia is common, with a decidedly prefrontal flavor, including apathy, lack of drive, mild depression, and alterations of mood (Libon et al., 1990; Loizou, Kendall, & Marshall, 1981). Binswanger's disease is relatively uncommon. Neuropathological features include extensive demyelination and destruction of subcortical white matter, with relative sparing of the cortical U fibers. Pathology is typically more pronounced in the temporal and occipital lobes. Criteria for clinical diagnosis were offered by Caplan and Schoene (1978) and include the presence of vascular risk factors, focal ischemic lacunar lesions in the white matter that are confluent on neuroimaging, age of onset between 55 and 75, subacute onset of focal neurological signs, and extensive white matter attenuation on T1 and hyperintensity on T2 weighted magnetic resonance images (MRI).

Dementia can also result from a strategically placed infarct—typically in the thalamus, frontal white matter, basal ganglia, or angular gyrus—that produces enough cognitive disturbance to produce functional decline. For example, in some individuals a single paramedian branch supplies both anteromedial thalamic regions. Occlusion of the paramedian artery in these cases will lead to bilateral infarction of the dorsomedial nucleus and the mammillothalamic tracts (Bogousslavsky, Regli, & Uske, 1998), disconnecting the prefrontal executive and limbic–diencephalic memory systems. Similarly, an infarct in the inferior genu of the internal capsule may strategically disrupt the inferior and medial thalamic peduncles carrying thalamo–cortical fibers related to cognition and memory (Tatemichi, Desmond, Prohovnik, et al., 1992; Tatemichi, Desmond, & Prohovnik, 1995). Kooistra and Heilman (1988) also reported on a lacune in the posterior limb of the left internal capsule resulting in a persistent verbal memory disorder.

A cerebrovascular syndrome that is receiving increasing attention as a cause of dementia is subcortical ischemic vascular disease. This syndrome is typically the result of occlusions of the deep penetrating arterioles and arteries that feed the basal ganglia, thalamus, white matter, and internal capsule. The lesions are small and are often referred to as *lacunes* or *lacunar infarcts;* the syndrome is sometimes known as *lacunar state dementia* or *état lacunaire*. Lacunes average 2 mm in volume but can range from 0.2 mm to 15 mm (Cummings, 1995). Although subcortical ischemic vascular dementia (SIVD) is typically associated with age and hypertension, there is also a variant of SIVD called *cerebral autosomal dominant arteriopathy with subcortical infarcts and leukoencephalopathy* (CADASIL). CADASIL is a genetic disorder linked to chromosome 19 (Davous, 1998). Although patients are typically free of classical vascular risk factors such as hypertension and diabetes, the disorder affects the small vessels of the brain and results in extensive subcortical infarcts and leukoencephalopathy.

The neuropsychology of SIVD is the primary focus of this chapter and is discussed in greater detail later.

DIAGNOSING VaD: THE PERSISTENT CHALLENGE

The prevalence of VaD depends on how it is defined and measured. In fact, there is debate about how *dementia* should be operationally defined. *The Diagnostic and Statistical Manual of Mental Disorders* (4th ed. [*DSM–IV*]; American Psychiatric Association, 1994) is one of the most widely used nosologies and requires the presence of multiple cognitive deficits but at minimum includes memory impairment and either aphasia, apraxia agnosia, or executive impairment. Deficits must be severe enough to cause impairment in occupational or social functioning. The emphasis on memory and cortical dementia symptoms such as aphasia and apraxia clearly reflects the Alzheimer's disease (AD) bias in these diagnostic criteria and may not work as well for subcortical syndromes. *The International Classification of Diseases* (10th revision [ICD–10]; WHO, 1993) uses different criteria, and low rates of agreement between the two nosologies for dementia have been reported (Erkinjuntti et al., 1997). For a diagnosis of VaD, *DSM–IV* requires that there be either focal neurological signs and symptoms or laboratory evidence indicative of cerebrovascular disease. Clinicians must judge the cerebrovascular disease to be etiologically related to the dementia, however, which may be difficult in cases where the infarcts are small and localized in subcortical regions.

Two other sets of diagnostic criteria for VaD have been proposed. The National Institute of Neurological Disorders and Stroke, in conjunction with the Association Internationale pour la Recherche et l'Enseignement en Neurosciences (NINDS–AIREN) published the NINDS–AIREN consensus criteria in 1993 (Roman et al., 1993). In the NINDS–AIREN system dementia is defined by cognitive decline manifested by impairment of memory and in two or more cognitive domains. Cerebrovascular disease is defined by the presence of focal signs on neurological examination and evidence of relevant cerebrovascular disease on neuroimaging. The cerebrovascular disease can be either a large cortical infarct, a single strategically placed infarct, or multiple subcortical or white matter lesions. The relationship between the dementia syndrome and the cerebro-vascular disease is more sharply defined than in *DSM–IV*, and is inferred when the dementia occurs within 3 months of a stroke, there is abrupt onset of cognitive impairment, or there is fluctuating or stepwise progression. NINDS–AIREN further established criteria for probable VaD and possible VaD, plus definite VaD that is established using postmortem neuropathological criteria.

A different diagnostic system was proposed by Chui et al. (1992) on the basis of the experience of the State of California Alzheimer's Disease Diagnostic and Treatment Centers (ADDTC). The ADDTC criteria focus on *ischemic* VaD. This system is somewhat unique in that memory impairment is not necessary for a diagnosis of dementia to be made. The key criterion for dementia is a deterioration from prior levels in two or more areas of intellectual functioning sufficient to interfere with the patient's customary affairs of life. A diagnosis of probable VaD is made when there is evidence of two or more ischemic strokes by history, neurologic signs, or neuroimaging studies or of a single stroke with a clearly documented temporal relationship to the onset of dementia.

PREVALENCE

The prevalence of VaD is a function not only of the diagnostic criteria used but also of the method by which the study samples are collected. Study samples can be derived from autopsy series, community surveys, dementia clinics, or general medical clinics. One recent autopsy study (Holmes, Cairns, Lantos, & Mann, 1999) evaluated 80 consecutive dementia cases brought to autopsy and illustrates the challenges associated with making a clinical diagnosis of VaD. The NINDS–AIREN criteria were used for making *in vivo* diagnoses. Only 8.8% of the sample met criteria for probable VaD; 1.3% had possible VaD, and 5% had mixed diagnoses (VaD with either AD or Lewy body dementia). On autopsy, of the 7 cases who met criteria for probable VaD, only 3 had infarctions alone, and 4 had infarctions concurrent with other pathology. Infarctions were found in 16 of the remaining 73 cases who were not thought to have a VaD on the basis of clinical considerations. The NINDS–AIREN criteria appear to have high specificity (i.e., patients who meet the criteria most likely have the disorder) but low sensitivity (i.e., the criteria miss a great many patients who in fact have the disorder). In a series of 50 autopsied cases of dementia, Tomlinson, Blessed, and Roth (1970) ascribed an arteriosclerotic cause in 18%. In a review of 8 autopsy series, O'Brien (1988) noted that at least one third of all patients with dementia have a significant vascular component. Mirsen and Hachinski (1988) reviewed 3 autopsy series and classified 15% to 19% with pure VaD and 9% to 18% with mixed dementia. Among the first 106 autopsies of patients enrolled in the Consortium to Establish a Registry for Alzheimer Disease with a clinical diagnosis of AD, 87% showed histological changes confirming a diagnosis of AD (Gearing et al., 1995). However, vascular lesions of varying nature and size were also present in 21%. The proportion of cases with mixed vascular and primary neuronal pathologies has been noted to increase with age. VaD was diagnosed in 15% of patients who died at ages younger than 70 years and in 22.5% of patients who died at ages older than 70 years (Katzman, Lasker, & Bernstein, 1988). Thus, data from hospital autopsy series indicate that vascular disease contributes to dementia in approximately one quarter of cases.

The ratio of AD to VaD is approximately 5 : 1 in hospital-based dementia clinics. A review of seven clinical series of patients with dementia ($n = 689$) revealed that the most common diagnosis by far was primary degenerative dementia (47%); a diagnosis of VaD was made in only 9% (Chui, 1989). This ratio is significantly higher than those found in community-based surveys. Lindsay, Hebert, and Rockwood (1997) reported prevalence rates of 7 per 1,000 in the community and 115 per 1,000 in institutions. Referral bias represents the most likely explanation for the discrepancy in prevalence rates between clinics and hospitals; patients with strokes tend to go to stroke clinics rather than to dementia clinics. Computation of prevalence rates are somewhat complicated, however, because they do not directly assess whether there is a causal relationship between dementia and stroke or in which direction the causal relationship runs. Ferrucci et al. (1996), for example, reported that patients with dementia are at greater risk of suffering a stroke than are cognitively normal elderly people, and that patients with severe cognitive impairment are twice as likely to suffer stroke than patients with only moderate cognitive impairment.

Another way of assessing the relationship between dementia and cerebrovascular disease is to evaluate the prevalence of dementia in patients with a known history of stroke. The prevalence of dementia among patients hospitalized with stroke tends to be high. On the basis of performance on the Wechsler Adult Intelligence Scale (WAIS), for example, 56.3% of 71 patients hospitalized with stroke were diagnosed with dementia (Ladurner, Iliff, & Lechner, 1982). Tatemichi et al. (1990) examined 726 patients with acute ischemic stroke and judged 15.9% to be demented. In a separate series of 251 stroke patients studied 3 months after acute infarction, Tatemichi, Desmond, Mayeux, et al. (1992) diagnosed dementia in 26.8% on the basis of modified DSM–III–R (American Psychiatric Association, 1987) criteria. Similarly, Suzuki, Kutsuzawa, Nakajima, and Hatano (1991) found dementia in 27.2% of 136 patients, and Pohjasvaara, Erkinjuntti, Vataja, and Kaste (1997) found dementia in 20% of 486 patients hospitalized with stroke. Thus, dementia is common after stroke, occurring in one quarter to one third of cases.

Demographic and patient-related variables should be considered when assessing the likelihood that a patient suffers from cerebrovascular disease. Age is the single strongest risk factor for stroke. Other known risk factors may include male gender and African American ethnicity (Sacco, Hauser, & Mohr, 1991). Risk of VaD is almost doubled if the patient has a history of arterial hypertension (Lindsay et al., 1997). Exposure to pesticides and fertilizer also has been suggested as a possible risk factor (Lindsay et al., 1997), as have atrial fibrillation, hypertension, cardiac disease, diabetes mellitus, smoking, alcoholism, and hyperlipidemia (Sacco, 1994; Schoenberg & Shulte, 1988; Tell, Crouse, & Furberg, 1988; Wolf, D'Agostino, Belanger, & Kannel, 1991). The effect size of each risk factor may differ for large versus small arteries. Hyperlipidemia and smoking primarily accelerate atherosclerosis of the larger arteries, whereas hypertension also increases arteriolosclerosis in small vessels. Diabetes mellitus enhances atherogenesis in both large and small arteries (Caplan, 1991). Cardiac emboli associated with atrial fibrillation tend to lodge in the early branches of the larger arteries (Feinberg et al., 1990; Wolf, Dawber, & Thomas, 1978).

SIVD

The primary focus of the remainder of this chapter is SIVD. The syndrome of dementia associated with multiple lacunar infarcts was first described by Marie (1901) and Ferrand (1902) in 50 residents of a chronic-care facility. Clinical features included sudden hemiparesis, dementia, dysarthria, pseudobulbar palsy and affect, crying, small-stepped gait, and urinary incontinence. Aphasia and heminopsia never occurred. Similar clinical features were confirmed by Fisher (1965). More recently, Cummings (1995) described several of the neuropsychological, neuropsychiatric, and motor features associated with SIVD and highlighted ways in which SIVD resembles the dementia associated with other subcortical syndromes. According to Cummings, anywhere between 13% and 51% of patients with VaD have subcortical lacunes. Loeb and Meyer (1996) reported that SIVD is the most common subtype of VaD.

Advances in neuroimaging during the last two decades have enabled researchers and clinicians to more accurately and reliably determine when subcortical ischemic vascular disease is present. Several issues continue to be debated, however. Key issues that we address in this chapter include (a) the relationship between subcortical lacunes and dementia, (b) differentiation between SIVD and AD, and (c) mechanisms by which SIVD impairs cognitive impairment.

Relationship Between SIVD and Dementia

The fact that a demented patient has one or more subcortical lacunes does not necessarily imply a causal relationship between the lacune and the dementia. Several studies have suggested that a great many well-functioning community-dwelling elderly people have had a lacunar infarct without obvious clinical impact. The Cardiovascular Health Study (Longstreth et al., 1998; Price et al., 1997) evaluated a large population-based sample aged 65 and older ($n = 3,660$) with brain MRI. Infarcts (lesions >3 mm) were found in 28% of the 3,397 participants who had no known history of stroke, indicating that the observed infarcts had been "silent" strokes. Older participants and those with a history of migraine headaches were more likely to have had a silent stroke. Shintani, Shiigai, and Arinami (1998) also found age to be a risk factor for silent strokes, along with systolic hypertension and duration of hypertension. Kobayashi, Okada, Koide, Bokura, and Yamaguchi (1997) scanned 933 neurologically normal adults covering a broader (and younger) age range and reported subcortical lacunes (also >3 mm) in only 10.6% of the sample. In addition to age and hypertension, diabetes and alcohol habits were risk factors. Autopsy studies have also demonstrated that silent infarcts can be found in over 10% of elderly individuals (Shinkawa et al., 1995).

Are silent infarcts necessarily associated with changes in cognition? Unfortunately, most studies that scan large numbers of seemingly normal elderly individuals do not extensively evaluate neuropsychological functioning. Bornstein et al. (1996) concluded that silent brain infarctions were not predictive of later dementia, but their study was restricted to patients who later on suffered a clinical ischemic stroke. Of possible relevance is a study designed to assess cognitive sequelae of TIAs using a brief neuropsychological test battery: Nichelli et al. (1986) failed to find an association between TIAs and later dementia. In contrast, Price et al. (1997) reported that silent subcortical lacunes were strongly associated with lower scores on a digit–symbol substitution test and more abnormalities on neurological examination. Studies from our laboratory also indicate that subcortical lacunes can be associated with subtle cognitive changes. In one study (Kramer, Reed, Mungas, Weiner, & Chui, 1999), 12 elderly patients with a clinical dementia rating of 0 (i.e., normal functioning in the community) and one or more subcortical lacunes, and 27 normal elderly individuals without lacunes, were evaluated. The presence of a subcortical lacune was established by MRI. All participants were administered a neuropsychological test battery, including the Stroop Interference Test (Stroop, 1935). The subcortical lacune and nonlacune groups were well matched in age, education, and Mattis Dementia Rating Scale (MDRS) total score (means of 137.3 for the lacune group and 139.9 for the control group). No group differences were found on measures of recent verbal memory, recent spatial memory, language, or spatial ability. On the Stroop Interference Test there were no group differences in the color naming or word reading conditions. In contrast, differences were found in the interference condition, in which participants were required to inhibit the overlearned reading response and instead name the color of ink in which each word was printed. Regression analyses indicated that the presence of a subcortical lacune predicted slower performance. The results suggest that SIVD is associated with subtle declines in executive functioning, even in nondemented patients. Mychack, Kramer, Schatz, and Reed (1998) also evaluated nondemented patients with subcortical lacunes, assessing executive functioning with the California Card Sort (Delis et al., 1999) and the Stroop Interference Test. Fifteen patients with subcortical lacunes were compared with 37 normal controls. The lacune group performed similarly to the control group on measures of language, visuospatial ability, and recognition memory. On the California Card Sort, however, the lacune group identified fewer correct sorts than the controls and gave significantly fewer correct responses in the interference condition of the Stroop test. Nondemented patients with CADASIL have also been reported to have subtle declines in executive functioning as measured by the Wisconsin Card Sorting Test (WCST) and the Trail-Making Test (Taillia et al., 1998).

Despite the evidence for an association between subcortical infarcts and cognitive impairment, some investigators still argue that lacunes do not cause dementia. Nolan, Lino, Seligmann, and Blass (1998), for example, studied 87 consecutive dementia patients at autopsy and concluded that dementia could not be attributed to the effects of cerebrovascular disease alone. The bulk of evidence does offer a clear link between small-vessel disease and dementia, however, although the patient's functional deficits may not be concurrent with the stroke. Loeb, Grandolfo, Croce, and Conti (1992) reported that 23% of patients who initially presented with a single lacunar infarct and who were followed for 4 years ultimately developed dementia, indicating that silent lacunes are a risk factor for the development of dementia.

In summary, the relationship between subcortical lacunes and dementia can be ambiguous. Clearly, a single lacune does not necessarily produce dementia, or even obvious cognitive impairment. A single lacune can disrupt normal cognition, however, and may be a risk factor for later development of dementia. Much more work is needed before it is better understood how lacune location, number, and volume interact with other factors to cause dementia.

Differentiation Between SIVD and AD

Differentiating SIVD from AD is often difficult clinically, because the two diseases can present so similarly. Both disorders are diseases of the elderly and have increasing prevalence with increasing age. Because small subcortical lacunes are so often "silent," SIVD, like AD, can begin quite insidiously. Progression in SIVD can also be slow. The classic way of differentiating VaD from AD relies on the presence of rapid-onset, stepwise progression; use of the Hachinski Scale (1975), which quantifies a list of potential cerebrovascular disease symptoms; and vascular risk factors. These clinical signs are typically more appropriate for large-vessel disease and have only limited applications to SIVD. Even traditional neuroimaging may not assist with differential diagnosis because of comorbidity. Many patients with AD have lacunes; some studies, in fact, have even suggested that AD patients may be at greater risk for cerebrovascular disease than their nondemented age peers. If presented with a moderately demented patient with a single, small infarct in the internal capsule, many clinicians will assume that the lacune is not a primary contributor to the dementia. The assumption that the lacune is only incidental is supported by the fact that a relatively large percentage of normal elderly individuals have lacunes. Consequently, it may not be possible to know with certainty what role the lacunes are playing in the patient's cognitive dysfunction.

One might expect that the patterns of neuropsychological deficits in SIVD and AD would be different as a function of differences in their underlying neuropathology (Mendez & Ashla-Mendez, 1991). AD involves neurofibrillary tangles and neuritic plaques in temporal limbic structures and the posterior association cortex, and it commonly entails impairment in memory, language, and conceptual abilities. In SIVD the presence of multiple subcortical lacunes is thought to affect subcortical–frontal circuits. Cummings (1995) described three subcortical–frontal circuits that mediate cognitive, motivational, and emotional processes. The dorsolateral prefrontal circuit includes the lateral convexity of the frontal lobe, the dorsolateral caudate, portions of the globus pallidus and substantia nigra, and ventral anterior and dorsomedial thalamic nuclei. The dorsolateral circuit plays a prominent role mediating executive functioning, including response inhibition, fluency, working memory, and retrieval from long-term memory. Shallice and Burgess (1991) identified the dorsolateral prefrontal cortex as an essential component of a supervisory attentional system that regulates selection among competing choices. They postulated that this supervisory or executive system is normally required for planning and decision making, error correction or troubleshooting, dealing with novel situations, and overcoming strong habitual or tempting responses.

Cummings (1995) also proposed an orbitofrontal circuit and a medial frontal circuit. The orbitofrontal circuit projects from the orbitofrontal cortex to ventral portions of the caudate, which in turn is connected with the amygdala, midbrain nuclei, ventrolateral and dorsomedial thalamus, and temporal lobe. The orbitofrontal circuit mediates the modulation of social behavior; lesions can produce tactlessness, indifference to others, and impulsive behavior. Obsessive–compulsive behaviors also may occur. The medial frontal circuit incorporates the anterior cingulate, nucleus accumbens, amygdala, dorsomedial thalamus, and midbrain structures. The medial frontal circuit is thought to mediate motivation; lesions are associated with apathy and disinterest.

Each subcortical loop is vulnerable to pathology in different vascular systems. For example, the basal ganglia and thalamus are perfused by small penetrating arteries that arise from or near the circle of Willis. In the basal ganglia, the "limbic" and lateral orbital circuits, which subserve attention and emotion, are positioned in the ventral–medial caudate and receive their blood supply primarily from perforating branches of the anterior communicating artery. The dorsolateral frontal–subcortical circuits are positioned more laterally and are fed predominantly from the lenticulostriate arteries and deep penetrating arteries, including the anterior choroidal artery and arteries near the posterior circle of Willis.

The strong anatomical and functional linkages between subcortical regions and the frontal lobes argue for a subcortical–frontal deficit model for SIVD. Such a model would predict that executive functioning and motor programming abnormalities would be disproportionately affected in SIVD and that memory and language would be disproportionately affected in AD. In support of this, Kertesz and Clydesdale (1994) found that patients with SIVD performed worse on tests that are influenced by frontal and subcortical mechanisms. For example, SIVD patients had greater difficulty on the MDRS-derived scale of Motor Performance, which measures motor perseveration and bimanual coordination deficits associated with frontal lobe dysfunction. SIVD patients also showed greater impairment on the WAIS–Revised (WAIS–R) Picture Arrangement subtest. This speeded task requires the sequential ordering of cards depicting various person–object and interpersonal interaction scenes and is sensitive to frontal lobe disease. Compared to the SIVD group, patients with AD were found to perform poorly on measures of memory (Wechsler Memory Scale–Revised immediate story recall) and language (Western Aphasia Battery, Repetition subtest).

Kemenoff et al. (1999) compared 27 patients with SIVD with 34 patients without lacunes on a broad range of neuropsychological measures. All SIVD patients met ADDTC criteria for VaD and had MRI evidence for one or more subcortical lacunes (Chui et al., 1992). No group differences were found on age, education, or total MDRS score. SIVD patients performed relatively better on the Memory versus the Conceptualization subscales of the MDRS, whereas AD patients demonstrated the opposite pattern. SIVD patients showed greater impairment on phonemic fluency relative to category fluency, whereas AD patients made more intrusion errors and exhibited poorer visual memory. After entering the discriminating neuropsychological variables into a logistic regression, Kemenoff et al. categorized SIVD and AD patients with 84% accuracy. Their results support the view that a subcortical–frontal pattern of neuropsychological performance is present in SIVD and may be useful for clinical diagnosis.

Lending further support to a subcortical–frontal deficit model, Wolfe, Linn, Babikian, Knoefel, and Albert (1990) tested the hypothesis that patients with multiple subcortical lacunes were selectively impaired on executive functioning measures. Executive abilities—including verbal fluency, semantic clustering, shifting of mental set, and response inhibition—were all compromised in patients with multiple subcortical lacunes on computer tomography (CT).

Tei et al. (1997) found that patients with early-stage AD had significantly lower scores on a test of visuospatial memory, whereas patients with multiple subcortical infarction with mild cognitive impairment demonstrated significantly worse performance on an executive functioning test sensitive to frontal lobe dysfunction (the WCST). Padovani et al. (1995) also explored the relationship between VaD and frontal lobe systems impairment. Patients with multiinfarct dementia were found to be more impaired on measures of frontal lobe functioning such as Controlled Oral Word Association Test (COWAT) and

WCST perseverative errors. AD patients were more impaired on measures of memory functioning (e.g., California Verbal Learning Test [CVLT] Total Recall and Delayed Recall, Spatial Recall Test) and on a measure of language comprehension.

Lafosse et al. (1997) used well-matched and well-defined samples of SIVD and AD patients, comparing them on select language and verbal memory tests. On the basis of the different patterns of neuropathological involvement in SIVD and AD, these researchers hypothesized that patients with SIVD would demonstrate better confrontation naming, worse verbal fluency (COWAT), and better memory performance. Although notable differences in confrontation naming were not found, SIVD patients had poorer verbal fluency but better free recall, fewer intrusions, and better recognition memory than AD patients. On the basis of their marked relative impairment in verbal fluency, Lafosse et al. (1997) suggested that the unifying feature of the SIVD patients' neuropsychological deficits was related to a failure of executive functions mediated by the frontal lobes. The pattern of deficit on verbal fluency tasks may also have utility in differential diagnosis. Carew, Lamar, Cloud, and Libon (1997) reported that SIVD patients and normal elderly controls performed better on category tasks than on letter fluency tasks, whereas the opposite was observed among AD patients. In addition, SIVD patients produced fewer responses than AD participants on letter fluency tasks, but there was no difference between AD and SIVD patients on category fluency.

Cummings (1995) proposed that patients with SIVD have deficits in new learning and spontaneous recall after delays, but because their deficit is largely one of retrieval (vs. encoding) they benefit from cues and recognition testing. We have found only marginal support for this hypothesis. We studied 13 patients with radiologically confirmed lacunes with total lacunar volume of at least 0.5 cm^3. We compared these SIVD patients with a sample of 15 AD patients well matched for age, education, and total MDRS score and with a sample of 22 neurologically normal controls. Both dementia groups had a mean age of 73 years and a mean MDRS score of 106. We administered to participants the Memory Assessment Scale (MAS) Verbal Learning test and the Biber Visual Memory Test (BVMT). Both the MAS and the BVMT contain several learning trials, delayed free recall trials, and recognition memory trials.

Recognition memory differences among the three groups were assessed. Both patient groups performed at levels significantly below the control group. For the MAS, a post hoc comparison between the SIVD and AD groups only approached significance, with the SIVD group performing better than the AD group. A similar pattern was found for the BVMT, with both patient groups performing less well than the controls but differences between the SIVD and AD groups only approaching significance.

More marked differences between the SIVD and AD groups were found when rates of learning and forgetting were analyzed. During the six learning trials on

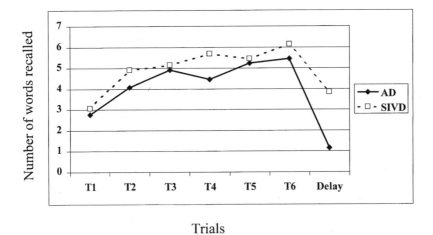

Trials

FIG. 14.1. Immediate and delayed recall of Alzheimer's disease (AD) patients and subcortical ischemic vascular dementia (SIVD) patients on the Memory Assessment Scale list learning task.

the MAS, there were no differences between the two demented groups in overall recall or rate of learning across the trials. Decline in recall over a 30-minute delay was then assessed. There was a significant Group × Trial interaction, reflecting the fact that the AD patients had a significantly steeper decline in recall over the delay than did the SIVD patients (see Fig. 14.1). The SIVD patients maintained information over the delay as well as the controls did. A similar pattern was found for visual memory, with no group differences during the learning trials, but a significant Group × Trial interaction, because of the more rapid rate of forgetting over the delay period by the AD patients.

Hassing and Backman (1997) also found greater memory impairment among AD patients versus VaD patients. They compared the two dementia groups on a series of episodic memory tasks, assessing face recognition, word recall, and object recall. Although no group differences were found for face recognition and object recall, VaD patients showed an advantage over AD patients in word recall. Hassing and Backman suggested that this selective word recall deficit may also be interpreted in terms of greater impairment of language-related functions in AD compared to VaD.

Libon et al. (1998) demonstrated that patients with AD and SIVD can be differentiated on the basis of differing patterns of impairment on tests of declarative and procedural memory. The used the CVLT to measure declarative memory and a rotor pursuit learning task to measure procedural memory. The SIVD group performed as poorly as the AD group on the CVLT List A immediate free recall test trials. By contrast, patients with SIVD showed a greater capacity to retain information, as evidenced by their significantly higher score on the CVLT recognition discriminability index. An opposite pattern of performance was demonstrated on the rotor pursuit task: AD patients exhibited greater learning than SIVD patients. These results are consistent with other reports of subcortical-dementia patients (e.g., those with Huntington's disease) exhibiting deficits in procedural memory (Knopman & Nissen, 1991).

Models of subcortical dementia also posit disproportionate difficulty with processing speed, concentration, and mental control. In support of this, mildly demented patients with SIVD (lacunes or extensive white matter lesions) who were comparable to AD patients on tasks of memory and abstract thinking were disproportionately impaired on tests of attention (Matsuda, Saito, & Sugishita, 1998). Similarly, in an investigation of sustained attention, vascular patients were slower in stimulus categorization time and made more omission and commission errors on a continuous-performance task (Mendez, Cherrier, & Perryman, 1997).

In summary, a review of the literature suggests that SIVD and AD patients differ in their patterns of performance on specific measures of cognitive functioning. Neuropsychological comparisons have generally reported relative deficits in SIVD compared to AD in subcortical–frontal executive functions such as verbal fluency, attention, sequencing, and problem solving (Rosenstein, 1998). Relative advantages in SIVD compared to AD have included better memory performance, fewer intrusions, and better comprehension and confrontation naming (Lukatela, Malloy, Jenkins, & Cohen, 1998).

Mechanisms of Impairment

SIVD is a complex and multifaceted disorder, and the ways in which it produces a dementia syndrome are only just beginning to be understood. Several different components of SIVD could potentially disrupt cognition. These include the specific nature of the subcortical pathology, disruption of subcortical–cortical circuits, and more diffuse brain dysfunction that extends beyond the specific regions infarcted. In addition, with any patient with suspected SIVD the possibility of comorbidity, particularly with AD, always exists.

Several studies have linked specific parameters of subcortical pathology to the severity or nature of the dementia. Lafosse et al. (1997), for example, were interested in discovering whether certain features such as number of infarcts and extent of white matter changes were related to SIVD patients' neuropsychological functioning. Consistent with a subcortical–frontal disconnection model, greater white matter change was associated with reduced fluency and poorer spontaneous recall, whereas increasing number of infarcts was associated with poorer recognition memory. Furthermore, ventricular enlargement was related to poorer delayed cued recall. Libon et al. (1998) differentiated AD and SIVD groups on the basis of MRI indexes of white matter alterations and size of the hippocampal formation. The body of the hippocampal formation and the para-hippocampal gyrus were consistently smaller in the AD group, and the size of the hippocampal formation was positively correlated with performance on the CVLT recognition discriminability index. In addition, patients with SIVD exhibited greater white matter alterations than patients with AD.

If the subcortical pathology has a direct bearing on cognitive impairment, three possible factors should be considered: the number or volume of lesions, the location of lesions, and the extent of white matter signal hyperintensities. Tomlinson et al. (1970) initially proposed that dementia follows when the volume of infarctions exceeds 100 ml. More recent autopsy and neuroimaging studies illustrate that dementia can occur with only 20 ml to 30 ml of infarcted brain tissue (Loeb & Meyer, 1996). Strong correlations between lacunar volume and cognitive functioning have not been routinely found, however. The location of the lesion(s) can also play a role. It is well established that strategically located lesions in the thalamus and frontal white matter can produce significant cognitive impairment (Erkinjuntti et al., 1996). What is less clear is the clinical significance of most small infarcts in the basal ganglia and internal capsule. Side of lesion may also be relevant. Caplan et al. (1990) reviewed 10 left- and 8 right-sided lesions involving the head of the caudate in the distribution of Heubner's artery. With the more extensive lesions, neurological signs included temporary motor weakness, decreased spontaneous and associative movements, and dysarthria. Contralateral neglect was noted with right-sided lesions, and speech and memory deficits were noted with left-sided ones.

Functional imaging studies tend to show that brain regions surrounding, or even remote from, the lacune are hypometabolic, indicating that brain dysfunction in SIVD spreads well beyond the infarcted tissue. These remote effects are thought to be related to disconnections within subcortical–cortical circuits. In light of the neuropsychological evidence supporting a subcortical–frontal model of dysfunction, it would be reasonable to hypothesize that the frontal lobes are particularly vulnerable to these disconnections. Using positron emission tomography (PET), Sultzer et al. (1995) found that the metabolic rate in the frontal cortex was lower in patients with a lacunar infarct of the basal ganglia or thalamus than in those without. Kwan et al. (1999) also found metabolic changes in the frontal cortex to be specific to cognitively impaired patients with subcortical lacunes. In their study, memory was associated with metabolism in different brain regions in SIVD versus AD. Participants were given a continuous verbal recognition memory task during the period of tracer uptake. A double dissociation was found. In cognitively impaired participants with subcortical lacunes but not AD, delayed-memory performance was associated with left dorsolateral frontal cortex metabolism. In AD patients, but not in subcortical lacune patients, memory was associated with left middle temporal gyrus and left hippocampal metabolism. MacKay et al. (1996), using Magnetic Resonance Spectroscopic Imaging (MRSI), also reported finding higher levels of creatine-containing metabolites, lower levels of N-acetyl aspartate (NAA), or both, in frontal white matter in patients with SIVD.

Several other studies have indicated that SIVD is associated with broader cortical dysfunction. In one study of SIVD in which PET was used, reduced cortical metabolism was generally associated with the severity of subcortical pathologic changes. Mean global cortical metabolism was lower in patients who had periventricular hyperintensities in anterior subcortical regions than in those without such lesions (Sultzer et al., 1995). Kwan et al. (1999) also showed that SIVD patients had lower whole brain Cortical Metabolic Rates-glucose (CMRglc) than controls or cognitively normal participants with lacunes. Structural imaging studies have also described widespread cortical changes in SIVD. Preliminary data from our group indicate that cortical gray matter is reduced in cognitively impaired and demented patients with lacunes compared to controls. In one set of analyses the extent of cortical gray matter reduction in SIVD patients was similar to that in AD patients, although the SIVD patients had greater ventricular size and more white matter lesions. Four patients with pathological confirmed absence of AD pathology indicates that comorbidity cannot explain the cortical gray matter reductions. Lafosse et al. (1997) reported that cortical atrophy in their SIVD participants was related to poorer performance on most of the neuropsychological measures. They argued that the pattern of correlations with cortical atrophy and their findings of greater cortical atrophy in the SIVD group than in the AD group suggests that a degenerative cortical process may be involved as well. Lafosse et al. concluded that characteristic deficits in SIVD may result from a combination of diminished executive functions based on direct ischemic damage to subcortical–frontal circuits and diffuse cortical dysfunction based on transsynaptic degeneration. Alternately, the diffuse cortical atrophy may be associated with microvascular ischemic changes in the cortex.

Hippocampal volume loss may also be present in SIVD. Our group (Kramer et al., 2000) has found that hippocampal volumes in SIVD were 25% less than those in controls, although atrophic changes in mesial temporal regions may be less in SIVD than in AD. For example, Libon et al. (1998) reported smaller hippocampi in AD versus SIVD. Kemenoff et al. (2000), using AD and SIVD groups well matched for dementia severity, also reported that the AD group had significantly smaller mean hippocampal volumes than the SIVD group, even after adjusting for total brain volume.

In summary, the dementia associated with SIVD is much more than a subcortical syndrome. Structural and functional imaging studies have documented changes in the cortex, particularly the frontal lobes, and in the hippocampus. Although the biological mechanisms that underlie these cortical changes have yet to be elucidated, they undoubtedly contribute to the dementia symptoms.

AREAS FOR FUTURE RESEARCH

An understanding of SIVD is only just beginning to evolve. Mild SIVD affects a large proportion of nondemented elderly people, and more severe forms of the disorder compose the second most common cause of dementia. A great deal of basic and applied research is clearly needed. We propose three areas where additional clinical research is sorely needed: diagnosis, neuropsychiatric symptoms, and treatment.

Our current base of knowledge about SIVD is hindered by the lack of uniformity in how SIVD is defined. When reviewing the behavioral literature on SIVD, we were struck by the several different ways in which study groups are defined. In some instances, VaD groups are defined on the basis of Hachinski scores and vascular risk factors without reliance on neuroimaging findings. Altogether too many researchers lump all VaD patients into a single group, paying little heed to the tremendous differences among multi-infarct dementia, SIVD, and Binswanger's disease. Even when a study is restricted to SIVD, there is wide variability in diagnostic criteria. CT scans may be less sensitive to white matter disease, for example, and some researchers do not distinguish between lacunes and extensive white matter signal hyperintensities. There is not even universal agreement on what constitutes a lacune, whether T1 or T2 MRI images are most reliable, or how large a lesion must be before it can be called a lacune. There is a considerable need for a consensus conference on diagnostic criteria for SIVD and a willingness on the part of researchers to use a common diagnostic standard.

Much of the clinical research on SIVD has focused on neuropsychological changes. Although this is important, and a great deal more research is needed, information about neuropsychiatric changes is lacking. We know from studies of depression that psychiatric symptoms are associated with subcortical hyperintensities (Simpson, Jackson, Baldwin, & Burns, 1997). Anxiety, depression, and the overall severity of neuropsychiatric symptoms in VaD patients have also been associated with the extent of white matter ischemia (Sultzer et al., 1995). Greater awareness of the neuropsychiatric features of SIVD can simultaneously improve patient care and guide understanding of brain–behavior relationships.

Finally, treatment aimed at primary prevention, secondary prevention, and tertiary care is needed. Primary intervention should dovetail with efforts aimed at reducing the prevalence of vascular disease in general. However, there are a large number of normal elderly people with so-called silent lacunes who are at greater risk than their peers for developing a dementia, and methods for preventing or delaying progression need to be developed. For patients who already have SIVD, more clinical trials are needed to assess the viability of medications that can improve cognitive functioning.

ACKNOWLEDGMENT

This work was supported by a grant (PO1 AG12435) from the National Institute on Aging.

REFERENCES

American Psychiatric Association. (1987). *Diagnostic and statistical manual of mental disorders* (3rd ed., rev.). Washington, DC: Author.

American Psychiatric Association. (1994). *Diagnostic and statistical manual of mental disorders* (4th ed.). Washington, DC: Author.

Babikian, V., & Ropper, A. H. (1987). Binswanger's disease: A review. *Stroke, 18*, 2–12.

Bogousslavsky, J., & Regli, F. (1986). Borderzone infarction distal to internal carotid occlusion: Prognostic implications. *Archives of Neurology, 20*, 346–350.

Bogousslavsky, J., Regli, F., & Uske, A. (1998). Thalamic infarcts: Clinical syndrome, etiology and prognosis. *Neurology, 38*, 837–848.

Bornstein, N. M., Gur, A. Y., Treves, T. A., Reider-Groswasser, I., Aronovich, B. D., Klimovitzky, S. S., Varssano, D., & Korczyn, A. D. (1996). Do silent brain infarctions predict the development of dementia after first ischemic stroke? *Stroke, 27*, 904–905.

Caplan, L. R. (1991). Diagnosis and treatment of ischemic stroke. *Journal of the American Medical Association, 266*(17), 2413–2418.

Caplan, L. R., Schmahmann, J. D., Kase, C. S., Feldmann, E., Baquis, G., Greenberg, J. P., Gorelick, P. B., Helgason, C., & Hier, D. (1990). Caudate infarcts. *Archives of Neurology, 47*, 133–143.

Caplan, L. R., & Schoene, W. C. (1978). Clinical features of subcortical arteriosclerotic encephalopathy (Binswanger disease). *Neurology, 28*, 1206–1215.

Carew, T. G., Lamar, M., Cloud, B. S., Grossman, M., & Libon, D. J. (1997). Impairment in category fluency in ischemic vascular dementia. *Neuropsychology, 11*, 400–412.

Chui, H. C. (1989). Dementia: A review emphasizing clinicopathologic correlation and brain behavior relationships. *Archives of Neurology, 33*, 568–575.

Chui, H. C. (1992). Criteria for the diagnosis of ischemic vascular dementia proposed by the state of California Alzheimer's disease diagnostic and treatment centers. *Neurology, 42*, 473–480.

Chui, H. C., Victoroff, J. I., Margolin, D., & Jagust, W. (1992). Criteria for the diagnosis of ischemic vascular dementia proposed by the State of California Alzheimer's Disease Diagnostic and Treatment Centers. *Neurology, 42*(3), Pt 1).

Cummings, J. L. (1993). Frontal–subcortical circuits and human behavior. *Archives of Neurology, 50*, 873–880.

Cummings, J. L. (1994). Vascular subcortical dementias: Clinical aspects. *Dementia, 5*, 177–180.

Cummings, J. L. (1995). Anatomic and behavioral aspects of frontal–subcortical circuits. *Annals of the Academy of Sciences, 769*, 1–13.

Davous, P. (1998). CADASIL: A review with proposed diagnostic criteria. *European Journal of Neurology, 5*, 219–233.

de Reuck, J. (1971). The human periventricular arterial blood supply and the anatomy of cerebral infarctions. *Neurology, 5*, 321–334.

Erkinjuntti, T. (1997). Vascular dementia: Challenges of clinical diagnosis. *International Psychogeriatrics* (Suppl. 1), 51–58.

Erkinjuntti, T., Benavente, O., Eliasziw, M., Mjunoz, D. G., Sulkava, R., Haltia, M., & Hachinski, V. (1996). Diffuse vacuolization (spongiosis) and arteriolosclerosis in the frontal white matter occurs in vascular dementia. *Archives of Neurology, 53*, 325–332.

Erkinjuntti, T., Ostbye, T., Steenhuis, R., & Hachinski, V. (1997). The effect of different diagnostic criteria on the prevalence of dementia. *New England Journal of Medicine, 337*(23), 1667–1674.

Feinberg, W. M., Seeger, J. F., Carmody, R. F., Anderson, D. C., Hart, R. G., & Pearce, L. A. (1990). Epidemiologic features of asymptomatic cerebral infarction in patients with nonvalvar atrial fibrillation. *Archives of Internal Medicine, 150*, 2340–2344.

Ferrand, J. (1902). *Essai sur l'hemiplegie des vieillards: les lacunes de desintegration cerebrale.* Paris: These.

Ferrucci, L., Guralnik, J. M, Salive, M. E., Pahor, M., Corti, M. C., Baroni, A., & Havlik, R. J. (1996). Cognitive impairment and risk of stroke in the older population. *Journal of the American Geriatric Society, 44,* 237–241.

Fisher, C. M. (1965). Lacunes: Small deep cerebral infarcts. *Neurology, 15,* 774–784.

Gearing, M., Mirra, S. S., Hedreen, J. C., Sumi, S. M., Hansen, L. A., & Heyman, A. (1995). The Consortium to Establish a Registry for Alzheimer Disease (CERAD): Part X. Neuropathology confirmation of the clinical diagnosis of Alzheimer's disease. *Neurology, 45,* 461–466.

Hachinski, V. C., Iliff, L. D., Zilhka, E., DuBoulay, G. H., McAllister, V. L., Marshall, J., Russel, R., & Symon, L. (1975). Cerebral blood flow of dementia. *Archives of Neurology, 32,* 632–637.

Hassing, L., & Backman, L. (1997). Episodic memory functioning in population-based samples of very old adults with Alzheimer's disease and vascular dementia. *Dementia and Geriatric Cognitive Disorders, 8,* 376–383.

Heaton, R. K., Chelune, G. J., Talley, J. L., Kay, G. G., & Curtiss, G. (1983). *Wisconsin Card Sorting Test Manual: Revised and Expanded.* Odessa: Psychological Assessment Resources, Inc.

Heiss, W. D. (1983). Flow thresholds of functional and morphological damage of brain tissue. *Stroke, 14,* 329–331.

Holmes, C., Cairns, N., Lantos, P., & Mann, A. (1999). Validity of current clinical criteria for Alzheimer's disease, vascular dementia and dementia with lewy bodies. *British Journal of Psychiatry, 174,* 45–50.

Katzman., R., Lasker, B., & Bernstein, N. (1988). Advances in the diagnosis of dementia: Accuracy of diagnosis and consequences of misdiagnosis of disorders causing dementia. In R. D. Terry (Ed.), *Aging and dementia* (pp. 17–62). New York: Raven.

Kemenoff, L. A., Kramer, J. H., Mungas, D., Reed, B., Willis, L., Weiner, M., & Chui, H. (2000, February). *Neuropsychological and neuroimaging differentiation of vascular and Alzheimer's dementia.* Abstract submitted for poster session to be presented at the annual meeting of the International Neuropsychological Society, Denver, Colorado.

Kemenoff, L. A., Kramer, J. H., Reed, B., Mungas, D., Willis, L., Weiner, M., & Chui, C. (1999, August). *Neuropsychological differentiation of vascular and Alzheimer's dementia.* Poster session presented at the 107th Annual Convention of the American Psychological Association, Boston.

Kertesz, A., & Clydesdale, S. (1994). Frontal lobe deficits prominent in vascular dementia. *Archives of Neurology, 51,* 1226–1231.

Knopman, D., & Nissen, N. J. (1991). Procedural learning is impaired in Huntington's disease: Evidence from the serial reaction time task. *Neuropsychologia, 29,* 245–254.

Kobayashi, S., Okada, K., Koide, H., Bokura, H., & Yamaguchi, S. (1997). Subcortical silent brain infarction as a risk factor for clinical stroke. *Stroke, 28,* 1932–1939.

Kooistra, C. A., & Heilman, K. M. (1988). Memory loss from a subcortical white matter infarct. *Journal of Neurology Neurosurgery and Psychiatry, 51,* 866–869.

Kramer, J. H., Reed, B. R., Mungas, D., Weiner, M., & Chui, H. (1999). *Executive dysfunction in subcortical ischemic vascular disease.* Manuscript submitted for publication.

Kramer, J. H., Reed, B. R., Mungas, D., Weiner, M. W., Schuff, N., & Chui, H. C. (2000). Rate of forgetting in Alzheimer's and subcortical vascular dementias (in review).

Kwan, L. T., Reed, B. R., Eberling, J. L., Schuff, N., Tanabe, J., Norman, D., Weiner, M. W., & Jagust, W. J. (1999). Effects of subcortical cerebral infarction on cortical glucose metabolism and cognitive function. *Archives of Neurology, 56,* 809–814.

Ladurner, G., Iliff, L. D., & Lechner, H. (1982). Clinical factors associated with dementia in ischemic stroke. *Journal of Neurol Neurosurg Psychiatry, 45,* 97–101.

Lafosse, J. M., Reed, B. R., Mungas, D., Sterling, S. B., Wahbeh, H., & Jagust, W. J. (1997). Fluency and memory differences between ischemic vascular dementia and Alzheimer's disease. *Neuropsychology, 11,* 514–522.

Libon, D. J., Scanlon, M., Swenson, R., & Coslet, B. (1990). Binswanger's disease: Some neuropsychological considerations. *Journal of Geriatric Psychiatry and Neurology, 3,* 31–40.

Libon, D. J., Bogdanoff, B., Cloud, B. S., Skalina, S., Giovannetti, T. Gitlin, H. L., & Bonavita, J. (1998). *Journal of Clinical and Experimental Neuropsychology, 20*, 30–41.

Lindsay, J., Hebert, R., & Rockwood, K. (1997). The Canadian study of health and aging: Risk factors for vascular dementia. *Stroke, 28*, 526–530.

Loeb, C., Grandolfo, C., Croce, R., & Conti, M. (1992). Dementia associated with lacunar infarction. *Stroke,* 1225–1229.

Loeb, C., & Meyer, J. S. (1996). Vascular dementia: Still a debatable entity? *Journal of Neurological Sciences, 143*, 31–40.

Loizou, L. A., Kendall, B. E., & Marshall, J. (1981). Subcortical arteriosclerotic encephalopathy: A clinical and radiological investigation. *Journal of Neurosurgery and Psychiatry, 44*, 294–304.

Longstreth, W. T. Jr., Bernick, C., Manolio, T. A., Bryan, N., Jungreis, C. A., & Price, T. (1998). Lacunar infarcts defined by magnetic resonance imaging of 3660 elderly people: The cardiovascular health study. *Archives of Neurology, 55*, 1217–1225.

Lukatela, K., Malloy, P., Jenkins, M., & Cohen, R. (1998). The naming deficit in Alzheimer's and vascular dementia. *Neuropsychology, 12*, 565–572.

MacKay, S., Ezekiel, F., Di Sclafani, V., Meyerhoff, D. J., Gerson, J., Norman, D., Fein, G., & Weiner, M. W. (1996). Alzheimer disease and subcortical ischemic vascular dementia: Evaluation by combining MR imaging segmentation and H-1 MR spectroscopic imaging. *Radiology, 198*, 537–45.

Marie, P. (1901). Des foyers lacunaires de desintegration et de differents autres etats cavitaires du cerveau. *Rev. Med., 21*, 281–298.

Matsuda, O., Saito, M., & Sugishita, M. (1998). Cognitive deficits of mild dementia: A comparison between dementia of the Alzheimer's type and vascular dementia. *Psychiatry and Clinical Neuroscience, 52*, 87–91.

Mattis, S. (1976). Mental status examination for organic mental syndrome in the elderly patient. In L. Bellack & T. B. Karasu (Eds.), *Geriatric psychiatry.* New York: Grunne & Stratton.

Mendez, M. F., & Ashla-Mendez, M. (1991). Differences between multi-infarct dementia and Alzheimer's disease on unstructured neuropsychological tasks. *Journal of Clinical & Experimental Neuropsychology, 13*(6).

Mendez, M. F., Cherrier, M. M., & Perryman, K. M. (1997). Differences between Alzheimer's disease and vascular dementia on information processing measures. *Brain Cognition, 34*, 301–310.

Mirsen, T., & Hachinski, V. (1988). The epidemiology and classification of vascular and multi-infarct dementia. In J. S. Meyer, H. Lechner, J. Marshall, & J. F. Toole (Eds.), *Vascular and multi-infarct dementia* (pp. 61–76). New York: Futura.

Moody, D. M., Bell, M. A., & Challa, V. R. (1990). Features of the cerebral vascular pattern that predict vulnerability to perfusion or oxygenation deficiency: An anatomic study. *American Journal of Neuroradiology, 11*, 431–439.

Mounier-Vehier, F., Leys, D., Godefroy, O., Rodepierre, P., Marchau, M., Jr., & Pruvo, J. P. (1994). Borderzone infarct subtypes: Preliminary study of the presumed mechanism. *European Neurology, 34*, 11–15.

Mull, M., Schwarz, M., & Thron, A. (1997). Cerebral hemispheric low-flow infarct in arterial occlusive disease: Lesion patterns and angiomorphological conditions. *Stroke, 28*, 118–123.

Mychack, P., Kramer, J. H., Schatz, J., & Reed, B. (1998, August). *Executive functioning deficits in nondemented vascular patients.* Poster session presented at the 106th Annual Convention of the American Psychological Association, San Francisco, CA.

Nichelli, P., Bonito, V., Candelise, L., Capitani, E., Manzoni, S., Prencipe, M., Sangiovanni, G., Sinforiani, E., Taiuti, R., & Fieschi, C. (1986). Three-year neuropsychological follow-up of patients with reversible ischemic attacks. *Italian Journal of Neurological Sciences, 7*, 443–446.

Nolan, K. A., Lino, M. M., Seligmann, A. W., & Blass, J. P. (1998). Absence of vascular dementia in an autopsy series from a dementia clinic. *Journal of the American Geriatric Society, 46*, 597–604.

O'Brien, M. D. (1988). Vascular dementia is underdiagnosed. *Archives of Neurology, 45*, 797–798.

Padovani, A., DiPiero, V., Bragoni, M., Iacoboni, M., Gualdi, G. F., & Lenzi, G. L. (1995). Patterns of neuropsychological impairment in mild dementia: A comparison between Alzheimer's disease and multi-infarct dementia. *Acta Neurologica Scandanavia, 92*(6), 433–432.

Pantoni, L. & Garcia, J. H. (1997). Pathogenesis of leukoaraiosis. *Stroke, 28*, 652–659.

Pojasvaara, T., Erkinjuntti, T., Vataja, R., Kaste, M. (1997). Dementia three months after stroke: Baseline frequency and effect of different definitions of dementia in the Helsinki Stroke Aging Memory Study (SAM) cohort. *Stroke, 28*, 785–792.

Price, T. R., Manolio, T. A., Kronmal, R. A., Kittner, S. J., Yue, N. C., Robbins, J., Anton-Culver, H., & O'Leary, D. H. (1997). Silent brain infarction on magnetic resonance imaging and neurological abnormalities in community-dwelling older adults: The Cardiovascular Health Study. CHS collaborative research group. *Stroke, 28*, 1158–1164.

Reitan, R. M., & Wolfson, D. (1988). *The Halstead-Reitan Neuropsychological Test Battery.* Tucson: Neuropsychology Press.

Román, G. C. (1987). Senile dementia of the Binswanger type. *Journal of the American Medical Association, 258*, 1782–1788.

Román, G. C., Tatemichi, T. K., Erkinjuntti, T., & Cummings, J. L. (1993). Vascular dementia: Diagnostic criteria for research studies: Report of the NINDS-AIREN International Workshop. *Neurology, 43*(2).

Rosenstein, L. D. (1998). Differential diagnosis of the major progressive dementias and depression in middle and late adulthood: A summary of the literature of the early 1990's. *Neuropsychology Review, 8*, 109–167.

Sacco, R. (1994). Ischemic stroke. In P. B. Gorelick & M. Alter (Eds.), *Handbook of neuroepidemilogy* (pp. 77–119). New York: Marcel Dekker.

Sacco, R. L., Hauser, W. A., & Mohr, J. P. (1991). Hospitalized stroke incidence in Blacks and Hispanics in northern Manhattan. *Stroke, 22*, 1491–1496.

Schoenberg, B. S., & Shulte, B. P. M. (1988). Cerebrovascular disease: Epidemiology and geopathology. In P. J. Vinkin, G. W. Bruyn, & H. L. Klawans (Eds.), *Handbook of clinical neurology, vascular diseases* (Part 1, Vol. 53, pp. 1–26). New York: Elsevier Science Publishers.

Sharbrough, F. W., & Burgess, P. (1973). Correlation of continuous electroencephalograms with cerebral blood flow measurements during carotid endarterectomy. *Stroke, 4*, 674–683.

Sharbrough, F. W., Messick, J. M., Jr., & Sundt, T. M., Jr. (1973). Correlation of continuous electroencephalograms with cerebral blood flow measurements during carotid endarterectomy. *Stroke, 4*(4), 674–683.

Shinkawa, A., Ueda, K., Kiyohara, Y., Kato, I., Sueishi, K., Tsuneyoshi, M., & Fujishima, M. (1995). Silent cerebral infarction in a community-based autopsy series in Japan: The Hisayama Study. *Stroke, 26*, 380–385.

Shintani, S., Shiigai, T., & Arinami, T. (1998). Silent lacunar infarction on magnetic resonance imaging (MRI): Risk factors. *Journal of Neurological Sciences, 160*, 82–86.

Simpson, S. W., Jackson, A., Baldwin, R. C., & Burns, A. (1997). Subcortical hyperintensities in late-life depression: Acute response to treatment and neuropsychological impairment. *International Psychogeriatric, 9*, 257–275.

Stroop, J. R. (1935). Studies of interference in serial verbal reaction. *Journal of Experimental Psychology, 18*, 643–662.

Sultzer, D. L., Mahler, M. E., Cummings, J. L., Van Gorp, W. G., Hinkin, C. H., & Brown, C. (1995). Cotrtical abnormalities associated with subcortical lesions in vascular dementia: Clinical and positron emission tomographic findings. *Archives of Neurology, 52*, 773–780.

Suzuki, K., Kutsuzawa, T., Nakajima, K., & Hatano, S. (1991). Epidemiology of vascular dementia and stroke in Akita, Japan. In A. Hartmann, W. Kuchinski, & S. Hoyer (Eds.), *Cerebral ischemia and dementia* (pp. 16–24). New York: Springer-Verlag.

Taillia, H., Chabriat, H., Kurtz, A., Verin, M., Levy, C., Vahedi, K., Tournier-Lasserve, E., & Bousser, M. G. (1998). Cognitive alterations in non-demented CADISIL patients. *Cerebrovascular Disorders, 8*, 97–101.

Tatemichi, T., Desmond, D. W., Mayeux, R., et al. (1992). Dementia after stroke: Baseline frequency, risks, and clinical features in a hospitalized cohort. *Neurology, 42*, 1185–1193.

Tatemichi, T. K., Desmond, D. W., & Prohovnik, I. (1995). Strategic infarcts in vascular dementia: A clinical and brain imaging experience. *Drug Research, 45*, 371–385.

Tatemichi, T., Desmond, D. W., Prohovnik, I., Cross, D. T., Gropen, T. I., Mohr, J. P., & Stern, Y. (1992). Confusion and memory loss from capsular genu infarction: A thalamocortical disconnection syndrome? *Neurology, 42*, 1966–1979.

Tatemichi, T., Foulkes, M. A., Mohr, J. P., Hewitt, J. R., Hier, D. B., Price, T. R., & Wolf, P. A. (1990). Dementia in stroke survivors in the Stroke Data Bank cohort: Prevalence, incidence, risk factors, and computed tomographic findings. *Stroke, 21*, 858–866.

Tei, H., Miyazaki, A., Makoto, I., Osawa, M., Nagata, Y., & Maruyama, S. (1997). Early stage Alzheimer's disease and multiple subcortical infarction with mild cognitive impairment: Neuropsychological comparison using an easily applicable test battery. *Dementia and Geriatric Cognitive Disorders, 8*, 355–358.

Tell, G., Crouse, J., & Furberg, C. (1998). Relation between blood lipids, lipoproteins, and cerebrovascular atherosclerosis: A review. *Stroke, 1*, 423–430.

Tomlinson, B. E., Blessed, G., & Roth, M. (1970). Observations on the brains of demented old people. *Journal of Neurological Science, 11*, 205–242.

Torvik, A. (1984). The pathogenesis of watershed infarction in the brain. *Stroke, 15*, 221–223.

Wechsler, D. (1981). *Manual for the Wechsler Adult Intelligence Scale–Revised*. San Antonio: The Psychological Corporation.

Wolf, P. A., D'Agostino, R. B., Belanger, A. J., & Kannel, W. B. (1991). Probability of stroke: A risk profile from the Framingham Study. *Stroke, 22*, 312–318.

Wolf, P. A., Dawber, T. R., Thomas, H. E., & Kannel, W. B. (1978). Epidemiologic assessment of chronic atrial fibrillation and risk of stroke: The Framingham Study. *Neurology, 28*, 973–977.

Wolfe, N., Linn, R., Babikian, V. L., Knoefel, J. E., & Albert, M. L. (1990). Frontal systems impairment following multiple lacunar infarcts. *Archives of Neurology, 47*, 129–132.

World Health Organization. Mental and Behavioral Disorders: Diagnostic Criteria for Research. In *The International Classification of Diseases* (10th ed., 1993, pp. 36–40). Geneva: World Health Organization.

CHAPTER FIFTEEN

Neuropsychological Aspects of Stroke

Gregory G. Brown
Lisa T. Eyler Zorrilla
*Veterans Administration San Diego Healthcare System
and University of California, San Diego*

Stroke, the sudden loss of a neurological function, was known to early Greek physicians (Clarke, 1963). However, few authorities connected the symptoms of stroke to disorders of circulation until Johanne Jacob Wepfer published his *Observationses Anatomicae* [Anatomical Observations] in 1658 (Donley, 1909). Wepfer's studies of the postmortem brain showed that the internal carotid arteries perforate the dura to enter the brain, where they branch into more finely articulated cerebral vessels (Benton, 1991). Wepfer was also the first author to show that stroke could be caused by occlusion of cerebral vessels or by subdural or intracerebral hemorrhage (Benton, 1991). Wepfer's distinction between cerebrovascular occlusive disease and cerebral hemorrhage remains one of the fundamental clinical distinctions in the differential diagnosis of stroke (Wiebe-Velazquez & Hachinski, 1991). A related etiologic distinction, between ischemic brain disease and brain hemorrhage, is important for the classification of neuropsychological studies of stroke. This chapter is a review of neuropsychological studies of stroke caused by ischemia or hemorrhage of large cerebral vessels. Neuropsychological dysfunction associated with other types of cerebrovascular and cardiovascular conditions, as well as the neuropsychological effects of stroke treatments, are discussed in other chapters. Meier and Strauman (1991) reviewed the literature on recovery of function following cerebral infarction.

This chapter aims to provide readers with a description of the cerebral vasculature needed to understand the pattern of neuropsychological effects of stroke. It also provides a broad outline of the pathophysiological effects of cerebral ischemia and hemorrhage. As neuropsychological studies increasingly focus on the cerebral metabolic–behavioral correlates of stroke, investigators will need to have a working knowledge of stroke pathophysiology. Last, this chapter reviews the neuropsychological effects of cerebral ischemia and hemorrhage. Because many investigators have studied stroke patients to test specific theories about localization of cerebral function, a review of stroke's effect on behavior could be as extensive as the field of neuropsychology itself. We restrict our review to studies specifically aimed at clarifying the effects of stroke on motor and sensory systems, memory, and general cognitive functioning.

DISTRIBUTION OF CEREBRAL VESSELS AND THEIR COLLATERALS

The topography of the major arteries and their interconnectedness generally determine the locus and severity of stroke. Pairs of carotid and vertebral arteries bring blood to the brain. At about the upper border of the thyroid cartilage the common carotid artery divides into external and internal segments (Gilroy & Meyer, 1969, p. 478). The internal carotid artery ascends to pierce the dura and bifurcates into the anterior and middle cerebral arteries at about the level of the optic nerve. The vertebral arteries ascend through the spinal vertebrae until they join at the lower border of the pons to form the basilar artery. At the upper border of the pons, the basilar artery divides to form a pair of posterior cerebral arteries (PCAs). The posterior artery ascends to the medial and lateral surfaces of the occipital and temporal lobes, where it provides blood flow to the inferior temporal gyrus, portions of the occipital lobe, and parts of the superior parietal lobule (Carpenter, 1972, pp. 237–238). Whereas the anterior division of the cerebral circulation provides blood supply to most of the forebrain, the posterior division, including the vertebrobasilar circulation and the PCAs, supplies the brainstem, the cerebellum, much of the thalamus, the occipital lobes, and the posterior medial temporal lobes. The low level of redundancy typically found in the final vascular pathway through which blood flows to a given brain location is one factor that produces focal neurologic dysfunction when blood flow is interrupted.

Neural damage caused by the interruption of blood flow to a circumscribed brain region depends not only on the duration of the interruption but also on the capacity of the cerebral circulation to compensate for the interruption of blood flow. Thomas Willis (1664) was the first author to describe the functional significance of the interconnectedness of the cerebrovasculature in providing a collateral path of blood flow when a single artery is blocked (A. Meyer & Hierons, 1962). Several of the many cerebrovascular connections are especially important to consider when interpreting results of neuropsychological studies of stroke. One set of connections, located at the base of the brain, was described in detail by Willis and appropriately bears his name. The anterior portion of the circle of Willis is formed by the two anterior cerebral arteries, which are connected by the anterior communicating artery (ACoA). Small branches from the ACoA, along with branches from the anterior cerebral artery, penetrate the brain to supply blood to the fornix, septal region, anterior perforated substance, optic chiasm, optic tract, optic nerve, and suprachiasmatic area (Dunker & Harris, 1976). The two PCAs, which are joined at the basilar artery, are in turn connected by the posterior communicating artery to their respective internal carotid arteries, just inferior to the bifurcation of the carotid artery into middle and anterior branches. The anterior and middle cerebral arteries and the PCAs are also joined at their ends by small vessels that pass through the leptomeninges. Further, the pericallosal branch of the anterior cerebral artery communicates with the posterior cerebral artery, as it bends around the splenium of the corpus callosum (Van der Drift & Kok, 1972). The external carotid artery has connections with the internal carotid artery, primarily through the ophthalmic artery (Osborn, 1980, pp. 78–85). Individual variability in this pattern of collateral supply is an important factor in determining the pattern and severity of damage in stroke. Nilsson, Cronqvist, and Ingvar (1979) showed that patients with occlusion of an internal carotid artery and collateral flow through the circle of Willis have normal regional blood flow values in the hemisphere ipsilateral to the occlusion, whereas those with collateral flow through the ophthalmic or leptomeningeal arteries had flow values 40% to 50% below normal. Thus, compensatory flow through the circle of Willis appears to be a more efficient source of collateral flow than the ophthalmic or leptomeningeal arteries. Moreover, the anterior portion of the circle of Willis is probably the critical route of compensatory flow because, typically, little blood is exchanged between the carotid artery and the PCA through the posterior communicating artery (Toole, 1990, p. 9).

CEREBRAL ISCHEMIA

Pathophysiology

Although the brain represents about 2% of total body weight, it receives 15% to 20% of the oxygenated blood pumped from the heart (Sokoloff, 1997). Mean cerebral blood flow (CBF) is about 50 ml/100 gm/minute, with mean gray matter CBF (80 ml/100 gm/minute) about three to four times the CBF of white matter (22 ml/100 gm/minute; Fieschi & Rosiers, 1976). Blood supplies the brain with glucose and oxygen while dispersing the heat and metabolic products of cerebral activity (Toole, 1990, pp. 28–29). The brain can tolerate only a brief cessation in the delivery of glucose and oxygen and the removal of metabolites before neural functioning is disrupted. Diminished cardiac output, clogged or ruptured blood vessels, reduced glucose and oxygen content of blood, or impaired autoregulation of blood flow all can disrupt normal circulatory function. *Cerebral ischemia* is the state of reduced blood flow to a brain region sufficient to alter neural metabolism and function (Ginsberg, 1997). Infarction occurs when the duration and severity of ischemia produce permanent functional and structural changes (Mohr, Fisher, & Adams, 1980). Because the early time course of ischemia's effects on the brain is very difficult to study in humans, most of what we know about early neuronal and metabolic effects of ischemia has come from animal studies. Within seconds after the onset of ischemia, glucose metabolism declines, depressing the production of adenosine triphosphate (ATP). With the reduction of high-energy phosphates following ischemia, energy-dependent ionic pumps collapse, permitting an influx of calcium into the cell (J. S. Meyer, Deshmukh, & Welch, 1976; Reivich & Waltz, 1980). The influx of calcium into the cell may stimulate a cascade of events that disrupts cell structure; alters the function of receptors and ionic channels; blocks the production of molecular energy; and, possibly, fragments DNA (Siesjo, 1990). The depression of molecular energy causes brain acidosis, vasodilation, a loss of autoregulation, altered neural excitability, and swelling of glial cells (Hødt-Rasmussen et al., 1967; Reivich & Waltz, 1980). Brain acidosis, in turn, suppresses the synthesis of molecular energy when blood flow returns after ischemia, and may potentiate the formation of free-radical molecules that cause membrane damage (Siesjo, 1985).

Presynaptic vesicles are altered and lost 3 to 4 minutes into the ischemic period (Williams & Grossman, 1970). These alterations are accompanied by the release of the neurotransmitters dopamine, serotonin, and norepinephrine into the extracellular space and cerebrospinal fluid (J. S. Meyer, Welch, Okamoto, & Shimazu, 1974). Disordered cholinergic transmission following acute stroke may add a neurogenic component to metabolic factors causing a disruption of autoregulation (E. O. Ott et al., 1975). Between the first and fourth hours after complete cerebral ischemia, the blood becomes stagnant, changes occur in the thin internal lining of the blood vessels, edema develops, and the regional collapse of autoregulation occurs. Although histologic changes continue to develop over the hours and days following ischemia, the type of change depends on the duration and severity of the ischemia as well as the chronicity (Garcia, 1995). Immediate acute changes (≥ 6 hr) involve shrinkage, scalloping, or swelling of neurons; delayed changes (6 hr–48 hr) include the alteration of the genetic material in neurons; subacute changes (2 days–2 weeks) involve an abundant reaction of inflammatory cells; and chronic changes (>2 weeks) consist of the liquefaction and cavitation of the infarcted tissue, with a surrounding zone of astrocyte proliferation (Garcia, 1995; Garcia & Brown, 1992).

Although depressed production of molecular energy appears to be the stimulus for the cascade of events leading to ischemic brain change, bioenergetic failure is not itself the cause of brain infarction. As Siesjo and Smith (1997) observed, brain infarction does not develop during hypoglycemic coma, despite the occurrence of bioenergetic failure. The list of candidate causes of neuronal death following ischemia include acidosis, abnormal calcium influx into nerve cells, free-radical production, glutamate-mediated excitotoxicity, dysregulated lipid metabolism, nitric oxide neurotoxicity, and activation of proteolytic enzymes. The primer edited by Welch, Caplan, Reis, Siesjo, and Weir (1997) can be consulted for reviews of each of these potential causes of ischemic neuronal death.

The ischemic region has a gradient of viability that varies with CBF. At the core is a focus where blood flow is not more than 10% to 20% of controls (Ginsberg, 1997). Neural tissue in the core is isoelectric and destined to progress to infarction (Welch & Levine, 1991). Surrounding the ischemic core is another isoelectric region, called either a *bordering* or *penumbral zone* (Astrup, Siesjo, & Symon, 1981; Meyer, Gotoh, & Tazaki, 1962), where flow is 20% to 40% of controls and tissue conditions fluctuate between those favoring and those opposing tissue viability. Although residual perfusion in the penumbra is probably sufficient to maintain near-normal concentrations of ATP, it seems insufficient to maintain normal lactate levels, adequate functioning of ionic pumps, and neurotransmitter synthesis (Welch & Levine, 1991). The ischemic penumbra is a target of some pharmacological stroke treatments. Surrounding the ischemic zone is a collateral region where neural tissue retains its normal electrical activity and its tissue viability and where CBF is higher than control states (Welch & Barkley, 1986).

In 1914, von Monakow (1914/1969) proposed the hypothesis that a focal lesion could depress neural functioning in distant brain regions, a phenomenon called *diaschisis*. In its narrow sense diaschisis is a transient depression of neuronal activity at brain sites distant from the lesion locus, although at times authors use the term to describe permanent depression. In support of the diaschisis hypothesis, regional CBF studies have shown that blood flow is mildly but significantly depressed in the hemisphere contralateral to the hemisphere containing the ischemic infarction (Fujishima, Tanaka, Takeya, & Omae, 1974; Lavy, Melamed, & Portnoy, 1975). Carefully conducted metabolic and imaging studies have shown that both ipsilateral and contralateral suppression of CBF occurs distant from the ischemic focus (J. S. Meyer, Naritomi, Saskai, Ishihara, & Grant, 1978). However, as typically used, diaschisis is a descriptive term with little explanatory value. To contribute to our understanding of the neurobiology of neuropsychological change following stroke, a mechanistic theory of diaschisis would need to be developed. One possible mechanism is represented by the *disconnection hypothesis,* which posits that ischemic infarction can destroy neuronal projections to a remote site, disconnecting that site from sources of neuronal innervation. In support of the disconnection hypothesis of diaschisis, Metter et al. (1985) reported on a patient with markedly reduced glucose metabolism in the left inferior frontal region. The patient died from a gastrointestinal bleed 10 days after the metabolic imaging study. At autopsy the left frontal region that showed depressed glucose metabolism was histologically normal. The reduction of glucose metabolism to the region was apparently due to an infarction in the left internal capsule in a region containing efferent and afferent fibers connecting the depressed frontal site to other brain regions.

Although disconnection appears to explain some cases of depressed blood flow and metabolism remote from the site of infarction, it is a passive mechanism that leaves the remote region functioning normally. A more active mechanism altering neuronal function remote from the site of infarction is *spreading depression*, a slowly propagating depolarization that can extend over an entire hemisphere (Hossmann, 1997). Spreading depression appears to propagate by the release of glutamate. The transient disruption of ionic homeostasis that spreading depression produces is reversed by the activation of CBF coupled with ionic transport (Hossman, 1997). Other pathological remote effects of stroke include anterograde degeneration, retrograde degeneration, and transsynaptic death (Tamura & Nakayama, 1997). A lesion of an axon has anterograde effects, causing the axon to degenerate and its myelin sheath and terminals to disintegrate. Axonal lesions can also impair functioning of the nerve cell body, producing retrograde degeneration. Both anterograde and retrograde degeneration can lead to death of cells joined with the lesioned cell at the synapse. Investigators have hypothesized that this transsynaptic death is caused by a reduction of neural stimulation below a level required by a neuron to survive or by diminished release of a trophic substance needed for neurons to survive (Tamura & Nakayama, 1997).

To summarize, interruption of the delivery of oxygen or glucose to neural tissue depresses the production of ATP and other energy-bearing molecules. Impaired molecular energy production triggers a cascade of cellular changes that alter neurotransmitter synthesis, cellular electrical activity, ionic channel stability, pH homeostasis and, ultimately, cell membrane integrity. Three zones of abnormal blood flow develop following cerebral ischemia: (a) the ischemic core, where tissue becomes infarcted; (b) the penumbra, where blood flow is diminished and tissue viability varies; and (c) the hyperemic zone, where blood flow is abnormally elevated and neural tissue remains intact. Although the precise mechanisms that cause cell destruction following ischemia are unknown, investigators have identified several possible mechanisms. Some of these pathological mechanisms—such as acidosis, glutamate-mediated excitotoxicity, and dysregulated lipid metabolism—can be studied with in vivo imaging methods. Although metabolic and blood flow reductions remote from the site of infarction can be observed among patients with ischemic stroke, the mechanisms underlying these changes are also unknown.

Behavioral Effects of Ischemic Stroke

Typically, strokes produce focal or multifocal neurobehavioral deficits. Because each carotid artery supplies blood to one cerebral hemisphere, lateralized deficits are common among stroke victims. In addition to producing focal or lateralized neuropsychological symptoms, stroke typically disrupts general behavioral functions that depend on the integrative activity of the entire brain (Hom, 1991).

Motor Impairment

The impact of lateralized strokes on motor functioning was reviewed by Brown, Baird, Shatz, and Bornstein (1996). The literature supports several generalizations about the motor performance of stroke patients. In righthanders, grip strength and finger tapping are selectively impaired on the hand contralateral to the hemisphere with the cerebrovascular lesion. Neither the right nor the left hemisphere predominates in the bilateral control of grip strength or finger flexion. Tests that depend heavily on intact motor steadiness or coordination show greater ipsilateral effects than do tests of finger tapping or grip strength. The left hemisphere may have greater bilateral control than the right on motor tests that involve a series of learned movements, especially when the patient is responding to verbal commands. However, the right hemisphere may have greater bilateral control over movements involving a spatial component.

Sensory Deficits

Reitan and Fitzhugh (1971) studied stroke-related lateralization of sensory deficits on tests of single- and double-simultaneous visual, auditory, and tactile stimulation; finger gnosis; and finger graphesthesia. Right-hemisphere stroke produced more contralateral sensory deficits than left hemisphere stroke did. Only the comparison between the right and left hands during double-simultaneous stimulation of the two hands produced a clear crossover effect, suggesting a strong lateralizing sign. Overall, the patterns of between- and within-group comparisons suggested greater bilateral control of tactile processing by the right hemisphere, greater contralateral loss in visual functioning after right-hemisphere lesions, and very little lateralization of simple auditory perception. Boll (1974) showed that for a mixed group of lateralized trauma, stroke, and tumor patients, right-hemisphere lesions were associated with a greater number of ipsilateral errors on tests of finger gnosis, finger graphesthesia, and tactile form recognition than were left-hemisphere lesions. He also reported a greater number of contralateral errors among patients with right-hemisphere lesion than among paitents with left-hemisphere lesions. More recently, Hom and Reitan (1982) confirmed poorer ipsilateral performance on sensorimotor measures following right-hemispheric lesions compared to left-hemisphere lesions.

General Cognitive Deficits

Investigators have used general intelligence tests, detailed neuropsychological batteries, or mental-status screening tests to study the prevalence of cognitive impairment following stroke. In a community-based study of patients with a first-ever stroke, House, Dennis, Warlow, Hawton, and Molyneux (1990) found that 26% of patients displayed impaired mental status on the Mini Mental State Examination 1 month following stroke. The percentage of patients with impaired mental status dropped to 21% at the 6-month follow-up and remained at this level at the 12-month evaluation. Impaired mental status was associated with greater age, physical disability prior to stroke, larger stroke volume, cerebral atrophy, white matter changes, and depression. Tatemichi et al. (1994) measured memory, orientation, verbal skills, visuospatial ability, abstract reasoning, and attentional skills in a sample of 227 patients 3 months following stroke. After adjusting all test scores for demographic factors, Tatemichi et al. used the fifth percentile of a stroke-free control group as a cutoff score to identify patients with cognitive impairment. If cognitive impairment was defined as failure on 4 or more of the 17 test items, 35.2% of the stroke patients and 3.8% of controls experienced cognitive impairment. Dependent living status was more than twice as likely if cognitive impairment was present, even after controlling for age and degree of physical impairment. Cognitive impairment that is sufficient to meet criteria for dementia following stroke is a risk factor for subsequent stroke (Moroney et al., 1997). Moreover, dementia following stroke is associated with a threefold increase in mortality among stroke patients older than 59 years of age, even after adjusting for the effects of demographic factors, cardiac disease, severity of stroke, stroke type, and recurrent stroke.

Reitan and Fitzhugh (1971) examined the effects of stroke on intellectual functions as measured by the Wechsler–Bellevue I. Although patients with left-hemispheric strokes scored worse on tests of verbal intelligence than patients with right-hemispheric strokes, there was no difference between the two groups on performance scores. Nonetheless, the within-group comparisons showed a more strongly lateralized pattern: patients with left-hemispheric stroke scored significantly worse on verbal tests than on performance tests, whereas patients with right-hemispheric stroke scored significantly worse on performance tests than on verbal tests. The between- and within-group findings together suggested that left-hemispheric vascular lesions affect both verbal and visuospatial intellectual functions, although verbal IQ is affected to a greater extent. In a similar study, which included a healthy control group, Reitan (1970) directly showed that left-hemisphere stroke depresses both verbal and visuospatial test scores, with verbal scores more severely depressed than visuospatial scores. He also found that right-hemispheric stroke patients had significantly lower verbal and visuospatial scores than controls, although, not surprisingly, visuospatial performance was more significantly impaired than verbal functions. Recently, Hom and Reitan (1990) replicated these findings using the Wechsler Adult Intelligence Scale (WAIS). The one exception was that even though the average verbal intelligence score of the right-hemisphere stroke patients was numerically smaller than that of healthy controls, the difference was not significant.

General Adaptive Functioning

Indexes of general adaptive functioning studied in stroke fall into two classes. The first is composed of indexes, such as the Halstead Impairment Index and the Average Impairment Index, that sum over scores obtained from separate tests. These indexes measure the additive effects of impaired discrete functions. The second class of indexes is composed of scores from single tests, such as the Halstead Category Test and the Trail-Making Test, that reflect the integrated, interactive behavior of the brain. Lateralized stroke lowers scores on both types of indexes, regardless of the side of the lesion. In particular, Hom and Reitan (1990) found that left- and right-hemispheric stroke produced similar levels of impairment on the Halstead Impairment Index; the Halstead Category Test; the Trail-Making Test, Form B; the Digit Symbol subtest from the WAIS; and the memory score from the Tactual Performance Test. These findings imply that lateralized stroke impairs general adaptive brain functions, such as abstraction and some measures of incidental memory and attention (Hom, 1991).

Memory Deficits

Patients have depressed memory performance following strokes to diverse parts of the brain. However, in many cases the poor memory performance can be attributed to impaired executive, language, or visuoperceptual functioning. Selective memory deficits, often severe enough to produce amnesia, are associated with stroke in specific brain areas. One such area is the territory supplied by the PCA and posterior communicating artery.

The posterior cerebral circulation provides blood to the posterior hippocampus, mamillary bodies, and much of the thalamus. Although the anterior choroidal artery, which branches from the internal carotid artery near the posterior communicating artery, provides blood to the hippocampus, branches of the PCA also supply the hippocampus, especially in posterior regions (Huther, Dorfl, Van der Loos, & Jeanmonod, 1998). A group of important posterior thalamo-perforating arteries, also referred to as the *posteromedial arteries* or the *paramedian arteries,* arise from the top of the basilar artery and from the PCA (Carpenter, 1972, p. 240; Grand & Hopkins, 1999; von Cramon, Hebel, & Schuri, 1985). When using the paramedian nomenclature to refer to the posterior thalamo-perforating arteries, authors should be careful to distinguish the thalamic paramedian arteries from the mesencephalic and pontine paramedian arteries (Carpenter, 1972, p. 241; von Cramon et al., 1985). To avoid confusion, we use the term *posterior thalamo-perforating arteries* to refer to the small arteries that arise from the basilar arteries or PCAs to penetrate the thalamus. Small branches of the posterior thalamo-perforating arteries also supply the mamillary bodies (Grand & Hopkins, 1999, p. 136). Although branches of the anterior choroidal artery supply ventrolateral portions of the thalamus, much of the blood supply to the thalamus is provided by the PCA system (Carpenter, 1972, pp. 240–241).

The caudal and lateral portion of the thalamus receives its blood supply mainly from thalamogeniculate perforating arteries, also called the *posterolateral arteries*, which arise from the P2 segment of the PCA (Carpenter, 1972, pp. 240–241; Grand & Hopkins, 1999, p. 137). The posterior thalamus, as well as periventricular and median nuclei of the thalamus, are supplied by the posterior thalamo-perforators described earlier (Grand & Hopkins, 1999). Branches of the medial posterior choroidal artery, which generally arises from the P2 portion of the posterior cerebral artery, supply the superior and medial surfaces of the thalamus (Carpenter, 1972, pp. 240–241; Grand & Hopkins, 1999, p. 137). Most studies of amnesic stroke have focused on two broad groups of patients: those with bilateral or unilateral infarct in the mesiotemporal lobe due to PCA stroke and those with infarction of the medial thalamus in the distribution of the posterior thalamo-perforating arteries.

Memory disturbances following bilateral and unilateral infarction of the PCA have been studied extensively. About 40% of patients with PCA stroke suffer from impaired learning and memory (Fisher, 1986; von Cramon, Hebel, & Schuri, 1988). The common feature distinguishing PCA stroke patients with amnesia from those without appears to be the involvement of mesiotemporal structures such as the hippocampus and parahippocampal gyrus (B. R. Ott & Saver, 1993; von Cramon et al., 1988). It was initially thought that bilateral damage to these structures was necessary to produce long-lasting, severe amnesia (Woods, Schoene, & Kneisley, 1982). Subsequent case reports of chronic, significant deficits following unilateral PCA infarction affecting the mesiotemporal lobe has forced a revision of this view (von Cramon et al., 1988). Dominant-hemisphere PCA strokes appear most likely to result in memory deficits. In the series reviewed by Fisher (1986), 24 of 25 memory-impaired patients had dominant-hemisphere lesions. B. R. Ott and Saver's (1993) literature review revealed that 44 of 48 reported cases involved left-sided damage. In von Cramon et al.'s (1988) series, none of the 10 right-hemisphere-lesion patients showed memory deficits despite involvement of the crucial mesiotemporal lobe structures in most of these patients. Unfortunately, all of the studies used verbal materials to test for learning and memory deficits, leaving open the possibility that right-hemisphere PCA infarction could lead to material-specific memory deficits for visual or spatial information. However, testing this possibility is made difficult by the visuoperceptual deficits (e.g., visual agnosia) that often accompany PCA infarction. Still, it is suggestive that in a study in which the PCA of nonhuman primates was occluded, the one macaque who suffered unilateral right mesiotemporal damage showed mild visual recognition memory deficits (Bachevalier & Mishkin, 1989).

Although the presence of memory deficits in cases of PCA infarction has been well documented, less attention has been paid to the specific nature of these deficits. Bilateral stroke in the mesiotemporal region appears to result in a profound amnesia that is obvious in daily life as well as on neuropsychological testing (Brindley & Janota, 1975; Victor, Angevine, Mancall, & Fisher, 1961; Woods et al., 1982). Perhaps relatedly, cases of transient global amnesia have been linked to temporary bilateral PCA occlusion resulting in widespread hypoperfusion of the territories supplied by the PCA (Stillhard, Landis, Schiess, Regard, & Sialer, 1990; Tanabe et al., 1991). Unilateral, dominant-hemisphere stroke of the PCA appears to lead to impaired verbal learning of word lists and paired associates (De Renzi, Zambolin, & Crisi, 1987; von Cramon et al., 1988) as well as deficient recall of word lists, stories, and objects (De Renzi et al., 1987; Mohr, Leicester, Stoddard, & Sidman, 1971; B. R. Ott & Saver, 1993; von Cramon et al., 1988). Remote, autobiographical memory also seems to be impaired in these patients, but auditory short-term memory is preserved (von Cramon et al., 1988). The severity of the deficit following unilateral damage is less than that seen as a consequence of bilateral infarction. Although the general profile of learning and memory deficits is consistent across case reports, the heterogeneity of severity and pattern of dysfunction remains to be explained. For instance, whereas all 12 memory-impaired patients in von Cramon et al.'s (1988) series showed learning deficits, only 6 were significantly impaired on recall measures. Further studies relating involvement of particular mesiotemporal structures to specific mnemonic abilities are needed to characterize fully the consequences of PCA infarction.

The second broad category of studies relating stroke of PCA to memory abilities includes patients with infarction of the posterior thalamo-perforating arteries resulting in selective lesions of the thalamus. General neurologic features common in medial thalamic stroke include decreased levels of consciousness, especially somnolence; supranuclear vertical gaze paresis; hemiparesis; hemiataxia; and delayed abnormal movements (B. R. Ott & Saver, 1993). Memory disturbance is a frequent outcome for these patients.

Studies of patients with selective thalamic lesions due to stroke have been of particular importance in the amnesia literature because they represent a pure test of the hypothesis that memory disturbance in so-called diencephalic amnesia (such as results from alcoholic Korsakoff's syndrome) is the result of damage to the diencephalon itself as opposed to other coincidentally damaged areas. The weight of accumulated evidence suggests that damage to the medial thalamus alone is sufficient to cause some components of the amnesia seen in alcoholic Korsakoff's patients. In particular, bilateral lesions of the thalamus have been shown to result in impaired recall for verbal and nonverbal material (Calabrese, Haupts, Markowitsch, & Gehlen, 1993; Graff-Radford, Damasio, Yamada, Eslinger, & Damasio, 1985; Katz, Alexander, & Mandell, 1987; von Cramon et al., 1985; Winocur, Oxbury, Roberts, Agnetti, & Davis, 1984) as well as impaired learning of verbal, visual, and spatial information (Stuss, Guberman, Nelson, & Larochelle, 1988; von Cramon et al., 1985). As in alcoholic Korsakoff's syndrome, immediate memory for verbal and spatial information is not impaired (Calabrese et al., 1993; Stuss et al., 1988; von Cramon et al., 1985; Winocur et al.,

1984); nor is motor learning (Graff-Radford, Tranel, Van Hoesen, & Brandt, 1990). Although patients with alcoholic Korsakoff's syndrome show a graded remote memory impairment, with more recent memories impaired more than remote memories, remote and autobiographical memory has only inconsistently been found to be impaired in patients with thalamic infarction (Graff-Radford et al., 1985, 1990; Katz et al., 1987; Stuss et al., 1988; von Cramon et al., 1985; Winocur et al., 1984). Thus, bilateral lesions of the medial thalamus can result in anterograde amnesia similar in severity to that seen in patients with alcoholic Korsakoff's syndrome. Thalamic stroke less consistently impairs remote autobiographical memory than does alcoholic Korsakoff's syndrome.

   Although thalamic stroke can produce anterograde amnesia, the degree and pattern of impairment may vary on the basis of the particular thalamic nuclei involved. For example, it has been suggested that damage to the mamillothalamic tracts is necessary to produce amnesia (Gentilini, De Renzi, & Crisi, 1987; von Cramon et al., 1985). Consistent with this hypothesis, Kritchevsky, Graff-Radford, and Damasio (1987) described a patient with partial bilateral damage to the mediodorsal nucleus sparing the mammilothalamic tracts who showed no signs of verbal or visual memory impairment. Similarly, the patient of Mennemeier, Fennell, Valenstein, and Heilman (1992) whose small unilateral lesion spared the mamillothalamic tract had subtle memory deficits that were revealed only when rehearsal and semantic encoding strategies were prevented. However, Calabrese et al. (1993) reported on a patient with bilateral medial thalamic infarct with no apparent mammilothalamic damage who evidenced considerable impairments in verbal learning and memory. Because small lesions restricted to particular thalamic nuclei are rare, further clarification of the role of the substructures of the thalamus in memory awaits other unfortunate accidents of nature.

   Unilateral lesions of the thalamus lead to deficits in learning and memory that are significant but less severe than the deficits seen with bilateral infarct. Left-hemisphere stroke in the thalamus has been shown to result in impairments of verbal learning and memory (Fensore, Lazzarino, Nappo, & Nicolai, 1988; Mori, Yamadori, & Mitani, 1986; Parkin, Rees, Hunkin, & Rose, 1994; Speedie & Heilman, 1982) and temporal-order memory (Parkin et al., 1994). In contrast, such patients have shown relatively preserved remote and autobiographical memory (Fensore et al., 1988; Parkin et al., 1994; but see Graff-Radford, Estlinger, Damasio, & Yamada, 1984) and few impairments of visual recall (Fensore et al., 1988; Mori et al., 1986; Parkin et al., 1994; Speedie & Heilman, 1982; but see Hennerici et al., 1989). Infarcts of the right medial thalamus have been less studied, but it is known that they can result in visuospatial memory deficits while sparing verbal learning and memory (Graff-Radford et al., 1984; Speedie & Heilman, 1983; Stuss et al., 1988). Other patients with right-thalamic lesions, however, have shown deficient memory in both verbal and visual modalities (Graff-Radford et al., 1984, 1985). Remote memory was normal in one reported patient (Speedie & Heilman, 1983) but deficient in two other cases (Graff-Radford et al., 1984). Thus, anterograde memory functions subserved by the thalamus appear to be broadly lateralized, with verbal memory deficits resulting from left-thalamic infarction and visuospatial or visuoperceptual memory deficits from right-thalamic lesions. The contribution of each hemithalamus to remote-memory abilities requires further study.

Summary

In about one fifth to one third of patients, ischemic stroke reduces cognitive functioning to a level of performance below all but the lowest 5% of healthy controls. Stroke impairs such general cognitive functions as intelligence, abstraction, incidental memory, and attention. Lateralized stroke produces predictable differences in verbal and performance intelligence test scores that are best detected by within-subject comparisons. Moreover, left-hemisphere stroke appears to more consistently produce general impairment of intellectual functioning than does right-hemisphere stroke. The question of what conditions must be met for strokes of the right hemisphere to disrupt intellectual functioning generally remains a lively issue. It is very likely to be unresolved until mediating factors such as intrahemispheric localization of the stroke, lesion size, and chronicity are accounted for in study designs. Asymmetries of motor performance following lateralized stroke are more consistently found on tests of finger tapping and grip strength than on tests of motor steadiness or fine motor coordination. Stroke produces more consistent lateralized sensory deficits on tests of single- and double-simultaneous stimulation in the visual and tactile modalities than in the auditory modality; however, even in the visual and tactile modalities right-hemispheric strokes tend to produce more sensory errors than left-hemispheric strokes do. Focal strokes produce circumscribed neuropsychological deficits; for example, circumscribed memory deficits commonly occur following stroke in the PCA distribution.

HEMORRHAGE

The neuropsychological literature discussed earlier primarily involved patients with ischemic stroke; this section focuses on the neuropsychological correlates of brain hemorrhage. The most common causes of nontraumatic, intracerebral hemorrhages are hypertension and vascular anomalies (Voelker & Kaufman, 1997). Because the neuropsychological effects of hypertension are reviewed elsewhere in this book, we review the neuropsychological effects of cerebral hemorrhage associated with vascular anomalies, especially cerebral aneurysms and arteriovenous malformations (AVMs).

Cerebral Aneurysms

An aneurysm is a thin-walled balloon-shaped dilatation of a vessel. Patients with aneurysms frequently present with hemorrhage; the rupture of an intracranial aneurysm may cause bleeding into brain parenchyma, the ventricular system, or subarachnoid spaces. Such patients frequently present with a neurological deficit that gradually develops over 5 to 30 minutes and with some change in alertness (Kase, Mohr, & Caplan, 1992). Other aneurysms are found incidentally on imaging studies of the head or on cerebral angiography when evaluating a patient for nonhemorrhagic neurologic disorders.

Aneurysms can disrupt cerebral functioning by rupturing, shedding emboli, producing mass effects, and causing hydrocephalus or spasm of the cerebral vessels (Mohr, Kistler, & Fink, 1992). The hemorrhage disrupts the normal supply of oxygen and glucose to brain tissue and disrupts removal of heat and byproducts from metabolic activities. Consequently, areas of infarction develop. The blood itself can be toxic to brain tissue, and this may be another source of neuronal dysfunction (Fein, 1975). Hemorrhage and the surgical removal of aneurysms can cause vasospasm. This constriction of cerebral vessels reduces CBF and disrupts energy metabolism (Powers & Grubb, 1987). The cascade of metabolic effects caused by vasospasm can eventually lead to brain infarction and, tragically, death.

Because the investigation of patients with ischemic stroke has provided neuropsychology with many of its principles of localization of functioning, the natural inclination is to assume that the site of cerebral hemorrhage has a powerful effect on the pattern of subsequent neuropsychological deficits. However, much of the evidence contradicts this assumption. Stabell (1991) reported that neither the site nor the side of a hemorrhage was associated with particular patterns of neuropsychological impairment in a sample of patients with subarachnoid hemorrhage due to cerebral aneurysms or AVMs. Similarly, Richardson (1991) found that patients studied 6 weeks following aneurysmal subarachnoid hemorrhage displayed disrupted performance on a broad range of neuropsychological tests, regardless of site. For example, Richardson found that patients with aneurysms of the left middle and left internal carotid arteries were no more impaired on measures of object naming latency, synonym vocabulary, fluent word generation, and verbal memory than were patients with aneurysms in the right hemisphere. Tidswell, Dias, Sagar, Mayes, and Battersby (1995) studied the neuropsychological function of 37 patients an average of 26.8 months following surgery to remove a cerebral aneurysm. Patients who had surgical removal of ACoA aneurysms did not differ from patients with aneurysms in nonfrontal regions on measures of intelligence, memory, executive function, neglect, vocational or cognitive complaints, or depression. Ogden, Mee, and Henning (1993) studied 89 patients with subarachnoid hemorrhage due primarily to aneurysmal bleed, first acutely and then 10 weeks and 12 months following hospitalization. Patients completed the WAIS–Revised, the Trail-Making Test, the Minnesota Test for the Differential Diagnosis of Aphasia, a copy trial of the Complex Figure Test, and a modified version of the Wisconsin Card Sorting Test. At none of the three assessment periods was site of hemorrhage related to performance on any neuropsychological measure.

Nonetheless, some investigators have found that either the severity or the pattern of neuropsychological deficit was associated with the rupture of or surgery on aneurysms at particular sites. For example, Bornstein, Weir, Petruk, and Disney (1987) found that, in a sample of patients with poor neuropsychological outcome following subarachnoid hemorrhage, patients with ACoA aneurysms were overrepresented. DeLuca and Cicerone (1991) found that only patients with hemorrhage associated with ACoA aneurysms displayed florid spontaneous confabulations, whereas patients with aneurysms in any cerebrovascular territory might display milder forms of confabulation. ACoA patients also tended to experience memory impairment and personality change. Barbarotto et al. (1989) concluded that patients with surgical removal of lateralized aneurysms of the middle and posterior communicating artery experience lateralized neuropsychological deficits. However, the authors qualified their conclusion by observing that in individual cases the extent of the neuropsychological deficit is broader than the pattern expected from the side of the aneurysm alone. Furthermore, the data analysis did not involve a direct comparison of the left- and right-hemispheric patients. Consequently, Barbarotto et al.'s article does not strongly contradict Stabell's (1991) finding that side of hemorrhage does not predict the pattern of subsequent neuropsychological deficit.

In summary, hemorrhage of cerebral aneurysms does not produce the clear patterns of laterality found following cerebral ischemia. However, severe impairment of neuropsychological dysfunction appears more often to be associated with aneurysms of the ACoA than aneurysms in the middle cerebral artery or PCA. Furthermore, hemorrhage of anterior cerebral artery aneurysms is often associated with the syndrome of florid confabulations, memory impairment, and personality change.

AVMs

An AVM is a congenital entanglement of blood vessels that forms an abnormal connection between the arterial and venous circulation (Adams & Victor, 1985, p. 622). AVMs are fetal abnormalities that arise about 3 weeks after conception, when primitive vessels divide into arteries and veins (Stein & Wolpert, 1980). An arrest at this early stage in the epigenesis of cerebral vessels produces a pipelike connection or fistula, which replaces the capillary bed. Blood is generally supplied to the nidus or core of an AVM by several feeding arteries and leaves the core through an enlarged draining vein. Although the majority of AVMs that become symptomatic present with hemorrhage, AVMs comprise only 2% to 9% of all hemorrhages (Gross, Kase, Mohr, Cunningham, & Baker, 1984; Perret, 1975; Perret & Nishioka, 1966) and about 1% of all strokes (Mohr, Hilal, & Stein, 1992). Hemorrhage due to AVM typically occurs in the second through fifth decades. The rarity of cases occurring in the first decade probably reflects the slow development of the abnormality (Stein & Wolpert, 1980).

Presurgical impairment of cognitive functioning varies widely in patients with AVMs. The impairment can be manifested as a specific neurobehavioral syndrome or as a general disruption of adaptive functioning (Reitan & Wolfson, 1985). In early studies of patients coming to surgery, the frequency of cognitive impairment ranged from none (Constans & Assal, 1971) to 50% (Olivecrona & Reeves, 1948). Perhaps the most important limitation of these studies was that none used well-validated measures of neuropsychological functioning.

A study by Waltimo and Putkonen (1974) represented a turning point in the neuropsychological analysis of AVMs. They administered the WAIS, the Benton Visual Retention Test, the Token Test, and tests of immediate and delayed memory to 40 patients with AVMs. A comparison of patients with left- and right-sided AVMs revealed no differences between them on any of the cognitive measures. Additional analyses did not indicate any relationship between overall intellectual performance (i.e., full scale IQ) and size, laterality, or symptoms of the AVM. However, there was a trend toward an association between neurobehavioral impairment and previous hemorrhage. In an additional analysis, patients were grouped on the basis of the uniformity of their cognitive performance. Those with obvious cognitive deficits and a large verbal–performance IQ difference were placed into one group ("high inequality"), and the remainder of the patients were placed into a second group. High inequality was found to be associated to a greater extent with right-sided malformations. Waltimo and Putkonen concluded that AVMs do not produce the kind of specific cognitive changes typically seen with acute focal lesions involving equivalent areas of the brain.

Waltimo and Putkonen's (1974) article does not indicate whether right-sided AVM patients with highly unequal verbal–performance IQ disparities generally had lower performance IQs than verbal IQs. Mahalick, Ruff, and U (1991) provided data to explore the question of differential effects of lateralized AVMs on verbal and performance IQs. Like Waltimo and Putkonen, Mahalick et al. failed to find a double dissociation between verbal and performance IQs when comparing patients with left-hemispheric AVMs and patients with right-hemispheric AVMs. In particular, mean verbal and performance IQs of patients with left-hemispheric AVMs—respectively 10 and 12 points below age- and education-matched healthy controls—did not significantly differ. However, a single dissociation was present. The mean performance IQ of patients with right-hemispheric AVMs was significantly below their mean verbal IQ. Although left-hemisphere AVMs are generally associated with mildly depressed verbal and performance IQs, right-hemisphere AVMs are often associated with moderately depressed performance IQs. What factors produce this uneven effect of lateralized AVMs on intellectual functioning is at present unknown.

Although only right-hemispheric AVMs produce lateralized deficits on intelligence tests, double dissociations have been reported on tests of other neuropsychological abilities (Close, O'Keefe, & Buchheit, 1977; Conley, Moses, & Helle, 1980). In addition to the studying the effects of lateralized AVMs on verbal and performance IQ, Mahalick et al. (1991) used a paired-test method to study the effects of lateralized AVMs on verbal, visuospatial, and figural tests. They found the predicted interaction in that patients with left-hemispheric AVMs were more impaired on the verbal member of test pairs and patients with right-hemispheric AVMs were more impaired on the figural or visuospatial pair member. Stabell and Nornes (1994) reported a similar finding: Patients with left-hemisphere AVMs scored more poorly than those with right-hemsiphere AVMs on digit span; verbal fluency; the Trial-Making Test, Form B; and initial learning of a 12-word list. Patients with right-hemisphere AVMs scored more poorly on the Picture Completion subtest of the WAIS.

The studies just reviewed suggest that lateralized AVMs produce less consistently lateralized neuropsychological effects than ischemic stroke. Brown, Spicer, Robertson, Baird, and Malik (1989) directly tested this hypothesis. They compared the accuracy of neuropsychological measures in predicting the laterality of AVMs with these measures' accuracy in predicting the laterality of ischemic stroke. Information from seven commonly used neuropsychological measures was analyzed using three techniques: discriminant function analysis, clinical judgment, and actuarial signs based on within-subject patterns of test scores. Although neuropsychological findings were significantly related to the laterality of ischemic stroke for all three methods, only clinical judgments were significantly related to laterality of AVMs for the complete sample. However, when neuropsychological evidence of lateralized dysfunction was clearly evident, actuarial signs and clinical ratings were as accurate in classifying the laterality of AVMs as they were in classifying the laterality of ischemic stroke.

Results from the studies just described suggest several summary generalizations. Although presurgical verbal IQs of patients with AVMs of either hemisphere generally fall within the normal range of intelligence, presurgical verbal IQs are typically about 0.75 *SD* below those of demographically matched controls. Performance IQs of patients with left-hemispheric AVMs are also about 0.75 *SD* below those of controls, compatible with a slight depression of verbal intellectual functioning. However, the mean presurgical performance IQ of patients with right-hemispheric AVMs falls 1.67 *SD* below that of controls, indicating mild to moderate impairment of visuospatial and visuoconstructional skills. Although patients with lateralized AVMs do not show the expected double dissociation between verbal and performance IQ found with other types of lateralized lesions, double dissociations between verbal functioning and visuoperceptual or visuospatial functioning are found for material-specific neuropsychological measures. Even on these more specific measures of lateralized functioning, lateralized AVMs do not as consistently produce a pattern of lateralized neuropsychological impairment as in patients with ischemic stroke. Nonetheless, when consistent evidence of lateralized dysfunction is present, the laterality of an AVM can be inferred as accurately as in ischemic stroke. Given the subtlety of the lateralized effects of AVMs and the broad influence of AVMs on intelligence, within-subject statistical designs are often necessary to detect the lateralized effects of AVMs.

FINAL COMMENTS

Since the publication of seminal studies in the early 1970s, the literature on the neuropsychological effects of strokes has grown rapidly. Neuropsychological studies of ischemic stroke have primarily focused on the neurocognitive and neurobehavioral correlates of the structural brain changes caused by infarction. This approach provides a limited characterization of the pathophysiology of brain ischemia, in part because ischemia alters brain function in regions outside of the region of infarction and in part because ischemia produces metabolic changes in addition to structural changes. Advances in the imaging of brain function make it possible to extend neuropsychological studies of ischemic stroke to the investigation of brain networks disrupted by stroke. Combining functional brain imaging with carefully chosen behavioral activation tasks administered while patients are being scanned will permit investigators to develop sophisticated accounts of the effects of ischemic stroke on cognitive, perceptual, and motor function. Similarly, in vivo metabolic imaging studies, such as proton and phosphorus spectroscopy, will permit investigators to investigate the neuropsychological–metabolic correlates of ischemic stroke. These correlates might be especially important in monitoring the effects of stroke medications and monitoring recovery of function. Theory accounting for the neuropsychological effects of brain hemorrhage may also become more sophisticated as it incorporates findings from functional and metabolic imaging methods. However as theory advances, neuropsychological studies of brain hemorrhage will need to continue to focus on practical issues, such as identifying factors predicting outcome and determining the neurobehavioral effects of surgical intervention. Assuming that technological advances in the study of brain function will continue to grow, the next century promises to be an even more productive period for neuropsychological studies of stroke than have the last three decades.

REFERENCES

Adams, R. D., & Victor, M. (1985). Principles of neurology (3rd ed.). New York: McGraw-Hill.

Astrup, J., Siesjo, B. K., & Symon, L. (1981). Thresholds in cerebral ischemia—The ischemic penumbra. *Stroke, 12,* 723–725.

Bachevalier, J., & Mishkin, M. (1989). Mnemonic and neuropathological effects of occluding the posterior cerebral artery in *Macaca mulatta. Neuropsychologia, 27,* 83–105.

Barbarotto, R., De Santis, A., Laiacona, M., Basso, A., Spagnoli, D., & Capitani, E. (1989). Neuropsychological follow-up of patients operated for aneurysms of the middle cerebral artery and posterior communicating artery. *Cortex, 25,* 275–288.

Benton, A. L. (1991). Cerebral vascular disease in the history of clinical neuropsychology. In R. A. Bornstein & G. G. Brown (Eds.), *Neurobehavioral aspects of cerebrovascular disease* (pp. 3–13). New York: Oxford University Press.

Boll, T. J. (1974). Right and left hemisphere damage and tactile perception: Performance of the ipsilateral and contralateral sides of the body. *Neuropsychologia, 12,* 235–238.

Bornstein, R. A., Weir, B. K. A., Petruk, K. C., & Disney, L. B. (1987). Neuropsychological function in patients after subarachnoid hemorrhage. *Neurosurgery, 21,* 651–654.

Brindley, G. S., & Janota, I. (1975). Observations on cortical blindness and on vascular lesions that cause loss of recent memory. *Journal of Neurology, Neurosurgery and Psychiatry, 38,* 59–64.

Brown, G. G., Baird, A. D., Shatz, M. W., & Bornstein, R. A. (1996). The effects of cerebral vascular disease on neuropsychological functioning. In I. Grant & K. M. Adams (Eds.), *Neuropsychological assessment of neuropsychiatric disorders* (2nd ed., pp. 342–378). New York: Oxford University Press.

Brown, G. G., Spicer, K. B., Robertson, W. M., Baird, A. D., & Malik, G. (1989). Neuropsychological signs of lateralized arteriovenous malformations: Comparison with ischemic stroke. *The Clinical Neuropsychologist, 3,* 340–352.

Calabrese, P., Haupts, M., Markowitsch, H. J., & Gehlen, W. (1993). The cognitive–mnestic performance profile of a patient with bilateral asymmetrical thalamic infarction. *International Journal of Neuroscience, 71,* 101–106.

Carpenter, M. B. (1972). *Core text of neuroanatomy.* Baltimore: Williams & Wilkins.

Clarke, E. (1963). Apoplexy in early Hippocratic writings. *Bulletin of the History of Medicine, 37,* 301–314.

Close, R. A., O'Keefe, A. M., & Buchheit, W. A. (1977). The determination of speech organization in a patient with an arteriovenous malformation. *Neurosurgery, 1,* 111–113.

Conley, F. K., Moses, J. A. Jr., & Helle, T. L. (1980). Deficits of higher cortical functioning in two patients with posterior parietal arteriovenous malformations. *Neurosurgery, 7,* 230–237.

Constans, J. P., & Assal, G. (1971). Evolution de la symptomalogie neuropsychologique d'une série d'anevrismes arterio–veineux opérés [Development of neuropsychological symptoms in a series of surgically treated arteriovenous aneurysms]. *Neurochiurgia, 14,* 201–216.

DeLuca, J., & Cicerone, K. D. (1991). Confabulation following aneurysm of the anterior communicating artery. *Cortex, 27,* 417–423.

De Renzi, E., Zambolin, A., & Crisi, G. (1987). The pattern of neuropsychological impairment associated with left posterior cerebral artery infarcts. *Brain, 110,* 1099–1116.

Donley, J. E. (1909). John James Wepfer, a renaissance student of apoplexy. *Bulletin, Johns Hopkins Hospital, 20,* 1–8.

Dunker, R. O., & Harris, A. B. (1976). Surgical anatomy of the proximal anterior cerebral artery. *Journal of Neurosurgery, 44,* 359–367.

Fein, J. M. (1975). Cerebral energy metabolism after subarachnoid hemorrhage. *Stroke, 6,* 1–8.

Fensore, C., Lazzarino, L. G., Nappo, A., & Nicolai, A. (1988). Language and memory disturbances from mesencephalothalamic infarcts: A clinical and computed tomography study. *European Neurology, 28,* 51–56.

Fieschi, C., & Rosiers, M. D. (1976). Cerebral blood flow measurements in stroke. In R.W. Ross Russell (Ed.), *Cerebral artery disease* (pp. 85–106). New York: Churchill Livingstone.

Fisher, C. M. (1986). The posterior cerebral artery syndrome. *Canadian Journal of Neurological Sciences, 13,* 232–239.

Fujishima, M., Tanaka, K., Takeya, Y., & Omae, T. (1974). Bilateral reduction of hemispheric blood flow in patients with unilateral cerebral infarction. *Stroke, 5,* 648–653.

Garcia, J. H. (1995). Mechanisms of cell death in ischemia. In L. R. Caplan (Ed.), *Brain ischemia: Basic concepts and clinical relevance* (pp. 7–18). New York: Springer-Verlag.

Garcia, J. H., & Brown, G. G. (1992). Vascular dementia: Neuropathologic alterations and metabolic brain changes. *Journal of Neurological Sciences, 109,* 121–131.

Gentilini, M., De Renzi, E., & Crisi, G. (1987). Bilateral paramedian thalamic artery infarcts: Report of eight cases. *Journal of Neurology, Neurosurgery, and Psychiatry, 50,* 900–909.

Gilroy, J., & Meyer, J. S. (1969). *Medical neurology.* London: MacMillan.

Ginsberg, M. D. (1997). Animal models of global and focal cerebral ischemia. In K. M. A.Welch, L. R. Caplan, D. J. Reis, B. K. Siesjo, & B. Weir (Eds.), *Primer on cerebrovascular diseases* (pp. 124–126). New York: Academic Press.

Graff-Radford, N. R., Damasio, H., Yamada, T., Eslinger, P. J., & Damasio, A. R. (1985). Nonhaemorrhagic thalamic infarction: Clinical, neuropsychological and electrophysiological findings in four anatomical groups defined by computerized tomography. *Brain, 108,* 485–516.

Graff-Radford, N. R., Eslinger, P. J., Damasio, A. R., & Yamada, T. (1984). Nonhemorrhagic infarction of the thalamus: Behavioral, anatomic, and physiologic correlates. *Neurology, 34,* 14–23.

Graff-Radford, N. R., Tranel, D., Van Hoesen, G. W., & Brandt, J. P. (1990). Diencephalic amnesia. *Brain, 113,* 1–25.

Grand, W., & Hopkins, L. N. (1999). *Vasculature of the brain and cranial base.* New York: Thieme.

Gross, C. R., Kase, C. S., Mohr, J. P., Cunningham, S. C., & Baker, W. E. (1984). Stroke in south Alabama: Incidence and diagnostic features—A population based study. *Stroke, 15,* 249–255.

Hennerici, M., Halsband, U., Kuwert, T., Steinmetz, H., Herzog, H., Aulich, A., & Feinendegen, L. E. (1989). PET and neuropsychology in thalamic infarction: Evidence for associated cortical dysfunction. *Psychiatry Research, 29,* 363–365.

Hødt-Rasmussen, K., Skinhøj, E., Paulson, O., Ewald, J., Bjerrum, J. K., Fahrenkrug, A., & Lassen, N. A. (1967). Regional cerebral blood flow in acute apoplexy: The "luxury perfusion syndrome" of brain tissue. *Archives of Neurology, 17,* 271–281.

Hom, J. (1991). Contributions of the Halstead–Reitan Battery in the neuropsychological investigation of stroke. In R. A. Bornstein & G. G. Brown (Eds.), *Neurobehavioral aspects of cerebrovascular disease* (pp. 165–181). New York: Oxford University Press.

Hom, J., & Reitan, R. M. (1982). Effect of lateralized cerebral damage upon contralateral and ipsilateral sensorimotor performance. *Journal of Clinical Neuropsychology, 4,* 249–268.

Hom, J., & Reitan, R. M. (1990). Generalized cognitive function after stroke. *Journal of Clinical and Experimental Neuropsychology, 12,* 644–654.

Hossmann, K.-A. (1997). Peri-infarct depolarization waves. In K. M. A.Welch, L. R. Caplan, D. J. Reis, B. K. Siesjo, & B. Weir (Eds.), *Primer on cerebrovascular diseases* (pp. 169–172). New York: Academic Press.

House, A., Dennis, M., Warlow, C., Hawton, K., & Molyneux, A. (1990). The relationship between intellectual impairment and mood disorder in the first year after stroke. *Psychological Medicine, 20,* 805–814.

Huther, G., Dorfl, J., Van der Loos, H., & Jeanmonod, D. (1998). Microanatomic and vascular aspects of the temporomesial regions. *Neurosurgery, 43,* 1118–1136.

Kase, C. S., Mohr, J. P., & Caplan, L. R. (1992). Intracerebral hemorrhage. In H. J. Barnett, J. P. Mohr, B. M. Stein, & F. M. Yatsu (Eds.), *Stroke pathophysiology, diagnosis and management* (2nd ed., pp. 561–616). New York: Churchill Livingstone.

Katz, D. I., Alexander, M. P., & Mandell, A. M. (1987). Dementia following strokes in the mesencephalon and diencephalon. *Archives of Neurology, 44,* 1127–1133.

Kritchevsky, M., Graff-Radford, N. R., & Damasio, A. R. (1987). Normal memory after damage to medial thalamus. *Archives of Neurology, 44,* 959–962.

Lavy, S., Melamed, E., & Portnoy, Z. (1975). The effect of cerebral infarction on the regional cerebral blood flow of the contralateral hemisphere. *Stroke, 6,* 160–163.

Mahalick, D. M., Ruff, R. M., & U, H. S. (1991). Neuropsychological sequelae of arteriovenous malformations. *Neurosurgery, 29,* 351–357.

Meier, M. J., & Strauman, S. E. (1991). Neuropsychological recovery after cerebral infarction. In R. A. Bornstein & G. G. Brown (Eds.), *Neurobehavioral aspects of cerebrovascular disease* (pp. 271–296). New York: Oxford University Press.

Mennemeier, M., Fennell, E., Valenstein, E., & Heilman, K. M. (1992). Contributions of the left intralaminar and medial thalamic nuclei to memory: Comparisons and report of a case. *Archives of Neurology, 49,* 1050–1058.

Metter, E. J., Mazziotta, J. C., Itabashi, H. H., Mankovich, N. J., Phelps, M. E., & Kuhl, D. E. (1985). Comparison of glucose metabolism, x-ray CT, and postmortem data in a patient with multiple infarctions. *Neurology, 35,* 1695–1701.

Meyer, A., & Hierons, R. (1962). Observations on the history of the "circle of Willis." *Medical History, 6,* 119–130.

Meyer, J. S., Deshmukh, U. D., & Welch, K. M. A. (1976). Experimental studies with the pathogenies of cerebral ischemia and infarction. In R. W. Ross Russell (Ed.), *Cerebral artery disease* (pp. 57–84). New York: Churchill Livingstone.

Meyer, J. S., Gotoh, G., & Tazaki, Y. (1962). Metabolism following experimental cerebral embolism. *Journal of Neuropathology and Experimental Neurology, 21,* 4–24.

Meyer, J. S., Naritomi, H., Saskai, F., Ishihara, N., & Grant, P. (1978). Regional cerebral blood flow, diaschisis, and steal after stroke. *Neurological Research, 1,* 101–119.

Meyer, J. S., Welch, K. M. A., Okamoto, S., & Shimazu, K. (1974). Disordered neurotransmitter function: Demonstration by measurement of norepinephrine and 5-hydroxytryptamine in CSF of patients with recent cerebral infarction. *Brain, 97,* 654–664.

Mohr, J. P., Fisher, C. M., & Adams, R. D. (1980). Cerebrovascular disease. In K. J. Isselbach, R. D. Adams, E. Braunwald, R. G. Petersdorf, & J. D. Wilson (Eds.), *Harrison's principles of internal medicine* (9th ed., pp. 1911–1942). New York: McGraw-Hill.

Mohr, J. P., Hilal, S. K., & Stein, B. M. (1992). Arteriovenous malformations and other vascular anomalies. In H. J. M. Barnett, J. P. Mohr, B. M. Stein, & F. M. Yatsu (Eds.), *Stroke pathophysiology, diagnosis, and management* (2nd ed., pp. 645–670). New York: Churchill Livingstone.

Mohr, J. P., Kistler, J. P., & Fink, M. E. (1992). Intracranial aneurysms. In H. J. M. Barnett, J. P. Mohr, B. M. Stein, & F. M. Yatsu (Eds.), *Stroke: Pathophysiology, diagnosis, and management* (2nd ed., pp. 617–644). New York: Churchill Livingstone.

Mohr, J. P., Leicester, J., Stoddard, L. T., & Sidman, M. (1971). Right hemianopia with memory and color deficits in circumscribed left posterior cerebral artery territory infarction. *Neurology, 21,* 1104–1113.

Mori, E., Yamadori, A., & Mitani, Y. (1986). Left thalamic infarction and disturbance of verbal memory: A clinicoanatomical study with a new method of computed tomographic stereotaxic lesion localization. *Annals of Neurology, 20,* 671–676.

Moroney, J. T., Bagiella, E., Tatemichi, T. K., Paik, M. C., Stern, Y., & Desmond, D. W. (1997). Dementia after stroke increases the risk of long-term stroke recurrence. *Neurology, 48,* 1317–1325.

Nilsson, B., Cronqvist, S., & Ingvar, D. H. (1979). Regional cerebral blood flow (rCBF) studies in patients to be considered for extracranial–intracranial bypass operations. In J. S. Meyer, H. Lechner, & M. Reivich (Eds.), *Cerebral vascular disease 2* (pp. 295–300). Amsterdam: Excerpta Medica.

Ogden, J. A., Mee, E. W., & Henning, M. (1993). A prospective study of impairment of cognition and memory and recovery after subarachnoid hemorrhage. *Neurosurgery, 33,* 572–586.

Olivecrona, H., & Reeves, J. (1948). Arteriovenous aneurysms of the brain: Their diagnosis and treatment. *Archives of Neurology and Psychiatry, 59*, 567–602.

Osborn, A. G. (1980). *An introduction to cerebral angiography.* New York: Harper & Row.

Ott, B. R., & Saver, J. L. (1993). Unilateral amnesic stroke: Six new cases and a review of the literature. *Stroke, 24*, 1033–1042.

Ott, E. O., Abraham, J., Meyer, J. S., Achari, A. N., Chee, A. N. C., & Mathew, N. T. (1975). Disordered cholinergic neurotransmission and dysautoregulation after acute cerebral infarction. *Stroke, 6*, 172–180.

Parkin, A. J., Rees, J. E., Hunkin, N. M., & Rose, P. E. (1994). Impairment of memory following discrete thalamic infarction. *Neuropsychologia, 32*, 39–51.

Perret, G. (1975). The epidemiology and clinical course of arteriovenous malformations. In H. W. Pia, J. R. W. Gleave, E. Grote, & J. Zierski (Eds.), *Cerebral angiomas: Advances in diagnosis and therapy* (pp. 21–26). New York: Springer-Verlag.

Perret, G., & Nishioka, H. (1966). Report on the cooperative study of intracranial aneurysms and subarachnoid hemorrhage: Section VI. Arteriovenous malformations. *Journal of Neurosurgery, 25*, 467–490.

Powers, W. J., & Grubb, R. L. Jr. (1987). Hemodynamic and metabolic relationships in cerebral ischemia and subarachnoid hemorrhage. In J. H. Wood (Ed.), *Cerebral blood flow: Physiologic and clinical aspects* (pp. 387–401). New York: McGraw-Hill.

Reitan, R. M. (1970). Presentation 15. In A. L. Benton (Ed.), *Behavioral change in cerebrovascular disease* (pp. 155–165). New York: Harper & Row.

Reitan, R. M., & Fitzhugh, K. B. (1971). Behavioral deficits in groups with cerebral vascular lesions. *Journal of Consulting and Clinical Psychology, 37*, 215–223.

Reitan, R. M., & Wolfson, D. (1985). *The Halstead–Reitan Neuropsychological Test Battery.* Tucson, AZ: Neuropsychology Press.

Reivich, M., & Waltz, A. G. (1980). Circulatory and metabolic factors in cerebrovascular disease. In *Cerebrovascular Survey Report* (pp. 55–134; NINCDS monograph available from National Institutes of Health, Building 31, Room 8A06, Bethesda, MD 20892-0002.

Richardson, J. T. (1991). Cognitive performance following rupture and repair of intracranial aneurysm. *Acta Neurologica Scandinavica, 83*, 110–122.

Siesjo, B. K. (1985). Acid–base homeostasis in the brain: Physiology, chemistry, and neurochemical pathology. In K. Kogure, K.-A. Hossmann, B. K. Siesjo, & F. A. Welsh (Eds.), *Progress in brain research* (Vol. 63, pp. 121–154). New York: Elsevier.

Siesjo, B. K. (1990). Calcium in the brain under physiological and pathological conditions. *European Neurology, 30* (Suppl. 2), 3–9.

Siesjo, B., & Smith, M.-L. (1997). Mechanisms of acidosis-related damage. In K. M. A. Welch, L. R. Caplan, D. J. Reis, B. K. Siesjo, & B. Weir (Eds.), *Primer on cerebrovascular diseases* (pp. 223–226). New York: Academic Press.

Sokoloff, L. (1997). Anatomy of cerebral circulation. In K. M. A. Welch, L. R. Caplan, D. J. Reis, B. K. Siesjo, & B. Weir (Eds.), *Primer on cerebrovascular diseases* (pp. 3–5). New York: Academic Press.

Speedie, L. J., & Heilman, K. M. (1982). Amnestic disturbance following infarction of the left dorsomedial nucleus of the thalamus. *Neuropsychologia, 20*, 597–604.

Speedie, L. J., & Heilman, K. M. (1983). Anterograde memory deficits for visuospatial material after infarction of the right thalamus. *Archives of Neurology, 40*, 183–186.

Stabell, K. E. (1991). *Neuropsychological investigation of patients with surgically treated aneurysm rupture at different cerebral sites.* Oslo, Norway: Institute of Psychology, University of Oslo.

Stabell, K. E., & Nornes, H. (1994). Prospective neuropsychological investigation of patients with supratentorial arteriovenous malformations. *Acta Neurochirurgica, 131*, 32–44.

Stein, B. M., & Wolpert, S. M. (1980). Arteriovenous malformations of the brain. I: Current concepts and treatment. *Archives of Neurology, 37*, 1–5.

Stillhard, G., Landis, T., Schiess, R., Regard, M., & Sialer, G. (1990). Bitemporal hypoperfusion in transient global amnesia: 99m-Tc-HM-PAO SPECT and neuropsychological findings during and after an attack. *Journal of Neurology, Neurosurgery, and Psychiatry, 53,* 339–342.

Stuss, D. T., Guberman, A., Nelson, R., & Larochelle, S. (1988). The neuropsychology of paramedian thalamic infarction. *Brain and Cognition, 8,* 348–378.

Tamura, A., & Nakayama, H. (1997). Neuronal damage in remote areas after focal cerebral infarct: Retrograde degeneration and transsynaptic death. In K. M. A. Welch, L. R. Caplan, D. J. Reis, B. K. Siesjo, & B. Weir (Eds.), *Primer on cerebrovascular diseases* (pp. 169–172). New York: Academic Press.

Tanabe, H., Hashikawa, K., Nakagawa, Y., Ikeda, M., Yamamoto, H., Harada, K., Tsumoto, T., Nishimura, T., Shiraishi, J., & Kimura, K. (1991). Memory loss due to transient hypoperfusion in the medial temporal lobes including hippocampus. *Acta Neurologica Scandinavica, 84,* 22–27.

Tatemichi, T. K., Desmond, D. W., Stern, Y., Paik, M., Sano, M., & Bagiella, E. (1994). Cognitive impairment after stroke: Frequency, patterns, and relationship to functional abilities. *Journal of Neurology, Neurosurgery, and Psychiatry, 57,* 202–207.

Tidswell, P., Dias, M. B., Sagar, D. M., Mayes, A. R., & Battersby, R. D. E. (1995). Cognitive outcome after aneurysm rupture: Relationship to aneurysm site and perioperative complications. *Neurology, 45,* 875–882.

Toole, J. F. (1990). *Cerebrovascular disorders* (4th ed.). New York: Raven.

Van der Drift, J. H. A., & Kok, K. D. (1972). Steal mechanisms between the carotid and vertebrobasilar systems. In J. S. Meyer, M. Reivich, H. Lechner, & O. Eichhorn (Eds.), *Research on the cerebral circulation: Fifth International Salzburg Conference* (pp. 325–336). Springfield, IL: Thomas.

Victor, M., Angevine, J. B., Mancall, E. L., & Fisher, C. M. (1961). Memory loss with lesions of hippocampal formation. *Archives of Neurology, 5,* 244–263.

Voelker, J. L., & Kaufman, H. H. (1997). Clinical aspects of intracerebral hemorrhage. In K. M. A. Welch, L. R. Caplan, D. J. Reis, B. K. Siesjo, & B. Weir (Eds.), *Primer on cerebrovascular diseases* (pp. 432–436). New York: Academic Press.

von Cramon, D. Y., Hebel, N., & Schuri, U. (1985). A contribution to the anatomical basis of thalamic amnesia. *Brain, 108,* 993–1008.

von Cramon, D. Y., Hebel, N., & Schuri, U. (1988). Verbal memory and learning in unilateral posterior cerebral infarction: A report on 30 cases. *Brain, 111,* 1061–1077.

von Monakow, C. (1969). Diaschisis (G. Harris, Trans.). In K. H. Pribram (Ed.), *Brain and behavior 1: Mood, states and mind* (pp. 27–36). Baltimore, MD: Penguin Books. (Reprinted from *Die lokalisation im Grosshirn und der abbau der Funktion durch korticale Herde [Localization in the cerebrum and functional impairment by cortical loci]* pp. 26–34, Wiesbaden: J. F. Bergmann. Original work published in 1914).

Waltimo, O., & Putkonen, A.-R. (1974). Intellectual performance of patients with intracranial arteriovenous malformations. *Brain, 97,* 511–520.

Welch, K. M. A., & Barkley, G. L. (1986). Biochemistry and pharmacology of cerebral ischemia. In H. J. M. Barnett, J. P. Mohr, B. M. Stein, & F. M. Yatsu (Eds.), *Stroke: Pathophysiology, diagnosis, and management* (Vol. 1, pp. 75–90). New York: Churchill Livingstone.

Welch, K. M. A., Caplan, L. R., Reis, D. J., Siesjo, B. K., & Weir, B. (Eds.). (1997). *Primer on cerebrovascular diseases.* New York: Academic Press.

Welch, K. M. A., & Levine, S. R. (1991). Focal brain ischemia and stroke: Pathophysiology and acid–base status. In R. A. Bornstein & G. G. Brown (Eds.), *Neurobehavioral aspects of cerebrovascular disease* (pp. 17–38). New York: Oxford University Press.

Wiebe-Velazquez, S., & Hachinski, V. (1991). Overview of clinical issues in stroke. In R. A. Bornstein & G. G. Brown (Eds.), *Neurobehavioral aspects of cerebrovascular disease* (pp. 111–130). New York: Oxford University Press.

Williams, V., & Grossman, R. G. (1970). Ultrastructure of cortical synapses after failure of presynaptic activity in ischemia. *Anatomical Record, 166,* 131–141.

Willis, T. (1664). *Cerebri anatome* [The anatomy of the brain]. London: J. Flesher.

Winocur, G., Oxbury, S., Roberts, R., Agnetti, V., & Davis, C. (1984). Amnesia in a patient with bi-lateral lesions to the thalamus. *Neuropsychologia, 22,* 123–143.

Woods, B. T., Schoene, W., & Kneisley, L. (1982). Are hippocampal lesions sufficient to cause lasting amnesia? *Journal of Neurology, Neurosurgery and Psychiatry, 45,* 243–246.

Author Index

Subject Index